ADVANCE PRAISE FOR

ESPN and the Changing Sports Media Landscape

"Much like ESPN assembles the best talent for delivery of its flagship *SportsCenter* program, Greg G. Armfield, John McGuire, and Adam Earnheardt have gathered respected scholars from around the world to examine the most pressing issues in the sports media industry. Foremost among the issues explored in this book is how ESPN and other media empires adapt to try to reach an audience distracted by a seemingly endless list of entertainment choices. These scholars help readers better understand how ESPN continues to rise to meet the challenges of this ever-changing industry and what strategies to use to stay ahead of the game. With each chapter expertly crafted by top scholars and thought-leaders—including interviews with ESPN heavyweights like John Walsh, Paul Melvin, and Kevin Blackistone, and *The Ringer*'s Bryan Curtis—it's easy to understand why this book will be one of this decades most influential collections of sports media studies. At 40 years old, ESPN has certainly grown into a sports media leader. Thanks to *ESPN and the Changing Sports Media Landscape*, we now have a guide for how ESPN might survive the next 40 years and how NBC, CBS, Fox, and others will continue to challenge the supremacy of the self-proclaimed 'worldwide leader in sports.'"

—James P. Tressel, President of Youngstown State University, College Football Hall of Fame inductee, and author of *The Winners Manual: For the Game of Life*

ESPN and the Changing Sports Media Landscape

COMMUNICATION, SPORT, AND SOCIETY

Lawrence A. Wenner, Andrew C. Billings, and Marie C. Hardin
General Editors

Vol. 2

The Communication, Sport, and Society series is part
of the Peter Lang Media and Communication list.
Every volume is peer reviewed and meets
the highest quality standards for content and production.

PETER LANG
New York • Bern • Berlin
Brussels • Vienna • Oxford • Warsaw

ESPN and the Changing Sports Media Landscape

Edited by Greg G. Armfield,
John McGuire, & Adam Earnheardt

PETER LANG
New York • Bern • Berlin
Brussels • Vienna • Oxford • Warsaw

Library of Congress Cataloging-in-Publication Data

Names: Armfield, Greg G., editor. | McGuire, John, editor. |
Earnheardt, Adam C., editor.
Title: ESPN and the changing sports media landscape /
edited by Greg G. Armfield, John McGuire, and Adam Earnheardt.
Description: New York: Peter Lang, 2019.
Series: Communication, sport, and society; v. 2 | 2576-7232
Includes bibliographical references and index.
Identifiers: LCCN 2019009923 | ISBN 978-1-4331-5170-5 (hardback: alk. paper)
ISBN 978-1-4331-5169-9 (paperback: alk. paper) | ISBN 978-1-4331-5172-9 (ebook pdf)
ISBN 978-1-4331-5173-6 (epub) | ISBN 978-1-4331-5174-3 (mobi)
Subjects: LCSH: ESPN (Television network) | Television broadcasting of sports.
Sports—Social aspects.
Classification: LCC GV742.3 .E76 2019 | DDC 070.4/49796—dc23
LC record available at https://lccn.loc.gov/2019009923
DOI 10.3726/b15990

Bibliographic information published by **Die Deutsche Nationalbibliothek**.
Die Deutsche Nationalbibliothek lists this publication in the "Deutsche
Nationalbibliografie"; detailed bibliographic data are available
on the Internet at http://dnb.d-nb.de/.

The paper in this book meets the guidelines for permanence and durability
of the Committee on Production Guidelines for Book Longevity
of the Council of Library Resources.

Printed in the United States of America

In appreciation of all the loved ones in our lives, but especially:
For Denise and the Minions (Skylar & Jake)
For my mom, Jane
For my loves, M. B. and Team EKSO
We dedicate this work,
Greg, John, and Adam

Contents

Tables and Figures

Preface: September 8, 2011

Greg G. Armfield, John McGuire, and Adam C. Earnheardt

September 8, 2011, will be remembered as one of the more memorable days in the history of ESPN, the dominant cable sports network in the United States. The network had just celebrated its 32nd anniversary the day before. On September 8, the network announced a new rights deal with the National Football League (NFL) to keep *Monday Night Football* and ancillary NFL programming like *NFL Insiders, NFL Live,* and *Sunday Morning Countdown* on ESPN into the early 2020s at the price of $1.9 billion per year, even if it was for just 20 or 21 live games a year (Hofheimer, 2011).

For company officials, retaining the rights to the country's most popular and most viewed sport on television was a crowning jewel (even if it costs nearly $2 billion per year) in their live sports programming inventory. One which already included college football's Bowl Championship Series (BCS), Major League Baseball (MLB), National Basketball Association (NBA), and the rights to numerous National Collegiate Athletic Association (NCAA) Division One conference championships. At the time, keeping the NFL on ESPN reinforced ESPN's supremacy in sports media. In hindsight, however, September 8, 2011 should be viewed as a turning point. As the rest of the 2010s unfolded, the sports media industry began changing, and ESPN with it.

The Rest of the 2010s

The world of traditional sports media, whether it be newspapers, magazines, or terrestrial and cable television, has been upended in the 2010s from a place of financial strength to one of a declining audience and rising costs. ESPN, despite still having the highest per-month subscriber rate among all national cable sports networks, has sustained multiple business setbacks and has been forced to rethink how to achieve its core mission (Gaines, 2017). While this book focuses in on the self-proclaimed "Worldwide Leader in Sports," the text offers other perspectives regarding the current sports media landscape in the U.S. and abroad as other media companies face the same competitive and financial pressures.

There is no singular cause or concern that created the upheaval in the sports media industry in the 2010s: in fact, there were many. It was and still is an ever-expanding sports media universe, with hundreds of Internet sites and its plethora of sports information and opinion shows you could once find only on ESPN and *SportsCenter*. It was mobile media that challenged the notion of how, when, and where you could watch sports highlights and get your sports news. It was social media sites, some of which traditional media people are still trying to wrap their heads around even as we write this. It was people who became cord-cutters, making use of new ways to get their entertainment outside of having cables running into their homes. In turn, it meant fewer cable and satellite subscribers (and fewer potential viewers) for regional and national sports networks. It was technology like DVRs and trends like second-day viewing, which meant live sports rights were at an even greater premium, meaning greater costs to acquire them. It was sports teams, leagues, and conferences with insatiable financial appetites, wanting skyrocketing rights fees to continue, come hell or high water. The NFL's expansion to a full slate of Thursday night games brought hundreds of millions of dollars for the owners, but it has also been criticized for diluting the Sunday/Monday NFL audience and diminishing the quality of the games on short weeks of rest for players (Ruiz, 2017). Traditional U.S. sports started suffering from an aging core audience while millennials showed less interest in baseball and more interest in new competitive esports and drone racing.

Technological changes are posing additional challenges for the future of regional and national cable sports networks. Part of the challenge stems from cord-cutting consumers, but the larger issue is new competition if, and when, Amazon, Facebook, Twitter, or others decide to compete for sports properties, likely resulting in higher rights fees that will exacerbate problems facing traditional network and cable outlets.

It was also old problems like athletes behaving badly (e.g., performance enhancing drug use in baseball and other sports) and when players did behave in a way that demonstrated the use of their First Amendment rights (e.g., NFL players kneeling during the National Anthem to protest police treatment of African-Americans), commentary over such actions dragged sports personalities (and the networks they worked for) into the cultural and political fulcrum that engulfed the United States during the latter part of the decade. ESPN and other sports media still had issues that had been raised long before the 2010s: particularly, the near absence of female athletes on information programs like *SportsCenter* and, to a lesser extent, live sports events.

As ESPN faces down its 40th anniversary in 2019, the company still has a global presence in its fifth decade, employing thousands of people all over the world. This book considers the way in which the company is once again reinventing itself (e.g., new broadcast facility in New York City, start-up of ESPN+, *SportsCenter* on Snapchat). In *The ESPN Effect* (2015), we made the observation that ESPN's pervasiveness, delivering programs and information 24 hours a day, 365 days a year, influenced "how sports fans think and feel about the people who play and control these games" (Armfield & McGuire, 2015, p. xvi). This book, in a way, is asking whether that still holds true heading into the 2020s. To be clear, ESPN still has an influential (some would argue too influential) role in how sports leagues and sports media operates in the United States, but the network's aura of invincibility circa 2011 has been chipped away by the factors stated above.

Maybe September 8, 2011, will not be remembered as well as September 7, 1979, the day ESPN launched, but it does provide a landmark in time to start our discussion. The 2010s have created such change that no one really has a grasp on what is to come in the world of sports media and where fans will find their favorite games or on what platforms they will watch them on. While it is beyond our abilities to make like "Jimmy the Greek" and prognosticate the future, this book will hopefully offer greater insight as to what has unfolded in the past decade and what is to come.

About the Volume

This endeavor explores the current and future sports media landscape at the end of the 2010s. The editors have included a deeper international perspective to shape this edition and reflect on the current media climate impacting ESPN and sports media internationally.

The chapters in this book focus on four areas of sports media. The first section examines changes and challenges in the sports media marketplace, both in the U.S. and abroad. Steve Dittemore starts the discussion with a retrospective about how the U.S. Congress has provided oversight of the American sports media industry. Aside from the governmental oversight of sports media, one cannot argue that ESPN is without question the leader in the United States. However, it has struggled to gain a stronghold in many parts of the world. David Bockino analyzes ESPN's struggle to gain any competitive advantage against their international competition. Paul Smith then takes a closer look into the worldwide struggles ESPN has encountered with the changing European marketplace for sports media rights. One area ESPN has gained a stronghold domestically is in fantasy sports. Brody J. Ruihley and Andrew C. Billings bring us into the fantasy sports world discussion through an examination of how ESPN continues to dominate the fantasy sports marketplace. Along with fantasy sports, the astronomical growth of esports viewing in the 2010s is well-documented. Steve Young and colleagues Sean Fourney and Braden Bagley conduct a value analysis of ESPN's emerging esports coverage. Kevin Hull and co-authors Miles Romney and David Cassilo round out this section with their discussion of streaming sports online. Utilizing diffusion of innovations theory, the authors offer insights as to the likely success of direct-to-consumer apps like ESPN+.

The book's second section is about changes and challenges in the sports media-political environment. This section begins with an exploration by Ryan Broussard and Jonathan Graffeo examining ESPN's perceived double standard in handling Jemele Hill's remarks about President Trump on Twitter compared to former ESPN baseball commentator Curt Schilling's controversial Facebook post regarding North Carolina's enactment of a law barring transgender individuals from using public restrooms according to their gender identity. Hill, the one-time ESPN on-air host and commentator, is the subject of two other chapters in this text: Katherine Lavelle takes us deep into an insightful analysis of public correction scholarship concerning Hill's political tweets. David Staton further explores ESPN's handling of Hill's case through the use of the Potter Box. Next, J. Scott Smith examines ESPN's crisis communication during the 2015 and 2017 company layoffs. The section concludes with the ESPN decision to eliminate the Ombudsman position with Xavier Ramon and co-authors José Luis Rojas and Andrew C. Billings look at the unique focus and role each Ombudsman has played at ESPN through the years.

The book's third section takes on changes and challenges in the sports media programming environment. If anyone ESPN entity can summarize the past, present, and future of ESPN, including the challenges that lay ahead, it is the network's flagship show *SportsCenter*. The longest-running sports highlight show still on the air in the U.S.. *SportsCenter* used to be one of the only places to find sports highlights. But today, social media and other media providers have altered sports fans' reality. We no longer must wait until a set time to see highlights, as they can be delivered to you instantaneously. John McGuire opens this section of the book with an analysis of how *SportsCenter* has evolved to meet the demands of serving its third generation of viewers and discusses the new Snapchat format of *SportsCenter*. Likewise, Jake Kucek and co-authors Zach Humphries, Adam C. Earnheardt, and Greg G. Armfield explore ESPN's dominance of the mobile app market and the technological advancements in sports media we enjoy today because of the risks ESPN assumed in their development of full, digital media platforms.

Jared Johnson takes a different look at how ESPN has tried to leverage the changing programming environment, targeting college sports fandom with a critical examination of the Longhorn Network. Next, William M. Kunz offers an examination of one of ESPN's primary competitors, Fox Sports, and its aggressive targeting and programming techniques during the past quarter century of local sports markets. Another area ripe for potential growth in sports media is a wider distribution of women's sports. Anji L. Phillips and Dunja Antunovic offer a review of historical trends and propose thought-provoking directions for the growth of women's sports. The section concludes by looking at one area where ESPN has had success with regard to women's sports and cultural issues is with the website espnW. Sara Wolter, well-known for her research on espnW and women's sports, provides a political economics analysis of espnW. While other ESPN forays into cultural and political arenas have experienced mixed results, espnW and its approach to covering women's sports has experienced much success.

The fourth and final section looks at some of the specific challenges that ESPN and other sports media companies face in the changing sports media landscape. While ESPN has decided the role of Ombudsman is no longer needed at the network, Michael L. Butterworth addresses this topic and others in an insightful interview with John Walsh, former Executive Vice President of ESPN. Although Walsh refrains from prognostication in his interview, he does provide some insight into the positive future and direction of ESPN. One interesting note is his belief that ESPN will continue dominating the business of sports media, and that the media giant is not behind the times when it comes to preparing for the future of sports media delivery. Speaking of digital innovations, Melvin Lewis brings us more insight into the possible directions ESPN is headed with a short interview with Paul Melvin, Senior Director of Communications for ESPN's Digital Media, Technology, International, and X Games groups. Melvin discusses the challenges ESPN faces in the evolving sports media landscape and the future vision of ESPN. Andreas Hebbel-Seeger and Thomas Horky then provide an exciting preview of the future of the sports viewing experience: from more overhead shots generated by drones and more first-person viewing experiences through virtual reality. While all technologies take time to emerge, we hope these don't go the way of ESPN 3D. Finally, we close with three media industry experts: Kevin Blackistone, Galen Clavio, and Bryan Curtis. "Visualizing 2020: The Future of Sports Media" highlights a panel discussion organized by the text's editors with the help of Galen Clavio for the International Association of Communication and Sports (IACS) 11th Summit on Communication and Sport at the University of Indiana in April 2018.

For those of us exploring and enjoying the sports media landscape, ESPN and other sports distributors have had a marked impact on our understanding of the field as well as our fanship. But for millennials and generations to come, these outlets may have less of a grip on those individuals than the baby boomers and GenXers. As we have seen in the 2010s, anything can happen. For researchers in the discipline of sports media, the idea that anything can happen is probably why we became sports fans.

References

Armfield, G. G., & McGuire, J. (2015). Preface: You've come a long ways baby. In J. McGuire, G. G. Armfield, & A. C. Earnheardt (Eds.), *The ESPN Effect: Exploring the worldwide leader in sports* (pp. xii–xviii). New York, NY: Peter Lang.

Gaines, C. (2017, April 27). Cable TV customers pay more than $9 per month for ESPN networks whether they watch or not. *Business Insider*. Retrieved from http://www.businessinsider.com/cable-satellite-tv-sub-fees-espn-networks-2017-4

Hofheimer, B. (2011, September 8). ESPN launches new NFL shows, expands others. *ESPN Press Room*. Retrieved from https://espnpressroom.com/us/press-releases/2011/09/espn-launches-new-nfl-shows-expands-others/

Ruiz, S. (2017, January 25). 6 reasons why Roger Goodell is wrong about 'Thursday Night Football.' *USA Today*. Retrieved from https://ftw.usatoday.com/2017/01/roger-goodell-thursday-night-footballs-quality-good-games

Section One

Changes and Challenges in the Sports Media Marketplace

1. *Sports Programming as a Public Good: A Complicated Congressional Legacy*

Stephen W. Dittmore

On November 2, 2016, the U.S. Justice Department sued DirecTV and AT&T, Inc., alleging it orchestrated a campaign to block broad carriage of a television channel owned by the Los Angeles Dodgers. In its filing, the Justice Department noted "a significant number of Dodgers fans have had no opportunity in recent years to watch their team play on television because overlapping and competitive pay television providers did not telecast Dodgers games" (*United States of America v. DirecTV*, 2016, p. 2). While the two parties settled the case on March 23, 2017, that the government was compelled to intervene in a case which, essentially, alleged collusion to limit consumer access to watching professional baseball, is illustrative of decades of conflicting public policy legacy and rhetoric to sports programming as a public good.

The Justice Department lawsuit also speaks to the complex nature of the sports media business generally. Professional sports leagues have enjoyed a Congressionally-approved exemption to antitrust laws when negotiating broadcast rights agreements since 1961. At that time, the impact of having leagues make its contests available to consumers on free-to-air broadcast networks was unknown. Leagues initially feared free broadcasts would negatively impact game attendance. National Football League (NFL) Commissioner Pete Rozelle, who led the lobbying effort in 1961, argued the exemption was necessary to prevent "open competition among its teams for broadcasting rights," which would create an environment in which rich clubs got richer, and poor clubs got poorer (Lowe, 1995, p. 93).

A half-century later, the benefits of selling broadcast rights are numerous. Hundreds of millions of dollars trade hands annually between networks and professional sports leagues, often with the goal of increasing the amount of available content to consumers. However, that content, in many cases, now comes with an increased cost which is passed directly on to consumers. Or, in extreme cases such as the Dodgers example, the content is simply not made available to all consumers in a given market.

The topic of sports programming on television has warranted significant Congressional review in the past 50-plus years. On at least 20 occasions, committees or subcommittees in Congress have held hearings on the subject. A similar number of bills have been introduced in Congress since the mid-1970s. Yet for all of the talk on the part of politicians, no laws have been passed to alter the current antitrust exemptions.

This chapter will consider in more detail the exact role of Congress in regulating sports programming, particularly in light of evidence supporting increased migration from free to pay television. What emerges through a review of proposed legislation and Congressional testimony is a lot of discussion on the part of public officials, but near-zero action. Members of Congress often use local constituents as examples of individuals in need of protection, but exhibit little willingness to back up threats to revamp legislation for consumer good. In this sense, American politicians project a confusing legacy as to whether the ability to view sports programming, something they often claim is central to American culture and lifestyle, is a public good.

1961—Granting Professional Sports an Antitrust Exemption

In July 1961, Federal District Judge Alan K. Grim ruled a two-year NFL contract with CBS in which the league sold the pooled rights of each team had gone too far in eliminating competition between individual teams and violated antitrust laws (Lowe, 1995). Congress moved swiftly to ensure the leagues were not adversely impacted by the court ruling. Representative Emanuel Celler (D-New York) sponsored a House bill while Senator Estes Kefauver (D-Tennessee) sponsored a sister bill in the Senate designed to exempt professional sports leagues from antitrust laws as it related to sale of broadcast rights (Lowe, 1995).

In a Senate Judiciary Committee hearing on August 28, 1961, politicians considered the "right" of citizens to watch sports. In the debate prior to the Act's vote, the Senate Committee on the Judiciary expressed, "the opinion that the public interest in viewing professional league sports warrants some accommodation of antitrust principles" (as quoted in *Blaich v. NFL*, 1962, p. 4).

The hearing lasted one day with NFL Commissioner Rozelle and MLB Commissioner Ford Frick both testifying to the need for the legislation in order to insure the viability of their leagues. So effective was the lobbying effort that the bill passed within two months of introduction and the Sports

Broadcasting Act of 1961 was signed into law by President John F. Kennedy (Lowe, 1995). The prospect of significant broadcast revenues, and its negative impact on in-stadium attendance, led to the adoption of rules which restricted interteam competition for the sale of broadcast rights (Horowitz, 1974).

Critics of this Congressionally-created monopoly suggested rights-pooling eliminated competition between televised games and created the right to televise "the only game in town" in each community (Horowitz, 1978, p. 415). Anderson (1995) called it "special-interest legislation" stating "it is difficult to see how an exemption to laws meant to protect the public could also benefit the public" (p. 958).

The Idea of "Public Good"

At its very basic, sports programming meets the definition of a public good, and therefore subject to government protection, in that "a viewer watching a game does not prevent other viewers from watching the same game" (Jeanrenaud & Kesenne, 2006, p. 13). Major League Baseball in particular has long enjoyed a place in America's public cultural consciousness, something Zimbalist (1994, p. 186) succinctly summarized as "how we treat baseball and how baseball treats us, reflects our values, our needs, and our direction." Indeed, Gaustad (2000) noted special characteristics of sports as television content, emphasizing (a) the time-sensitive nature of the product; (b) the unique nature of the product, which makes it hard to substitute with other forms of programming; and (c) the strong cultural connection to sport programming, arguing these characteristics created a strong public good element for televised sports.

Whether sports programming meets the threshold of being in the public interest is an entirely different discussion, one which has manifested itself in several ways. Several countries, including Australia and members of the European Union, have passed legislation aimed at protecting the rights of citizens to watch live sporting events. These measures, known as *anti-siphoning* or *anti-migration* rules, are aimed at slowly, if not stopping, the migration of broadcast sports from traditional free-to-air television to pay television (Lefever & Van Rompuy, 2009).

Countries which have passed major events legislation perceive their citizens have a right to watch certain sporting events on free-to-air television (Evens, Iosifidis, & Smith, 2013). Indeed, the European Court of Human Rights has inferred that the right to information includes anything which plays an important role in the development of citizens, and sports can fulfill that role by bringing people together and stimulating conversation (Lefever, 2012). Essential to this condition, however, is the ability for all citizens to simultaneously have access to the sport programming. In other words, "access to the broadcasting of these events should not be restricted to a limited number of people" (Lefever, 2012, p. 69).

Iosifidis and Smith (2013) stressed because the European Union considers sport as an area of society which brings people within the Union together, free-to-air broadcasting of sport is essential: "A necessary precondition for the achievement of sport's social and cultural benefits is for sport to be available and affordable to all—hence, the importance of free-to-air sports broadcasting" (p. 114). Their view suggests watching sport is a public good.

Through its Australian Communications and Media Authority agency and the Minister for Communications, the government of Australia regulates television content through an anti-siphoning list. Events on the list may be simulcast or repeated on free-to-air broadcaster's digital channels, but the events may not be shown first on those platforms ("Sport (anti-siphoning)," 2015). Programming on Australia's anti-siphoning's list includes Olympic Games, Commonwealth Games, the Australian Open, the Australian and United States Masters golf tournament, and many international cricket, rugby and soccer matches.

Early Anti-Siphoning Movement

Similar to how professional sports team owners' fear of free, over-the-air broadcasts of their games led to the Sports Broadcasting Act early in the decade, by the end of the 1960s the owners now feared a new technology, cable television. Klatell and Marcus (1988) argued that sports rights-holders and the networks opposed sports on cable because "moving sports to cable would be akin to stealing from the public, and holding at ransom, its precious TV games" (p. 83).

An early example of how cable could impact sports programming came in *United States v. Southwestern Cable*. The government alleged that a San Diego cable system was transmitting signals from Los Angeles stations into the San Diego market. Included in the channel line-up was a station carrying Los Angeles Dodgers baseball games. San Diego, at the time, did not have a Major League Baseball franchise, though the Padres began play in 1969. Although not explicitly tasked with regulating cable television at the time, the FCC sought to assert itself over the industry in a 1968 case. This siphoning issue came before the U.S. Supreme Court in 1968 which upheld a U.S. Court of Appeals, D.C. Circuit decision vacating anti-siphoning rules passed by the FCC in the late 1960s (*United States v. Southwestern Cable*, 1968). Shortly after the decision in *U.S. v. Southwestern Cable*, the FCC adopted an "anti-siphoning" regulation and the move of sport programming to cable slowed.

In *Home Box Office, Inc. v. FCC* (1977), the U.S. Court of Appeals D.C. Circuit vacated the anti-siphoning rules passed by the FCC in the late 1960s. In joining the court's opinion, Judge Stanley Weigel emphasized the FCC lacked the power to regulate programming which originated with cablecasters as though programs are not retransmitted from over-the-air signals.

Senator Wendell Ford (D-Kentucky) was one of the first members of Congress to take an interest in protecting sports programming on broadcast networks. He introduced S. 2954 on April 19, 1978, a bill amending the 1934 Communications Act "to require the Federal Communications Commission to make such rules and regulations as are necessary and appropriate with regard to major sports programming that may be provided by pay television" ("S. 2954," 2018, para. 1). His bill was referred to the Senate Commerce, Science and Transportation committee, never to be heard from again.

Siedlecki (1978) suggested anti-siphoning restrictions should be lifted from all programming except sports programs for three reasons. First, sports have great entertainment value only at the time of their occurrence. Second, the supply of sports events is inelastic, meaning if they were siphoned, there would be no similar substitute. And third, sports leagues controlled the percentage of events to be televised through a "government sanctioned cartel" (p. 822).

Thirty years later, Hylton (2011) noted, "there has been a movement to protect the public's right to 'free' broadcasts of major sporting events" (p. 53). While acknowledging teams are under no obligation to make their games available on free television, Hylton argued the historical precedent of games being available on broadcast networks coupled with the notion these events are "communal events, it is understandable that the public would develop an expectation that such events would continue to be available for public viewing without additional charges" (p. 54).

If that "movement" to protect free broadcasts of major sporting events were to become a reality, it would be up to Congress to develop legislation revoking the Sports Broadcasting Act, something Wolohan (2009) suggested would have severe consequences for leagues and conferences. For example, if the leagues were no longer able to pool the broadcasting rights of all their teams, the teams from smaller media markets would all of a sudden find it very difficult to compete financially with those teams from larger media markets (p. 586).

1989—The First Real Threat to Revoke

One of the early critics of baseball's television policy was Senator Howard Metzenbaum, (D-Ohio), who served from 1976 to 1995. Called an "abrasive, ultraliberal Democrat" by his biographer (Diemer, 2008, p. xii), Metzenbaum was pro-labor and a staunch supporter of antitrust regulations. Both figured into his interest in televised baseball in late 1989 when, as chair of the Senate Judiciary Subcommittee on Antitrust, Monopolies and Business Rights, he held a hearing titled "Sports Programming and Cable Television" on November 14, 1989. In his opening remarks, Metzenbaum stated, "Given this level of fan support, team owners ought to take steps to ensure that access to sports on TV does not become solely dependent upon an individual's ability to pay. If they won't take such steps, Congress may do it for them (*"Sports Programming,"* 1989, pp. 3–4).

The event which served as a flash point for the 1989 hearing was a deal between the New York Yankees and Madison Square Garden Network to show all of the team's games on cable television at a time when cable penetration across the country was just 56% (*"Sports Programming,"* 1989). So incensed that his constituents would not be able to watch the Yankees on television, Representative Charles Schumer (D-New York) on June 8, 1989 introduced the "Baseball Viewers Protection Act of 1989," which stipulated, among other provisions, "at least 50 percent of team's televised games are broadcast by one or more regular over-the-air broadcasting stations serving the home city of that team" ("H.R. 2593," 1989, para. 1). Schumer's bill was referred to the House Judiciary Subcommittee on Economic and Commercial Law but was never acted upon (Table 1.1 contains a comprehensive chronological list of bills introduced in Congress which concerned sport broadcasting).

Table 1.1: Chronological list of bills on sports and television introduced in Congress, 1978 to present.

Date	Title
April 4, 1978	A bill to provide that antitrust laws shall apply ... (H.R. 11940)
April 19, 1978	A bill to amend the Communications Act of 1934 ... (S. 2954)
Jan. 22, 1979	A bill to provide that antitrust laws shall apply ... (H.R. 1239)
June 15, 1987	A bill to make antitrust laws applicable ... (H.R. 2687)
June 8, 1989	Baseball Viewers Protection Act of 1989 (H.R. 2593)
May 8, 1991	Public Access to National Sport Events Act (S. 1015)
Aug. 4, 1992	To express the sense of the Congress with respect to sports blackouts (H.R. 5760)

Date	Title
May 5, 1993	Right to View Professional Sports Act of 1993 (H.R. 1988)
March 15, 1995	Right to View Professional Sports Act of 1995 (H.R. 935)
Feb. 5, 1997	Give Fans a Chance Act of 1997 (H.R. 590)
Feb. 3, 1999	Give Fans a Chance Act of 1999 (H.R. 532)
Nov. 8, 2001	Give Fans a Chance Act of 2001 (H.R. 3257)
July 8, 2002	Baseball Fan Protection Act (H.R. 5062)
July 15, 2003	Baseball Fan Protection Act (H.R. 2745)
Nov. 12, 2013	Furthering Access and Networks for Sports (FANS) Act (H.R. 3452)
Nov. 18, 2013	Furthering Access and Networks for Sports (FANS) Act (S. 1721)
Dec. 4, 2014	Sustained Promotion of Responsibility in Team Sports (SPORTS) Act (S. 2974)
Dec. 17, 2015	Furthering Access and Networks for Sports (FANS) Act (S. 2414)

Source: Author.

During the hearing, the views of Senators Metzenbaum and Schumer were reinforced by fellow Senators Joseph Lieberman (D-Connecticut) and Herbert Kohl (D-Wisconsin). In his opening statement, Lieberman opined that he did not know that he "could quite construct a constitutional right to equal access to sports, but I think there must be something derived from the pursuit of happiness that we are all promised as Americans" ("*Sports Programming*," 1989, p. 8). Lieberman expressed concern with the "cableization of New York Yankees baseball" and that he supported Congress's efforts to ensure that Americans "will not lose their right to equal access to sports; that sports will not become a luxury or a privilege for those who can afford it, but will remain a basic right" ("*Sports Programming*," 1989, p. 9).

To illustrate the partisan nature of the debate at this hearing, sports industry leaders would attempt to use one of Lieberman's quotes against him. Lieberman stated:

> What is happening now, because of the growing power of cable television, is that the American people are losing some of their options and possibilities. It remains for those of us who hold positions of authority in Government to step in and try to draw some rules to protect people's access to baseball and other sports. ("*Sports Programming*," p. 9)

Witnesses called by the Subcommittee to testify at the hearing, including MLB Commissioner Fay Vincent, NFL Commissioner Paul Tagliabue, and

ESPN President Roger L. Werner, Jr. all argued that the shift of programming to cable television had, in fact, increased consumer options. Vincent testified that, when removing exclusive national contract windows, an individual MLB team could telecast 130 out of 162 games per year, thereby increasing the possibility for fans to watch their local team's games ("*Sports Programming*," p. 29).

Similarly, Tagliabue noted the NFL's contract with ESPN "has brought additional games to fans across the country and has yielded consistently strong ratings, reflecting viewer preferences and viewer acceptance" ("*Sports Programming*," 1989, pp. 40–41).

While not assigned to the Judiciary Committee in 1989, Senator John McCain (R-Arizona) would also take an interest in televised sport a few years later as a member of the Senate Commerce, Science, and Transportation Committee. On May 8, 1991, McCain introduced the "Public Access to National Sporting Events Act" which would have amended the Communications Act of 1934 to require live telecast of the Super Bowl and the World Series over a national broadcast network ("*Public Access*," 1991). Like previous bills, this bill never made it out of committee.

While McCain's bill singled out the Super Bowl and World Series, the language in section two of the bill spoke directly to the changing landscape of cable television and sports: (a) there is a growing trend toward making sports events available only through media other than live broadcast television; (b) access to these events is becoming increasingly costly to the consumer; (c) as this trend develops, whether the consumer has access to sports events will be determined by the ability of the consumer to pay; (d) many consumers have benefited from the constant availability of sports programming through subscription media; (e) nonetheless, the access by members of the public to certain sports events should not be dependent upon their ability to pay for that access ("*Public Access*," 1991). Additional language in the bill made it clear the antitrust exemptions afforded to the NFL and MLB have allowed the leagues to prosper but that: "Limited access to viewing the Super Bowl and the World Series would deprive citizens of the ability to enjoy these events which have become an American tradition, and which benefit from the antitrust exemptions conferred upon them by Congress and the Federal courts" ("*Public Access*," 1991).

Now, more than 25 years later, there appears to be significant evidence of migration of both professional and college sports, not to mention Olympic sport, from free to pay television. Recent media rights agreements have moved marquee sporting events such as college football bowl games, the NCAA Men's Basketball tournament, and MLB and NBA playoffs from traditional terrestrial networks to subscription-based networks.

The FCC Punts on Migration

Representative John Dingell of Michigan offered H. Amdt.742 to the 1992 Cable Television Act (H.R. 4850) on July 23, 1992 requiring the FCC to study the extent to which exclusive contracts between college athletic conferences and regional sports programming networks artificially and unfairly restrict the ability to broadcast local college sporting events on local television stations (*"Cable Television,"* 1992). The Senate version of the 1992 Cable Television Act (S. 12), despite being vetoed by President George H. W. Bush, would become Public Law No: 102–385. Section 26 of the Act required the FCC to provide a final report to Congress by July 1, 1994 which summarizes the Commission's analysis of trends in migration of sports programming from broadcast stations to cable networks, including economic and social consequences of such trends.

The Commission released that report to Congress on June 30, 1994 and concluded, in general, no significant evidence of migration of professional sports existed, although the report did acknowledge concern about migration of college football (*"Sports Programming,"* 1994). As the Commission reported, "the purpose of sports siphoning rules would be to give those not served by cable broader access to sports programming and to maintain a consistent level of free sports programming for the general viewing public" (*"Sports Programming,"* 1994, para. 144). Because the Commission concluded there was little evidence of sports migration in 1994, it did not recommend adoption of siphoning legislation or regulation.

At the time of the Commission's report in 1994, networks had not yet fully taken advantage of the cable television business model where networks received revenue from two sources, subscriber fees and advertisers. Terrestrial, or over-the-air, networks received revenue only from one source, advertisers (Gratton & Solberg, 2007). Indeed, one can even argue the FCC's retransmission consent rules now created a situation where terrestrial networks would receive the benefit of additional revenue from subscriber fees previously reserved for pay networks. Despite this evidence, the FCC appeared to be reticent to revisit sports siphoning rules.

In its 2012 annual report assessing competition in the market for delivering video programming, the FCC noted, "one recent trend has been the migration of some major sports, including the NBA and MLB, to cable networks" (*"Annual Assessment,"* 2012, para. 375). Indeed, Toms (2010, para. 2) noted, "fewer and fewer [MLB] games are available on local 'over the air' channels as sports continue to migrate to the more lucrative 'dual revenue' (sub fees and ads) model of cable TV." Instead of advocating for re-opening dialogue on sports siphoning rules, the FCC instead focused on a benefit of the CBS/TNT joint bid for the NCAA Men's Basketball tournament rights, suggesting the partnership is beneficial in "providing additional outlets for sports programming" ("Annual Assessment," 2012, para. 375).

If, indeed, viewing professional sports is in the public interest, then the indifference exhibited by Congress, as well the FCC, toward migration of sports programming to pay television begs the question as to whether or not the public interest is being harmed. Even if Congress or the FCC had pushed the envelope and stemmed the migration of sports programming from broadcast to cable networks, the question of whether this programming was really "free" to consumers would remain. When Congress, in the 1992 Cable Act, granted broadcasts networks the ability to negotiate retransmission consent from cable and satellite companies, it signaled a preference for consumers to subscribe to cable and satellite providers.

Retransmission Fees Change Everything

A chief concern following the advent of cable television in the early 1970s was the retransmission of broadcast signals by a cable or satellite provider, known as a multichannel video programming distributor (MVPD). As cable operators transitioned from facilitating broadcast signals into rural areas to a distributor of programming, local television station owners became fearful they would lose audience and advertising dollars if people could receive programming directly into their homes via cable rather than through terrestrial signals (Deninger, 2012). In response to the concerns, the FCC adopted "must carry" rules in 1972 which required cable systems to include every television station within a 60-mile radius (later revised to 50 miles) as part of the basic cable package. Stations were guaranteed carriage on cable, but they could not demand compensation from the cable distributor (Deninger, 2012). The issue of compensation would be revisited by Congress in 1992 with the adoption of retransmission consent rules.

A condition of the 1992 Cable Act required multichannel video programming distributors (MVPDs) to seek permission from broadcasters before carrying their programming. Alternatively, MVPDs could include networks in their service under must carry rules in which MVPDs with more than 12 channels must set aside one-third of their channel capacity for local, free-to-air broadcasters. At that time, some 40% of U.S. households relied on free-to-air broadcasters for their television programming (Teeter & Loving, 2008).

Permission to retransmit a broadcast network's signal on an MVPD became known as "retransmission consent" or "carriage fees." Should an MVPD and a broadcast network not reach agreement on an appropriate carriage fee, the MVPD may remove, or *blackout*, the network from its system (or vice versa), thereby depriving consumers the ability to see certain programming. Often, live sports content is at the center of these debates. For example, Sunbeam Television Corporation operated WHDH, the NBC affiliate in Boston. On January 14, 2012, Sunbeam denied DirecTV access to its signal after the company refused to pay a 300% increase in retransmission fees. The timing of the blackout occurred prior to popular NFL divisional playoff games. The dispute was settled on January 27, one week before the New England Patriots played in Super Bowl XLVI, a game for which NBC had broadcast rights ("Sunbeam," 2012).

Retransmission fees allowed broadcast networks to receive compensation from MVPDs which retransmitted their signal, enabling broadcast networks to receive similar dual revenue streams (fees and advertising) to cable networks which were already receiving carriage fees from MVPDs and advertising revenues. Much like the recent issues with retransmission consent, cable networks have long struggled to negotiate carriage deals with MVPDs, or risk their network not being carried to interested consumers. In attempt to prevent unscrupulous business practices, Congress, through the 1992 Cable Act, instructed the FCC to "adopt regulations prohibiting cable companies from discriminating in carriage agreements between affiliated and nonaffiliated networks" (Hutson, 2008, p. 413). The intent of these carriage anti-discrimination laws was to prevent an MVPD from gaining too much market power over nonaffiliated networks.

The first complaint made under the FCC's carriage agreement regulations occurred in 1997 when Classic Sports Network (Classic), an independent cable network broadcasting vintage sporting events, complained that Cablevision, a cable company with, at the time, 2.8 million subscribers, used coercive bargaining tactics to require an ownership stake in the network as a condition of carriage (Hutson, 2008, p. 417). Classic claimed that, in negotiations, Cablevision CEO James Dolan demanded an equity stake in Classic in exchange for carriage. The sides settled out of court, and eventually the dispute became a footnote as Classic was bought by ESPN.

The issue of carriage debates first caught the attention of Congress prior to the start of the 2006 MLB season, the second year of existence for the Washington Nationals following their relocation from Montreal. Representative Tom Davis (R-Virginia), chairman of the House Committee on Government Reform, called a hearing to examine why Nationals fans in an around Washington, D.C. were not able to watch Nationals games on their chosen cable or satellite system. In particular, Davis wanted to understand why subscribers to Comcast, the region's dominant cable provider, did not have access to 75% of Nationals games.

During the unprecedented hearing to focus on the carriage of one MLB team, the Washington Nationals, Representative Dutch Ruppersberger (D-Maryland), synthesized the issue, noting again the right of baseball fans to be able to watch their hometown team, as follows: "I have been a Baltimore Orioles fan all my life. I love going to Camden Yards to watch the games, and when I cannot see them, I enjoy watching them on TV. As we know now, many Nat fans cannot do that right now. And if you are a baseball fan, that is just not right" (*"Out at home,"* 2006, p. 12).

On one hand, this hearing can be viewed as nothing more than a politician, Representative Davis, using his power as chair of a House Committee to solve a personal problem. But on another hand, the hearing can be examined from the perspective that elected officials were beginning to understand the myriad of problems related to growing migration of sports programming to pay television.

MLB President and Chief Operating Officer Bob Dupuy testified during the hearing that the league was "very proud of how well we serve the television viewing public through a combination of national telecasts, regional telecasts, out-of-market telecasts for displaced fans, and games and highlights streamed on the Internet" (*"Out at home,"* 2006, p. 18). Dupuy noted that virtually all 2,400 of league games are available in local markets through a variety of platforms. He clarified to the committee that Nationals games were available in the local market, but on different MVPDs such as DirecTV, Charter, Cox, Verizon, and RCN.

Finally, Dupuy hoped that for the benefit of Nationals fans who were Comcast subscribers, an agreement could be reached quickly between MASN and Comcast. By articulating it this way, Dupuy sought to absolve MLB of any wrongdoing in this case.

In his opening remarks, Representative Elijah Cummings (D-Maryland had acknowledged that other providers carried MASN but sought to ask different questions. We should ask why five out of six cable providers in the Washington region have been able to reach a contractual agreement with the Mid-Atlantic Sports Network but Comcast has refused. What impact has Major League Baseball's antitrust exemption had in creating this situation? (*"Out at home,"* 2006, p. 7).

Less than a year later, Dupuy would find himself once again back in Washington, D.C. to defend the business practices of MLB. When the league entered into an agreement with DirecTV for exclusive carriage of its Extra Innings pay package in February 2007, it caught the attention of "Red Sox Nation" (Stewart, 2007). In an attempt to placate concerned constituents, Senator John Kerry (D-Massachusetts) asked the FCC to investigate the exclusive nature of the agreement. In his letter to FCC chairman Kevin Martin, Kerry stated, "In the case of my hometown team, Red Sox Nation stretches all across our country from coast to coast. I am concerned that this deal ... will separate fans from their favorite teams" (Stewart, 2007, p. D1). Without acknowledging either Senator Kerry or the possible FCC investigation, MLB and DirecTV, nonetheless, announced on March 8, 2007 an "expanded multi-year agreement" in which incumbent MVPDs Dish Network and InDemand would be allowed to carry the Extra Innings package ("MLB, DIRECTV," 2007).

Nevertheless, on March 27, 2007, Kerry convened the Senate Commerce Committee for a hearing titled "Exclusive Sports Programming: Examining Competition and Consumer Choice." At one point in the hearing, during an exchange with Chase Carey, President and CEO for DirecTV, Inc., and MLB's DuPuy, Kerry explained the reason for the hearing, "It's the public interest, it's the sports interest, it's baseball's interest ... And it's hard to marry the deeply felt, and I think, earnest belief of the Commissioner, that this is a social institution with enormous historical and cultural ties to the country and a larger public interest with the economic interest that's represented here" (*"Exclusive sports,"* 2007, p. 58). The effort of Kerry and his committee bore fruit, as shortly after the hearing, MLB made its Extra Innings package available to other MVPDs.

The relative stability lasted less than a year when Representative Ed Markey (D- Massachusetts) convened a hearing on March 5, 2008 for the House Subcommittee on Telecommunications and the Internet titled "Competition in the Sports Programming Marketplace" (See below for a listing of Congressional hearings focused on sport broadcasting).

List of Congressional Hearings on Sports and Television

A. October 3–5, 1972—*Blackout of sporting events on T.V.* Subcommittee on Communications, Senate Commerce Committee.

B. July 31, 1973—*Professional sports blackouts.* Subcommittee on Communications and Power, House Interstate and Foreign Commerce Committee.

C. October 3, November 2–3, 1977—*Network sports practices.* Subcommittee on Communications, House Interstate and Foreign Commerce Committee.

D. November 14, 1989—*Sports programming and cable television.* Subcommittee on Antitrust, Monopolies, and Business Rights, Senate Judiciary Committee.

E. January 31, 2006—*Video content.* Senate Commerce Committee.

F. April 7, 2006—*Out at home: Why most Nats fans can't see their team on TV.* House of Representatives, Committee on Government Reform

G. November 14, 2006—*Competition in sports programming and distribution: Are consumers winning?* Senate Judiciary Committee

H. December 7, 2006—*Vertically integrated sports programming: Are cable companies excluding competition?* Senate Judiciary Committee

I. March 27, 2007—*Exclusive sports programming: Examining competition and consumer choice.* Senate Commerce Committee

J. March 5, 2008—*Competition in the sports programming marketplace.* Subcommittee on Telecommunications and the Internet, House Energy and Commerce Committee

K. December 16, 2009—*Piracy of live sports broadcasting over the Internet.* House Judiciary Committee

L. November 17, 2010—*Television viewers, retransmission consent, and the public interest.* Subcommittee on Communications, Technology, and the Internet, Senate Commerce, Science, and Transportation Committee

M. September 10, 2013—*Satellite Television Laws in Title 17.* Subcommittee on Courts, Intellectual Property and the Internet, House Judiciary Committee.

N. December 4, 2014—*The FANS Act: Are sports blackouts and antitrust exemptions harming fans, consumers, and the games themselves?* Senate Judiciary Committee.

The 2008 hearing's purpose, Markey stated, was to examine the effectiveness of policy provisions such as the 1992 Cable Act in regulating the marketplace for sports programming as well as "assess the continued migration of sports programming from broadcast television to pay TV services, exclusive programming packages, the nature of cable carriage for sports programming, the emergence of conference or league channels and program carriage issues generally" ("*Competition,*" 2008, p. 2). While Markey was acknowledging the existence of sports programming migration, Representative Anna Eshoo (D-California) worried about the impact on the consumer, stating, "For an industry that is so heavily subsidized by the public, I am concerned that it is the public that may ultimately pay the price again" ("*Competition,*" 2008, p. 4).

In a written statement prepared for the 2008 hearing, Representative John Dingell (D-Michigan), the Congressman who, in 1992, insisted on inserting language into the 1992 Cable Act which would require the FCC to examine sports programming migration, again voiced concern. Clearly,

Dingell believed, in the 15-plus years since the Cable Act, the problem of migration had not changed.

> Many of this country's greatest sporting events have been broadcast free on over-the-air television for all consumers to enjoy ... Today's hearing asks whether these events will continue to be removed from free, over-the-air broadcast television to the detriment of our local communities ... Taxpayers have a vested interest in this question. Taxpayers finance public universities and approve public financing for professional sport venues. Cities, counties, and states have provided support in other ways, including financial incentives and the use of public resources. It is therefore logical and fair that taxpayers should be able to enjoy the fruits of their investments and continue to see local teams in free, over-the-air broadcasts. I am concerned by the ever-increasing migration of sports programming to pay TV ... I urge my colleagues to keep a close eye on this disturbing trend. (*"Competition,"* 2008, p. 108)

Conclusion

In the more than half-century since the Sports Broadcasting Act became law, much of the broadcast industry and its business models have changed. With each change, consumer conflicts have arisen. Congress, to its credit, has sought to understand those conflicts and issues by introducing 17 different bills focused on sports and television and holding 14 different Congressional hearings. From a review of hearing transcripts and bill languages, three different themes can be discerned. These themes provide insight into the perspectives of elected officials.

By electing not to declare sports programming a public good and enact legislation to prevent siphoning of sports content from free television to pay television, significant migration has occurred. This fact was acknowledged not only on multiple occasions by politicians, but also by the FCC in 2012 in its annual assessment of competition in the marketplace. While this migration has led to increased league and team revenues, the negative byproducts of this migration include rising consumer costs and increasing conflicts among networks, MVPDs, and the leagues themselves.

A fair question to ask, following the 1992 Cable Act which enabled retransmission consent, is whether free television still exists. Consumers can still purchase an antenna, hook it up to their television, and receive a terrestrial signal without any additional fees. According to a 2017 study by the Video Advertising Bureau, only 12% of U.S. households watched video content using over-the-air (OTA) digital broadcast antennas (Granados, 2018).

On multiple occasions, members of Congress have expressed concern over consumers' inability to watch their hometown team without paying more for special channels. The politicians have noted the cultural significance of sport to Americans, particularly baseball, and have suggested watching sports programming is, at least, in the public interest, if not a public right.

Perhaps that connection fueled a second theme to emerge, the not-too-surprising finding that politicians pander to their constituents. This idea of localism led directly to the convening of three Congressional hearings. The first of these occurred in 1989 when an agreement between the New York Yankees and Madison Square Garden network to broadcast games on the cable network led to the initial concern regarding migration to pay television. While that hearing was chaired by a Senator from Ohio, it was New York Senator Charles Schumer who introduced legislation in 1989 titled, the "Baseball Viewers Protection Act of 1989."

In 2006, Virginia Representative Tom Davis called for a hearing to examine the carriage issues around his local MLB team, the Washington Nationals, and the region's dominant cable provider, Comcast. Similarly, in 2007, Massachusetts Senator John Kerry called a hearing after receiving feedback from his "Red Sox Nation" constituents concerned they would not be able to watch Red Sox games following an exclusive deal between MLB and DirecTV.

Finally, politicians have consistently employed similar rhetoric toward revoking the antitrust exemption which leagues enjoy through the Sports Broadcasting Act, while failing to ever actually act on that threat. Senator Joe Lieberman threatened Congressional action as far back as the 1989 hearing. It is a mantra which has been repeated so frequently in front of league officials, it is worth questioning whether or not league representatives even take the threat seriously.

In making the threat, but failing to act, Congress has left behind a confusing legacy about the importance of the public's ability to watch sports programming. Politicians seem united in protecting the public interest and consider sports an important part of our culture. Yet, they also seem reticent to act on behalf of the public in making sports programming less costly and more widely available.

In fact, recent mergers approved by the U.S. Department of Justice suggest the problem will only become more widespread. Scholars who study the political economy of media have bemoaned the trend toward a mass media oligopoly (e.g., Dart, 2014; Law, Harvey, & Kemp, 2002) in which few providers compete for sports content. AT&T's purchase of Time Warner further reduces the numbers of buyers in the space, though alternative media companies such as Amazon, Netflix, and Google may emerge in the wake of this consolidation.

Thus far, Congress has not taken the United States the way of Australia and the EU, despite most sporting events not named the Super Bowl or the

World Series moving to pay television. Until the NFL decides to take the Super Bowl and place it on the NFL Network, depriving millions of Americans access to the league's self-made holiday, it seems unlikely Congress will do anything.

References

Anderson, D. L. (1995). The sports Broadcasting act: Calling it what it is—special interest legislation. *Hastings Communication and Entertainment Law Journal, 17,* 945–959.

Annual assessment of the status of competition in the market for the delivery of video programming. (2012, July 20). *Federal Communications Commission (FCC 12–81).* Washington, DC: Author.

Blaich v. The National Football League. 212 F. Supp. 319 (S.D. N.Y. 1962).

Cable Television Consumer Protection and Competition Act of 1992. (1992). H.Amdt. 742, 102nd Cong.

Competition in the sports programming marketplace: Hearings before the subcommittee on telecommunications and the internet, of the house committee on energy and commerce. (March 5, 2008). 110th Cong. 98.

Dart, J. (2014). New media, professional sport and political economy. *Journal of Sport and Social Issues, 38*(6), 528–547.

Deninger, D. (2012). *Sports on television: The how and why behind what you see.* New York, NY: Routledge.

Diemer, T. (2008). *Fighting the unbeatable foe: Howard Metzenbaum of Ohio, The Washington Years.* Kent, OH: The Kent State University Press.

Evens, T., Iosifidis, P., & Smith, P. (2013). *Political economy of television sports rights: Between culture and commerce.* New York, NY: Palgrave Macmillan.

Exclusive sports programming: Examining competition and consumer choice: Hearings before the Senate Committee on Commerce, Science, and Transportation. (March 27, 2007). 110th Cong. 1067.

Gaustad, T. (2000). The economics of sports programming. *Nordicom Review, 21*(2), 101–113. https://content.sciendo.com/view/journals/nor/21/2/article-p101.xml

Granados, N. (2018, March 30). 2017 report: A quarter of U.S. households only stream video or use digital antenna. *Forbes.com.* Retrieved from https://www.forbes.com/sites/nelsongranados/2018/03/30/2017-report-a-quarter-of-u-s-households-only-stream-video-or-use-digital-antenna/#175e73ad51b6

Gratton, C., & Solberg, H. A. (2007). *The economics of sports broadcasting.* Abingdon, UK: Routledge.

H. R. 2593 (101st): Baseball Viewers Protection Act of 1989. (2018). *govtrack.us.* Retrieved from https://www.govtrack.us/congress/bills/101/hr2593/summary#libraryofcongress

Home Box Office, Inc. v. Federal Communications Commission. 567 F.2d 9 (D.C. Cir. 1977).

Horowitz, I. (1974). Sports broadcasting. In R. G. Noll (Ed.), *Government and the sports business* (pp. 275–323). Washington, DC: The Brookings Institution.

Horowitz, I. (1978). Market entrenchment and the Sports Broadcasting Act. *American Behavioral Scientist, 21*(3), 415–430.

Hutson, D. (2008). Paying the price for sports TV: Preventing the strategic misuse of the FCC's carriage regulations. *Federal Communications Law Journal, 61*, 407–430.

Hylton, J. G. (2011). The over-protection of intellectual property rights in sport in the United States and elsewhere. *Journal of Legal Aspects of Sports, 21*, 43–73.

Iosifidis, P., & Smith, P. (2013). Television sports rights: Between culture and commerce. In K. Donders, C. Pauwels, & J. Loisen (Eds.), *Private television in Western Europe: Content, markets, policies* (pp. 136–150). Basingstoke, UK: Palgrave Macmillan.

Jeanrenaud, C., & Kesenne, S. (2006). *The economics of sport and the media.* Cheltenham, UK: Edward Elgar Publishing.

Klatell, D. A., & Marcus, N. (1988). *Sports for sale: Television, money and the fans.* New York, NY: Oxford University Press.

Law, A., Harvey, J., & Kemp, S. (2002). The global sport mass media oligopoly: The three usual suspects and more. *International Review for the Sociology of Sport, 37*(3–4), 279–302.

Lefever, K. (2012). *New media and sport: International legal aspects.* The Hague, The Netherlands: TMC Asser Press.

Lefever, K., & Van Rompuy, B. (2009). Ensuring access to sports content: 10 years of EU intervention. Time to celebrate? *Journal of Media Law, 1*(2), 243–268.

Lowe, S. R. (1995). *The kid on the Sandlot: Congress and professional sports, 1910–1992.* Bowling Green, OH: Bowling Green State University Popular Press.

MLB, DIRECTV expand multi-year agreement. (2007, March 8). *mlb.com.* Retrieved from http://mlb.mlb.com/content/printer_friendly/mlb/y2007/m03/d08/c1833910 .jsp

Out at home: Why most Nats fans can't see their team on TV: Hearing before the House Committee on Government Reform. (April 7, 2006). 109th Cong. 152.

Public Access to National Sporting Events Act, S. 1015, 102d Cong. (1991).

S. 2954 (95th): A bill to amend the Communications Act of 1934 in order to protect the rights of the general public in the television broadcasting of major sports events. (2018). *govtrack.us.* Retrieved from https://www.govtrack.us/congress/bills/95/ s2954/summary

Siedlecki, M. A. (1978). Sports anti-siphoning rules for pay cable television: A public right to free TV? *Indiana Law Journal, 53*(4), 821–840.

Sport (anti-siphoning). (2015, Oct. 9). *acma.gov.au.* Retrieved from http://www.acma.gov. au/Industry/Broadcast/Television/TV-content-regulation/sport-anti-siphoning- tv-content-regulation-acma

Sports programming and cable television: Hearing before the Subcommittee on Antitrust, Monopolies, and Business Rights, of the House Committee on the Judiciary. 101st Cong. 1209 (Nov. 14, 1989).

Sports programming migration final report. (1994, June 30). *Federal Communications Commission (FCC 94–149).* Washington, DC: Author.

Stewart, L. (2007, Feb. 3). Baseball TV deal contested. *Los Angeles Times.* Retrieved from http://articles.latimes.com/2007/feb/03/sports/sp-extrainnings3

Sunbeam television shuts out DirecTV NFL fans in Miami in attempt to extract 300 percent pay increase. (2012, Jan. 14). *Thestreet.com.* Retrieved from https://www.thestreet.com/story/11376257/1/sunbeam-television-shuts-out-directv-nfl-fans-in-miami-in-attempt-to-extract-300-percent-pay-increase.html

Teeter, Jr., D. L., & Loving, B. (2008). *Law of mass communications: Freedom and control of print and broadcast media* (12th ed.). New York, NY: Foundation Press.

United States v. Southwestern Cable Co., 392 U.S. 157 (9th Cir. 1968).

United States of America v. DirecTV Group Holdings, LLC and AT&T, Inc. (2016, Nov. 2). Case No. 2:16-cv-08150, Complaint, Document 1.

Wolohan, J. T. (2009). United States. In I. Blackshaw, S. Cornelius, & R. Siekmann (Eds.), *TV rights and sport: Legal aspects* (pp. 567–586). The Hague, The Netherlands: TMC Asser Press.

Zimbalist, A. (1994). *Baseball and billions: A probing look into the big business of our national pastime.* New York, NY: Harper Collins.

2. ESPN's Search for a Sustained Global Competitive Advantage

David Bockino

In June 2009, the Irish-based television broadcaster Setanta failed to make a $16 million (US) payment to the English Premier League (EPL), subsequently freeing up a package of television rights to what was arguably the world's most popular soccer league (Davoudi, 2009). ESPN, which had for years proclaimed itself the "Worldwide Leader in Sports," quickly pounced on the opportunity, ponying up an estimated $400 million (US) for the right to air EPL games in the United Kingdom over a four-year period (2009–2013). Less than two months after securing those rights and after a few frantic weeks of preparation, ESPN launched an eponymous television network in the United Kingdom (Grossman, 2010). At the time, Russell Wolff, Executive Vice President and Managing Director of ESPN International, explained that securing rights to the country's most popular soccer league was paramount to ESPN's investment in the region: "The key to growing a global brand is to become as relevant as you can be locally. … It's hard to be relevant unless you're serving sports fans in their own markets" (Garrahan, 2009, para. 7).

But just four years after it entered the market, ESPN sold much of its UK and Ireland television business to the British-based BT Group for a reported $15 million (US) (Szalai, 2013). While ESPN continued to publicly emphasize its commitment to the region, especially with its digital products, the deal was a remarkable about-face for a company that only a few years before viewed its new UK venture as the foothold it needed to maintain a sustained level of relevance across the European sports media landscape.

In many ways, ESPN's foray into and subsequent exit from the United Kingdom television market is a useful starting point from which to examine the company's international strategy over the past 30-plus years. This chapter contextualizes ESPN's global decision making within the framework of

Barney's model of sustained competitive advantage (Barney, 1991). First, it introduces Barney's model and examines ESPN's success in the United States as a function of resource heterogeneity, namely its lucrative relationship with U.S.-based cable carriers. Second, it analyzes an ESPN International success story, the company's 2007 acquisition of Cricinfo, in an effort to understand the nature of sustained competitive advantage when expanding overseas. Third, it analyzes ESPN's entrance into the United Kingdom through the lens of Barney's model, arguing that the company's most celebrated resource—its rights to the English Premier League—failed to provide the company with the competitive advantage it needed to compete in an overheated sports television marketplace. Fourth, it looks at ESPN's multimedia strategy in Australia in order to analyze where the company may be headed next. Finally, it summarizes ESPN's current global strategy, discussing whether the company will ever truly realize its goal of becoming the "Worldwide Leader in Sports."

Sustained Competitive Advantage

In analyzing a firm's capacity to maintain a sustained competitive advantage, Barney (1991) advocated a conceptual shift from an environment-based view of firms toward a resource-based view (see Wernerfelt, 1984), a theoretical framework that emerged from the larger discipline of strategic management. The resource-based view "assumes that each firm is a collection of unique resources that provide the foundation for its strategy and lead to the differences in each firm's performance" (Albarran, Chan-Olmsted & Wirth, 2006, p. 164). With this conceptual shift, an analysis of a firm or industry becomes internal-facing, focusing more on the capabilities of each individual firm rather than the opportunities or threats presented by the environment. The term *resources*, furthermore, becomes an umbrella phrase, referring to "all assets, capabilities, organizational processes, firm attributes, information, knowledge, etc. controlled by a firm that enable the firm to conceive of and implement strategies that improve its efficiency and effectiveness" (Daft, 1983 as cited by Barney, 1991, p. 101).

Barney goes on to propose two assumptions in order to ground his resource-based view of sustained competitive advantage. The first is that "firms within an industry (or group) may be heterogeneous with respect to the strategic resources they control" (p. 101). The second is that "these resources may not be perfectly mobile across firms, and thus heterogeneity can be long lasting" (p. 101). Furthermore, for a firm resource to become a potential source of sustained competitive advantage, Barney suggests that it must have four attributes: "(a) it must be valuable, in the sense that it exploit opportunities and/or neutralizes threats in a firm's environment; (b) it must be rare among a firm's current and potential competition; (c) it must be imperfectly imitable; and (d) there cannot be strategically equivalent substitutes for this resource that are valuable but neither rare or imperfectly imitable" (p. 106).

Since its inception in 1979, ESPN has enjoyed unparalleled success in the U.S. cable and satellite environment. Retroactively, we can conclude that the company has enjoyed a sustained competitive advantage. But how? While at least one scholar has documented the company's rise through "a broader set of law and policy developments that have affected sports, cable, and satellite television industries since the early 1960s" (Corrigan, 2015, p. 38), most analyses of ESPN's rise focus on the internal decisions made by the company's executives (see Fortunato, 2015).

One way to understand ESPN's nearly four-decade competitive advantage is to conceptualize the company's relationship with cable and satellite companies, and specifically, the revenue generated carrier per subscriber, as a heterogeneous firm resource within Barney's model. First, this relationship is *valuable* in that it has been able to "exploit opportunities in the firm's environment" (Barney, 1991, p. 106). While exact numbers are difficult to come by, estimates by the third-party research firm SNL Kagan showed ESPN went from generating an average of $1.14 per U.S. subscriber in 2000 to $7.21 per subscriber in 2016 ("How Much More," 2016). When combined with the conceivable revenue for all of its networks (ESPN, ESPN2, ESPNU, and the SEC Network), the company's subscriber fees translate to potential affiliate revenue of over $9 billion per year (US), even when accounting for the loss of 13-million subscribers since a 2011 peak ("How Much Bigger," 2018).

Second, the amount of revenue ESPN generates through these relationships is *rare*. According to the 2016 SNL Kagan estimates, the NFL Network generated the second highest monthly affiliate fee per subscriber for cable sports networks at $1.39. TNT, a network that airs both entertainment and sports programming, has been estimated to generate close to $2 per subscriber (Bi, 2015). And Fox Sports 1(FS1), the national sports network launched by FOX in 2013, was third at $1.15, more than $6 per subscriber less than ESPN ("How Much More," 2018). Based on these estimates, ESPN would have generated more than $6.5 billion (US) more through subscriber fees in 2016 than FS1.

Third, these relationships are *imperfectly imitable* in that "firms that do not possess these resources cannot obtain them" (Barney, 1991, p. 107). There are, according to Barney, a few ways by which a valuable and rare resource can become imperfectly imitable. Most relevant to the case of ESPN is the suggestion that this process can come about as a result of the firm's "unique historical position" (Barney, 1991, p. 107). How ESPN came to command such lucrative affiliate fees is an often-told tale. It started back in March 1983, when three ESPN executives walked into the Cablevision offices in New York City and demanded 10-cents per subscriber per month for the right to air the network. After some intense negotiations, they got it. And from there a precedent was set, a structure for increased subscriber fees that would soon become the envy of all cable networks. As one scholar has noted, "By securing not only annual rate increases but also compounding increases, ESPN ensured itself exponential carriage fee growth" (Corrigan, 2015, p. 47).

Finally, at least for the first three decades of ESPN's existence, there have been no "strategically equivalent substitutes for this resource" (Barney, 1991, p. 111). Generally speaking, there are two ways in which media companies make money: through subscriptions and through advertising. Newspapers, for example, have traditionally generated 80% of their revenue through advertising (Meyer, 2004). ESPN, however, has historically generated about two-thirds of its revenue from affiliate fees which, at their core, are nothing more than subscriptions (Thompson, 2013). These fees have always been ESPN's cash cow, a continuously increasing, contractually guaranteed, and difficult to duplicate flow of subscriber dollars. But as more consumers abandon traditional cable television and satellite providers for a blend of online streaming services, these relationships with cable carriers may finally become *substitutable*. And those substitutes will undoubtedly take the form of stand-alone, subscription-based services, a situation that executives at ESPN are well aware of (Steinberg, 2018).

ESPN leadership also surely understands that most resources within the sport media environment are far from heterogeneous. Live rights, to use one example, change hands often, sometimes at the most unexpected times. In 2010, for instance, ESPN received significant accolades for its coverage of the FIFA World Cup, capturing "a total of 38 industry awards for its coverage … including three Sports Emmy Awards" ("ESPN's World Cup," 2011, para. 1). But in 2011, the company was outbid by FOX Sports for the rights to the FIFA World Cup and Women's World Cup from 2015 through 2022 ("Fox Wins Bid," 2011). Even more fluid than live sports rights is the talent involved to produce, editorialize, and present those games. Just from 2015 to 2016, ESPN lost such notable contributors as Bill Simmons, Mike Tirico, Skip Bayless, and Colin Cowherd (Roberts, 2016).

What sport media companies must understand, then, is that sustained competitive advantages cannot be built on live rights or talent alone. There must be some other resource, another asset or process or relationship, which remains both valuable and rare *and* difficult to emulate, a lesson that ESPN has undoubtedly learned as it has attempted, with mixed results, to expand overseas during the last four decades. And it is a lesson that becomes abundantly clear when you track the progression of three of ESPN's international ventures: ESPNcricinfo, ESPN UK, and ESPN in Australia.

A Statistical Advantage

In an online article written in 2013, Badri Seshadri recounted the origin of what would become one of the most popular sports websites in the world:

> We were graduate students in the US. I was at Cornell University. The problem was getting hold of cricket scores of any kind. Today to imagine a pre-internet era is really difficult. There was no television that broadcast cricket, the [foreign] newspapers were received a week to ten days after the matches actually happened. No Internet, of course, though the university had Internet connectivity and email. Cricinfo was the culmination of a series of attempts that were made to simply inform a guy that a match had happened a day or five days back and this was the result. (Seshadri, 2013, para. 1)

This situation led Seshadri and a group of willing collaborators to create an online portal named Cricinfo where cricket fans could both check in on current scores and access an unprecedented digital archive of previous results. As Seshadri recalled, "[Soon] a bunch of statisticians, people who had access to *Wisden Almanacks*, started coming in. I remember one name, John Hall. He came up with this idea: why don't we type and archive every Test scorecard ever? This idea was floated … and volunteers came and joined" (Seshadri, 2013, para. 30).

The site was the first of its kind and turned out to be wildly popular with cricket's stat-obsessed fans. Throughout the next decade, Cricinfo continued to grow and in 1997 it received its first advertiser, Titan Watches, followed quickly by Kingfisher and Intel (Shetty, 2013). In 2000, Cricinfo launched its popular Statsguru feature, described today as "the world's premier online tool for analyzing cricket statistics" (Statsguru, 2018, para. 1). The database would become one of the defining features of Cricinfo, a true differentiator among a growing list of online competitors. Eventually, the site would have the ability to capture approximately two-dozen variables for every ball bowled during a match (Writer, 2015). And during the 20-year anniversary celebration of Cricinfo, the British comedian Andy Zaltzman would declare Statsguru its crown jewel:

> If cricket stands undisputed as the greatest creation in the history of humanity, which it does, then Statsguru is the talking penguin in its zoo of marvels. … Statsguru is one of those few inventions that makes such a permanent, immutable change to the planet that it swiftly becomes impossible to imagine life without it: the wheel, the printing press, the aeroplane, the novelty revolving bow-tie, the television, the television remote control, the threat to confiscate the television remote control, childbirth, the gherkin, and the bagel. (Zaltzman, 2013, para. 5)

In 2007, recognizing an opportunity to expand its international foot-print, ESPN jumped in and purchased Cricinfo, rebranding it ESPNcricinfo. com (Kiss, 2007). In an article posted directly on the site, ESPN explained Cricinfo's appeal in a growing digital age:

> Cricket lends itself perfectly to online coverage: the length of matches and the statistics-rich nature of the game combine to drive high global usage and build loyalty, and that's where Cricinfo has scored. Beginning with scorecards and live scores, the portal pioneered audio and video streaming of cricket matches. ("Cricinfo Staff," 2007, para. 8)

John Kosner, the head of ESPN's digital offerings at the time was so impressed with the site that he said he wanted "a Cricinfo for every sport" ("How Do You," 2008, para. 5). The Cricinfo staff, meanwhile, was told that the site would maintain its identity and independence, and would essentially be run outside the normal ESPN operations (Kiss, 2007).

What ESPN recognized is that ESPNcricinfo's sophisticated data-driven foundation provided the site with a sustained competitive advantage (see Barney, 1991). Its statistical backbone is valuable in that it attracts an engaged and loyal fan base (which can then be turned into advertising dollars), rare in that no other site has a similar level of depth, and difficult to emulate because of its unique historical conditions, coming to fruition during the early days of the Internet and propped up by the expertise of the team at *Wisden Almanacks,* sometimes referred to as the "Bible of Cricket" (Robinson, 2013). This unique resource has contributed to ESPNcricinfo becoming the most popular cricket website in the world and the undis-puted global category leader in "unique audience, total time spent, vis-its, page views, and average minutes per visitor" (ESPNcricinfo Factsheet, 2015, para. 2).

Just a few months after its 2007 purchase of Cricinfo, George Boden-heimer, the President of ESPN, hinted to a reporter that the company was ready to embark on an international spending spree. He explained the com-pany's international strategy as follows: "We're going to work on getting as local as we can. We want to deliver product that is relevant in each country. It's a country-by-country approach. We want to be investors wherever the top sports product is" (Garrahan, 2007, para. 7). He noted that the English Premier League was a prime target. It's a "fabulous property," he said to a reporter, "we are absolutely interested in it" (Garrahan, 2007, para. 3). Eigh-teen months later, Setanta would miss its payment to the league, the rights would come up for auction, and ESPN would have the opening in the United Kingdom it had been waiting for.

It's Great to Be Here

From the beginning, ESPN knew it faced an uphill battle to build a dedicated audience in the United Kingdom. In order to promote its newly launched standalone network as well as spread awareness of its foray into English Premier League programming, the company flew over several executives from its U.S.-based marketing team and launched a multimillion-dollar ad campaign with the slogan "It's Great to be Here" (Sweney, 2009). The campaign included shots from well-known EPL stadiums as well as "images of rainy days, local football pitches and fans wearing team shirts in their everyday surroundings" (Johnson, 2009, para. 4). The campaign was a manifestation of the strategy mentioned above: harness the power of the ESPN machine but be as local as possible.

Several pundits thought ESPN was well positioned to succeed. One writer commented that, "the timing is right for ESPN to expand into the U.K. Gone are the days when Britain was solely for the British, as international brands are everywhere" (Grossman, 2010, para. 10). But it would be a performance largely reliant on help from others. Because although ESPN had the rights to air the English Premier League, everything involved with live game production, advertising, and subscriptions had been handed off to BSkyB, the region's most popular sports broadcaster and, in many ways, a direct competitor of ESPN ("ESPN Expands," 2009).

Still, things seemed to be going well for ESPN as late as 2012. In April, the company reported its twelfth consecutive month of ratings growth, noting that audiences were up 18% (Gibson, 2012). According to Ross Hair, who was serving as ESPN's managing director for Europe, the Middle East, and Africa, ESPN was showing more live soccer than any other network in the country. It had added the FA Cup, the Europa League, and the Scottish Premier League to a roster that already included its crown jewel, the English Premier League, as well as the top Italian and German leagues. "We've come an awful long way in the short time we've had," Hair told a reporter in 2012, "We are still in investment mode, we're still building our business" (Gibson, 2012, para. 22). Speaking to the future, Hair also said that ESPN would "bid 'aggressively' for 'more games' of 'better quality'" (Gibson, 2012, para. 7).

A few months after that interview, ESPN's momentum was abruptly halted. In a surprising turn of events, BT, a UK telecommunications company, decided it wanted to secure its own package of EPL rights, thus initiating an aggressive bidding war. When the dust settled, BT and BSkyB were the two companies left standing, spending approximately $4.7 billion (US)—a 40% increase from the previous three-year deal—to air games for the next three years (Sabbagh, 2012). The drastic price increase was unexpected and left ESPN without its most valuable resource. As one journalist wrote at the time:

> Many thought the value of Premier League TV rights had peaked. That they had not done so is due to unexpectedly aggressive bidding – not least from BT, previously better known as a phone company, which has snatched the rights to air the remaining games from ESPN. (Sabbagh, 2012, para. 2)

Without its core property, ESPN began putting together an exit strategy. Company executives knew that UK sports fans would never pay extra for a channel that no longer aired the most popular league in the country. In early 2013, ESPN sold its UK and Ireland-based television channels to the same company that outbid it for the EPL rights, BT. According to an article in *The Guardian*, the deal was reportedly in the "low tens of millions" (Deans & Gibson, 2013, para. 1). Two years later, in 2015, ESPN and BT signed what was essentially a programming and licensing deal. The seven-year agreement allowed BT to show up to 5,000 hours a year of ESPN programming on its network and gives the company "the opportunity to use the ESPN brand in a range of different ways" (Lees, 2015, para. 2). A few months later, BT renamed one of its channels BT Sport ESPN.

Why was ESPN able to find so much success with ESPNcricinfo but fail so quickly with ESPN UK? The short answer is that ESPN UK had no resources: No "assets, capabilities, organizational processes, firm attributes, information, knowledge, etc." able to provide the company with a sustained competitive advantage (Barney, 1991, p. 101). Production, advertising sales, and affiliate agreements had been handed off to outside entities. The ESPN *brand*, meanwhile, could not be counted on to prop up an otherwise unimpressive programming slate. And their most important asset, live rights to English Premier League matches, was available to any company willing to spend the money.

ESPNcricinfo, on the other hand, does not rely on live sport rights. Instead, it relies on a proprietary statistical database developed over the last few decades and comprehensive enough to attract and maintain an engaged and loyal audience. In fact, ESPN has sometimes chosen *not* to air live cricket on ESPNcricinfo, even when presented with the opportunity. In 2015, for example, ESPN secured the rights to air the 2015 ICC Cricket World Cup in the United States but decided to distribute them separately from ESPNcricinfo, both as a stand-alone fee-based streaming service called ESPNcricket2015. com and as a pay-per-view to cable and satellite television subscribers (Adler, 2015). It was a strategic move by ESPN management in two ways. First, it allowed ESPN to test a stand-alone streaming service, a priority for the company in an era where cord-cutting by cable subscribers has become a major concern. As one analyst wrote at the time, "The move is important because it's the first time ESPN will sell some of its stuff directly to consumers instead of wholesaling it to pay-TV providers" (Kafka, 2014, para. 5). And second, it kept cricket's premiere event off ESPNcricinfo, thus preventing the site's dedicated following from developing an expectation for high-level live cricket, an expectation largely dependent on continuously securing rights to air those matches.

In 2012, just as ESPN was being outbid for the English Premier League rights in the UK, Disney Chairman and Chief Executive Bob Iger seemed to walk back George Bodenheimer's 2007 comments regarding ESPN's global strategy when he told a group of investors, "ESPN's international business has never been particularly large, nor has it been a huge priority for the company" (Henderson, 2012, para. 2). The aggressive bidding for live sports rights, Iger stated, continued to stymie ESPN's growth and its experience in the UK was perhaps a signal that ESPN's global strategy would have to change. As Iger said, "It's kind of tough to be as aggressive buying live sports. So, the opportunities for ESPN internationally, I think, are somewhat limited. Not to say that they don't exist, but it's never going to be a big part of ESPN's business" (Henderson, 2012, para. 7).

Strategy Down Under

So where does ESPN International go from here? A good place to look is Australia, where ESPN has seen significant success in growing its business since the turn of the century. The company's presence in the region is significant. It operates two television networks—ESPN and ESPN2—which reach over two million households and cater mostly to an Australian-based audience interested in American (e.g., NBA, NFL, MLB) and international sport (e.g., global soccer). In 2017, the network aired the NBA Finals, the Super Bowl, the MLB World Series, the X Games, the FA Cup Final and the 2018 World Cup qualifiers ("2017 International," 2017). Decisions on what games to air often come down to how relevant the matchup is to an Australian audience. The network, for example, has been known to air multiple St. Mary's of California basketball games per year because the school has had at least one Australian on its roster since 2001 (Brown, 2016). In addition to its television business, ESPN also operates a thriving digital network, mostly populated with websites designed to cater to sport-specific audiences including ESPNcricinfo (cricket), ESPNFC (soccer), and ESPNscrum (rugby).

The company's strength in the region is buoyed by two factors: (a) its expertise with American sport; and (b) its robust digital offerings. According to the ESPN International marketing team, ESPN is "the #1 channel and ESPN.com is the #1 website for providing the 'best range of American sport'" ("2017 International," para. 7). Its digital portfolio, meanwhile, ranks first "amongst all sports properties in terms of time spent and page views" (para. 1).

In 2016, ESPN continued to expand its investment in Australia by launching a localized version of its eponymous website (ESPN.com.au). According to Haydn Arndt, the general manager of ESPN Australia/New Zealand, the site was designed to be "authentically ESPN but distinctly Australian" (Bodey, 2016, para. 4). On the site's first day, Managing Editor Andy Withers referred to two Australian athletes competing in the United States to support his promise that ESPN.com.au would continue to cover Australians competing on the world stage:

> We're committed to bringing you more because we know you want more. We want more. And we want to give it with passion. You want more thoughtful analysis and reports of the Aussies in Action overseas. Can we explain the slump of Ben Simmons' LSU Tigers? Can we envision the Bogut's-eye view of Steph Curry's wizardry? (Withers, 2016, para. 4)

But Withers also announced that the company would expand its coverage to include the most popular Australian leagues:

> AFL [Australian Football League], NRL [National Rugby League], V8 Supercars and netball now sit proudly alongside NBA, NFL, Major League Baseball, soccer, cricket, rugby union, college sports, tennis, golf, Formula 1 … all covered in-depth with the rigour and diligence, style and swagger, that you expect from ESPN. (Withers, 2016, para. 2)

Accompanying this strategy was ESPN's announcement that they had signed several high-profile Australia-based analysts to its team such as Brett Kimmorley, who would be covering the NRL, and Brad Haddin, who would be covering all things related to Australian cricket.

With this investment, ESPN was utilizing lessons learned from its UK experiment and attempting to become locally relevant in a much subtler and more cost-effective way. Instead of investing big dollars in the live rights to Australia's most popular sports leagues (e.g., AFL, NRL), the company was hoping to build on its existing digital presence in order to create a one-stop shop for *all* Australian sports fans. By doing so, ESPN was relying on two specific resources as a way to develop a sustained competitive advantage in the region. First, it took advantage of its brand, known across the world as the preeminent *American* sports media company. When tasked with delivering local sport at a local level, as it tried to do in the United Kingdom, this brand strength means little. But when asked to deliver American sport at a local level, ESPN's brand becomes an authoritative and difficult to emulate resource.

Second, ESPN took advantage of its strong digital infrastructure, one that was already reaching millions of Australian sports fans. Although it was promoting a new domain name—ESPN.com.au—ESPN by no means created this site from scratch. The site would look and operate, for instance, exactly like the company's main site, ESPN.com. And much of the content was populated from other channels. For American sports coverage, ESPN linked to news from its flagship site. For cricket coverage, ESPN pulled articles and recaps from the world's most popular cricket website, ESPNcricinfo. com. For soccer coverage, ESPN pulled information from its soccer-specific site ESPNFC.com. The only new material, in fact, was the Australian-specific coverage, such as recaps and analysis for the AFL or NRL. On a macro scale, it was the same strategy that had been deployed in the United Kingdom— locally relevant sports content—but because it didn't include live rights, and because it built upon a foundation already in place, the strategy had a much smaller price point.

The International Future of ESPN

In a 1997 article, scholar Robert McChesney wrote how, "ESPN International dominates televised sport, broadcasting on a 24-hour basis in 21 languages to over 165 countries. ... In Latin America the emphasis is on soccer, in Asia it is table tennis, and in India ESPN provided over 1,000 hours of cricket in 1995" (McChesney, 1997, para. 27).

But while McChesney got ESPN's strategy right (i.e., global but locally relevant), his statement was a gross exaggeration. ESPN has never "dominated" televised sport on a global scale. In fact, over its 40-year history, ESPN has had more than its share of international missteps. It failed to establish a sustained competitive advantage in the United Kingdom television market and was forced to sell its eponymous network only a few years after launch. Around the same time, it sold its 50% stake in ESPN Star Sports, a joint venture that ran over a dozen television networks throughout Asia, to News Corp. for a reported $250 million (US) (Szalai, 2012). It was also forced to shut down two other networks—ESPN America and ESPN Classic—across Europe, the Middle East, and Africa (Fang, 2013). As of 2018, ESPN had failed to gain much traction in the country with the world's biggest population (China) and its most successful venture in the country with the world's second biggest population (India) had been a website that ESPN simply renamed.

Many of these missteps can be conceptualized within Barney's resource-based view of sustained competitive advantage. For example, in some regions, ESPN has found that live rights can be valuable and rare but easily attained by a firm willing to spend the money. In other regions, ESPN has found that its brand, although strong in the United States, is nearly worthless when broad-casting local sport in a different country. Finding a resource that will provide a sustained competitive advantage, then, has become a region-by-region exercise.

Furthermore, if ESPN's overarching international strategy has been to become locally relevant, that strategy has manifested itself in different ways. In a few regions, ESPN remains a programming and production juggernaut. Across Latin America, for example, where ESPN entered the cable market early, the network retains a significant multimedia audience through its local-ized news coverage (e.g., *SportsCenter*) as well as its schedule of local soc-cer (e.g., Mexican League, Copa America), American sport (e.g., NFL and MLB), and international sport (e.g., professional golf and tennis).

In other regions, however, ESPN has pursued various licensing or partner-ship deals. After exiting the UK, for example, ESPN allowed BT Group—the company that outbid it for a new package of EPL rights—to use the ESPN brand on its American-based sports network (Lees, 2015). In 2016, ESPN negotiated a deal with Tencent, a company that one news outlet has called "the Chinese Internet colossus" (Stone & Chen, 2017, para 1), to show ESPN-branded content and programming such as the NBA and X Games across Tencent's wide array of social and digital based platforms (Huddleston, 2016).

At the end of the 2010s, ESPN was still very much a global entity. Accord-ing to the company's marketing materials, it reached sports fans in over 200 countries and territories in five different languages and had offices and/or production facilities in at least nine of those regions (the United States, India, Argentina, Hong Kong, the United Kingdom, Australia, Brazil, Singapore and Canada). The company's specific media holdings included "32 television networks, 13 websites, 90+ broadband networks, 7 radio properties" as well as various print, mobile, consumer product and event management extensions all over the world ("About," 2018). But the idea of *reach* suggests availability rather than dominance. In many of those 200 countries, ESPN maintains a solid but unremarkable presence, delivering its content through niche digital channels or low-maintenance partnerships. And with the price of global sport rights escalating quickly, it is unlikely that ESPN, which faces decreasing prof-itability in the United States, will attempt to muscle its way into a region by emulating its UK strategy—bidding for a region's most popular sports league and subsequently launching a linear television network.

But that is not to say ESPN and its parent company Disney will not pursue opportunities outside the United States if and when they emerge. Whether it succeeds, however, depends on how well the company utilizes its heterogeneous resources. And if history has shown anything, ESPN will need a lot more than live rights to maintain a sustained global competitive advantage.

References

2017 International Planning Guide—Aus & NZ. Retrieved from http://worldofespn. com/uploads/900009/1508776940777/ESPN_PlanningGuide2017_Australia. pdf

About. (2018). *World of ESPN*. Retrieved from http://www.worldofespn.com/about

Adler, K. (2015, January 30). ESPN coverage of ICC Cricket World Cup to be on ESPNcricket2015.com. *ESPN MediaZone.com*. Retrieved from https://espnmediazone.com/us/press-releases/2015/01/espn-coverage-icc-cricket-world-cup-espncricket2015-com/

Albarran, A. B., Chan-Olmsted, S. M., & Wirth, M. O. (2006). *Handbook of media management and economics*. Mahwah, NJ: Lawrence Erlbaum Associates.

Barney, J. (1991). Firm resources and sustained competitive advantage. *Journal of Management, 17*(1), 99–120. https://doi.org/10.1177/014920639101700108

Bi, F. (2015, January 8). ESPN leads all cable networks in affiliate fees. *Forbes.com*. Retrieved from https://www.forbes.com/sites/frankbi/2015/01/08/espn-leads-all-cable-networks-in-affiliate-fees/

Bodey, M. (2016, February 29). Coming in to bat: ESPN set to launch local website. *The Australian*. Retrieved from https://www.theaustralian.com.au/business/media/coming-in-to-bat-espn-set-to-launch-local-website/news-story/4e3fa6e4b 371127f00e8f147ec493616

Brown, C. L. (2016, October 21). How Saint Mary's Australian pipeline got started. *ESPN. com*. Retrieved from http://www.espn.com/mens-college-basketball/story/_/id/ 17841484

Corrigan, T. (2015). Digging the moat. In J. McGuire, G. Armfield, & A. Earnheardt (Eds.), *The ESPN effect: Exploring the worldwide leader in sports* (pp. 37–51). New York, NY: Peter Lang.

Cricinfo Staff. (2007, June 11). ESPN acquires Cricinfo. *ESPNCricinfo*. Retrieved from http://www.espncricinfo.com/ci/content/story/297655.html

Daft, R. (1983). *Organization theory and design*. Boston, MA: Cengage.

Davoudi, S. (2009, June 21). Struggling Setanta runs out of rescue options. *FT.com*. Retrieved from https://www.ft.com/content/76f79502-5e84-11de-91ad-00144feabdc0

Deans, J., & Gibson, O. (2013, February 25). BT buys ESPN'S UK and Ireland TV channels. *The Guardian*. Retrieved from http://www.theguardian.com/media/2013/ feb/25/espn-bt-vision

ESPNCricinfo Factsheet. (2015). *ESPNMediaZone.com*. Retrieved from https://espnme-diazone.com/espnuk/espncricinfo-june-13-factsheet/

ESPN expands in United Kingdom. (2009, August 22). *Variety*. Retrieved from http://variety.com/2009/tv/features/espn-expands-in-united-kingdom-1118007587/

ESPN's World Cup coverage wins three Sports Emmy awards. (2011, June 3). *SoccerAmerica*. Retrieved from https://www.socceramerica.com/publications/article/42433/espns-world-cup-coverage-wins-three-sports-emmy-a.html

Fang, K. (2013, May 13). ESPN quietly shutting down international channels. *Awfulannouncing.com*. Retrieved from http://awfulannouncing.com/2013/espn-quietly-shutting-down-international-channels.html

Fortunato, J. (2015). Changing the competitive environment for sports broadcast rights. In J. McGuire, G. Armfield, & A. Earnheardt (Eds.), *The ESPN effect: Exploring the worldwide leader in sports* (pp. 24–35). New York, NY: Peter Lang.

Fox Sports wins bid to televise World Cup in 2018, '22. (2011, October 21). *ESPN.com*. Retrieved from http://www.espn.com/sports/soccer/news/_/id/7130785/fox-sports-wins-bid-espn-nbc-televise-world-cup-2018-22

Garrahan, M. (2007, December 9). ESPN eyes UK rights to premier league. *Financial Times*. Retrieved from https://ftalphaville.ft.com/2007/12/10/9494/espn-eyes-uk-rights-to-premier-league/

Garrahan, M. (2009, June 23). ESPN set to tackle English football. *FT.Com*. Retrieved from https://www.ft.com/content/6073375a-601e-11de-a09b-00144feabdc0

Gibson, O. (2012, May 2). FA Cup the springboard as ESPN plots Premier League expansion. *The Guardian*. Retrieved from https://www.theguardian.com/football/2012/may/02/fa-cup-espn-premier-league

Grossman, B. (2010, December 20). In a flyover state: Where there is a little upstart called ESPN. *Broadcasting & Cable, 140*(47), 26. Retrieved from https://www.broadcastingcable.com/news/flyover-state-where-there-little-upstart-called-espn-111480

Henderson, R. (2012, May 9). ESPN could quit UK. Retrieved from https://www.pocket-lint.com/tv/news/115417-espn-could-quite-uk-fa-cup

How do you view? (2008, July 31). *The Economist*. Retrieved from https://www.economist.com/node/11825546

How much bigger is ESPN than FS1? February 2018 Cable Coverage Estimates. (2018, January 30). *Sports TV Ratings*. Retrieved from https://sportstvratings.com/how-much-bigger-is-espn-than-fs1-october-2017-cable-coverage-estimates-2-2/8703/

How much more does ESPN make in affiliate revenue than the other sports networks? (2016, August 30). *Sports TV Ratings*. Retrieved from https://sportstvratings.com/how-much-more-does-espn-make-in-affiliate-revenue-than-the-other-sports-networks/5737/

Huddleston, T. (2016, February 3). How ESPN plans to conquer China. *Fortune*. Retrieved from http://fortune.com/2016/02/03/espn-tencent-china/

Johnson, S. (2009, August 5). ESPN focuses on "British" identity. *Marketing*, 8. Retrieved from https://search.proquest.com/docview/214959450?rfr_id=info%3Axri%2Fsid%3Aprimo

Kafka, P. (2014, October 5). Why ESPN thinks it can sell NBA games on the Web without breaking up its pay TV bundle. *recode.net*. Retrieved from https://www.recode.net/2014/10/5/11631606/why-espn-thinks-it-can-sell-nba-games-on-the-web-without-breaking-up

Kiss, J. (2007, June 11). ESPN buys Cricinfo website from Wisden Group. *The Guardian*. Retrieved from http://www.theguardian.com/media/2007/jun/11/digitalmedia.sport

Lees, W. (2015, April 24). BT SPORT and ESPN deepen relationship with long-term collaboration. *ESPNMediazone.com*. Retrieved from https://espnmediazone.com/espnuk/press-releases/2015/04/bt-sport-and-espn-deepen-relationship-with-long-term-collaboration/

McChesney, R. W. (1997, November 1). The global media giants. *Fair.org*. Retrieved from https://fair.org/extra/the-global-media-giants/

Meyer, P. (2004). *The vanishing newspaper: Saving journalism in the information age*. Columbia, MO: University of Missouri Press.

Roberts, D. (2016, May 12). How ESPN's talent exodus could actually save ESPN. *Yahoo! Finance*. Retrieved from https://finance.yahoo.com/news/how-espn-exodus-of-expensive-tv-talent-simmons-olbermann-cowherd-tirico-bayless-could-save-it-190031820.html

Robinson, J. (2013, April 12). The Bible of Cricket turns 150. *Wall Street Journal*. Retrieved from https://www.wsj.com/articles/SB10001424127887323741004578416490298585144

Sabbagh, D. (2012, June 13). Premier League strikes gold with BT talking telephone numbers. *The Guardian*. Retrieved from http://www.theguardian.com/media/blog/2012/jun/13/premier-league-strikes-gold-bt

Seshadri, B. (2013, September 26). A bot called Cricinfo. *ESPNCricinfo*. Retrieved from http://www.espncricinfo.com/cricinfoat20/content/current/story/674431.html

Shetty, R. (2013). The first two decades. *ESPNCricinfo*. Retrieved from http://www.espncricinfo.com/cricinfoat20/content/site/cricinfoat20/timeline.html

Statsguru. (2018). *ESPNCricinfo.com*. Retrieved from http://stats.espncricinfo.com/guru

Steinberg, B. (2018, March 27). ESPN's Jimmy Pitaro on cord-cutting, new takes on sports coverage and the NFL. *Variety*. Retrieved from http://variety.com/2018/tv/news/jimmy-pitaro-espn-nfl-streaming-politics-1202736559/

Stone, B., & Chen, L. (2017, June 28). Tencent dominates in China. Next challenge is rest of the world. *Bloomberg.com*. Retrieved from https://www.bloomberg.com/news/features/2017-06-28/tencent-rules-china-the-problem-is-the-rest-of-the-world

Sweney, M. (2009, August 3). ESPN plugs Premier League coverage in ads for UK sports channel. *The Guardian*. Retrieved from http://www.theguardian.com/media/2009/aug/03/espn-premier-league-campaign

Szalai, G. (2012, June 6). News Corp. to buy out ESPN's stake in Asian TV venture. *The Hollywood Reporter*. Retrieved from https://www.hollywoodreporter.com/news/news-corp-buy-espn-asia-stake-334177

Szalai, G. (2013, February 25). ESPN to sell U.K., Ireland TV channels to British telecom giant BT. *The Hollywood Reporter*. Retrieved from https://www.hollywoodreporter.com/news/espn-sell-uk-tv-channels-424219

Thompson, D. (2013, June 28). How ESPN makes money—in 1 graph. *The Atlantic*. Retrieved from https://www.theatlantic.com/business/archive/2013/06/how-espn-makes-money-in-1-graph/277342/

Wernerfelt, B. (1984). A resource-based view of the firm. *Strategic Management Journal*, 5(2), 171–180. https://doi.org/10.1002/smj.4250050207

Withers, A. (2016, March 1). ESPN: Serving Australian sports fans now better than ever. Retrieved from http://www.espn.com/afl/story/_/id/14874766

Writer, P. (2015, February 19). ESPNcricinfo launches "Insights" to further strengthen its content offering. *PaulWrtier.com*. Retrieved from https://paulwriter.com/espncricinfo-launches-insights-strengthen-content-offering/

Zaltzman, A. (2013, June 19). In praise of Statsguru. *ESPNcricinfo*. Retrieved from http://www.espncricinfo.com/cricinfoat20/content/current/story/637682.html

3. *A Whole New Ball Game? The Changing European Sports Rights Marketplace*

PAUL SMITH

During the early 1990s, Rupert Murdoch's embryonic British pay-TV service, Sky (then called BSkyB), agreed a landmark exclusive live television rights deal with the newly established English Premier League (EPL) and proclaimed the arrival of a new era for English football (and British television) with the slogan: *It's a whole new ball game!*

Some 25 years later, Sky (in the United Kingdom (UK), Germany, Italy and Ireland), together with other established pay-TV broadcasters across Europe, such as Canal Plus (France), Mediaset (Italy) and Eurosport (various), is itself facing a potentially game changing scenario; namely, the growing use of online delivery for sports content. Put another way, the European sports rights market is in a state of flux, positioned somewhere between the traditional "broadcast model" and a new "networked model" for sports content (Hutchins & Rowe, 2009). Focusing on the European Union's (EU) "big five" (France Germany, Italy, Spain and the UK), this chapter examines how key media and sports organisations are both shaping and responding to Europe's changing sports rights market.

Following a brief account of the historical development and key features of sports broadcasting in Europe, the rest of the chapter is divided into two main parts. The first part focuses on how the delivery of sports content via the Internet is threatening to disrupt the dominance of Europe's sports rights market by a handful of national pay-TV companies. This section highlights the ongoing challenge facing media and sports organisations from the availability of (and willingness of consumers to watch) live sports content transmitted (i.e., streamed) illegally online. It also details the increased competition faced by Europe's established pay-TV companies from (actual and/or potential) new entrants to the sports rights market, using the Internet to deliver sports content directly to consumers, over-the-top (OTT). The second part of the chapter moves on to consider how some of Europe's main pay-TV operators have responded to increased competition by launching their own OTT services and/or restructuring their conventional bundled pay-TV sports channel offerings. This section also analyses how various national and international sports organisations are attempting to balance potential commercial opportunities from the launch of their own OTT services with a desire to avoid undermining the value of existing lucrative national rights deals with established broadcasters. Taken together, it is argued that these developments are producing an increasingly complex European sports rights market, characterised by a myriad of interlocking relationships and rivalries between established broadcasters, new entrants and sports organisations, which encompass single or multiple delivery technologies, and for the most part remain organised along national market lines, even though many media and sports organisations operate within multiple European countries (and beyond).

Sport and Television in Europe: From National Events to Pay-TV

From the 1950s until around the middle of the 1980s, television and sport in Europe developed in parallel: Both were organised at a national level with one public TV-channel and one federation (per sport) per country ("The European Model," 1998). During this period, sport was an important part of the mix of public service programming offered by state owned broadcasters, such as the BBC (UK), ARD and ZDF (Germany), RAI (Italy) and France Television. However, sports coverage was limited to a relatively small number of major national and international sporting events, including national and continental football cup finals, the Olympic Games and FIFA World Cup football matches involving their respective national teams. This was partly due to the limited amount of time available to dedicate to coverage of sporting events alongside other forms of programming. But it was also the result of a widely held belief amongst sporting organisations that television coverage would lead to reduced attendance at live events and thus reduced revenue.

During the 1980s and 1990s, deregulation at the national level and liberalisation at the pan-European level via the Television without Frontiers Directive ("Directive," 1989), alongside the development of cable and satellite television delivery technologies, facilitated the emergence of commercial (free-to-air and subscription) television across Europe. This led to a significant growth in the amount of sports coverage available to European viewers. Across Europe as a whole, between 1989 and 1995, "sports coverage increased from 24,000 hours to some 58,000 hours" per year (Maguire, 1999, p.144). During the late 1990s, the launch of dedicated sports channels in numerous European countries increased the amount of sport on television still further. In 1995, there were only three sports channels available in Europe; by 2000, there were about 60 different sports channels in operation around the continent (Papathanassopoulos, 2002, p.189).

During the 1990s and 2000s, increased coverage of live sport on television in Europe was primarily driven by pay-TV broadcasters, who, in Rupert Murdoch's much quoted phrase, used exclusive sports rights as a "battering ram" to open up national markets (Milliken, 1996, para. 1). With this approach, by the early 2000s, pay-TV services were established across Europe, most notably by BSkyB and On Digital (UK); Canal Plus and Télévision Par Satellite (TPS) (France); Canal Satélite Digital and Via Digital (Spain); Premiere (Germany); and Telepiù and Stream (Italy) (Cave & Crandall, 2001). However, intense competition for premium sports rights resulted in monopolistic pay-TV market structures and major corporate failures (Leandros & Tsourvakas, 2005). During the early 2000s, in an attempt to establish and/or challenge a dominant market position, a whole host of European pay-TV broadcasters overpaid for sports rights and faced the "winners curse" of heavy losses and/or bankruptcy, including On Digital (renamed ITV Digital) and Setanta (UK), Premiere (Germany) (taken over by BSkyB), Telepiù and Stream (Italy) (merged to form Sky Italia), TPS (France) (merged with Canal Plus) and Quiero TV (Spain). By the early 2000s, Europe's national pay-TV markets had become "winner-takes-all-markets," largely dependent on the exclusive ownership of key sports rights (Cudd, 2007). The last decade or so, has witnessed more new entrants to Europe's major pay-TV markets, with traditional (former state owned) telecommunications companies, British Telecom (BT) (UK), Deutsche Telekom (Germany), Orange/France Telecom (France) and Telefonica (Spain), investing in premium sports rights in their respective national markets. Here, sports rights have been used as a vital part of "triple play" strategies employed to ensure a competitive position in the increasingly converged pay-TV and broadband markets (Smith, Evens, & Iosifidis, 2016). Finally, the Qatari government financed broadcaster, beIN Sport, launched pay-TV services in France and Spain, accompanied by heavy investment in sports rights.

The strategic importance attached to key sport rights by Europe's pay-TV operators has led to a major escalation in value of rights since the 1990s. For example, between 1992 and 2010–12, the value of European television rights for the Olympic Games increased by 700% ("Study on Sports,"

2014). Similarly, between 1990 and 2010, the value of the European rights to the FIFA World Cup increased by over 1100% ("Study on Sports," 2014). Even more importantly, the rights for domestic European football leagues have also experienced significant inflation over the last couple of decades. A defining feature of the vast majority of European sports rights markets is the overwhelming popularity and therefore commercial value of a single sport, namely football, and in particular domestic club football. Across the EU's "big five," football accounts for 79% of the total spending on sports rights, with the acquisition of rights to domestic football leagues accounting for more than half of all spending ("Study on Sports," 2014). Formula One is the second most valuable sport (4.4%), followed by rugby (4%), the Olympic Games (2.2%) and tennis (1.9%) ("Study on Sports," 2014). It is hardly surprising therefore that the exclusive live rights for domestic football have experienced some of the biggest increases in value over recent years. This has been most marked in the case of the EPL (see Table 3.1), but Europe's other major domestic football leagues have also attracted significant and escalating payments from pay-TV operators within their respective national markets (Smith et al., 2016). Furthermore, the increasing value of television rights has also meant that major sporting organisations in general, and football clubs in Europe's major leagues in particular, have become increasingly reliant on the sale of live television rights for a significant proportion of their total income. For clubs in Europe's big five football leagues, the sale of domestic media rights accounted for an average of 39% of total revenue and increases to 49% when revenue from the sale of television rights for UEFA European level competitions are also taken into account ("The European club," 2018).

Table 3.1: The value of (UK) live Premier League football rights.

Years	Value (£ millions)
1992–1997	191
1997–2001	670
2001–2004	1,200
2004–2007	1,024
2007–2010	1,706
2010–2013	1,773
2013–2016	3,018
2016–2019	5,136
2019–2022	4,654

Sources: Data adapted from "Premier League in," (2015); O'Halloran (2018); Biddiscombe (2018).

Finally, it should be noted that the "battering ram" strategy employed by national pay-TV operators have long attracted the attention of Europe's media policy makers and competition regulators, at both national and EU level (Smith, Evens, & Iosifidis, 2015). First, during the early 2000s, the use of exclusive football rights as a source of market power within Europe's pay-TV markets led to introduction of measures designed to ensure greater competition for rights, most notably the division of television rights into a number of smaller packages, three year limits on the lengths of exclusive contracts and the unbundling of new media rights (from live television rights) ("Commission Clears," 2003). Second, to prevent live television coverage of major international and national sporting events migrating from free-to-air to pay-TV, during the late 1990s, the European Commission introduced major events legislation within the EU. While far from all member states have implemented this co-ordinating, but not compulsory, measure, most of the biggest, including the UK, Germany, France, and Italy have taken the opportunity to ensure access to a host of sporting events is preserved for free-to-air viewers (Evens, Iosifidis, & Smith, 2013).

New Issues and New Players

The online delivery of sports content poses a number of challenges for Europe's established pay-TV operators and leading sports organisations. To start with, both have become increasingly concerned at the use of the Internet to illegally distribute live sports coverage, which it is feared could reduce viewing figures for official broadcasters and undermine the commercial value of rights. These fears are not entirely without foundation. While by its very nature the exact scale of illegal streaming by sports fans is difficult to ascertain, survey evidence suggests the practice is widespread, particularly amongst younger fans. According to an extensive BBC survey ("Premiere League: Third," 2017), more than a third of EPL football fans say they regularly watch matches live online via unofficial streams, and the proportion increases to over 60% for younger fans (age 18–34). Similarly, a European Union Intellectual Property Office (EUIPO) survey, found that illegal viewing was most common in Spain, with around 33% of respondents using illegal sources to access online content, including live football matches (Clancy, 2016). Fears over the impact of illegal viewing were also given credibility when the beginning of the 2016–17 Premier League season was accompanied by a fall in television audiences for live matches of around 20% (Gibson, 2016).

In response, Europe's national football leagues and pay-TV operators have made a concerted effort to tackle copyright infringement. First, this has meant making full use of the courts to prosecute those involved in illegal streaming and/or the selling of illicit set-top boxes designed to facilitate access to illegal streams, which, in the UK, has resulted in heavy fines and even suspended prison sentences for some offenders (Mann, 2017). Second, Europe's football leagues, including La Liga (Spain) and the Pro League (Belgium) are making use of technology specially designed to identify and close down illegal streams. In 2015, La Liga introduced its *Marauder* tool and since then claims to have removed over 268,000 videos, blocked 9,000 accounts and taken 140 mobile applications and 500 URLs, which shared illegal links to images of the competition, offline (Holmes, 2018). And third, both of these initiatives have been given legal support at EU and national level. In April 2017, a ruling from the European Court of Justice, clarified that existing EU copyright law was applicable to "temporary reproduction" via Internet streaming, as well as downloading ("The Sale," 2017). Tackling illegal streaming is likely to remain a constant battle; but taken together, these measures have ensured that the availability of live sports coverage remains largely controlled by sports organisations and authorised broadcasters. Any loss of value for Europe's leading sports organisations from breaches of copyright via illegal Internet streaming has therefore been relatively limited and there is little evidence to suggest a collapse in the value of European sports rights market any time soon.

On the contrary, for Europe's leading pay-TV operators, an arguably more significant concern is the prospect of competition for premium sports rights from United States (U.S.) based social and digital media giants, namely one or more of the so-called FAANG (Facebook, Apple, Amazon, Netflix and Google) group. From around 2012, Europe has witnessed the launch of OTT Subscription Video On-Demand (SVOD) services from both Netflix and Amazon. In some national markets, notably the UK and Germany, there has been significant growth for both of these services. By 2017 in the UK, Netflix and Amazon Prime Video had attracted around 6-million and 3.8-million subscribers respectively, and, in Germany, 2.5-million and 6-million respectively ("International Communications," 2017). However, arguably reflecting their relative lack of "home" produced/language programming, U.S. based SVOD services have been less successful in other countries, including France, Spain and Italy, where, by 2017, subscriber numbers for Netflix and Amazon combined were 2.4-million, 1.8-million and 1.2-million respectively ("International Communications," 2017). Furthermore, the uptake of SVOD in Europe has largely supplemented, rather than replaced, existing broadcast and pay-TV services. Unlike in the U.S., there has been little evidence of viewers abandoning pay-TV services, commonly referred to as "cord-cutting" ("The Communications," 2016). Whether or not this pattern continues may depend in no small part on whether one or more of the FAANG group look to secure exclusive premium sports rights in one or more European markets.

It is certainly the case that FAANG each possess the financial resources to easily outbid even Europe's largest pay-TV operators. For instance, Amazon's annual revenue of around £100 billion is around three times that of Sky and BT combined (Rumsby, 2018). Whether there is any realistic prospect of a bid for key European sports rights from a U.S. based OTT new entrant is less certain. Netflix has consistently stated that it has no intention to bid for live sports rights. In 2015, Netflix's Chief Content Officer, Ted Sarandos, declared that "there [are] a lot of irrational bidders for sports. We're not anxious to become another one" (Mann, 2015, para. 2). In 2018, Netflix did launch a "fly on the wall" docuseries focused on Italy's most popular (and successful) football club, Juventus, and it has announced plans for a similar series in partnership with the Formula One motor-racing competition (Carp, 2018), but these initiatives appear more in keeping with Netflix's wider strategy to invest in original content than any burgeoning intent to enter the sports rights market. By contrast, other potential bidders for European sports rights have openly declared their interest in offering live (and non-live) sports content. Facebook has been keen to point out that "sports are inherently social" and has described itself as a "natural home for sports" (Malyon, 2017, para. 21). Just as, if not more significantly, in 2017, Facebook launched its new "Watch" tab as part of a general strategy to maintain/increase its popularity (and attractiveness to advertisers) by greatly expanding its offering of audio-visual content, including sports. In the U.S., during the first six months of 2017, Facebook aired over 3,500 different live sports events and it is looking to expand to cover sport in Europe (Joseph, 2017). In a similar vein, Amazon has made no secret of the fact that it views sports rights as an important part of a drive to increase membership of Amazon Prime, which, for an annual fee, offers subscribers access to music, television/movies and free next day delivery on home shopping purchases from Amazon. In the U.S., Prime members have been found to spend almost twice as much per year as Amazon customers who are not Prime members (Hellier & Soper, 2018). Speaking at the 2017 Edinburgh international television festival, the head of Amazon Studios, Roy Price, commented: "People love sports—it's big, it's engaging, it really motivates people, so I think that's a good opportunity. ... it's definitely an opportunity we'll explore" (Ruddick, 2017, para. 5).

Since around 2016, the prospect of U.S. based digital giants entering the European sports rights market has also appeared increasingly credible because of the array of high profile deals agreed by Facebook and Amazon, as well as Twitter, with leading U.S. sports organisations, including the NFL (American football), MLB (baseball) and MLS (football) for OTT coverage in the U.S. (Spangler, 2018). Most of these have been either non-exclusive, or for a limited number of events. In 2017, however, Facebook's $600 million (US) bid (albeit unsuccessful) for the exclusive global digital rights for Indian Premier League cricket indicated a willingness to countenance major exclusive deals beyond the U.S. (Garrahan & Stacey, 2017). It came as only a limited surprise therefore when, in August 2017, Amazon agreed to an exclusive £50 million, five-year deal with the ATP to cover elite men's tennis (apart from Grand Slams) in the UK and Ireland, then followed up with a similar £40 million deal for the exclusive UK and Ireland rights for the U.S. Open Grand Slam tennis tournament (Sweney, 2017a). While these deals for tennis rights were relatively small scale, they were enough to fuel speculation during early 2018 that Amazon could seriously rival Sky and BT for exclusive live UK rights for EPL football (for three seasons, 2019/20 to 2021/22) (Rumsby, 2018). Sky and BT secured contracts worth more than £4.5 billion combined for all but one of the EPL match packages. In June 2018, Amazon paid an estimated £100 million for the exclusive streaming rights to the remaining 20-match package starting with the 2019/20 season (Biddiscombe, 2018; O'Halloran, 2018).

To date, a non-U.S. based new entrant OTT SVOD services, DAZN, has arguably had a more significant impact on the European sports rights market. DAZN is owned by the UK-based Perform Group sports rights agency, which, in turn, is part of the Access Industries holding company, backed by billionaire Len Blavatnik (Williams, 2016). In 2016, focusing on markets with relatively low levels of pay-TV subscription and high broadband speed capacity, DAZN launched in German-speaking Europe—a bloc known collectively as DACH that comprises Germany, Switzerland, and Austria—as well as Japan, and in 2017, Canada. In each of these markets, DAZN has set about replicating the successful Netflix streaming model by offering an array of sports content for a relatively low monthly fee and with no long-term contract. With this in mind, DAZN's chief executive, James Rushton, has described DAZN's strategy as looking to compliment, rather than replace existing pay-TV broadcasters. According to Ruston, "you can see quite easily in Germany a Sky Deutschland subscriber continuing with a Sky Deutschland package but then supplementing that with DAZN at €9.99" ("OTT: The Shifting," 2017, pp.15–16). To a large degree, this is reflected in the portfolio of second order (rather than premium) non-domestic rights assembled by DAZN for the DACH region, including live football from the top divisions in England, Spain, France and Italy, as well as the basketball (NBA) and football (NFL) from the U.S.

In a similar vein, when, in 2017, Sky Deutschland secured exclusive rights (for Germany and Austria) for live UEFA's Champions League (2018/19 to 2020/21) football, Europe's premier pan-European club competition, it agreed to a sub-licensing deal for matches it did not plan to cover with DAZN (Carp, 2017a). At the same time, however, DAZN is also a direct competitor for Sky Deutschland in the DACH region. Since its launch, DAZN has not released subscriber figures, but industry observers have estimated these to be relatively low (around 200,000) by comparison with Sky Deutschland's around 5-million subscribers (Jellis, 2018). To narrow this gap, DAZN has already demonstrated its willingness to continue to invest heavily in sports rights for DACH. In 2017, DAZN agreed a deal to show all 205 of the UEFA Europa League games, Europe's second-tier club football competition. That figure included 190 exclusive contests (Dudley, 2017). In 2016, DAZN was also reported to have bid aggressively against Sky for exclusive live rights to the Bundesliga, Germany's domestic football league (Jellis, 2017). Sky Deutschland, secured the rights to over 90% of matches (for seasons 2017/18 to 2020/21) with Eurosport winning the rights to the remaining matches. However, at least partly due to competition from DAZN, the cost of the rights increased by 85% from the last auction in 2012, to a record €4.6 billion (Bond, 2016).

Finally, it should be noted that new entrants to the European sports rights market looking to utilise OTT face a significant technological challenge, namely delivering a high-quality viewing experience over broadband networks of variable speed and reliability. In the UK, "superfast" broadband, recommended for SVOD services, is defined as offering a download speed of between 30 and 300 megabytes per second. By 2017, almost half of households in Spain (49%) and the UK (45%) were able to access superfast broadband, but the proportion falls to 31% for Germany and then to 18% and 12% respectively for France and Italy ("International Communications," 2017). Furthermore, streaming live sport causes particular difficulties. The speed of movement and action in sports, combined with the desire for mass live consumption, places intense demands on broadband networks. For recorded content, like drama and movies, withholding transmissions to allow for buffering is a feasible option for SVOD providers; but any delay in transmission during live sport is unlikely to be tolerated by consumers (Lopez-Gonzalez, Stavros, & Smith, 2017). It is perhaps not surprising therefore that SVOD operators in Europe have experienced technological problems when offering live coverage of sports events. In Germany for example, Eurosport's live coverage of Bundesliga matches at the start of the 2017–18 season via its new OTT Eurosport Player (see below) was overshadowed by technical problems, which caused delays and interruptions for viewers (Krieger, 2017). In the short term at least, concerns over the limitations of existing broadband networks, and the possibility of reputational damage that could stem from problems with the live streaming, may be enough to deter OTT providers (and European sporting organisations) from agreeing a major exclusive rights deal, such as for domestic football.

Old Players With New Tactics

Over the last few years, established pay-TV operators in Europe have responded to the potential of OTT delivery in two main ways. First, OTT delivery has been utilised to attract additional subscriptions from potential viewers put off by the prices and long-term contracts conventionally associated with pay-TV. Most, if not all, of Europe's pay-TV operators have launched OTT services designed to complement their existing pay-TV platforms, such as MediaSet Infinity and beIN Sports Connect. Most significantly, as early as 2012 in the UK, Sky launched Now TV, offering movies and other popular recorded content without a contract. In 2014, Sky added live sports coverage to Now TV with the launch of the Now TV Sports Pass and, no doubt with sports fans in mind, a "day pass" and "weekly pass" were made available at the cost of £6.99 and £10.99 respectively (Plunkett, 2017). Subsequently, Sky has adopted the same approach with its European pay-TV services in Germany and Italy, and most recently has launched Now TV in Spain, as a test bed for its expansion into other European countries where Sky does not have an existing pay-TV service (Krieger, 2016). Owned by U.S. based Discovery, Incorporated, Eurosport has also responded to the growing potential for OTT delivery by launching an OTT service, the Eurosport Player. Originally launched in 2011 and revamped in 2015, as part of Discovery's general strategy to grow OTT subscriber numbers, Eurosport Player offers Eurosport's existing channels OTT, plus more extensive coverage of particular sports events, such as coverage of additional courts at the French Grand Slam tennis ("Eurosport," 2015). Eurosport has also agreed carriage deals with Amazon to make Eurosport Player available via Amazon Prime in the UK, Germany and Austria for €4.99 per month (Carp, 2017b).

With the real, or at least potential threat of OTT, and with new entrants to the sports rights (and/or general pay-TV) market in mind, the second way Europe's pay-TV operators have responded to the growth of OTT has been more defensively minded. Specifically, pay-TV operators have begun to restructure the traditional bundling of channels in the hope of avoiding, or at least lessening, the cord-cutting evident in the United States. Most notably, in July 2017, Sky announced a major restructuring of its Sky Sports channels in the UK, moving from a set of bundled channels, to 10 different channels, dedicated to specific sports (e.g., cricket, football, golf) or sports organizations (e.g., EPL, Formula One) and available to viewers as a bundled offering, or as individual channels at a cost of £18 per month, considerably less than the £49.50 fee previously charged for the Sky Sports bundle ("New Sky," 2017). Just as significant, in an attempt to dampen the spiralling costs of acquiring exclusive sports rights, European pay-TV operators have also been looking to reduce the intensity of competition for rights, between themselves at least, by agreeing on cross platform delivery deals for their respective sports channels. In the UK, just a few months before the 2018 auction for EPL rights, Sky and BT agreed a deal for BT to market and sell Sky's Now TV service as part of BT TV, and in return, for BT to wholesale its BT Sport channels to Sky, allowing the media company to sell those channels directly to Sky satellite customers for the first time (Sweney, 2017b). As a result, the 2018 EPL rights auction was the first for several years not to produce a major escalation in the cost of the rights. Albeit with less success, a similar approach was also adopted in France. In 2016, pay-TV Canal Plus agreed a five-year exclusive distribution agreement for the sports channels of its rival, beIN Sports. However, the deal was blocked by the French competition authority. Subsequently, Canal Plus has been allowed to offer one (but not all) of its rival's premium sports channels to Canal Plus subscribers (Ross, 2017). Most recently, in Italy, in 2018, Sky Italia agreed to a content and carriage deal with its main rival, Mediaset, which will make Mediaset's premium channels available to Sky Italia subscribers and allow Sky Italia to offer its pay-TV service via digital terrestrial television using bandwidth rented from the Mediaset Group (Mann, 2018).

For European sports organisations, the potential to deliver sports content OTT has been a wholly welcome development. To start with, the prospect of increased competition from OTT new entrants has enabled sports organisations to extract maximum value from the sale of their rights. As discussed above, in some cases, such as the UK rights to ATP tennis, an OTT new entrant has paid a significant increase on the previous fee paid by a pay-TV operator. In others, such as the 2016 auction for exclusive live domestic Bundesliga rights, competition from an OTT provider has forced incumbent pay-TV operators to significantly increase their payments. And, finally, as in the case of the EPL's 2018 domestic rights auction, the mere potential of a rival bid from an OTT provider has been enough to ensure that major increases in value of rights gained during recent years have at least been preserved. The continued high value of exclusive live sports rights is also underpinned by the prospect of sports organisations offering live coverage of their events and/or competition OTT directly to consumers. At the very least, sports organisations are able to use this option as a way to keep pay-TV operators (OTT or not) "honest" in their bids for rights. For example, in February 2018, La Liga announced the launch of a multi-sport OTT streaming service that will initially be offered free of charge to viewers. The service will offer past La Liga games, interviews and documentaries, but not live streams of La Liga matches. However, no doubt with pay-TV operators in mind, the League's President, Javier Tebas, commented that he does not rule out live match coverage "in the mid to long term" and stressed that whether this is option is pursued will be "determined by the market" (Briel, 2018, para. 6).

La Liga's decision not to offer live matches, at least for the time being, is also a good illustration of the "double game" being played by sports organisations in the new OTT environment, whereby they are looking to explore potential new revenue streams, but at the same time not undermine the value of lucrative and guaranteed rights fees from established broadcasters (Hutchins & Rowe, 2009, p. 356). For example, in August 2016, following the end of the Rio Summer Olympics, the IOC launched the Olympic Channel, available OTT "anytime, anywhere and on any device" offering live and recorded coverage of a range of different Olympic sports between the Games, but not the actual Olympics (Owen, 2016, para. 7). The stated purpose of the channel is to be the place "Where The Games Never End," which translates as coverage of Olympic sports, but not the Olympic Games, thus preserving the value of the IOC's major source of revenue. In a similar way, in February 2018, Formula One confirmed the launch of its OTT service, F1 TV, in a number of international markets, including France and Germany (Cooper, 2018). The service offered subscribers advertising- free coverage of races, plus build-up and additional coverage. However, its launch has been carefully negotiated around existing and new rights contracts. Consequently, the service is not available in the UK or Spain due to rights deals with Sky and Telefonica respectively. While in Germany and France F1 TV will offer non-exclusive coverage with races also available via free-to-air commercial television via RTL and TF1 respectively.

Europe's leading football organisations are also playing the "double game" with OTT. In 2017 the UK's English Football League (EFL), the competition below the EPL, launched its OTT service iFollow offering fans of particular team's live coverage of all their matches throughout the season at a cost of £110 per season. However, the service has only been made available to fans outside the UK in order not to undermine the EFL's domestic pay-TV deal with Sky, its main source of broadcast revenue ("iFollow," 2017). Albeit at a more elite level, similar logic has informed UEFA's decision to refuse a partnership with Facebook to offer live coverage of UEFA Champions League football to countries not covered by existing UEFA broadcast contracts, such as India (Forrester, 2017). UEFA feared that to enter such a partnership and give away live coverage of its premium competition would dilute the value of the competition's brand in markets where it does have broadcast contracts.

Finally, it should be noted that for many minority sports without major broadcasting deals, OTT distribution, either independently or in partnership with existing broadcasters, provides an opportunity to better reach existing fans and even attract new fans. For example, in November 2017, the BBC announced a wide-ranging partnership with host of relatively small sporting organisations in the UK, including British Swimming, British Basketball and the Women's Super League (football), to make available over 1,000 additional hours of live sport via its BBC Sport app and the BBC i-player OTT service ("More Sport," 2017).

Conclusion

Using examples from France, Germany, Italy, Spain and the UK, this chapter has analysed how the potential to deliver live sports content OTT is changing the European sports rights market. It has highlighted how the European sports rights market is in the midst of a period of change, with OTT delivery offering new market entrants, from the U.S., or Europe, as well as existing pay-TV operators and sports organisations, a new means to deliver content to sports fans. However, this period of change is best understood as of process of evolution, rather than revolution. With this in mind, it is worth emphasising several key points. First, Europe's sports rights market is still defined by traditional national/regional exclusive live rights deals. There has been no discernible move towards large scale pan-European, or even global, rights deals with content delivered OTT. Nor has there been a shift away from high value deals for exclusive live rights to the revenue sharing approach commonly employed within online media markets by major players, such as Facebook and Amazon. From this, a second key point to be stressed is that live rights to exclusive premium content, mostly domestic football leagues, remain a key source of market power within Europe's national pay-TV and wider communications markets. In fact, the interest of new entrants in OTT services acquiring the rights to key European sporting events and competition is testament to the continuing strategic value attached to live sports coverage within an increasingly competitive media environment. Third, for the immediate future at least, the technical limitations associated with OTT mean that control over, or at least access to, traditional (terrestrial, satellite and/or cable) electronic media infrastructure remains a major competitive advantage for established pay-TV operators within Europe's national sports rights markets. Finally, while not discussed here, all of the above suggests a vital future role for Europe's media policy makers and competition regulators. Whether established pay-TV operators or OTT new entrants, the high cost of premium rights means that the sports rights market is likely to be dominated by a handful of major media organisations. Intervention from competition regulators is likely to be required to ensure fair and effective competition in the sports rights market and wider related pay-TV/communications markets. Just as significantly, the enormous commercial value attached to premium sports rights means there is little prospect of a reversal to the trend for coverage of popular sporting events and competitions to migrate from free-to-air to pay-TV. On the contrary, the growth of OTT delivery may well facilitate significant growth in the amount of sports content (live and recorded) available to European sports fans, but access to much of this content is likely to be dependent on the ability and/or willingness to pay for it. A major future challenge for policy makers in Europe is to resist pressure from at least some media and sports organisations to remove, or at least water down, existing major events legislation, which guarantees live coverage of key national and international sports events on free-to-air television.

References

Biddiscombe, R. (2018, June 12). Analysis: Has Amazon scored with its Premier League package? *IBC365*. Retrieved from https://www.ibc.org/production/analysis-has-amazon-scored-with-its-premier-league-package/2873.article#.WyDrDwkZGiw. twitter

Bond, D. (2016, June 9). Sky and Eurosport secure Bundesliga rights at €4.6bn. *Financial Times* (London), 17. Retrieved from https://www.ft.com/content/851559f4-2e29-11e6-bf8d-26294ad519fc

Briel, R. (2018, February 19). Spanish La Liga to launch OTT sports platform. *Broadband TV News*. Retrieved from https://www.broadbandtvnews.com/2018/02/19/spanish-la-liga-to-launch-ott-sports-platform/

Carp, S. (2017a, June 13). DAZN partners with Sky for Champions League rights. *Sport Pro*. Retrieved from http://www.sportspromedia.com/news/dazn-partners-with-sky-for-champions-league-rights?utm_source=daily_deal&utm_medium=article&utm_ campaign=dazn-partners-with-sky-for-champions-league-rights

Carp, S. (2017b, August 16). Amazon secures Eurosport streaming deal. *SportsPro*. Retrieved from http://www.sportspromedia.com/news/amazon-secures-eurosport-streaming-deal?utm_source=daily_deal&utm_medium=article&utm_campaign=amazon-secures-eurosport-streaming-deal

Carp, S. (2018, March 26). Formula One to star in Netflix docuseries. *SportsPro*. Retrieved from http://www.sportspromedia.com/news/f1-netflix-original-docuseries?utm_

source=daily_deal&utm_medium=article&utm_campaign=f1-netflix-original-docuseries

Cave, M., & Crandall, R. (2001). Sports rights and the broadcast industry. *Economic Journal, 111*(469), 4–26. doi.org/10.1111/1468-0297.00596

Clancy, M. (2016, April 10). EU: Piracy rampant throughout Europe. *Rapid TV News.* Retrieved from http://www.rapidtvnews.com/2016041042411/eu-piracy-rampant-throughout-europe.html?utm_campaign=eu-piracy-rampant-throughout-europe&utm_medium=email&utm_source=newsletter_914#axzz45REXH4UM

Commission clears UEFA's new policy regarding the sale of media rights to the Champions League. (2003, July 24). *EC (European Commission).* Retrieved from http://europa.eu/rapid/press-release_IP-03-1105_en.htm?locale=en

Cooper, A. (2018, March 1). F1 eyes 5m potential subscribers for OTT service. *motorsport.com.* Retrieved from https://www.motorsport.com/f1/news/f1-tv-five-million-subscribers-ott-1010165/

Cudd, A. E. (2007). Sporting metaphors: Competition and the ethos of capitalism. *Journal of the Philosophy of Sport, 34*(1), 52–67. doi: 10/1080/00948705.2007.9714709

Directive 89/552/EEC on the coordination of certain provisions laid down by law, regulation or administrative action in Member States concerning the pursuit of television broadcasting activities (1989). *European Council.* Retrieved from https://eur-lex.europa.eu/legal-content/EN/TXT/?uri=CELEX%3A31989L0552

Dudley, G. (2017, October 5) DAZN gets German and Austrian rights to Europa League. *SportsPro.* Retrieved from http://www.sportspromedia.com/news/dazn-gets-german-and-austrian-rights-to-europa-leagueEvens, T., Iosifidis, P., & Smith, P. (2013). *The political economy of television sports rights.* Basingstoke, England: Palgrave Macmillan.

Eurosport relaunches Player in OTT push. (2015, June 5). *Digital TV Europe.* Retrieved from https://www.digitalveurope.com/2015/06/05/ eurosport-relaunches-player-in-ott-push/

Forrester, C. (2017, October 11). Facebook wanted "free" Champions League. *Advanced Television.* Retrieved from https://advanced-television.com/2017/10/11/facebook-wanted-free-uefa-champions-league/

Garrahan, M., & Stacey, K. (2017, September 5). Murdoch's Star wins IPL with $2.6bn bid. *Financial Times* (London), p.11.

Gibson, O. (2016, October 24). Is the unthinkable happening—are people finally switching the football off? *The Guardian.* Retrieved from https://www.theguardian.com/football/2016/oct/24/sky-sports-bt-sport-people-switching-football-off

Hellier, D., & Soper, S. (2018, January 5). Amazon plans bid for Premier League streaming rights. *Bloomberg Technology.* Retrieved from https://www.bloomberg.com/news/articles/2018-01-05/amazon-is-said-to-plan-bid-for-premier-league-streaming-rights

Holmes, E. (2018, March 20). Pro League teams up with La Liga to fight illegal match-streaming. *SportsPro.* Retrieved from http://www.sportspromedia.com/news/

pro-league-la-liga-fight-illegal-match-streaming?utm_source=daily_deal&utm_medium=article&utm_campaign=pro-league-la-liga-fight-illegal-match-streaming

Hutchins, B., & Rowe, D. (2009). From broadcast scarcity to digital plenitude: The changing dynamics of the media sport content economy. *Television and New Media*, *10*(4), 354–370. doi: 10/1177/1527476409334016

iFollow: Live streaming platform unveiled for global EFL fans. (2017, May 3). *EFL (English Football League)*. Retrieved from https://www.efl.com/news/2017/may/ifollow-live-streaming-platform-unveiled-for-global-efl-fans/

International Communications Market Report 2017. (2017). *Ofcom*. Retrieved from https://www.ofcom.org.uk/__data/assets/pdf_file/0032/108896/icmr-2017.pdf

Jellis, R. (2017, February 1). German TV market waits on two big deals. *TV Sports Markets*. Retrieved from https://www.sportbusiness.com/tv-sports-markets/german-tv-market-waits-two-big-deals

Jellis, R. (2018, February 7). German market set for quieter period following blockbuster year. *TV Sports Markets*. Retrieved from https://www.sportbusiness.com/tv-sports-markets/german-market-set-quieter-period-following-blockbuster-year

Joseph, S. (2017, October 11). Facebook looks to emerging markets for streaming rights to sports. *Digiday UK*. Retrieved from https://digiday.com/marketing/facebook-looks-emerging-markets-streaming-rights-sports/?utm_medium=email&utm_campaign=digidaydis&utm_source=uk&utm_content=171011

Krieger, J. (2016, August 26). Sky Deutschland launches new OTT platform. *BroadbandTV News*. Retrieved from https://www.broadbandtvnews.com/2016/08/26/sky-deutschland-launches-new-ott-platform/

Krieger, J. (2017, August 27). Eurosport to compensate viewers for Bundesliga outage. *BroadbandTV News*. Retrieved from https://www.broadbandtvnews.com/2017/08/27/eurosport-to-compensate-viewers-for-bundesliga-outage/

Leandros, N., & Tsourvakas, G. (2005). Intensive competition and company failures in subscription television: Some European experiences. *International Journal on Media Management*, *7*(1–2), 24–38. doi:10.1080/14241277.20059669414

Lopez-Gonzalez, H., Stavros, C., & Smith, A. (2017). Broadcasting sport: Analogue markets and digital rights. *International Communication Gazette*, *79*(2), 175–189.

Maguire, J. (1999). *Global sport: Identities, societies, civilizations*. Cambridge, UK: Polity Press.

Malyon, E. (2017, March 2). How Facebook could change the face of Premier League broadcasting—and why the television giants should be scared. *The Independent*. Retrieved from https://www.independent.co.uk/sport/football/premier-league/premier-leagues-television-rights-bubble-might-burst-facebook-a7608356.html

Mann, C. (2015, October 15). Netflix: "News, but not sports." *Advanced Television*. Retrieved from https://advanced-television.com/2015/10/15/netflix-news-but-not-sports/

Mann, C. (2017, October 26). Fines for illegal Sky Sports streamers. *Advanced Television*. Retrieved from https://advanced-television.com/2017/10/26/fines-for-illegal-sky-sports-streamers/

Mann, C. (2018, April 3). Sky Italia, Mediaset content and carriage deal. *Advanced Television*. Retrieved from https://advanced-television.com/2018/04/03/sky-italia-mediaset-content-and-carriage-deal/?utm_source=Newsletter&utm_campaign=ba75f95353-EMAIL_CAMPAIGN_2018_04_03&utm_medium=email&utm_term=0_17fb4fdd18-ba75f95353-44001637

Milliken, R. (1996, October 16). Sport is Murdoch's "battering ram" for pay TV. *The Independent* (UK). Retrieved from https://www.independent.co.uk/sport/sport-is-murdochs-battering-ram-for-pay-tv-1358686.html

More sport for more people as the BBC announces biggest increase of live sport in a generation. (2017, November 3). *BBC*. Retrieved from http://www.bbc.co.uk/mediacentre/latestnews/2017/live-sport

New Sky Sports line-up gives customers more choice and channels at the same price and individual channel packs for the first time. (2017, July 10). *Sky*. Retrieved from https://www.skygroup.sky/corporate/media-centre/articles/en-gb/new-sky-sports-line-up-gives-customers-more-choice-and-channels-at-the-same-price-and-individual-channel-packs-for-the-first-time

O'Halloran, J. (2018, February 14). Sky, BT retain principal Premier League football rights for £4.5BN. *Rapid TV News*. Retrieved from https://www.rapidtvnews.com/2018021350894/sky-bt-retain-principal-premier-league-football-rights-for-4-5bn.html?utm_campaign=sky-bt-retain-principal-premier-league-football-rights-for-4-5bn&utm_medium=email&utm_source=newsletter_1638#axzz576bfkU84

OTT: The Shifting Broadcasting Landscape. (2017) *Leaders*. Retrieved from https://leadersinsport.com/sport-business/digital-and-media/leaders-special-report-rise-ott/

Owen, D. (2016, July 27). Olympic channel to launch on August 21. *Inside the Games*. Retrieved from https://www.insidethegames.biz/articles/1040035/olympic-channel-to-launch-on-august-21

Papathanassopoulos, S. (2002). *European television in the digital age*. Cambridge, UK: Polity Press.

Plunkett, J. (2015, June 16). Now TV to launch monthly sports-pass to coincide with start of Premier League season. *The Guardian*. Retrieved from https://www.theguardian.com/media/2015/jun/16/now-tv-to-launch-monthly-sports-pass-to-coincide-with-start-of-ashes

Premier League in record £5.14bn TV rights deal. (2015, February 10). *BBC News: Business*. Retrieved from http://www.bbc.co.uk/news/business-31379128

Premier League: Third of fans say they watch illegal streams of matches—survey. (2017, July 4). *BBC Sport*. Retrieved from http://www.bbc.co.uk/sport/football/40483486

Ross, M. (2017, June 22). Canal Plus no longer obliged to sell on free-to-air rights to major events. *Sportcal*. Retrieved from https://sportcal.com/News/FeaturedNews/111496

Ruddick, G. (2017, August 25). Amazon TV hints at significant expansion into sport broadcasting. *The Guardian*. Retrieved from https://amp.theguardian.com/tv-and-radio/2017/aug/25/amazon-tv-hints-at-significant-expansion-into-sport-broadcasting

Rumsby, B. (2018, January 4). Amazon holds talks over Premier League UK TV rights. *The Telegraph*. Retrieved from https://www.telegraph.co.uk/football/2018/01/04/amazon-holds-talks-premier-league-uk-tv-rights/

Smith, P., Evens, T., & Iosifidis P. (2016). The next big match: Convergence, competition and sports media rights. *European Journal of Communication, 31*(5), 536–550.

Smith, P., Evens, T., & Iosifidis P. (2015). The regulation of television sports broadcasting: A comparative analysis. *Media, Culture and Society, 37*(5), 720–736.

Spangler, T. (2018, January 30). Big media, Silicon Valley battle for multibillion-dollar sports TV rights. *Variety*. Retrieved from http://variety.com/2018/digital/ features/ olympics-rights-streaming- nbc-winter-games-1202680323/

Study on sports organisers' rights in the European Union: Final Report for the European Union. (2014). *Asser Institute*. Retrieved from http://ec.europa.eu/sport/news/2014/ docs/study-sor2014-final-report-gc-compatible_en.pdf

Sweney, M. (2017a, November 15). Amazon US tennis deal sparks speculation over Premier League bid. *The Guardian*. Retrieved from https://www.theguardian.com/media/ 2017/nov/15/amazon-us-open-tennis-deal-premier-league-uk-bt-sky

Sweney, M. (2017b, December 15). BT customers get to binge on Game of Thrones after landmark Sky deal. *The Guardian*. Retrieved from https://www.theguardian.com/business/2017/dec/15/bt-sky-deal-atlantic-and-sport-channels-customers

The Communications Market Report. (2016). *Ofcom*. Retrieved from https://www.ofcom.org.uk/__data/assets/pdf_file/0024/26826/cmr_uk_2016.pdf

The European club footballing landscape: Club licensing benchmarking report Financial Year 2016. (2018). *uefa.com*. Retrieved from http://www.uefa.com/MultimediaFiles/Download/OfficialDocument/uefaorg/Clublicensing/02/53/00/22/2530022_DOWNLOAD.pdf

The European Model of Sport. (1998). *EC (European Commission)*. Retrieved from http://www.bso.or.at/fileadmin/Inhalte/Dokumente/Internationales/EU_European_Model_Sport.pdf

The sale of a multimedia player which enables films that are available illegally on the internet to be viewed easily and for free on a television screen could constitute an infringement of copyright. (2017, April 26). *ECJ (European Court of Justice)*. Retrieved from https://curia.europa.eu/jcms/upload/docs/application/pdf/2017-04/cp170040en.pdf

Williams, C. (2016, August 20). Blavatnik's perform group rebuffs tech investors to build "Netflix for sport." *The Telegraph*. Retrieved from https://www.telegraph.co.uk/business/ 2016/08/20/blavatniks-perform-group-rebuffs-tech-investors-to-build-netflix/

4. *Ascending as the Fantasy Giant: ESPN Fantasy, Mainstreaming Fantasy Gaming, and the Role of Goliath*

Brody J. Ruihley and Andrew C. Billings

If there is a 60-million-person industry that still somehow flies under the mainstream radar, fantasy sport is that industry. With a wider number of regular participants than Twitter or Instagram and more dollars being generated within it than all but the most major of sports leagues, fantasy sport has ascended to the level of a giant. Decades ago, fantasy sport providers were ancillary to the mainstream sport networks; once the potential of the industry was realized, virtually any network (e.g., FOX Sports, NBC Sports Group) or publication outlet (e.g., *USA Today, Sporting News*), sought a way to capitalize on its potential. Inevitably, that included the self-proclaimed (and yet rarely challenged) Worldwide Leader in Sports: ESPN.

Considering its role within ESPN, fantasy sport quickly enters the discussion when addressing the changing landscape of sports, technological advancements, and digital trailblazing taking place in the sports environment. From the mainstream sports of football, baseball, basketball, and hockey to the more niche areas of golf, auto racing, and even bass fishing, fantasy sport, as an industry, is reaching many sport fans across North America. Offerings of season-long play and daily fantasy sport (DFS) are providing sport fans ample opportunity to compete, socialize, gather information, and enjoy sport at an amplified level (Billings & Ruihley, 2014). Even more than that, and applicable to ESPN, participants of fantasy sports are inevitably becoming consumers of ESPN television programming, ESPN's web offerings, and more.

Touting an industry size of 59.3 million North American participants and constant annual growth (Billings & Ruihley, 2014; Fantasy Sports Trade

Association, 2018), the fantasy sport industry is changing the sports landscape in many unique ways. First, data analytics and statistics are becoming part of everyday conversation around sports. While statistics have always been a part of sport consumption, fantasy sport is allowing those more complicated models and formulas to become part of common analysis and dialogue. As a result, communication outlets, fantasy sport publications, and fantasy sport analysts are paving a unique road for those that want to glean more out of the numbers. Even more than that, since fantasy sport users want statistics to match a players' inherent value, new statistics are given greater relevance while older, less reliable measures of performance are deemphasized; for example, moving out are heavy weights placed on a baseball pitchers' wins, moving in are more accurate measures of value, such as walks and hits per innings pitched (WHIP). In sum, the need for accurate fantasy games created fans (and leagues) that embraced more accurate measures of performance.

A second way fantasy sport is changing sports coverage is the way fans consume sports broadcasts. As outlined in Billings and Ruihley (2014), fantasy sport professionals have and are advocating for information and content to cater—even if subtly done—to the fantasy sport user. This primarily comes in the form of key fantasy sport statistics highlighted, bottom line scrolls, highlights, and representing the information important to the fantasy audience. Major sport communication outlets from Fox Sports and *USA Today*, to Yahoo!, ESPN, and SiriusXM have all had fantasy professionals advocating for key statistic graphics, on-air time, or fantasy information included in publication all to serve the fantasy sport public.

A third way fantasy is changing sport coverage is by amplifying consumption of sporting contests. By simply having a stake in a season-long or DFS contest, fantasy participants are tuning in, tracking, and consuming more sport coverage than traditional sport fans (Billings & Ruihley, 2014). Consuming more sport can take the form a fantasy sport participant following games not associated with their favorite team because: (a) they want to keep up with their fantasy competition and/or, (b) their favorite team is out of contention or poorly performing and their fantasy team is another outlet for sport consumption. In fact, we have discovered nearly 60% more sport consumption for both male and female fantasy sport participants when compared to traditional sport fans (Billings & Ruihley, 2014). There is no doubt that fantasy sport and its subsequent consumption is transforming the sport environment. A major player—arguably now the *most* major player—in this transformation is none other than the Worldwide Leader in Sports, ESPN. This chapter will outline how the network ultimately moved fantasy sport technologies to the forefront of their transition to mobile networks and changing business models.

ESPN & Fantasy Sport Technologies

While popular and accepted now, ESPN has not always embraced fantasy sport as they believed the activity was too much of a unique niche for only a select group of sport fans and would, hence, alienate many core consumers. Interviewing ESPN directors, Billings and Ruihley (2014) found that considerable effort and jockeying for airtime was necessitated to allow fantasy sport to grow as a viable format (also see Ruihley, Hardin, & Billings, 2015). In the past decade, that tune has changed with ESPN Fantasy receiving airtime, attention, and accolades, including a 28-hour fantasy sport marathon every August as a precursor for the upcoming NFL season.

As a top provider in the fantasy sport landscape of nearly 60 million participants, a personal interview with Kevin Ota, Director of Communications at ESPN, provided a sense of ESPN's oversized share of that market and the ancillary elements of their programming strategy. ESPN lays claim to 20 million unique users, a figure that doubled from 2013 to 2017 (K. Ota, personal communication, 2018). What is even more impressive is that half of that growth came in 2017, even after the meteoric rise of DFS in 2015. Another positive participation trend includes a dominance of attention to fantasy sport during the NFL season. Ota reports that on National Football League Sundays, ESPN Fantasy accounts for 50% of all minutes across ESPN digital platforms (K. Ota, personal communication, 2018). Such a statistic cannot be overstated: when the NFL is playing games, more users are operating under the ESPN "Fantasy" tab than the regular ESPN "NFL" tab. This popularity is, undoubtedly, a result of fantasy sports' escalated coverage and attention given to the activity. In many ways, reaching the fantasy sport consumer is exactly what it sounds like. Companies must *reach* them *where they are*. This puts great emphasis on videos, social media, mobile use, and television time slots; and ESPN is doing just that with their television presence, podcasts availability, and fantasy application for tablets and phones. The reason for this is quite simple: In an age of splintering media consumption, niche programming, and ubiquitous screen options, the major way to drive consumption higher is by garnering the same user more than once. This means embracing second-screen activities (Cunningham & Eastin, 2017) and social TV functions (Lim, Hwang, Kim, & Biocca, 2015) that allow users to have "multiple identities" (Larkin & Fink, 2016, p. 643). They do so by consuming live or televised games all while interacting on mobile applications to garner more information and interact with friends and family, diminishing Fear of Missing Out (Larkin & Fink, 2016).

ESPN Fantasy Sport Television

ESPN is no stranger to televising sport coverage. Since 1979, ESPN has been providing many different types of sports entertainment, live sporting contests, debate shows, and highlights. This history of ESPN televising fantasy sport coverage began when Matthew Berry and John Diver arrived at ESPN to launch fantasy sport play. This history of ESPN Fantasy is beyond the scope of this chapter, but can be explored more in a chapter titled "ESPN and the Fantasy Sport Experience," in the preceding book in this series, *The ESPN Effect: Academic Studies of the Worldwide Leader in Sports*. The focus rather, is how ESPN is transitioning coverage of fantasy sport in a new technological and digital era. Fantasy sport has found its way into ESPN television programming in several ways. First, ESPN did the previously unthinkable: They counter-programmed their *Sunday NFL Countdown* show with *Fantasy Football Now*, a show entirely dedicated to preparing fantasy participants for the NFL slate of games. This was a move that John Diver believed advanced fantasy sport at ESPN because administrators now saw "fantasy is a viable play for content, and just not going around the horn talking about the weather and if the defensive lineman has a hurt foot" (Ruihley et al., 2015, p. 229).

A second television-oriented way ESPN promoted fantasy sport came in 2017 when ESPN added another show called *The Fantasy Show with Matthew Berry*. The show claims to provider viewers "with a mix of news and analysis, as well as special guests and segments, all presented with Berry's smart, irreverent style" (Ota, 2017a, para. 22). Again, this show counter-programmed against two staples of ESPN television, *Around the Horn* and *Pardon the Interruption*. In addition to these two fantasy-specific shows, Matthew Berry makes appearances on *Sunday NFL Countdown* and *Monday Night Countdown* to provide the fantasy perspective.

A third way fantasy sport was infused into ESPN television broadcasting was a unique and unconventional idea to host a fantasy football marathon. In 2016, ESPN conducted a momentous 28-hour televised fantasy football marathon on several ESPN platforms, drawing from many hosts and personalities, and drawing attention to the activity in effort to gain one million new fantasy football registrations. It worked. ESPN announced that 1.75 million teams were drafted as a result (Ota, 2016). The effort paid off once again in 2017, as another 28-hour marathon drew in more than two million teams (Ota, 2017b; Ota, personal communication, 2018).

ESPN Radio and Podcasts

ESPN is also utilizing audio platforms to promote fantasy sport. On ESPN Radio, fantasy sport has voices across the United States. From drop-in on key

ESPN Radio shows with guests discussing fantasy implications to full-blown fantasy shows, a fantasy sport voice is being heard on ESPN airwaves. Specifically, *Fantasy Focus Baseball*, a fantasy baseball show featuring Eric Karabell, and other fantasy football-type shows have been present on ESPN Radio over the past several years. On the podcast-front, fantasy sport is represented well with the aforementioned *Fantasy Focus Baseball* and the highly-popular *Fantasy Focus Football* podcast featuring Matthew Berry, Field Yates, and Stephania Bell. These two shows, offered in audio and video (at times), are showcasing fantasy sport in a way that reaches consumers where they are and in a digestible manner.

Such a strategy highlights the ultimate approach for ESPN as they move from linear to digital delivery systems. By finding seemingly inexhaustible interest in fantasy from millions of their core consumers, ESPN finds ways to still have a presence in radio and other traditional forms of audio while packaging these same programs into the formats likely to thrive in the new economy; perhaps terrestrial radio is slowly losing steam, but the desire for audio-only content for a drive to and from work or even to listen while walking the dog will still be present for many. As such, fantasy products in this vein are easily adaptable, serving dual purposes for dual audiences (and likely different age demographics) in whichever manner appears more frictionless for the consumer. It is important to note that Sirius XM satellite radio offers a station fully-devoted to fantasy sport. While not owned or operated by ESPN, many ESPN voices are heard through this radio outlet.

ESPN Fantasy App

One of the biggest innovations for ESPN Fantasy arrived in August 2016 when ESPN consolidated all fantasy sports and gaming into one single application or "app" (Ota, 2017c; Ourand, 2017). In fact, when asked about success factors of fantasy sport at ESPN, Ota stated that the consolidating of multiple fantasy apps including football, baseball, basketball, hockey, *Streak for the Cash*, and more truly assisted in capturing and engaging fans year-round (K. Ota, personal communication, 2018). The ESPN Fantasy app alone continues to increase consumption of fantasy play. As evidence of this, consider the following points:

- During September through December 2016 (the first four months of existence), the app increased unique monthly consumption by more than 76% when compared to ESPN's standalone fantasy football app in 2015. "This year the ESPN Fantasy App produced more minutes in September than the Yahoo Fantasy, NFL Fantasy, DraftKings, and CBS Fantasy apps combined" (Ota, 2017c, para 6).

- In November 2016 (four months after release), the app accumulated 2.4 billion minutes and was the second-ranked sports app for monthly unique users with 12.2 million (Spangler, 2017).
- In September 2017, the app drew 9.1 million unique users, a figure that is 2.7 million more than Yahoo! fantasy app (Ota, 2017c).
- From August 2016 and through the end of 2017, total participation for ESPN Fantasy's other major games, not named Fantasy Football or Fantasy Baseball, increased significantly with basketball participation increasing 67% hockey participation increasing 36%, and ESPN Streak for the Cash increasing 68% (Ota, 2017c).
- Even combining the digital/video/television worlds, Matthew Berry accounts for "nearly half of the 40% growth in video starts enjoyed by the ESPN Fantasy App" (Ota, 2017c, para. 8).

To stress the importance of the advancement of the singular app even further, staggering numbers have been discovered as it relates to mobile use in the fantasy sport experience. In a 2016 presentation, ESPN Senior Director of Product Development—and one of the innovators of ESPN Fantasy— John Diver, claimed that 80% of fantasy traffic was mobile, compared to 20% desktop/laptop based (J. Diver, personal communication, 2016). This is a number that is surprising to those that were not born in the cellphone generation and remember the fantasy experience without automatic statistics and computer-based live drafting. When inquiring about this figure in 2018, it was learned that the number has since grown to an 88% share of fantasy traffic for mobile devices (K. Ota, personal communication, 2018). When asked if any of the ESPN Fantasy staff found this figure to be surprising, Ota responded:

> Not surprising at all. This trend began with NFL Sundays skewing higher for mobile usage. With the exception of a fantasy league draft, where a larger screen lends itself to doing more in-depth player research, setting a lineup, monitoring a team, following live scores, etc. are all activities that are easily done on a mobile device. (K. Ota, personal communication, 2018)

This is all quite relevant, but also shows how strategies for consumer penetration have moved from such heavy reliance on securing programming contracts from major American sports leagues. For instance, ESPN has never secured rights for any Sunday afternoon NFL game contracts—and yet now has found a mechanism for ensuring that millions of fans are nonetheless interacting with an ESPN product during these games. This is, arguably, a larger opportunity for growth than the transmission of the games themselves; while television will feature advertisements rendered to millions of viewers, ESPN's app-based advertisements will be more interactive, allowing for greater consumer engagement and even the ability to purchase an item or service on the same mobile device during the experience.

Fantasy Sport Importance and Success

The advancements, attention, and resources surrounding ESPN Fantasy activities are impressive but also carry an important purpose. As John Diver noted to Billings and Ruihley (2014), creating games and activities are part of the way to gain consumer attention:

> Part of our job is to create habits. We want people to have bookmarks, go check their fantasy basketball page, go look at tomorrow's lineup, make sure they don't have any bench players, make sure no one's hurt, pick your *Streak for the Cash*, go look at your English Premier Soccer League team. If someone has 45 minutes a day that they sit in on their computer or cellphone, we want to try to get a percentage of that. (p. 72)

Creating habits, routine, and information/activities consumers desire. These functions are important to many technology-based organizations. For ESPN, Kevin Ota now believes those activities have been cemented within ESPN products and are assisting in advancing their products to an advanced consumer. He notes:

> According to the 2017 ESPN Sports Poll, fans who play fantasy sports are more likely to attend games, read sports news, watch sports highlights and spend money on sports compared to fans who aren't fantasy players. Simply put, there are no more engaged and avid sports fans than those who play fantasy. (K. Ota, personal communication, 2018)

With the aforementioned success evident, we inquired about how some of the success came to be. Ota and associates responded with four major success factors (K.Ota, personal communication, 2018). The first success factor was the fact that fantasy sports were made a priority at ESPN. This meant ESPN was "applying resources from nearly every aspect of the company toward ensuring world-class game development, content innovation and reach toward new and younger audiences" (K. Ota, personal communication, 2018). This unfolds in the technological advancements, hiring of fantasy sport-specific staff and on-air talent, and allowing for airtime. The talent gets better, the viewers get smarter, and the general sense is that a rising tide lifts all boats, serving ESPN's most essential mission: to entertain sports fans. A second success factor was the decision to consolidate the multiple fantasy apps into the single ESPN Fantasy App. This decision was key to creating a similar look, feel, and experience for all the ESPN gaming options. In addition, it allowed for some uninitiated fantasy sport users to see and know that the fantasy experience is just as accessible as other ESPN gaming options. Moreover, as other fantasy sport providers were slower to follow in this desire for consolidation, ESPN made the argument for ease of use to many new fans: you can sign up and use the following six sources to serve your fantasy purposes … or you can have a single multi-function application by selecting ESPN as your fantasy sport host provider.

A third ESPN Fantasy success factor was the idea that ESPN invested *primetime* programming toward "explicit promotion" of fantasy games including the Fantasy Football Marathon and Tournament Challenge Marathon (a similar marathon to the fantasy sport where the goal was to increase bracket entries for the NCAA Men's Basketball Tournament). This explicit promotion included dedicated commercial space and events broadcasted on ESPN and ESPN2, use of many ESPN analysts and hosts, and utilization of a studio and equipment. Moreover, wall-to-wall coverage on a major cable network sends one clear message: fantasy sport is no longer niche; not only that, we can create 28 hours of programming and we *know* we have the audience who will desire it.

In a similar vein, the fourth success factor Ota described was the fact that ESPN was continuing to develop TV shows and segments dedicated to fantasy sport. This includes *The Fantasy Show with Matthew Berry, Fantasy Football Now*, and segments on *NFL Live, Sunday NFL Countdown*, etc. (K. Ota, personal communication, 2018). Fantasy coverage, by its very nature, is bite-sized and digestible in short (1–2 minute) segments. ESPN has recognized the value of such content, as it readily translates to app and web offerings where one can scroll or toggle through similar-length content offerings in a relatively short—yet meaningful to the fan—span of time.

Through all the successes that fantasy sport is providing for ESPN, Ota and his associates are pleased about the future of fantasy sport at ESPN. When asked about this, he stated:

> Fantasy is going to continue to grow and be a significant driver of our overall product consumption. We continue to make significant investments in product, technology, and content initiatives for fantasy. We are expanding to new audiences and introducing them to our games while continuing to serve our dedicated fan base. (K. Ota, personal communication, 2018)

The Missteps

When determining any elements that impeded the development of the ESPN Fantasy model, it is clear that two stand out ahead of all others. The first was the massive expansion of DFS, which ESPN decided to embrace via not only an exclusive advertising deal with DraftKings but also through daily sport content placed within the aforementioned programs. The ensuing legal battles surrounding such leagues hurt ESPN's brand while not contributing to the financial bottom line as the DFS games produced a "sharks and minnows" concept (Harwell, 2015). The "sharks" not only won 91% of all the money to be gained, but also used advanced analytics to the point that they did not need ESPN's advice or products. The "minnows" quickly lost money, finding the game frustrating while lamenting broadly-defined "fantasy sport" in a manner that hurt ESPN's core traditional business. Such leagues imploded in 2016 (Van Natta, 2016), with ESPN's *Outside the Lines* left to chronicle the downfall.

The second misstep involved the element of their fantasy strategy that was most heralded: The unified ESPN Fantasy application. Not ready to handle the immense traffic occurring with the start of the 2016 NFL season, the system crashed for four-and-a-half-hours, frustrating millions of fans wishing to check scores and adjust lineups. The application crash was short-lived, but nevertheless planted a seed in the minds of some sports fans who perhaps began to question whether ESPN's newfound #1 placement in the fantasy hierarchy was to their own benefits as fantasy sport users. It appears ESPN was able to respond adequately and avoid similar frustrations in the coming years, but such a crisis hindered the overall brand that ESPN Fantasy had worked exceedingly hard to cultivate.

Conclusion

Just a decade ago, ESPN was demonstrably trailing its fantasy sport competitors, whether that was Yahoo! (in total number of players/leagues) or sites like *Rotoworld* (in total number of fantasy page views). The transformation of ESPN from "one of the guys" to the Goliath among industry leaders is as noteworthy as it is strategic. From the hiring of Matthew Berry, to the creation of fantasy sport segments, to the advancement of fantasy sport shows, to the now dominance of fantasy within mobile platforms, ESPN was able to bet on the future and see a 20-million-participant industry (in the mid 2000s) and project a potential reach of triple that amount in 2018. In doing so, ESPN was able to blunt other choices that are, in hindsight, less economically viable, including agreeing to pay for mass increases in league contracts or offering more for its *Monday Night Football* contract than for any of the other NFL contracts; and yet without being part of the rotation to televise a Super Bowl. For ESPN, fantasy sport moved from bit player to stalwart defender of the ESPN brand. As ESPN moves toward its fifth decade of existence, gaming is as prominent as games within a new strategy to reinvent ESPN's economic model.

References

Billings, A. C., & Ruihley, B. J. (2014). *The fantasy sport industry: Games within games.* London: Routledge.

Cunningham, N. R., & Eastin, M. S. (2017). Second screen and sports: A structural investigation into team identification and efficacy. *Communication & Sport, 5*(3), 288–310. doi:10.1177/2167479515610152.

Fantasy Sports Trade Association. (2018). Industry demographics: Actionable insights & insightful data. Retrieved from https://fsta.org/research/industry-demographics/

Harwell, D. (2015, Oct. 12). All the reasons you probably won't win money playing daily fantasy sports. *Washington Post.* Retrieved from https://www.washingtonpost.com/news/the-switch/wp/2015/10/12/all-the-reasons-you-probably-wont-win-money-playing-daily-fantasy-sports/?noredirect=on&utm_term=.f6234bd5f955

Larkin, B. A., & Fink, J. S. (2016). Fantasy sport, FoMO, and traditional fandom: How second-screen use of social media allows fans to accommodate multiple identities. *Journal of Sport Management, 30*(6), 643–655. doi:10.1123/jsm.2015-0344.

Lim, J. S., Hwang, Y. C., Kim, S., & Biocca, F. A. (2015). How social media engagement leads to sports channel loyalty: Mediating roles of social presence and channel commitment. *Computers in Human Behavior, 46,* 158–167. doi:10.1016/j.chb.2015.01.013.

Ota, K. (2016, August 17). ESPN's fantasy football marathon spurs two days of record sign ups. *ESPN Media Zone.* Retrieved from http://espnmediazone.com/us/press-releases/2016/08/espns-fantasy-football-marathon-spurs-two-days-record-sign-ups/

Ota, K. (2017a, August 9). ESPN fantasy football: Bigger and better than ever for 2017 [Press Release]. *ESPN Media Zone.* Retrieved from https://espnmediazone.com/us/press-releases/2017/08/espn-fantasy-football-bigger-better-ever-2017/

Ota, K. (2017b, August 16). ESPN fantasy football marathon II: More than 2 million teams drafted. *ESPN Media Zone.* Retrieved from https://espnmediazone.com/us/press-releases/2017/08/espn-fantasy-football-marathon-ii-2-million-teams-drafted/

Ota, K. (2017c, November 28). ESPN's fantasy success: It's all real [Press Release]. *ESPN Media Zone.* Retrieved from http://espnmediazone.com/us/press-releases/2017/11/espns-fantasy-success-real/

Ourand, J. (2017, November 27). After bundling games in one app, ESPN watches fantasy take off. *Sports Business Daily.* Retrieved from https://www.sportsbusinessdaily.com/Journal/Issues/2017/11/27/Media/Sports-Media.aspx

Ruihley, B. J., Hardin, R., & Billings, A. C. (2015). ESPN and the fantasy sport experience. In J. McGuire, G. G. Armfield, & A. Earnheardt (Eds.), *The ESPN Effect:*

Academic Studies of the Worldwide Leader in Sports (pp. 225–236). New York, NY: Peter Lang.

Spangler, T. (2017, May 12). ESPN to debut fantasy football week day show with Matthew Berry. *Variety.* Retrieved from https://variety.com/2017/digital/news/espn-fantasy-football-show-matthew-berry-1202423985/

Van Natta, D. (2016, August 24). "Outside the Lines" investigates: The implosion of daily fantasy sports leaders Draft Kings and FanDuel. *ESPN's Outside the Lines.* Retrieved from http://www.espn.com/espn/feature/story/_/id/17374929/otl-investigates-implosion-daily-fantasy-sports-leaders-draftkings-fanduel

5. ESPN and esports: Capturing and Joining a Rising Sport

STEVE YOUNG, SEAN FOURNEY, AND BRADEN BAGLEY

> And it has an audience, and it's an audience that isn't necessarily duplicated with what ESPN is doing. So to wade into a debate about whether or not it's sports is irresponsible from a content creation perspective, because then we're not serving the audience, which is all we're supposed to be doing. I don't think the audience cares.
>
> —Peckham (2016, para. 11)

The above quote comes from former ESPN Editor-in-Chief, Chad Millman, who explained his company's decision to invest in esports' growing popularity in 2015 as somewhat of a no-brainer. As a "massive, global series of video game competitions" (Robison, 2018, para. 2), esports has an estimated following of nearly 150 million while revenue projections see the industry worth $1.5 billion by 2020 (Patel, 2017). Esports is clearly not just for competitors (although purses range in the tens of millions) but fans who enjoy the "personalities and culture … This has led to sponsorships of teams, players and competitions, as well as giveaways, which are creating massive global visibility for brands" (Patel, 2017, para. 2). The growing number of sponsors and advertisers—from Red Bull to Arby's to the NFL and NBA—invest because it "remains much cheaper than doing so on more traditional sports" (Rapaport, 2017, para. 10). Although playing video games for a living at one time seemed like a joke (Tassi, 2013), esports commercial popularity has taken "another step toward mainstream acceptance of professional video gaming" (Gaudiosi, 2016, para. 1).

Once considered the "Worldwide Leader in Sports" because of its extensive network of global and local coverage (Wood, 2015), ESPN dominated cable, print, and web in the 1990s and 2000s. Layoffs, declining ratings, political criticism, a sexual harassment scandal, and a digital-streaming market ill-suited for cable threatened to knock the sports giant from its pedestal. It is possible in the near future that the network "gets outbid for key sports by rich, content-hungry tech giants such as Facebook and Amazon—leaving the company hollowed out, with little of value to offer" (Hruby, 2017, para. 27). So how does ESPN regain some of its viewership? Esports offers a unique opportunity to cover a sport as it evolves, and the network already broadcasts its events alongside an editor and two full-time reporters for its website coverage (Gaudiosi, 2016). This study seeks to identify what exactly ESPN covers in its esports content from a cultural-value analysis lens. As Bien-Aimé, Whiteside, and Hardin (2017) adequately note, the business of covering sports is a tricky one that involves following audiences' desires while at the same time promoting that which a network and its partners' coverage stand to profit from. With these pressing concerns in mind, how exactly is ESPN covering esports?

Esports and ESPN

Esports are an entirely new entertainment experience for most Americans. They involve individual and team-based competitions through video games, and imply a public and now mainstream dimension of the larger realm of video games and gaming. Esports takes a game that various individuals have experience playing or watching and integrates it with technical innovation and aspirational qualities to introduce it to mainstream audiences (Taylor, 2012). Common synonyms for esports include professional gaming, competitive gaming, cyber sports, and cyber athletics among others (Weiss & Schiele, 2013).

Competitive video gaming is distinct in comparison to casual or leisurely gaming. Martončik (2015) examined the differences between various types of video gamers including team leaders, team members, non-members of a team, and solo players in a research questionnaire. Esports was defined as "the area of game playing in which the player's goal is to continually advance, regularly train, compete, and participate in leagues and tournaments" (p. 208). A similar study conducted by Seo (2016) highlighted the differences between occasional and competitive gaming by stating, "It is not which games are played for esports, but how these games are played that primarily differentiates competitive gaming from other forms of playing computer games" (p. 266). Today's youth have grown up in a digital age where computer use was the norm whether for research, social interaction, or play. As such, playing video games on computers and consoles is a natural aspect of life for them. To this point, Adamus (2012) offered a theoretical framework of esports as a youth subculture. The author emphasized that esports were predominantly played and consumed by adolescents.

A distinctive feature of esports is that consumers regularly watch others playing various games via streamed online matches and also by attending real-life tournaments (Taylor, 2012). Watching esports is similar to watching traditional sports in the sense it involves "its own nexus of understandings, tools, skills, and competencies that are used by consumers to coordinate this practice" (Seo & Jung, 2016, p. 643). In order to fully grasp an esport event, viewers must understand video game competition as a form of sport consisting of a competitive performance involving skilled cyber athletes and their narratives. The knowledge and skills required to play video games competitively are also needed when consuming esports and understanding what is happening. Esports leagues and tournaments "authenticate the consumption of esports in a real world, traversing the boundaries between what consumers do inside the computer games and how they engage with esports offline" (Seo & Jung, 2016, p. 646).

Over the past 10 years, several Asian and European countries adopted professional gaming as a legitimate form of competition. Esports were accredited as sports in China, Russia, Bulgaria, Sweden, and Taiwan (Stein & Scholz, 2014). Recently, "esports have rapidly gained popularity among youth cultures around the world and accumulated cult-like followings of player celebrities" (Wagner, 2007, p. 183). In South Korea, children grow up in a culture where the norm is people playing video games outside of the home. Internet cafes, also known as LAN centers and PC bangs, are a fundamental aspect of teenage culture. For many teens and young adults in South Korea, esports replaces traditional sports fandom in the sense that matches are held in large stadiums and on television (Erzberger, 2016). Top esports players are widely considered to be superstars. They are viewed as celebrities and are mobbed on the street whenever they are recognized (Heaven, 2014). While Europe, North America, and the rest of the world are slowly adopting esports as a legitimate form of competition, the heart of esports remains South Korea (Erzberger, 2016).

In America, competitive video gamers often lack the support needed to practice and become masters of their craft (Shaw, 2012). The perception of video gaming as a hobby still overshadows the idea of making a living through competitive gaming. Thiborg (2009) maintained major governing organizations play a vital role in gathering social support and legitimacy for esports as a form of professionalized sports. He suggested a greater distinction between competitive gaming and other forms of gaming ought to be stressed in order for esports to acquire such support and recognition.

The formal organization of competitive video game tournaments and leagues at both amateur and professional levels has played an integral role in the professionalization of esports (Taylor, 2012). As Taylor (2012) explained, the popularity of esports has "undergone a transformation over the last decade where small, grassroots play intermingles with large-scale coordinated commercial efforts" (p. 136). As the number of esports leagues increased, various communities of gamers became motivated to create and join teams to compete for large prize pools and recognition within gamer communities.

In the mid-to-late 2010s, esports seemingly exploded onto the mainstream stage of American entertainment. With television shows such as *ELeague* on TBS, official esport leagues (e.g., Overwatch League), and large tournaments (e.g., The Dota 2 International, League of Legends Worlds), esports have drawn so much attention and curiosity, that individuals are actually leaving their homes to view esports events in-person. Players, fans, and spectators of various skill levels and understandings now pack large stadiums to watch professional gamers compete for extremely large prize pools in the millions of dollars (Taylor, 2012). Although gamers have stereotypically been defined by a certain "geeky" style as unpopular, unattractive, technology savvy individuals (Shaw, 2010), the increasing popularity of video games in general and esports in particular, in addition to investment by high-profile individuals and sport-related networks such as ESPN, may be shifting this gamer stereotype in a more positive mainstream-accepted direction. ESPN can not only attract a new audience to their brand but also help legitimize the esports industry.

ESPN is no stranger to the world of esports. In January 2016, ESPN added esports to its repertoire of sports (Rovell, 2016). On the ESPN.com website, esports has its own section next to football, baseball, and other traditional sports. The esports division of the ESPN.com website offers individuals seven sections of content: "Home," "Esports [Events] Calendar," "League of Legends," "Overwatch," "CS:GO," "Dota 2," and "Tickets," with League of Legends, Overwatch, CS:GO, and Dota 2 being popular competitive esports titles. Various contributors provide content on the esports division of ESPN. com including professional esport players, coaches, investors, academics, and others who have a vested interest in esports.

With in-depth investigative journalism, interviews, and behind-the-scenes coverage of the competitive gaming culture, ESPN produces top quality illustrations of esports for its viewership of over 94 million households in more than 200 countries around the world (Baron, 2015; Vogan, 2015). The esports section of ESPN's website is meant to serve the needs of competitive video game consumers who watch esports—an activity that is considered one of the fastest growing spectator sports worldwide (Rovell, 2016).

Media act fundamentally as narrators of change in our society (Campbell, Jensen, Gomery, Fabos, & Frechette, 2014), and depictions of video gaming have a major effect on their consumption. Esports bring together organized audiences that were largely neglected throughout American history. Today, like-minded individuals who share a common understanding and appreciation of competitive video games are able to consume esports in ways that were unavailable just a few years ago thanks to television broadcasts such as the *Street Fighter 5 Finals* on ESPN2 (ESPN, 2017b) and Internet sites like ESPN.com/esports.

The ways in which ESPN builds their relationship with the gaming community is a fascinating concept that demands deeper investigation. Through various Web publications containing text, images, and videos, ESPN.com/esports illustrates competitive video gaming in a particular pattern. As ESPN reaches new audiences with ESPN.com/esports, it is important to investigate how they are portraying esports culture to their astoundingly large, global audience.

Method

On its face, there are many interpretations of ESPN.com/esports articles. The content in these articles does more than simply report scores and news; it often takes a critical stance on esports culture. To explore how esports culture is situated in ESPN.com/esports articles, a value analysis was employed.

A culture is often characterized by the values it asserts and what it ignores. Value analysis is a methodology used to view cultures or subcultures in their broader implications (Sillars & Gronbeck, 2001). A major strength of value analysis is its ability to bring attention and understanding to certain values and value systems that organizations and individuals communicate. Values may be understood as devices of oppression that constrain thoughts and behavior. They can also be seen as ideologies that deprive groups of individuals to the desire of others who are more powerful. Value analyses have been applied in various contexts, including sport and media studies (Sandeen, 1997; Trujillo & Ekdom, 1985), to recognize and describe patterns within a text. Critics who use value analysis explore which topics, elements, and ideas are included more than others in a text. They focus on selection, ordering, and emphasis determined directly from the text (Sillars & Gronbeck, 2001).

For this study, the researchers investigated ESPN.com/esports articles from March 2017 (when the esports section was launched) to February 2018. By examining 100 of the most popular articles (based on Twitter "retweets"), the researchers highlighted stated and implied beliefs, values, and value systems "as a means of defining the culture and its human orientations to the material world" (Sillars & Gronbeck, 2001, p. 186). Because ESPN. com/esports is available for public consumption, the researchers accessed popular articles directly from ESPN's website for analysis.

In order to identify the most popular ESPN.com produced esports articles, the researchers measured the potential articles by the amount of Twitter engagements they received when included in a tweet by the official ESPN esports Twitter account, @ESPN_Esports. Twitter measures engagement by counting any clicks on a tweet, including retweets, replies, follows, favorites, links, cards, hashtags, embedded media, username, profile photo, or tweet expansion (Lee, 2017a). Socialbearing, a Twitter insights and analytics software, was used to gather the data and sort it by engagements. Socialbearing has been used in academic literature as a tool to study observations, opinions, and experiences on social media (Upadhyay & Upadhyay, 2017).

The data collection process was executed through the following steps: (a) Searched "@ESPN_Esports" by @Handle at https://socialbearing.com/ search/user; (b) Selected "load more" until all tweets within our selected timeframe were loaded; (c) Selected "Sort tweets by engagement;" and (d) Selected the 108 most engaged tweets that included a link to an ESPN. com published article. The Twitter data included 3,222 tweets composed or retweeted by @ESPN_Esports between March 25, 2017 and February 1, 2018. Only articles coming directly from tweets composed by @ESPN_ Esports were selected, meaning retweets were skipped over in the process. The sample was also purged of duplicate articles and expired URL's leaving a final total of 100 articles to code. After coding of the 100 articles was complete, we concluded that an acceptable standard of saturation had been reached, as there was adequate information to replicate the study, and we were no longer obtaining additional information (Fusch & Ness, 2015).

Analysis

Developing Narratives

The majority of articles (43%) involved human interest stories about esports players, staff (coaches, statisticians, analysts) teams, leagues, and tournaments. We describe this theme as *developing narratives* because of the writer's underlying focus on stories involving specific individuals, teams, leagues, and tournaments.

Particular language was employed in developing narratives by ESPN. com/esports writers to illustrate various players, teams, tournaments, and leagues. Players and teams were referred to as gods, god slayers, kings, legends, prodigies, players to watch for, odds-on favorites, regulars at the grand finals, and top competitors. Writers highlighted various characteristics of players and teams such as passion, consistency, fearlessness, adaptiveness, patience, aggressiveness, consistency, focus, intelligence, creativity, trickiness, style, and efficiency. Tournaments and leagues were written about in ways that highlighted their uniqueness and attractiveness to esports fans and spectators. In a piece about the League of Legends All-star weekend for example, Moser (2017) claimed "no other event expresses why fans love their favorite players so well" (para. 18).

Esports player and team articles covered a wide variety of subjects including pursuit of greatness, familial impact, cultural significance, and age. Pursuit of greatness narratives were often portrayed in the context of tournament and league wins, although some articles touched on concepts such as a player's career, retirement, and giving back to esports. These pieces often portrayed a rags-to-riches storyline in which players followed their dreams, against tremendous odds, to be professional gamers. DR Ray, a *Street Fighter V* player from the Dominican Republic, for example, was covered in a "real life underdog story" (Lee, 2017b, para. 23), as someone who does not let his struggle define his story, despite the clear hardships that Dominican players face.

Familial impact narratives typically revolved around individual players. Khan (2017a) explained how professional esports player Tokido consulted his father when considering pursuing a career in professional gaming, and how his father helped him become the professional esports player he is today. In the same article, Khan (2017a) explained how as a child growing up, Tokido discovered his passion for *Street Fighter* (the game he plays professionally) by playing the game whenever he visited his cousin's house.

Cultural significance played a major role in many developing narrative articles. Khan (2017a) explained how Tokido faced many hardships pursuing an esports career in Japan because it is a very conservative country where parents push their children to seek traditional careers: "Most students in Japan aim to land a job in their third year of college. These jobs are usually set for life, and those who aren't able to secure a job … are looked down upon" (para. 17). Other articles mentioned international players experiencing difficulty or being prohibited from entering the United States due to visa or other travel-related issues: "DR Ray believed the main reason for his country's invisible presence has more to do with the strict standards and procedures to secure a visa than the skill level of the players" (Lee, 2017b, para. 3). Cultural aspects of players, teams, leagues, and tournaments were also mentioned to provide perspective. Lee (2017b) described Dominican Republic esports players as "representing one of the smallest communities in the fighting game scene" (para. 2).

Developing narratives recurrently spoke of age, and more specifically, youth in esports. Many articles mentioned players' exact ages and highlighted how young they were when they began playing video games competitively. For example, *Street Fighter V* player DR Ray illustrated the hardships of pursuing a professional career in video gaming at an early age, "I was very young at the time—17-years-old—and it was incredibly difficult to secure funds" (Lee, 2017b, para 5). Age was also spoken of to provide perspective. Jae Jeon (2017) highlighted the significance of youth in esports by suggesting, "few players in any esport can remain capable of competing toe-to-toe against prodigies 10 years younger than them" (para. 15). Finally, age was discussed in a cultural and familial context to suggest that esports payers could not play games forever. Competitive gamers who started young were expected to go to college, get a "real" job, get married, move on with their life, and be looking to make the next major step—whether that be transitioning to a new esport title, a new role within esports (coaching, broadcasting, etc.), or retiring from esports altogether.

Video game tournaments and leagues were prime subjects of many developing narratives. Major tournaments such as the Evolution Championship Series (Evo) were described as spectacles involving thousands of live viewers, and even greater numbers of online spectators. Banusing (2017b) covered the 2GGC: Greninja Saga Smash Bros. tournament highlighting how, "nearly every notable Greninja specialist is headed to the Esports Arena ... With more than 300 attendees" (para. 2). Erzberger (2017) emphasized the 200,000-person spectator count of the Tyler1 Championship Series and stated that it was "A number unreachable for most esports tournaments, even ones backed by multimillion-dollar companies and sponsorships" (para. 3). Tournament narratives were also illustrated as rags-to-riches stories. Evo, now considered the biggest fighting game event worldwide, was written about from a historic perspective—highlighting how the first iteration of Evo took place at a university, and is now held at Mandalay Bay events center for thousands of spectators.

Transactional Dynamism

A significant portion (34%) of activity encompassing coverage of esports comes in the form of business dealings. We labeled this theme *transactional dynamism* for its complex mixture of organizational establishment and entrepreneurial speculation. Specifically, actions of investment, bidding, acquiring, earning, expanding, drafting, purchasing, and finalizing characterize a flurry of activity from multiple entities of interest in the business of esports.

At first glance, the activity associated with league development seems confusing and overwhelming. Articles are continually referencing the beginning and abandoning of leagues from which teams are constantly jumping. Announcements like "OpTic Gaming will join the North American League of Legends Championship Series" (Wolf, 2017c, para. 1) are quickly followed by the reality that OpTic is also in an *additional* league (Overwatch League). However, Overwatch League is also reorganizing itself. Teams' agreements "will not be valid for the league, meaning teams that participate in the Overwatch League will have to sign their players to new contracts" (Wolf, 2017c, para. 3).

Organizing this activity comes from entertainment organizations that create leagues and construct teams to play in them. Organizations like Cloud 9, Immortals, OpTic Gaming, and NRG have multiple teams in leagues like "Overwatch, Counter-Strike: Global Offensive, Super Smash Bros., Hearthstone, Rocket League, Vainglory, and other titles" (Wolf, 2017b, para. 7). Leagues that become popular and profitable, such as Overwatch League, traditionally grow and will "feature 12 teams, each of which paid $20 million for a franchise spot ... will represent a city ... similar to a traditional sport" (ESPN, 2018b, para. 1). Such activity in esports organizational discourse displays the dynamic nature of an industry forming from just one game:

> Riot Games announced changes to the North American League Championship Series in June that included team permanence, a secondary academy league, a players' association and revenue-sharing options for both teams and players. With it, the 10 previously participating teams were not guaranteed to return to the league, but instead had to go through a meticulous application process that lasted from July to September. (Wolf, 2017c, para. 6)

The entrepreneurial interest in esports has captured investors from a myriad of traditional sports and entertainment industries. Investments from the New York Mets, Cleveland Cavaliers, the NFL, Silicon Valley, and Disney represent the crossover appeal of esports. ESPN, Disney, and the NFL held a Madden NFL tournament featuring "players representing all 32 NFL franchises" (ESPN, 2018a, para. 3) that is "just the beginning of business opportunities ... for audience overlap between the NFL and the Madden player base" (Wolf, 2017a, para. 12). Additionally, "the NBA announced 17 of its 30 teams would participate, at a cost of reported $750,000 on three-year agreements" (Wolf, 2017c, para. 6). Former athletes such as Shaquille O'Neal and Alex Rodriguez and NFL running back Marshawn Lynch have invested in teams (Wolf, 2017b). The oldest venture capital firm in the United States, Bessemer, is also a player in esports. Having already invested $15 million in Twitch—the streaming platform with 20 million esports viewers

(Lawler, 2012)—Bessemer placed a $25 million bid on an esports team that would:

> ... now recruit additional investors for the round, which are likely to include other esports-interested firms or wealthy entrepreneurs, as well as the possibility of professional sports teams ... is ultimately expected to be larger than the $25 million that Bessemer will contribute. (Wolf, 2018b, para. 3)

As a result, the activity surrounding investment in esports gives the strong sense of opportunity for traditional sports as well as entertainment and technology companies to cash-in on a burgeoning industry that has a fervor and excitement on the horizon.

Gameplay Reporting

The final theme that emerged from the data centered on the reporting of game and tournament related results, previews, and news. In all, 22% of the articles fell under this category. The most common among these articles was tournament results. These were often simple reporting pieces on competitive events relaying final scores, wins, and losses. For example, Donigan (2018) reported, "It may have taken a while, but SK Telecom TI closed out the second day of the 2018 League of Legends Champions Korea Spring Split with a 2–1 win" (para. 1). In addition to this simple reporting, the articles often put the tournament results into a bigger picture, like when Timothy Lee put a win by "ZeRo" into perspective, "In Smash 4, it was the continuation of the ZeRo dynasty as Team SoloMid's Gonzalo 'ZeRo' Barrios took down another major tournament" (Lee, 2017c, par. 2).

Authors of these articles also did their best to communicate the excitement and importance of specific moments during these events. For example, in one article recapping the plays of the year, the author sets up the play with the following colorful preview:

> It was the biggest stage of Salem's life, Evo 2017. Thousands of live spectators at the Mandalay Bay Arena and tens of thousands more online were on the edge of their seats as he, the man who once slayed titans in his prime, was attempting to take out ZeRo, the god of gods. (ESPN, 2017a, para. 6)

Additionally, Khan shares the following experience, "Rudolph is brash. Before a grand finals set, he'll take the microphone, call out his opponent and proclaim that he's the greatest. It's entertaining, and very not-Japanese" (Khan, 2017b, para. 13). Inserts like these give the articles life.

While most articles in this category were recaps, some of them were previews. For example, before the Clash of Smash major, Banusing gave his readers an article outlining what to expect at the tournament in Japan:

This weekend, 468 players will make their way to Tokyo to compete in the Ume-bura Japan Major, the country's largest tournament to date. With nearly every top Japanese player and a select few of the West's best confirmed, the path to first place will be laden with challenges for veterans and amateurs alike. (Banusing, 2017a, para. 1)

In addition to tournament recaps and previews, this category also included writer generated power rankings of teams and players. The team power ranking articles typically followed the same outline, beginning with a few paragraphs of introduction such as "from the kings to the teams wondering when it can sign new players in the midseason transaction window, here are the rankings that follow Round 2 of the Overwatch League" (Erzberger, 2018, para. 3). Following the introductions, authors ranked teams from first to last, with recaps of their week, such as this recap of the Seoul Dynasty's second week of action, "This week felt like the Dynasty was on cruise control, sweeping both the Florida Mayhem and Boston Uprising to keep its perfect record intact" (Erzberger, 2018, para. 5). Player rankings followed a similar structure, like a piece from Banusing ranking all of the available free agents in the Super Smash Bros League, where he lists "five free agents in Melee and Smash 4 that teams have yet to recruit, but should consider" (Banusing, 2017c, para. 8).

Finally, there were several other articles categorized in this theme that covered other miscellaneous events that affected the game-to-game and tournament-to-tournament gameplay. For example, in January 2018, Wolf reported that a Dallas Fuel player was suspended for making disparaging remarks:

xQc's punishment comes after he directed anti-gay slurs at Houston Outlaws tank Austin "Muma" Wilmot, who is openly gay. The Dallas Fuel player made those comments on his personal Twitch livestream Thursday following the Fuel's 4–0 loss to the Outlaws. Blizzard Entertainment, the operator of the Overwatch League, said that xQc's actions violated the league's code of conduct. (Wolf, 2018a, para. 4)

As demonstrated by this theme, readers are often interested in simple news stories that keep them current on the leagues and players that interest them. These gameplay reporting articles compliment those found in the first theme, developing narratives, which instead focus on the broader picture and stories of different entities within the industry. The articles in the transactional dynamism theme, on the other hand, strike a balance between the two, highlighting up-to-date news that have long-term impact on the state of the leagues being discussed. Together, these three themes explain the variety of ways that ESPN, and its writers, have covered the relatively new and growing industry of esports. Further discussion of these findings, and the implications that accompany them, are explored in the following section.

Discussion

ESPN's dual investment of esports—coverage and promotion—represents a turn towards both proclaiming and solidifying a new player in sports and entertainment. The excitement with which competitions are covered, the rapid pace in which transactions occur, the drama that envelops individual and team stories, and the youthful vigor with which participants enact and investors pursue, all point toward a new frontier on the horizon. Thusly, ESPN's coverage of esports situates itself as the capturing progenitor of sports, capitalism, and the American Frontier.

In 1893, historian Frederick Jackson Turner penned *The Significance of the Frontier in American History* which outlined America's identity as a confluence of initiation and adaptation (Bonazzi, 1993). Unlike the hierarchical formality of their European brethren—where individuals are born into social structures—Americans are driven by political ideology which encourages them to explore, tame, and conquer new worlds. As Carveth and Metz (1996) explain, a frontier mindset embodied a distinctly different civilization from ones of the past:

> The ideal of the frontier society was the self-made individual, and wealth and power won by competitive skill were much admired. What offended the frontiers people was wealth and power obtained through special privilege. They believed in a natural aristocracy, rather than an aristocracy by birth, education or special privilege. (p. 79)

Exploration of nature, however, *initiates* man to the frontier, and strips him of his assumptions "by destroying his inherited culture ... it offers the pioneer new opportunities, new ideals once he has overcome the ordeal of being mastered by the wilderness" (Bonazzi, 1993, p. 155). Once man has tamed the frontier, he then *adapts* incrementally and in coordination with fellow man to conquer a new frontier. Thus, initiating and adapting provides "why America reads like a palimpsest of social evolution ... the two structures of the Frontier Thesis reinforce each other and live in symbiosis" (Bonazzi, 1993, p. 158).

The presence of esports on the international sports stage is certainly growing, but the value that drives ESPN's venture into esports is truly that of an initiation of opportunity. The continual investment from celebrities, Silicon Valley, traditional sports owners and players, and, of course, the network that covered them so heavily for so long, exemplifies a frontiersman's perspective that gold is to be had in esports. Such initiation represents both an eschewing of an "inherited culture"—video games are for not sports and therefore not worthy of coverage—and an excitement in a new market for sports entertainment. ESPN's initiation positions themselves as front-and-center to the rush of excitement as leagues develop seemingly overnight, stadiums are packed, sponsors flock, young players "slay" one another, and traditionally competitive spatial boundaries be damned. In this way, the American Frontier is not about land but a renewed purpose found in one's *energy*. Frontiers may begin with an initiation of economic opportunity, but its source of power is manifested by "a spiritual quality, the true mark of the original human condition. As such it is an explosion of pure energy coming from the renewed union with the fountainhead of life" (Bonazzi, 1993, p. 159). Therefore, ESPN's coverage of esports shows the youthful energy and vigor strongly associated with attitudes of a burgeoning frontier.

Frontiers eventually need to be organized for settlement, however, and this requires cooperation amongst settlers. ESPN's coverage of match results, team synopses, league rules and, especially, player profiles, work to organize the frontier into a comprehensible and habitable place for consumption. From rags-to-riches stories, to cultural impediments of esports' hopefuls, to establishment of player, league, and organization contractual rights, ESPN is presenting esports not unlike traditional sports. That is, along with initiation, ESPN simultaneously presents the frontier in a familiar way to audiences as a way to *adapt* them. The decline of the company's popularity is much noted (Gaudiosi, 2016; Hruby, 2017). Also, rumors that ESPN will soon drop *Monday Night Football*—their only link to broadcasting America's most popular sport—increasingly surface (Duffy, 2017). The esports frontier which they are creating, then, will need settlers, and what better way to build homes for them then through traditional sports' narratives of individuals' overcoming adversity, teams' scurrying to get the latest prodigy, and guarantees of bombastic and passionate competition. In this way, ESPN solidifies the new frontier through tried-and-true methods as it potentially leaves behind the safety of its last home:

> The Frontier Thesis is meant to be a gateway to a consciousness of historical continuity through change ... Evolutionism shows that there is nothing inherently tragic in the passing of the frontier: the real tragedy would be to keep fast to old customs and ideas. This is how history works as the self-consciousness of America. (Bonazzi, 1993, p. 163)

Therefore, ESPN positions itself as a major player in the esports phenomenon through initiating excitement and adapting its audience to traditional methods of sports reporting. In essence, ESPN is capturing, capitalizing, and normalizing esports as just another sport.

Esports provides a new frontier for ESPN to explore, tame, and utilize in its defense against network competitors and consumer cord-cutters. The question of what to call esports—sport, entertainment, video gaming, or competitive video gaming—is irrelevant. With the help of ESPN and the company's capital, esports is now a player in emerging popular culture. Through a value analysis, ESPN's coverage of esports displays an exciting phenomenon as an exploration into individual and organizational initiative while at the same time relying on predictable sports tropes to adapt its viewers. ESPN frames esports as a frontier that, like other sports, has its settlers. To further develop that frontier, though, ESPN has to offer excitement and opportunity to encourage migration. Let the investors and fans flock.

References

Adamus, T. (2012). Playing computer games as electronic sport: In search of a theoretical framework for a new research field. In J. Fromme & A. Unger (Eds.), *Computer games and new media cultures* (pp. 477–490). Dordrecht: Springer. https://doi.org/10.1007/978-94-007-2777-9_30

Banusing, J. (2017a, May 5). Clash of Smash at Umebura Japan major. *ESPN.* Retrieved from http://www.espn.com/Esports/story/_/id/19309712/clash-smash-umebura-japan-major

Banusing, J. (2017b, May 19). Greninja specialists unite at 2GGC Saga. *ESPN.* Retrieved from http://www.espn.com/Esports/story/_/id/19411671/greninja-specialists-unite-2ggc-greninja-saga

Banusing, J. (2017c, August 17). The biggest free agents in Smash. *ESPN.* Retrieved from http://www.espn.com/Esports/story/_/id/20358704/super-smash-bros-essential-free-agents

Baron, S. (2015, February 22). List of how many homes each cable network is in as of February 2015. *ESPN.* Retrieved from http://tvbythenumbers.zap2it.com/2015/02/22/list-of-how-many-homes-each-cable-network-is-in-as-of-february-2015/366230/

Bien-Aimé, S., Whiteside, E., & Hardin, M. (2017). Sport as journalistic lens. In A. C. Billings (Ed.), *Defining sport communication* (pp. 223–234). New York, NY: Routledge.

Bonazzi, T. (1993). Frederick Jackson Turner's frontier thesis and the self-consciousness of America. *Journal of American Studies, 27*(2), 149–171. https://doi.org/10.1017/S0021875800031509

Campbell, R., Jensen, J., Gomery, D., Fabos, B., & Frechette, J. (2014). *Media in society*. Boston, MA: Bedford St Martin's Press.

Carveth, R., & Metz, J. (1996). Frederick Jackson Turner and the democratization of the electronic frontier. *The American Sociologist, 27*(1), 72–90. https://doi.org/10.1007/BF02691999

Donigan, W. (2018, January 17). Wolf debuts in the jungle against ROX during SKT win, KT drops to Afreeca. *ESPN.* Retrieved February from http://www.espn.com/Esports/story/_/id/22133133/wolf-debuts-jungle-rox-skt-win-kt-drops-afreeca

Duffy, T. (2017, July 5). We'll find out much about ESPN's future when the Monday Night Football deal gets renegotiated. *Awful Announcing.* Retrieved from http://awfulannounci   ng.com/espn/well-find-much-espns-future-monday-night-football-deal-gets-renegotiated.html

Erzberger, T. (2016, January 23). South Korea has been doing this a while. *ESPN*. Retrieved from http://espn.go.com/Esports/story/_/id/14628446/south-korean-Esports-lifestyle

Erzberger, T. (2017, November 29). League of Legends returns to grassroots with Tyler1 Championship Series. *ESPN*. Retrieved from http://www.espn.com/Esports/story/_/id/21599629/opinion-Esports-returns-grassroots-tyler1-championship-series

Erzberger, T. (2018, January 24). Overwatch League week 2 power rankings. *ESPN*. Retrieved from http://www.espn.com/Esports/story/_/id/22188834/overwatch-league-week-2-power-rankings

ESPN. (2017a, December 27). 2017 ESPN Esports Awards: Play of the year. *ESPN*. Retrieved from http://www.espn.com/Esports/story/_/id/21804729/2017-espn-Esports-awards-play-year

ESPN. (2017b, July 15). ESPNU and DisneyXD to air Smash at Evo, Street Fighter on ESPN2. *ESPN*. Retrieved from http://www.espn.com/Esports/story/_/id/19962785/espnu-disney-xd-air-smash-evo-street-fighter-espn2

ESPN. (2018a, January 26). ESPN, Disney, NFL ink multiyear deal for Madden broadcast rights. *ESPN*. Retrieved from http://www.espn.com/Esports/story/_/id/22217917/espn-disney-nfl-announce-multi-year-deal-broadcast-madden-nfl-18-championship-series

ESPN. (2018b, October 30). Overwatch League Season 1—everything you need to know. *ESPN*. Retrieved from http://www.espn.com/Esports/story/_/id/21331089/everything-need-know-overwatch-league-season-1-teams-roster-calendar-news-recaps

Fusch, P. I., & Ness, L. R. (2015). Are we there yet? Data saturation in qualitative research. *The qualitative report*, *20*(9), 1408–1416. Retrieved from https://nsuworks.nova.edu/tqr/vol20/iss9/3

Gaudiosi, J. (2016, January 22). Why ESPN is investing in ESports coverage. *Fortune*. Retrieved from http://fortune.com/2016/01/22/espn-invests-in-Esports-coverage/

Harwell, D. (2015, December 28). Disney has a money problem that even "Star Wars" can't fix. *The Washington Post*. Retrieved from https://www.washington-post.com/news/the-switch/wp/2015/12/28/disney-has-a-money-problem-that-even-star-wars-cant-fix/

Heaven, D. (2014). Rise and rise of esports. *New Scientist*, *223*(2982), 17. https://doi.org/10.1016/S0262-4079(14)61574-8

Hruby, P. (2017, December 7). ESPN: Can the worldwide leader in sports manage its own decline? *The Guardian*. Retrieved from https://www.theguardian.com/sport/2017/dec/07/espn-revenue-viewership-politics-layoffs

Jae Jeon, Y. (2017, November 27). From Overwatch to PUBG: A conversation with EscA. *ESPN*. Retrieved from http://www.espn.com/Esports/story/_/id/21586747/overwatch-pubg-esca-interview

Khan, I. (2017a, August 25). Creating a champion: How a father's trip abroad led Tokido to the Top. *ESPN*. Retrieved from http://www.espn.com/Esports/story/_/id/20444277/creating-champion-how-father-trip-abroad-led-tokido-top-fighting-game-community

Khan, I. (2017b, July 27). Why Rudolph, the best Melee player in Japan, is struggling to stay afloat. *ESPN*. Retrieved from http://www.espn.com/Esports/story/_/id/20163709/daiki-rudolph-ideoka-best-melee-player-japan-faces-roadblocks-abroad

Lawler, R. (2012, September 19). With more than 20m gamers tuning in, Twitch raises $15m from Bessemer Venture Partners. *TechCrunch*. Retrieved from https://techcrunch.com/2012/09/19/twitch-15m-bessemer-venture-partners/

Lee, K. (2017a, May 4). How to use Twitter analytics: 17 simple-to-find stats to help you tweet better. *Buffer*. Retrieved from https://blog.bufferapp.com/twitter-analytics.

Lee, T. (2017b, December 21). Putting the Dominican Republic on the Street Fighter map. *ESPN*. Retrieved from http://www.espn.com/Esports/story/_/id/21827498/street-fighter-v-drmap

Lee, T. (2017c, May 15). ZeRo and Mango reign supreme at Royal Flush. *ESPN*. Retrieved from http://www.espn.com/Esports/story/_/id/19387720/royal-flush-2017-super-smash-bros-zero-mango-reign-supreme-royal-flush

Martončik, M. (2015). e-Sports: Playing just for fun or playing to satisfy life goals? *Computers in Human Behavior*, *48*, 208–211. https://doi.org/10.1016/j.chb.2015.01.056

Moser, K. (2017, December 7). One-on-one tourney is the highlight of All-Star weekend. *ESPN*. Retrieved from http://www.espn.com/Esports/story/_/id/21691517/league-legends-all-star-event-one-one-tournament-loved-players-fans

Patel, D. (2017, August 1). What the emergence of the ESports industry means for brands. *Forbes*. Retrieved from https://www.forbes.com/sites/deeppatel/2017/08/01/what-the-emergence-of-the-esports-industry-means-for-brands/#4e246bb911b5

Peckham, M. (2016, March 1). Why ESPN is so serious about covering esports. *Time*. Retrieved from http://time.com/4241977/espn-esports/

Rapaport, D. (2017, February 9). What to expect from the booming esports industry in 2017. *Sports Illustrated*. Retrieved from https://www.si.com/tech-media/2017/02/09/Esports-industry-expectations-billion-dollar

Robison, N. (2018, January 30). Esports is the new college football. *Forbes*. Retrieved from https://www.forbes.com/sites/moorinsights/2018/01/30/esports-is-the-new-college-football/#11bc3f611855 Rovell, D. (2016, January 16). Esports is having a moment. *ESPN*. Retrieved from http://espn.go.com/Esports/story/_/id/14551519/Esports-having-moment

Sandeen, C. (1997). Success defined by television: The value system promoted by PM Magazine. *Critical Studies in Media Communication*, *14*(1), 77–105. doi:10.1080/15295039709366997

Seo, Y. (2016). Professionalized consumption and identity transformations in the field of Esports. *Journal of Business Research, 69*(1), 264–272. https://doi.org/10.1016/j.jbusres.2015.07.039

Seo, Y., & Jung, S. U. (2016). Beyond solitary play in computer games: The social practices of Esports. *Journal of Consumer Culture, 16*(3), 635–655. https://doi.org/10.1177/1469540514553711

Shaw, A. (2010). What is video game culture? Cultural studies and game studies. *Games and Culture, 5*(4), 403–424. https://doi.org/10.1177/1555412009360414

Shaw, A. (2012). Do you identify as a gamer? Gender, race, sexuality, and gamer identity. *New Media & Society, 14*(1), 28–44. https://doi.org/10.1177/1461444811410394

Sillars, M. O., & Gronbeck, B. E. (2001). *Communication criticism: Rhetoric, social codes, cultural studies.* Prospect Heights, IL: Waveland Press.

Stein, V., & Scholz, M. T. (2014). The intercultural challenge of building the European Esports League for video gaming. In C. Barmeyer & P. Franklin (Eds.), *Case studies in intercultural management: Achieving synergy from diversity* (pp. 1–13). Basingstoke, UK: Palgrave Macmillan.

Tassi, P. (2013, July 14). The U.S. now recognizes Esports players as professional athletes. *Forbes.* Retrieved from https://www.forbes.com/sites/insertcoin/2013/07/14/the-u-s-now-recognizes-esports-players-as-professional-athletes/#6dcdcb3f3ac9

Taylor, T. L. (2012). *Raising the stakes: E-sports and the professionalization of computer gaming.* Cambridge, MA: MIT Press.

Thiborg, J. (2009). Esport and governing bodies—An outline for a research project and preliminary results. Paper presented at the Kultur-Natur Conference, Norrkoping, Sweden.

Trujillo, N., & Ekdom, L. (1985). Sportswriting and American cultural values: The 1984 Chicago Cubs. *Critical Studies in Media Communication, 2*(3), 262–281. https://doi.org/10.1080/15295038509360085

Upadhyay, N., & Upadhyay, S. (2017). #RighttoBreathe why not? Social media analysis of the local in the capital city of India. *Procedia Computer Science, 108*, 2542–2546. https://doi.org/10.1016/j.procs.2017.05.017

Vogan, T. (2015). *ESPN: The making of a sports media empire.* Urbana, IL: University of Illinois Press.

Wagner, M. (2007). Competing in metagame space—eSports as the first professionalized computer metagame. In F. von Borries, S. Walz, & M. Böttger (Eds.), *Space time play—Computer games, architecture, and urbanism* (pp. 182–185). Basel: Birkhäuser.

Weiss, T., & Schiele, S. (2013). Virtual worlds in competitive contexts: Analyzing Esports consumer needs. *Electronic Markets, 23*(4), 307–316. https://doi.org/10.1007/s12525-013-0127-5

Wolf, J. (2017a, August 21). All 32 NFL teams to participate in Madden Club Championship. *ESPN.* Retrieved from http://www.espn.com/Esports/story/_/id/20398998/all-32-nfl-tteams-participate-madden-club-championship

Wolf, J. (2017b, September 29). Lynch, Strahan, J.Lo part of $15 million investment in NRG Esports. *ESPN*. Retrieved from http://www.espn.com/Esports/story/_/ id/20851460/marshawn-lynch-rod-part-15-million-investment-round-nrg-Esports

Wolf, J. (2017c, October 18). OpTic Gaming to join North American League of Championship Series. *ESPN*. Retrieved from http://www.espn.com/Esports/story/_/ id/21045921/sources-optic-gaming-join-north-american-league-championship-series

Wolf, J. (2018a, January 20). Dallas Fuel suspend xQc for anti-gay slurs; Overwatch league fines player. *ESPN*. Retrieved from http://www.espn.com/Esports/story/_/ id/22156350/dallas-fuel-suspends-felix-xqc-lengyel-following-use-anti-gay-slurs-stream

Wolf, J. (2018b, January 9). Sources: TSM to receive $25 million investment from Bessemer. *ESPN*. Retrieved from http://www.espn.com/esports/story/_/id/22016269/ sources-team-solomid-parent-company-receive-25-million-investment-bessemer-venture-partners

Wood, S. P. (2015, November 2). ESPN is no longer the "worldwide leader in sports'" following Grantland closure. *Adweek*. Retrieved from https://www.adweek.com/ digital/espn-is-no-longer-the-worldwide-leader-in-sports-following-grantland-closure/

Section Two

*Changes and Challenges in the Sports
Media Political Environment*

6. Tune It or Stream It? Can Millennials and the Internet Save ESPN?

Kevin Hull, Miles Romney, and David Cassilo

Since 1979, sports fans have turned on their cable or satellite television and dialed up ESPN for the latest sports scores, news, highlights, and live games. However, the number of fans watching the sports network began decreasing in 2011 (Gaines, 2016). Specifically, millennial sports fans (those ages 18–34) are shunning cable and turning to online streaming services for video (McCoy, 2015). For ESPN, this created a problem. The network earned billions of dollars each year from cable and satellite subscriptions, and when consumers began canceling their packages, revenue was not as high as forecasted due to subscriber loss (Nocera, 2017). When the Walt Disney Company (the owner of ESPN) announced earnings had dropped in 2017, it was ESPN that was prominently blamed for the fall (Lafayette, 2017).

In February 2018, ESPN finalized plans for ESPN+, the network's first ever direct-to-consumer streaming option. For $4.99 a month, sports fans would be able to stream live programming "not available on current channels" (Aiello, 2018, para. 3). According to Walt Disney Corporation CEO and Chairman Bob Iger, the service will show about 10,000 sporting events each year, including games from Major League Baseball, National Hockey League, college sports, and tennis' Grand Slam events (Aiello, 2018). However, fans looking for the top sports shown on ESPN's broadcast television network (e.g., the College Football national championship) would still need to pay up for a cable or satellite subscription. Professional football and basketball, plus the top-tier college football games, will not be on the service. With those limitations, one writer predicted: "It will not be a big hit" (Kafka, 2018, para. 1).

However, Iger hinted this could just be the beginning. When announcing the service, he said, "If anything points to what the future of ESPN looks like, it will be this" (Lang, 2018, para. 2). Perhaps that is an indication that this initial service is more of a trial run to see if a fully streaming ESPN, available without a cable/satellite subscription, is a viable option in the future. ESPN's first attempt at online streaming, WatchESPN, allowed only some games to be viewed without a cable package, essentially requiring sports fans to still subscribe to cable if they wanted to watch the events on the main channels such as ESPN, ESPN2, and ESPNU (Pomerantz, 2014).

Now ESPN must hope that the next generation of consumer, one that is already showing a lack of interest in subscribing to cable, will pay for this streaming service (Raine, 2017). This chapter will examine how college-aged students, those who might have Mom and Dad paying their bills and who still have an opportunity to decide how they plan to watch the big games in the future, feel about streaming sports options. Using diffusion of innovation as a guide, future sports-paying consumers were surveyed about ESPN, streaming sports online, and opinions regarding the financial and economic impact watching sports may have on their own budget.

Literature Review

Streaming Television and Sport

Alternative television viewing options, such as streaming devices and services, have caused traditional television ratings, pay-TV subscriptions, and television advertising revenue to decline (Kaplan, 2015). This decrease in television ratings has not meant an overall decrease in media viewing, however. In fact, viewers age 18 and over consumed 28 more hours of content per week in 2017 than they did in 2002 (Nielsen, 2018). People are simply finding new ways to watch more events. The time U.S. adults spent on computers, smartphones, and tablets increased 45% from 2015 to 2016. U.S. adults ages 18 to 24 spent 35.6% of their media time on smartphones, compared to 27.1% on television (Nielsen, 2017). Furthermore, viewers have expressed that they see more similarities than differences between streaming television and traditional television, which gives a leg up to streaming devices among cord-cutters (those who are getting rid of cable) because it is the less expensive of the two options (Logan, 2011). Streaming television also offers other advantages that traditional television does not. Jones (2009) stated that streaming devices allow the viewer to watch programming from wherever they want, have potential for a more social experience, and allow the user to select their own programming. With the streaming options for television holding advantages that the traditional format does not, it is no surprise that the computer has become equally as popular as television screens among younger viewers (Bury & Li, 2015).

There is less research on the tablet as a television-viewing device. As McCreery and Krugman (2015) explained, the tablet's ease of portability makes it a larger version of a smartphone. That quality does not just make it easier to use to view television programming than a traditional television screen, but also easier than a computer. The tablet allows more spatial freedom for television viewing than prior technologies without sacrificing too much in screen size.

But the decline of traditional television viewers is not just a result of easier-to-use devices. It is the content within those devices that allow options outside of traditional cable television packages. Services such as Netflix and Amazon Prime allow consumers access to thousands of television shows and movies without the need for cable. Meanwhile, other services are tied to current cable channels or offer similar content along with digital native programming. Services like Hulu and HBO Go allow users to pay for access to cable and digital content without a subscription. At first, these services—whether tied to a cable company or not—provided cable content to subscribers, but now they are creating original content and competing with cable networks for movies (Thielman, 2013).

However, in a changing television world, sports remain one of the medium's biggest moneymakers. The National Football League (NFL), the financial king of sports, earned $7.6 billion in television revenue during the 2016 season (Wagner-McGough, 2017). It appeared to be money well spent for television networks, as the NFL had 204 million unique viewers during the 2016 season (Leung, 2017). This symbiotic relationship is known as the sports/media complex, which refers to the cultural importance of sports leading to financial benefit of all stakeholders within the relationship between sports and media (Jhally, 1984). According to Jhally, the cultural importance of sports leads to financial benefit of all stakeholders within the relationship between sports and media. Because of the high level of cultural importance for sports, it is a commodity that is able to maintain economic prosperity for all stakeholders involved. This can be seen easily in television where the leagues, teams, television companies, and advertisers all prosper from their relationship with one another (Lefever, 2012).

For viewers, new technology means new ways to watch sports. Because of the high demand for sports and the money involved, network and cable companies have found ways to meet the needs of sports fans on these new devices. While NBC tape-delayed its coverage of the 2012 Summer Olympics on traditional television, viewers were able to stream the events live on their mobile devices (Burroughs & Rugg, 2014), a trend that continued in subsequent Olympics (Pedersen, 2018). Regardless of medium, sport continues to draw viewers and bring people together (Boyle, 2014). Boyle added that as new screens and new audiences develop through technological shifts, advertisers are closely watching, intrigued with reaching new audiences in new ways. Sports, unlike other television content, has the ability to be something that is viewed both collectively in front of a large screen and privately in front of a small screen (Whannel, 2014).

Evolution of ESPN

When ESPN, an all-sports television network, launched in 1979, its flagship news and highlight program was *SportsCenter*. The daily show was unlike anything else at the time and it was solely devoted to showing sports highlights and talking about sports (Farred, 2000). Farred noted that as a result, sports talk was born, and it became "cool" to talk about sports and have television content devoted to it. *SportsCenter* transformed sports on cable and network television, as there was now daily sports programming that did not require a live sporting event to get people to watch.

However, digital technology and social platforms have captured the interest of sports fans, and in many cases, it is no longer necessary to watch an hour-long program like *SportsCenter* to get news, information, or game highlights. Industry observers note that *SportsCenter* viewership was down 10% in 2015, while a similar show on ESPN, *NFL Countdown*, was down 13% (2015), and dropped another 15% from 2016 to 2017 (Klinski, 2017; Smith & Shaw, 2015).

ESPN attempted to create some new excitement for struggling shows by rebranding them. *SportsCenter with Scott Van Pelt* went to a new format for the show that combined popular elements from Van Pelt's ESPN Radio sports talk show with a traditional sports highlight show (Miceli, 2015). Ratings for that show started low, but in late 2017 were the highest among male viewers age 18–34 in that time slot among all television shows (Guthrie, 2017; Miceli, 2015). While Van Pelt's addition was a success, a 6:00 p.m. *SportsCenter* rebrand with Jemele Hill and Michael Smith (dubbed *SC6*) resulted in stagnant ratings before both hosts left the show after only 13 months (Deitsch, 2018). ESPN has made other efforts to keep up with the times, such as launching a twice-daily *SportsCenter* on the popular social media outlet Snapchat (Jarvey, 2017).

ESPN also invested heavily in live sports programming. The network spent billions of dollars to broadcast NBA, NFL, MLB, and college sports

(Ourand, 2017). Executives justified the cost because they viewed live sporting events as "DVR-proof," meaning that people wanted to watch games live and, therefore, would be forced to watch the advertisements as well (Dickey, 2017). While that may be true, what ESPN did not foresee was viewers eliminating cable/satellite completely (Ourand, 2017). With fewer subscribers, ratings fell for all of ESPN's live sports programming, including a 10-year low for their flagship live program, *Monday Night Football* (Putterman, 2017).

Theoretical Base: Diffusion of Innovation

The theoretical base for this study comes from the book *Diffusion of Innovation* (Rogers, 2003). Rogers explained the process of the adoption of a new innovation and the different stages involved in having an innovation adopted, with that adoption cycle being demonstrated by implementation of technology among the public. Rogers (2003) argued in order to have an impact on society the innovation must: (a) have an advantage over the current practice; (b) be compatible with existing needs; (c) not be too complex; (d) be able to be tested before adoption; and (e) have observable results and outcomes.

The rate of successful adoption of a new technology depends on the type of user. Rogers (2003) divided users into five different adopter categories: (a) innovators, (b) early adopters, (c) early majority; (d) late majority; and (e) laggards. Innovators are the first to adopt an innovation. In research previous to Rogers, Beal and Bohlen (1957) found these people tended to be more educated, more prosperous, and more risk-oriented. Early adopters are traditionally younger and well-educated, but tended to be less prosperous than the innovators. The early majority, traditionally more conservative, adopt the innovation after the innovators and early adopters. Individuals in the late majority are older and conservative and will adopt an innovation after about half the population has discovered it. Finally, laggards are the last to use an innovation: this group of people are very conservative, older, and are the least educated (Beal & Bohlen, 1957; Rogers, 2003).

Diffusion of innovations theory has been widely used in the social sciences, including research on adopting technologies such as computers (Lin, 1998), the Internet (Jeffres & Atkin, 1996), and interactive, multimedia cable (Lin & Jeffres, 1998). The theory is also popular among research involving journalism and media companies (English, 2016; Garrison, 2001; Singer, 2004; Tremayne, Weiss, & Alves, 2007). Researchers have examined how newsrooms adopted new technologies (Singer, 2004) and determined that larger corporations are more likely to be early adopters of technology than smaller organizations (Termayne et al., 2007). Studies on news consumption found that young adults were more likely to adopt technology if it was easy to use and had advantages over previous technologies (Chan-Olmsted, Rim, & Zerba, 2013). Lin (2001) suggested that online media can displace traditional media with "better content, superior technical benefits, and greater cost efficiency" (p. 36). While millions of Americans use streaming video services (Steel & Marsh, 2015), this research is one of the first to address how sports consumers view these products and if these innovations have an opportunity to be a lasting part of sports viewership.

Research Questions

To determine the long-term interest in ESPN's streaming service, a survey was distributed to college students at two large universities in the United States. Students were chosen as the target demographic for three reasons: (a) they are reflective of the audience most sought by executives; (b) they represent the future of video viewing (Lane, 2018); and (c) their age group spent over 57 hours per week consuming media in 2016 (Nielsen, 2017). While most college graduates have already decided about purchasing a cable package or streaming service(s), college students could still be using a family member's account. By surveying college students, this research sought to understand how prevalent live sports streaming is among college students, where and how they stream programming, and project future trends in live sports streaming. Therefore, the following research questions were proposed:

RQ$_1$:   Do college students watch more programming (all programming, not just sports) on streaming services or on traditional broadcast television?

RQ$_2$:   What factors will motivate college students to abandon traditional television for digital options?

RQ$_{3A}$:   Do sports streaming services that do not offer their marquee sports properties available online face negative perceptions about their brand?

RQ$_{3B}$:   Will college students spend money on services that do not contain games marquee sports properties?

RQ$_4$:   Do students view streaming as a viable way to watch sports online now and in the future?

Methods

In order to determine how college-aged consumers view ESPN, ESPN's streaming service, and cable/satellite packages as a whole, a 41-question survey was created. The survey was based on a previous study that examined video streaming (CSG Systems International, 2017). The survey included general questions about watching traditional television, streaming video online (including sports), and sports fandom. Based on diffusion of innovation (Rogers, 2003), additional questions were asked relating to online viewing in regards to how streaming (the innovation) can have an impact on society based on the five traits an innovation must have.

Following a brief explanation of ESPN's proposed streaming service, participants were also asked questions about their interest level in that service. The survey was administered in December 2017 and January 2018, before ESPN officially announced details of the streaming service that was set to start in the spring of 2018. At the time of the survey, only vague details on the ESPN streaming service were available and that information was provided. Participants were then asked about their plans for watching sports after graduation. Finally, basic demographics questions were asked.

The online survey was sent to college students at two large universities in the United States (one in the Southeast and one in the West). Participants were provided class credit for completing the study. Following the initial recruitment email and a reminder a week later, the survey generated 306 valid responses. This number of participants is in line with previous research on ESPN (Bissell & Zhou, 2004) and the sports media (Hardin & Shain, 2005).

Results

Sample Description

The majority of the respondents in the convenience sample (N = 306) were female (205, 67%), which is unsurprising as the students targeted in the survey were enrolled in their university's respective communication/journalism schools. These programs generally see a higher percentage of female enrollees (York, 2017). The average age of respondents was 20.3 years old (SD = 1.59). To determine how interested they would be in the content offered by ESPN, participants were asked about their sports fandom. The majority either agreed or strongly agreed with the statement, "I consider myself a diehard sports fan" (180, 58.8%), with most strongly agreeing (102, 33.3%). Only 84 students (27.4%) disagreed with the statement, with the remaining neither agreeing or disagreeing (42, 13.7%). The vast majority (145, 80.1%) said they enjoy watching sports either on broadcast television or on online.

Streaming Habits

The first research question asked if students viewed programming primarily on streaming services or on traditional television. The results from this study corroborate wider market research findings that indicate audiences, especially college-age students, are shifting towards streaming services. Respondents reported they primarily watch video content over the Internet (67.9%), compared to just 5.9% who said they primarily watch traditional television. The remaining 80 participants (26.1%) reported about a 50/50 split between traditional television and online streaming viewing. A t-test determined that the difference between male (M = 1.6, SD = .92) and females (M = 2.0, SD = .97) was significant t (301) = 2.998, p = .003. Just over half of those surveyed (52.3%) pay for a streaming service themselves, while 37.5% borrow another persons login. Most of the streaming occurs on a laptop (34.4%), phone (28.5%) or TV streaming device, like Apple TV or Amazon Firestick (29.3%). Television shows were the most frequently streamed content (61.4%). When asked specifically about live sports, the findings suggest that college students have fully embraced streaming services. Nearly all of the respondents had previously viewed a live sporting event online (87.2%).

Diffusion of Innovation and Online Streaming

The second research question explored, based on diffusion of innovation, what factors might motivate college students to abandon traditional television for digital streams. Based on Rogers' (2005) five elements needed for new adoption innovation, respondents found that online streaming of sports fit with three of them: (a) streaming was considered less complex than traditional television; (b) participants said that streaming had advantages over traditional television; and (c) streaming was compatible with existing needs to get sports news.

Nearly half of the participants (48%) said they found streaming less complex to use than traditional television. A t-test found that the difference between male (M = 2.2, SD = .77) and female (M = 2.5, SD = .97) was significant t (303) = 3.307, p = .001. For the other students who did not report streaming to be easier to use, 36.9% believed there was little difference between the two, indicating that they feel equally comfortable navigating both platforms. When asked in an open-ended response why they would consider having only streaming options and not a cable package, participants frequently cited their perceived advantages of the streaming option. One wrote, "I prefer my easily accessible streaming services," while another commented, "I would not have to pay for something that I do not ever watch." A hockey fan wrote, "I basically only watch NHL games and I would instead subscribe to NHL Center Ice Live, which I currently do to watch out of market games and I am very pleased with the service." NHL Center Ice Live allows fans to watch most hockey games online, without the need for a cable television subscription (NHL Center Ice, n.d.). Finally, when presented with a brief description of the ESPN streaming service, the majority of participants (54.3%) responded that they would be interested in subscribing. This demonstrates that fans believe the ESPN streaming option would be compatible with their needs and provide coverage that they can currently get from a cable package.

The data presented a second motivating factor: social influences. Students were presented a scenario in which someone they know gave a positive review about a streaming service. Almost 22% of respondents said they *strongly agreed* that it would impact their decision to try the service, and 55.8% said they *somewhat agreed* that it would be a motivating factor. Conversely, the data shows that college students would likely not be the first adopters of new streaming technology—especially if it requires a subscription. The respondents indicated they would likely wait for a service to gain popularity in their social circles before making the leap. In a follow-up question, the students reinforced their hesitancy to be early adopters to subscription streaming services by indicating that even if a sports network offered all major sports on their app or streaming service, they would wait for their peers to first try out the service before paying for the technology. Most students said they would wait for positive reviews from a *few* people first (46%) before jumping in, while others were more hesitant, waiting for *a lot of* people (29.7%) to join before committing to a service. A t-test determined that the difference between males (M = 3.9, SD = 1.5) and females (M = 4.7, *SD* = .96) was significant $t(303) = 5.808$, $p = .000$.

However, whether an early adopter or a laggard, Lin's (2001) suggestion that online media can displace traditional media with "better content, superior technical benefits, and greater cost efficiency" (p. 36), could result in streaming services coming up short. The participants' identified two primary drawbacks detrimental to user growth: (a) the cost of the service, and (b) a lack of marquee programming from top sports leagues available on the service.

Challenges Facing Live Sport Streaming Services

That lack of top sports leagues on the service was addressed in research question three. It had two components: (a) Will sports streaming services that choose not to offer their marque sports properties face negative perceptions from the surveyed demographic about their brand? and (b) Will students consider spending money on a service that does not contain games from top leagues? The data reveals an uphill battle to win Millennial approval for networks choosing to not livestream their full slate of sports programming.

At face value, a majority of students claimed to be interested in the ESPN streaming service (54.2%). A chi-square test for independence found that die-hard sports fans were statistically more likely to be interested in the service than those who did not identify as diehard sports fans (x^2 (df = 1) = .46, p = .000). However, respondents were clear that any interest they had in the service was dependent upon the network including their marque sports properties such as the NFL and the NBA. Students were asked of all the sports available to stream, which one sport would need to be included in a streaming service for them to subscribe. College football drew the highest number of responses (36.9%). This is perhaps unsurprising considering the sport's popularity, but is also likely influenced because the responses were drawn from students attending large universities where college football is an important thread in the social fabric of life on campus. Other sports that drew interest include the NFL (22.8%), college basketball (11.1%), MLB (8.5%), and NBA (8.1%).

When informed ESPN was considering having subscribers pay for a cable sports package to view games from the NBA and NFL and not make games from those leagues available on the streaming service (a position that was ultimately adopted by the network), student interest in the service dropped precipitously. A majority of students (71.5%) reported themselves less interested in a service without major sports leagues. Indeed, students perceived the ESPN service sans major sports with apathy.

The good news for sports executives is that if major leagues are included and the cost was palatable—such as less than $20 per month—college students would be willing to consider subscribing. Just over 30% (30.3%) said they would pay between $10-$20 dollars a month for a live streaming service that included all sports; an additional 23.5% said they would subscribe if the service was $10 or less. Combined, that results in a majority of college students (53.8%) who are willing to pay for a streaming service–if the price is right and if the most popular leagues are included. Sports networks must consider these ramifications when developing streaming content. There does not appear to be blind loyalty to networks or their streaming offerings. Only two respondents said that they would sign up for the ESPN streaming service *no matter* the price. The important factor is the marquee properties. The survey indicates that students are ambivalent towards a streaming service without the network's most prominent leagues and would be less likely to spend money on a service if it did not include them.

Are Live Sports Streaming Services Viable?

The final question examined if students view live sports streaming as a viable way to watch sports online. The data is clear on this point: yes. As outlined previously, a majority of students already subscribe to a video streaming service (52.3%); they overwhelmingly consume content online, including sports (15.3%), and many find streaming services less complex to use (48.0%) or just as easy as traditional television (36.9%). Most respondents (87.2%) have streamed a live sporting event before and have done so for many years. Nearly 20% of students said they have streamed content for at least two to three years, 21.5% reported having used a streaming service for three to four years, and 22.5% have utilized a streaming service for four years or more.

The data should be encouraging to sports media entities. The brand awareness for their streaming services are registering with college students. Respondents were provided a list of the 11 top sports streaming services and asked with which brands they were most familiar and if they currently subscribed to any of the services on the list. Every streaming service presented to the students was familiar to at least one of the respondents. The highest registered response was the *familiar, but do not subscribe* option. The services that scored the highest recognition among students were the WWE Network (46%), WatchESPN (45.4%), FOX Sports GO (44.7%), NFL Network Game Pass (43.7%), and NBA League Pass (38.5.%). Every service was subscribed to by at least one student in the sample, with the exception of MLS Live Major League Soccer. The three sports networks that saw the highest total number of current student subscribers were WatchESPN (34.3%), FOX Sports Go (18.3%), and NFL Network Game Pass (10.4%).

Ultimately, ESPN's streaming service may end up as the only way the sports network will be able to reach younger consumers. When students were asked if they planned to subscribe to a cable television package after graduation, 41.1% of the sample said yes, 31.3% said no, and 27.4% said they were unsure. Perhaps more troubling for ESPN is the fact that only 49% of those who strongly agreed with the statement "I consider myself a diehard sports fan" (50 of 102) said they planned to subscribe to a cable television package. This move away from cable subscriptions further demonstrates the importance of ESPN's plan to create a streaming service.

Discussion

This chapter examined the viability and demand of an ESPN streaming service. Alternative forms of viewing have negatively impacted television ratings (Kaplan, 2015). However, much of this prior research has been focused on scripted television content (Bury & Li, 2015; Kaplan, 2015; Logan, 2011; Nielsen, 2017, 2018). Programming, especially live sports, historically one of traditional television's most consistent and highest-earning moneymakers, has remained one of the few areas of television content that has survived. Still, the signs of a shift are there. Several sports leagues and networks have created their own online streaming services (e.g.: FOX Sports Go, NBA League Pass, etc.), and ESPN launched its own standalone streaming service ESPN+ in 2018. From the data gathered in this study, it is clear that the interest is there to make this a successful venture for ESPN, assuming that service includes one important form of programming—live sporting events from high profile leagues, otherwise the survey indicates users' manifest an ambivalence towards streaming services that offer anything less than access to their marquee live properties.

Rogers (2003) argued that emerging innovations must meet several key benchmarks in order to thrive in the marketplace, and this study reveals ESPN's streaming service meets three of the five: (a) complexity; (b) relative advantage; and (c) compatibility. The service has great potential to succeed with college-aged students because these three elements have already been demonstrated by other streaming services such as Netflix and Hulu. Participants likely believe a sports streaming service is a viable way to view sports content because they have experienced the benefits of: (a) reduced complexity; (b) relative advantage; and (c) compatibility with scripted television content services such as Netflix and Hulu. For college students who are generally more digitally literate, streaming platforms may seem more native to their media consumption habits. This familiarity could be a driving factor for why most students decide to watch sports programming online instead of on television. Furthermore, their experiences with other streaming platforms could have influenced their responses and expectations in regards to the timing for adoption (e.g., waiting for early adopters to show platform's viability and popularity) as well as willingness to pay a certain price.

One discernable difference between this study and previous research on streaming services is the inclusion of live, unscripted television, which in this context is sports. With the broadcasting of live marquee sports being such an important part of ESPN's content, respondents essentially described it as a deal breaker when it comes to subscribing to an ESPN streaming service. Returning to Rogers (2003), this is where the importance of relative advantage in diffusion is illustrated. If live sports are more easily accessible, or only accessible through a traditional television viewing platform, then respondents indicated that adopting an ESPN streaming service would be less likely. Such responses suggest that factors influencing diffusion of innovation (e.g., complexity, compatibility) might not all carry the same weight. Although respondents signified that they felt a streaming service was less complex than traditional television content and more compatible with their lives, there was still resistance to adopt an ESPN service if there were no live marquee sports, thus suggesting the importance of relative advantage compared to other influences.

Limitation and Future Research

One limitation did emerge within the study: the majority of respondents were female. Research indicates that men make up a higher percentage of sports viewers (Jones, 2015) and that men and women have different television viewing habits (Nathanson, Perse, & Ferguson, 1997). Accounting for such differences could be beneficial for future research. Also, while the survey design met the desired goals for this research, future research on streaming services should be designed with observability of the platforms to account more fully for other areas of Rogers' (2003) diffusion of innovation.

Future researchers may wish to revisit this study following the implementation of ESPN+. The survey for this study was administered after the plans for the network were finalized and before the service began. By completing a similar study after the streaming service has been running for some time, researchers may have an updated vision of the impact of streaming options for millennials.

References

Aiello, C. (2018, February 6). ESPN streaming service to cost $4.99 per month: Disney CEO Iger. *CNBC.com*. Retrieved from https://www.cnbc.com/2018/02/06/disney-ceo-iger-espn-streaming-service-to-cost-4-point-99.html

Beal, G. M., & Bohlen, J. M. (1957). *The diffusion process*. Special report. Agricultural Extension Service, Iowa State College, Ames, Iowa.

Bissell, K. L., & Zhou, P. (2004). Must-see TV or ESPN: Entertainment and sports media exposure and body-image distortion in college women. *Journal of Communication, 54*(1), 5–21. doi:10.1111/j.1460-2466.2004.tb02610.x

Boyle, R. (2014). Television sport in the age of screens and content. *Television & New Media, 15*(8), 746–751. doi:10.1177/1527476414529167

Burroughs, B., & Rugg, A. (2014). Extending the broadcast: Streaming culture and the problems of digital geographies. *Journal of Broadcasting & Electronic Media, 58*(3), 365–380. doi:10.1080/08838151.2014.935854

Bury, R., & Li, J. (2015). Is it live or is it timeshifted, streamed or downloaded? Watching television in the era of multiple screens. *New Media & Society, 17*(4), 592–610. doi:10.1177/1461444813508368

Chan-Olmsted, S., Rim, H., & Zerba, A. (2013). Mobile news adoption among young adults: Examining the roles of perceptions, news consumption, and media usage. *Journalism & Mass Communication Quarterly, 90*(1), 126–147. doi:10.1177/1077699012468742

CSG Systems International. (2017). Going with the flow: How to captivate video streamers. Retrieved from https://www.csgi.com/resources/going-flow-captivate-video-streamers/

Deitsch, R. (2018, March 8). Michael Smith to leave 6pm SportsCenter. Retrieved from https://www.si.com/tech-media/2018/03/08/michael-smith-espn-leaving-sportscenter-sc6

Dickey, J. (2017, December 18). John Skipper build a tremendous legacy but leaves ESPN facing an uncertain future. *Sports Illustrated.* Retrieved from https://www.si.com/tech-media/2017/12/18/john-skipper-espn-president-legacy-journalism

English, P. (2016). Twitter's diffusion in sports journalism: Role models, laggards and followers of the social media innovation. *New Media & Society, 18*(3), 484–501. doi:10.1177/1461444814544886

Farred, G. (2000). Cool as the other side of the pillow: How ESPN's SportsCenter has changed television sports talk. *Journal of Sport & Social Issues, 24*(2), 96–117. doi:10.1177/0193723500242002

Gaines, C. (2016, May 31). ESPN continues to lose subscribers at an alarming rate. *Businessinsider.com.* Retrieved from http://www.businessinsider.com/espn-bleeding-subscribers-2016-5

Garrison, B. (2001). Diffusion of online information technologies in newspaper newsrooms. *Journalism, 2*(2), 221–239. doi:10.1177/146488490100200206

Guthrie, M. (2017, November 14). ESPN signs Scott Van Pelt to new deal (exclusive). *Hollywoodreporter.com.* Retrieved from https://www.hollywoodreporter.com/news/espn-signs-scott-van-pelt-new-deal-1056545?

Hardin, M., & Shain, S. (2005). Strength in numbers? The experiences and attitudes of women in sports media careers. *Journalism & Mass Communication Quarterly, 82*(4), 804–819. doi:10.1177/107769900508200404

Jarvey, N. (2017, November 13). ESPN launches "SportsCenter" on Snapchat. *Hollywoodreporter.com.* Retrieved from https://www.hollywoodreporter.com/news/espn-launches-sportscenter-snapchat-1057282

Jeffres, L., & Atkin, D. (1996). Predicting use of technologies for communication and consumer needs. *Journal of Broadcasting & Electronic Media, 40*(3), 318–30. doi:10.1080/08838159609364356

Jhally, S. (1984). The spectacle of accumulation: Material and cultural factors in evolution of the sports/media complex. *Critical Sociology, 12*(3), 41. doi:10.1177/089692058401200304

Jones, E. (2009, April). *Network television streaming technologies and the shifting television social sphere.* Paper presented at Media in Transition 6: Stone and Papyrus, Storage and Transmission, Cambridge, MA.

Jones, J. M. (2015, June 17). As industry grows, percentage of U.S. sports fans steady. *Gallup.com.* Retrieved from http://news.gallup.com/poll/183689/industry-grows-percentage-sports-fans-steady.aspx

Kafka, P. (2018, February 6). ESPN's new subscription app will cost $5 a month. It will not be a huge hit. *recode.net.* Retrieved from https://www.recode.net/2018/2/6/16982032/espn-plus-subscription-streaming-service-five-dollars

Kaplan, D. (2015, August 23). The streaming revolution is now hurting cable networks as well as broadcast networks. *New York Daily News.* Retrieved from https://www.nydailynews.com/entertainment/tv/streaming-revolution-hurting-cable-networks-article-1.2332493 Klinski, F. (2017, November 8). ESPN, other NFL pre-game shows see big decline in viewers: report. *New York Daily News.* Retrieved from http://www.nydailynews.com/sports/football/espn-nfl-pre-game-shows-big-decline-viewers-report-article-1.3619532

Lafayette, J. (2017, August 8). Disney earnings drop as profits at ESPN plunge. *Broadcasting and Cable.* Retrieved from http://www.broadcastingcable.com/news/currency/disney-earnings-drop-profits-espn-plunge/167777

Lane, C. (2018, February 3). Advertisers say the influential male demographic is waning. *npr.org.* Retrieved from https://www.npr.org/2018/02/03/583037137/advertisers-say-the-influential-male-demographic-is-waning

Lang, B. (2018, February 6). ESPN streaming service coming this Spring for $4.99. *Variety.* Retrieved from http://variety.com/2018/digital/news/espn-streaming-service-price-1202689709/

Lefever, K. (2012). *New media and sport.* The Hague, Netherlands: TMC Asser Press.

Leung, D. (2017, August 3). NFL: More TV viewers than ever last season amid digital offerings. *SportTechie.* Retrieved from https://www.sporttechie.com/nfl-more-tv-viewers-ever-last-season-digital/

Lin, C. A. (1998). Exploring personal computer adoption dynamics. *Journal of Broadcasting & Electronic Media, 42*(1), 95–112. doi:10.1080/08838159809364436

Lin, C. A. (2001). Audience attributes, media supplementation, and likely online service adoption. *Mass Communication & Society, 4*(1), 19–38. doi:10.1207/S15327825MCS0401_03

Lin, C. A., & Jeffres, L. W. (1998). Factors influencing the adoption of multimedia cable technology. *Journalism & Mass Communication Quarterly, 75*(2), 341–352. doi:10.1177/107769909807500209

Logan, K. (2011). Hulu.com or NBC? Streaming video versus traditional TV: A study of an industry in its infancy. *Journal of Advertising Research, 51*(1), 276–287. doi:10.2501/JAR-51-1-276-287

McCoy, T. (2015, January 6). The ESPN streaming deal and how TV is becoming entertainment for old people. *Washington Post.* Retrieved from https://www.washingtonpost.com/news/morning-mix/wp/2015/01/06/the-espn-streaming-deal-and-how-tv-is-becoming-entertainment-for-old-people/?utm_term=.a7b5821c418a

McCreery, S. P., & Krugman, D. M. (2015). TV and the iPad: How the tablet is redefining the way we watch. *Journal of Broadcasting & Electronic Media, 59*(4), 620–639. doi:10.1080/08838151.2015.1093483

Miceli, M. (2015, September 25). New look, same ratings for late night SportsCenter. *USnews.com.* Retrieved from https://www.usnews.com/news/articles/2015/09/25/new-look-same-ratings-for-late-night-sportscenter

Nathanson, A. I., Perse, E. M., & Ferguson, D. A. (1997). Gender differences in television use: An exploration of the instrumental-expressive dichotomy. *Communication Research Reports, 14*(2), 176–188. doi:10.1080/08824099709388659

NHL Center Ice. (n.d.). *nhl.com*. Retrieved from https://www.indemand.com/sport-package/nhl-center-ice/

Nielsen. (2017). Year in sports media report: 2016. *Nielsen.com*. Retrieved from http://www.nielsen.com/us/en/insights/reports/2017/the-year-in-sports-media-report-2016.html

Nielsen. (2018). Year in sports media report 2017. *Nielsen.com*. Retrieved from http://www.nielsen.com/us/en/insights/reports/2018/2017-year-in-sports-media.html

Nocera, J. (2017, August 11). ESPN's surrender to grim new reality. *Bloomberg.com*. Retrieved from https://www.bloomberg.com/view/articles/2017-08-11/espn-s-surrender-to-grim-new-reality

Ourand, J. (2017, June 26). Taking the pulse of ESPN. *Sports Business Journal*. Retrieved from https://www.sportsbusinessdaily.com/Journal/Issues/2017/06/26/Media/ESPN-main.aspx

Pedersen, E. (2018, February 8). How to watch the Winter Olympics on TV & online. *Deadline.com*. Retrieved from http://deadline.com/2018/02/watch-winter-olympics-live-stream-online-twitter-facebook-1202279951/

Pomerantz, D. (2014, January 27). ESPN tries to have it both ways. *Forbes*. Retrieved from https://www.forbes.com/sites/dorothypomerantz/2014/01/27/espn-tries-to-have-it-both-ways/#3e58ac1148de

Putterman, A. (2017, December 28). "Sunday Night Football," "Monday Night Football" both reportedly drew their worst viewership in years. *Awfulannouncing.com*. Retrieved from http://awfulannouncing.com/nba/sunday-night-football-monday-night-football-reportedly-saw-worst-viewership-years.html

Raine, L. (2017, September 13). About 6 in 10 young adults in U.S. primarily use online streaming to watch TV. *Pew.org*. Retrieved from http://www.pewresearch.org/fact-tank/2017/09/13/about-6-in-10-young-adults-in-u-s-primarily-use-online-streaming-to-watch-tv/

Rogers, E. M. (2003). *Diffusion of innovation* (5th ed.). New York, NY: Simon & Schuster.

Singer, J. B. (2004). Strange bedfellows? The diffusion of convergence in four news organizations. *Journalism Studies, 5*(1), 3–18. doi:10.1080/1461670032000174701

Smith, G., & Shaw, L. (2015, December 16). ESPN's dilemma in mobile age where fans see clips all day. *Bloomberg.com*. Retrieved from https://www.bloomberg.com/news/articles/2015-12-16/espn-s-dilemma-in-mobile-age-where-fans-can-watch-clips-all-day

Steel, E., & Marsh, B. (2015, October 3). Millennials and cutting the cord. *The New York Times*. Retrieved from https://www.nytimes.com/interactive/2015/10/03/business/media/changing-media-consumption-millenials-cord-cutters.html?_r=0

Thielman, S. (2013, April 29). After streaming kills cable, where will the content come from? *Adweek.com*. Mutually assured survival. Retrieved from http://www.adweek.com/brand-marketing/after-streaming-kills-cable-where-will-content-come-148961/

Tremayne, M., Weiss, A. S., & Alves, R. C. (2007). From product to service: The diffusion of dynamic content in online newspapers. *Journalism & Mass Communication Quarterly, 84*(4), 825–839. doi:10.1177/107769900708400411

Wagner-McGough, S. (2017, July 12). Packers disclosure shows NFL teams split a record $7.8B in national revenue in 2016. *CBSsports.com*. Retrieved from https://www.cbssports.com/nfl/news/packers-disclosure-shows-nfl-teams-split-a-record-7-8b-in-national-revenue-in-2016/

Whannel, G. (2014). The paradoxical character of live television sport in the twenty-first century. *Television & New Media, 15*(8), 769–776. doi:10.1177/1527476414551180

York, C. (2017, September 18). Women dominate journalism schools, but newsrooms are still a different story. *Poynter.org*. Retrieved from https://www.poynter.org/news/women-dominate-journalism-schools-newsrooms-are-still-different-story

7. ESPN's Double Standard? The Politics of Frame and Tone in Sports

RYAN BROUSSARD AND JONATHAN GRAFFEO

ESPN has come under fire from conservatives who believe the "Worldwide Leader in Sports" has become too politically oriented in its coverage and has taken a liberal slant to boot (Crouch, 2017). "Stick to sports" has become the mantra of those who feel ESPN has strayed too far from its sports focus (Brady, 2017, para. 1). Clavio and Vooris (2017) found that political affiliation impacts a person's belief that ESPN is politically biased, with right-leaning respondents perceiving ESPN as more biased and hostile than left-leaning respondents.

But as Strenk (1979) noted, "sports are politics," and have been for centuries (p. 129). When today's athletes voice controversial political views, news media often draw parallels to precursors, such as Muhammad Ali protesting the Vietnam War or Jackie Robinson breaking the color barrier in Major League Baseball. Still, the question remains whether ESPN and the broader media favor one political viewpoint over another when sports and politics inevitably collide. Events at ESPN provide for an interesting case comparison in this respect.

On April 18, 2016, former Major League Baseball pitcher Curt Schilling, then a color commentator on the network's baseball broadcasts, shared on his personal Facebook page an image seen as derogatory toward transgender individuals. The meme Schilling shared showed actor Danny DeVito dressed in sheer women's clothing, ripped nylons and a blonde wig that said. The meme said "LET HIM IN! To the restroom with your daughter or else you're a narrow minded, judgmental, unloving racist bigot who deserves to die." The word "die" appeared in red, and all letters were capitalized. Schilling included a personal observation: "A man is a man no matter what they call themselves. I don't care what they are, who they sleep with, men's room was designed for the penis, women's not so much. Now you need laws telling us differently? Pathetic" (Grautski, 2016). The Facebook post came amid political controversy over North Carolina's enactment of the so-called "bathroom bill," which barred transgender individuals from using public restrooms according to their gender identity (Kopan & Scott, 2016). Schilling, an avowed conservative, had previously made other politically-charged comments while working for ESPN, but the network fired him two days after he shared this Facebook post. Schilling subsequently blasted ESPN in interviews with other media outlets, claiming he was fired because his conservative views were unwelcomed at the network (Heck, 2016).

Then on September 11, 2017, *SportsCenter* anchor Jemele Hill tweeted, "Donald Trump is a white supremacist who has largely surrounded himself w/ other white supremacists" (Hill, 2017). Hill's remarks came in the wake of a protest in Charlottesville, Virginia, over the removal of a statue of Confederate General Robert E. Lee, during which one person was killed as white supremacists clashed with counter-protesters. Many in the media accused Trump of providing cover for white supremacists by virtue of remarks he made in the immediate aftermath of the deadly protest (Thrush & Haberman, 2017). Like Schilling, Hill had made inflammatory remarks prior to this incident. Unlike Schilling, however, Hill received a reprimand from ESPN executives but retained her job at the network, even in the face of pressure from the White House to fire her (Nakamura, 2017).

In light of its seemingly inconsistent handling of these incidents, ESPN itself came under scrutiny from the broader media as conservatives leveled charges of hypocrisy and liberal bias against the network and chastised it for not sticking to sports (Hookstead, 2016). Some defended ESPN's actions, saying Schilling was repeatedly warned to refrain from making political statements, but that did not stop the barrage from conservatives or Schilling himself (Gaines, 2017; Pepin, 2016). As pressure mounted, ESPN President John Skipper addressed the controversy in a memo to the network's employees. Skipper stated, "ESPN is not a political organization" and stressed that while company executives would not dictate which political views employees could express, the company would foster an environment of tolerance and inclusion (Stelter, 2017, para. 12–13).

This chapter examines whether the print media's framing of the Schilling and Hill incidents mirrored the difference in ESPN's treatment of each individual. Since ESPN fired Schilling for his remarks, the chapter explores whether the broader print media's coverage of the incident further marginalized Schilling and his political views. By contrast, ESPN reprimanded but retained Hill after her remarks. Accordingly, the chapter also explores whether the framing of print media coverage tended to excuse or validate Hill and her political views. Finally, the chapter examines how print media portrayed the political leanings of ESPN and whether these portrayals underscore or contradict the view of conservatives, who claim ESPN has taken a liberal slant in its policies and coverage.

Literature Review

Framing

Framing has theoretical roots in sociology (Gitlin, 1980; Goffman, 1974), economics (Kahneman & Tversky, 1979) and psychology (Kahneman & Tversky, 2013; Tversky & Kahneman, 1985). Entman (1993) wrote framing is "select[ing] some aspects of a perceived reality and mak[ing] them more salient in a communicating text, in such a way as to promote a particular problem definition, causal interpretation, moral evaluation, and/or treatment recommendation" (p. 52). Goffman (1974) introduced frame analysis and examined how situations are defined. Frames, Goffman noted, are schemata that allow people to "locate, perceive, identify, and label" events in their life (p. 21). The framing approach is beneficial for journalism studies because it offers a window into what makes an item or event newsworthy and the value judgments that go into reporting and writing stories with certain frames (Brüggemann, 2014).

This chapter focuses on episodic and thematic frames put forth by Iyengar (1990, 1991, 1996). Episodic frames are those with an emphasis on the particular instance, a person's point of view, or the individual level of a larger problem. Thematic frames are those in which the story provides information on general trends, the societal level in a crisis, and the broader context for the event or issue at hand. Iyengar (1991) showed thematic framing caused readers to feel that responsibility rested at the societal level, while episodic framing caused them to feel that it rested at the individual level. Similarly, Coleman and Thorson (2002) found that participants in an experiment were more likely to associate responsibility for crime and violence with society rather than individuals involved when broader context about public health problems was included in news stories. When stories were framed thematically in this way, participants tended to see violence and crime as a consequence of larger societal forces, in this case neglect of public health challenges. As these two studies demonstrated, both responsibility for problems and a relatively negative valence are associated with individuals at the center of stories framed episodically. Conversely, responsibility for problems is associated with society, and a relatively positive valence is associated with the individuals involved, when stories are framed thematically.

The concepts of episodic and thematic framing have been applied to various topics: poverty (Iyengar, 1990), child abuse (Hove, Paek, Isaacson, & Cole, 2013), elderly abuse (Mastin, Choi, Barboza, & Post, 2007), recalled Chinese drywall (Hong, 2013) and same-sex marriage in the U.S. (Li & Liu, 2010). In their study about the coverage of elderly abuse, Mastin et al. (2007) noted how the nature of the current news cycle encouraged reporters and editors to cover societal issues episodically, a practice that favored newsroom protocols over providing readers a full view of how the issue at hand affects society. But rarely have episodic and thematic frames been applied to sports. One such study by Lee, Kim and Love (2014) looked at how journalists covered the Gay Games. They found an overwhelming use of thematic frames in stories, with most of the stories featuring topics such as LGBT social group identity and optimistic images throughout the event coverage.

The aforementioned literature on framing, and the concepts of episodic and thematic framing, especially the findings by Coleman and Thorson (2002) about how the responsibility for problems and a negative valence are associated with individuals in stories framed episodically, while responsibility for problems is associated with society, and a positive valence is associated with the individuals when stories are framed thematically are taken into account here. Given that ESPN fired Schilling for his social media post, but took no action against Hill at that time, would journalists frame Schilling and Hill the same in the way, or would there be any difference? We offer the following hypotheses:

> **H1:** Stories in which Jemele Hill is the main subject are more likely to be framed episodically than stories in which Curt Schilling is the main subject.

> **H2:** Stories in which Curt Schilling is the main subject are more likely to be framed thematically than stories in which Jemele Hill is the main subject.

> **H3:** Stories are more likely to be framed thematically than episodically if political ideology is mentioned.

Tone of News Coverage

Tone of news coverage has been used as part of attributes in second-level agenda setting research (Kim & McCombs, 2007). Issue attributes have two aspects: Information about the characteristics or traits about the object or issue in question, and an affective part regarding the positive, negative, or neutral tone of the object or issue when it appears on the news agenda.

Researchers have also noted how the tone of news coverage can be influenced by news routines (Eshbaugh-Soha, 2014; Fogarty, 2005). Tuchman (1972, 1973) defined the concept of news routines as professional norms, a way journalists bring normality into their day. Routines, like news beats and deadlines are followed by journalists in the daily production of news. Shoemaker and Reese (1996) incorporated routines into their Hierarchy of Influences, a model that describes the daily constraints and pressures on reporters and news organizations.

The concept of tone in news coverage has been studied in other settings, particularly economic (Fogarty, 2005; Hester & Gibson, 2003; Soroka, 2006) and political news (De Vreese, Banducci, Semetko, & Boomgaarden, 2006; Eshbaugh-Soha, 2014; Hopmann, Vliegenthart, De Vreese, & Albæk, 2010). But the literature seems lacking on tone research pertaining to sports with the exception of gender studies and coverage of women's sports (Eastman & Billings, 2000; Messner, Duncan, & Cooky, 2003).

In political literature, tone of news coverage, along with visibility of coverage has been shown to influence party choice in European elections (Hopmann et al., 2010). Tone and visibility were also shown to lead to a person's reconsideration of views if they disagreed with the views featured in the news, and to a possible change in opinion from one side of an issue to another. A study of news on European Union elections by De Vreese et al. (2006) in which the news was coded for valence (positive/negative/neutral) showed the tone of most of the news studied was neutral, but when the news was more evaluative—containing opinions from outside parties—the news was generally negative.

Given the prior coverage on the tone of news coverage in stories that are political in nature, especially De Vreese et al. (2006), we pose the following research questions:

RQ1: Is there a difference in an article's tone (critical, supportive or neutral) depending on the main subject?

RQ2: Is there a difference in an article's tone (critical, supportive or neutral) toward the main subject when political ideology is mentioned?

Intersection of Sports and Politics

The long-held assumption among many in the U.S. is that sports and politics are separate spheres of life and should never cross, but as Strenk (1979) noted, "sports are politics" (p. 129), and have been for centuries, dating back to when the ancient Greeks and Romans discussed sports in the context of politics (Gift & Miner, 2017). The Olympic Games every two years are a political flashpoint, with successful national teams touted by their governments as proof that their nation is superior (Strenk, 1979). And, with the amount of money involved, sports is political (Gift & Miner, 2017). Sports are the closest aspect of society to a civic religion; they reflect political values, sensibilities and priorities (Gift & Miner) and have been called a "microcosm of society" (Marston, 2017, p. 68). Politicians even use sports in an effort to attract voters, as Republican presidential candidate Carly Fiorina did during the 2016 Iowa caucuses when she publicly supported the University of Iowa's football team against Stanford, her alma mater, in the upcoming Rose Bowl (Gift & Miner, 2017).

But some argue sports can be non-political. Thiel, Villanova, Toms, Friis Thing, and Dolan (2016) in an editorial illustrated their argument that sports can be a non-political entity with the example of NFL players protesting racial injustice during the national anthem before games. Acknowledging the negative reactions provoked by these protests, Thiel et al. maintain that "deny[ing] them their right to [protest] is by no means a justified strategy to secure the neutrality and political autonomy of sport" (p. 254). However, athletes starting social movements is not a new phenomenon. The so-called Ali Summit in 1967, which occurred when prominent athletes like Jim Brown and Kareem Abdul-Jabbar (then known as Lew Alcindor) met with Muhammad Ali to discuss his stance as a conscientious objector to the Vietnam War, is a crucial early moment for athlete activism in the United States, as was John Carlos and Tommie Smith raising their gloved fists while on the medal podium of the 1968 Mexico City Summer Olympics (Vasilogambros, 2016).

Rowe (2007) has contended that sports departments are the "toy department of the news media" (p. 385) and thus not subjected to the same standards and scrutiny as other journalists. Rowe added that this is because sports departments bring in readers, particularly men. Because of that importance, sports departments are governed by "ingrained occupational assumptions about what 'works' for this readership, drawing it away from the problems, issues and topics that permeate the social world to which sport is intimately connected" and that "most sports journalism eschews problematic social issues ..." (p. 400).

The clamor over ESPN's perceived political leanings is still new. Clavio and Vooris (2017) found, through a survey of 470 U.S. residents, political affiliation impacts a person's belief that ESPN is politically biased, with right-leaning respondents perceiving ESPN as more biased and hostile than left-leaning respondents. "This is to be expected since ESPN's purposeful entry into covering issues with a political or social basis removes the expectation that audiences are perceiving ESPN's content as neutral" (Clavio & Vooris, 2017, p. 11). Media and business reporters are quick to note that ESPN's drop in viewership is mostly due to cord-cutting, but the narrative that the company's perceived political leanings are the culprit for ESPN's money woes is still pushed (see Burke, 2018; Swan, 2017)

Based on prior research by Clavio and Vooris (2017), the narrative of ESPN's perceived political leanings hurting its bottom line, and how people on both ideological sides view ESPN's coverage of politics, we offer the following research question:

RQ3:   Are ESPN's perceived political leanings mentioned in stories in which the network was the main subject?

Method

Sample

To address the hypotheses and research questions proposed, the authors used a purposive sample of newspaper articles pulled from the online search engine ProQuest over a four-week period beginning from the respective posts by Schilling and Hill. The ProQuest database included members of the prestige press, including *The New York Times* and *The Washington Post*; smaller newspapers, such as *The Journal-Advocate* in Sterling, Colorado; and student newspapers from colleges and universities across the country. That gives this study a well-balanced approach with opinions and viewpoints from across the country, not just from the long-standing titans of the industry. The searches returned 97 results for the Schilling sample and 212 for the Hill sample. Using a random number generator, 97 stories were pulled from the Hill sample to compare to the 97 stories in the Schilling sample.

A four-week sampling window was used following Schilling and Hill's respective controversial social media posts: Schilling's sharing of a meme viewed as disparaging to transgender people on April 19, 2016, at the height of the polarizing N.C. bathroom bill debate, to May 17, 2016, and Hill's tweet calling President Donald Trump a "white supremacist" on Sept. 11, 2017, during a back-and-forth with several people that originated from a story about Kid Rock running for the U.S. Senate, to Oct. 9, 2017. This four-week sample was utilized because in today's 24/7 news cycle, stories tend to fall from the public's consciousness quickly, limiting the time frame from which to draw samples (Saltzis, 2012). Four weeks also allowed the authors to gather enough articles for Schilling to be able to make statistical inferences, since his story did not have the prominence that Hill's tweet did. To find as comprehensive of a sample as possible on ProQuest during those four-week periods, multiple keyword searches were used. For Hill, combinations of the terms "Jemele Hill," "Donald Trump," "white supremacist," and "ESPN" were used. For Schilling, a combination of "Curt Schilling," "ESPN firing," "Facebook," and "NC bathroom bill." All duplicate articles were culled from newspapers, wire feeds, blogs, podcasts, and websites from within the search parameters.

Coding

Each article (n = 194, 97 each) was coded throughout, but emphasized the wording and framing at the top of the article, because research has shown that most people read only the first few paragraphs or skim the top of the story (Purcell, Buchanan, & Friedrich, 2013; Wastler, 2013). The authors served as coders, with one coding the entirety of articles from the Schilling timeline and the other coding the entirety of articles from the Hill timeline. The final coding sheet featured questions about the five main variables in the study: (a) type of article; (b) main subject of the article; (c) whether perceived political affiliation of the main subject is mentioned; (d) whether article is critical or supportive of the main subject; and (e) type of frame (episodic/thematic) used in the article. The first four variables are categorical, while the final is continuous. It is measured using a 5-point Likert-type scale going from episodic framing only to thematic framing only.

The original social media posts by Hill and Schilling were excluded in the analysis as the posts could skew the data analysis both in terms of how the article was framed and the tone of the article. This allowed the researcher to analyze how the media covered the incident and its backlash. Including those comments in every article could conceivably bias the coding because of the episodic effects each comment would present and how the tone of the article could be changed based on those comments being included.

Five single indicator variables were employed in this study. To measure the first categorical variable, the type of story, we classified each story in one of three categories: (a) hard news; (b) editorials, op-eds, commentary and/or letters to the editor; and (c) sports columns. To measure the second categorical variable, the main subject of each story, we identified three main categories of subjects—Curt Schilling, Jemele Hill or ESPN executives—and coded each story based on: (a) person or persons the journalist featured as the main subject of the article; (b) whether that be through the repeated use of that person or persons in the lead and throughout the first few graphs; or (c) through a delayed lead in which the writer draws the reader in with bits of information before identifying the main subject. The third categorical variable, whether the perceived political affiliation of the main subject was mentioned, was coded for presence or absence of outright stating the perceived political affiliation of the subject or language that could be reasonably inferred or interpreted to imply the political affiliation of the main subject of the article. For example, if a reporter writes "Supporters of Donald Trump are railing against Jemele Hill" or "Conservative media outlets are once again aiming their arrows at ESPN, accusing the sports media giant of bias." The fourth categorical variable, tone of the story, was coded to be critical, supportive, or neutral toward the main subject by counting sources and seeing whether there were more sources that were critical than supportive or vice versa. As with the other variables, an emphasis on source placement at the top of the story and opposing source viewpoints, a lack of opposing sourced views, or completely one-sided sourcing was coded. Sources were how tone was measured. The fifth, and only continuous, variable, coded whether the stories were framed episodically or thematically by using a 5-point Likert scale developed by Zhang, Jin, and Tang (2015): (1) entirely episodic; (2) episodic and thematic with an emphasis on episodic; (3) an equal combination of episodic and thematic; (4) thematic and episodic with an emphasis on thematic; or (5) entirely thematic.

Twenty stories from each batch of 97 were pulled to measure intercoder reliability. To calculate intercoder reliability, the researchers used the first 10 and last 10 stories from each sample. Using Krippendorff's Alpha, reliability ranged from .70 to .82. The original reliability figures were lower, forcing a collapsing of some of the measures. Lombard, Snyder-Duch, and Bracken (2002) noted intercoder levels of .70 and .80 are acceptable for exploratory studies, of which this study is due to the lack of prior research on the subject.

Results

As stated above, an equal number of stories were used for each sample (n = 97) based on search terms related to Hill and Schilling. Results from coding for variable two, the main subject of the story, showed unbalanced numbers. Schilling was the main subject in 82 articles, Hill and ESPN executives tied with 55 and "others" were the main subject in two articles (see

Table 7.1). H1 states stories in which Jemele Hill (n = 55) is the main subject are more likely to be framed episodically than stories in which Curt Schilling (n = 82) is the main subject. A one-sample t-test, $t(54) = 16.27$, $p < .001$, supporting H1.

H2 states stories in which Curt Schilling is the main subject are more likely to be framed thematically than stories in which Jemele Hill is the main subject. A one-sample t-test, $t(81) = 27.88$, $p < .001$, supporting H2.

H3 states stories are more likely to be framed thematically (n = 36) than episodically (n = 39), with three stories sharing equal emphasis, if political ideology is mentioned. When the perceived political ideology of the main subject is mentioned (n = 78), the stories were framed more thematically (M = 2.95, SD = 1.08), compared to stories framed more episodically when political ideology is not mentioned (M = 2.42, SD = 1.08). An independent samples t-test, $t(192) = -3.33$, $p < .001$ confirming H3.

Table 7.1: Frequencies and Chi-Squares of categorical variables.

		MAIN SUBJECT[a]			
		Schilling	Hill	ESPN	Total
KIND OF ARTICLE	Fact-Based Article	39 40.6%	22 22.9%	35 36.5%	96 100%
	Opinion	43 44.8%	33 34.4%	20 20.8%	96 100%
POLITICS OF MAIN SUBJECT	Not Mentioned	41 36.0%	39 34.2%	34 29.8%	114 100%
	Mentioned	41 52.6%	16 20.5%	21 26.9%	78 100%
TONE OF ARTICLE[b]	Critical	24 42.9%	10 17.8%	22 39.3%	56 100%
	Neither	35 46.7%	14 18.7%	26 34.6%	75 100%
	Supportive	23 37.7%	31 50.8%	7 11.5%	61 100%
	Total	82 42.7%	55 28.65%	55 28.65%	192 100%

[a]Two articles had main subjects classified as "other" and were not included in these calculations
[b]p < 0.001.
Source: Authors.

RQ1 asks whether there was a difference in the articles' tone (positive, negative, or neutral) depending on the main subject. A chi-square analysis found most of the articles about Curt Schilling (n = 35, 43%) and ESPN (n = 26, 47%) to be neutral in tone and the articles about Jemele Hill to be supportive (n = 31, 56%). A chi-square analysis found this difference to be statistically significant, $\chi^2(6) = 26.21, p < .001$.

RQ2 asks whether there was a difference in tone (critical or supportive) toward the main subject when political ideology was mentioned. Of the 194 articles, political affiliation was not mentioned in the majority (n = 116, 60%), and most of the articles were neutral in tone (n = 76, 39%), as opposed to critical (n = 56, 29%), or supportive (n = 62, 32%). A chi-square analysis, $\chi^2(2) = 2.55, p = .28$, however, found no statistical significance in these differences.

RQ3 asks whether ESPN's perceived political leanings were mentioned in stories when the network was the main subject. Of the 55 stories that ESPN was the main subject, its perceived political leanings were mentioned 38% (n = 21) of the time. A chi-square analysis, $\chi^2(3) = 7.54, p = .57$, found no statistical significance. Figure 7.1 illustrates the relationships between the variables tested in this study.

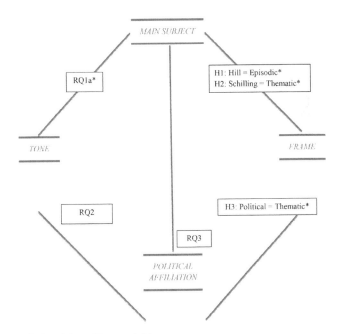

Figure 7.1: Relationships of key variables.

Discussion

In applying framing theory (Gitlin, 1980; Goffman, 1974), this study contributes to the scholarly literature on sports and politics by providing a better understanding of how the media covers such issues. In the process, this chapter makes further contribution by suggesting that established understandings about the implications of episodic and thematic framing may not necessarily hold when politics enters the sports arena.

This study set out to determine whether print media portrayals of Curt Schilling and Jemele Hill mirrored the difference in their treatment by ESPN. Results indicate this was the case in certain respects. First, there was a statistically significant difference in the tone of articles depending on the main subject. In particular, stories about Hill were more likely to be supportive rather than critical when compared to stories about Schilling. More than half of the stories in which Hill was the main subject (56%) carried a supportive tone towards her, whereas less than a third of the stories about Schilling (28%) were supportive toward him. This divergence indicates that the tone of journalists' stories generally reflected the difference in ESPN executives' decisions pertaining to each person: Schilling was marginalized and Hill was excused.

It is noteworthy that of the 55 articles in which ESPN executives were the main subject of the story, only seven (13%) carried a supportive tone toward the network. Moreover, although the relationship between the main subject of the story and the mention of their political affiliations was not statistically significant, it is worth noting ESPN's perceived political leanings were mentioned in 38% of the articles in which ESPN was the main subject. More revealing, in all instances, ESPN was characterized as liberal-leaning. This finding seemingly undermined ESPN President John Skipper's claim that the network is not a political organization and indicates one reason why he may have found it necessary to issue the statement in the first place (Stelter, 2017).

In addition, there was a statistically significant difference in the way articles about Schilling and Hill were framed, with stories about Schilling framed thematically and stories about Hill more likely to be framed episodically. Our results found a statistically significant relationship between the mention of the main subject's political affiliations and the type of frame used in the story. Specifically, when the main subject's political affiliations were mentioned, stories were more likely to be framed thematically than episodically. This finding contributes to the literature on sports and politics by providing empirical evidence of how journalists frame stories when the two intersect. When politics enter the sports realm, journalists tend to add background information about the political context, providing a more thematic frame.

The implications of another finding are less clear, yet worthy of further exploration for theoretical reasons. Previous research indicated thematically framed stories tended to be more favorable to the main subject relative to episodically framed stories (Iyengar, 1990). This is because when additional context is provided about the larger circumstances surrounding the immediate conflict in which the main subject is involved, less responsibility or blame appears to rest solely on that individual (Coleman & Thorson, 2002; Iyengar, 1990). Our findings indicate this may not necessarily be the case when it comes to sports and politics. On one hand, we did not find a statistically significant relationship between the tone of the article and the frame used. On the other hand, statistically significant results did indicate articles about Schilling were more likely to be framed *thematically* and carry a *critical* tone, relative to stories about Hill. In light of the finding, stories are also more likely to be framed thematically when the main subject's political affiliations are mentioned, further research may find that when it comes to sports and politics, the main subject's situation may more likely be framed *thematically* and portray the main subject in a *less favorable* light when their personal political views are mentioned. Such findings would run contrary to established understandings of episodic and thematic framing, which hold that thematic framing casts the main subject of a story in more positive light relative to an episodic frame.

Limitations

One limitation of this study relates to the robustness and reliability of our measures. As it relates to robustness, each of our variables depended on a single-item measure. Tone, for example, was assessed by counting the number of sources in the story (either on background or on-the-record) and characterizing each as either critical or supportive of the main subject. The researchers then determined the tone of the entire story was either supportive or critical of the main subject based on which category had the greater total (unless they were even). As it relates to reliability, the range of Krippendorff's alpha for our variables ranged from 0.70 to 0.82. While these levels are acceptable, the researchers aimed to achieve reliability across all variables at 0.80 and above (De Swert, 2012; Lombard et al., 2002).

A second limitation relates to the time frame and composition of the sample. The sampling time frame ran four weeks from the day that Schilling and Hill posted their respective comments on social media. Four weeks was chosen because this was the length of time, based on ProQuest search results, needed to reach the threshold number of stories about Schilling necessary to draw valid statistical inferences. To be consistent, we applied this same time frame to Hill. Once we had collected both samples and began coding, news broke that ESPN suspended Hill for additional comments she made on a separate matter. It is conceivable the sample for Hill's tweet also included some stories regarding her tweet about Dallas Cowboys Owner Jerry Jones, which resulted in her suspension. Results could have been different had stories about Hill's suspension been included in the sample. At the same time, the fact remains that Schilling was fired and Hill was not. It is therefore equally conceivable that the results may not have changed.

Future Research

In light of increasing levels of political polarization in the U.S., scholarly literature on crisis communication provides an intriguing avenue for future research on ESPN's handling of situations involving hot-button political issues. In particular, Situational Crisis Communication Theory (SCCT) (Coombs, 2007) provides the framework to gauge audience reactions to corporations' handling of crisis situations. SCCT centers on the amount of crisis responsibility a corporation bears based on the type of situation involved (e.g., whether the corporation is a *victim* of the crisis, the crisis is the result of an *accident* made by the corporation, or the crisis is the result on an *intentional* act by the corporation) (Coombs, 2007). The corporation's level of crisis responsibility combines with its crisis history and the strength of its reputation among key stakeholder groups to determine the reputation threat the organization faces in a given situation and dictates the way the corporation should respond (Coombs, 2007).

SCCT shares an important theoretical link with the episodic and thematic frames used in this study. As discussed above, episodic and thematic frames (Iyengar, 1990, 1991, 1996) narrow or broaden the focus of a news story and shape the audience's view of who or what is responsible for a negative situation. Similarly, SCCT is grounded in Attribution Theory, which states people search for the cause(s) of negative events and attribute blame for them (Weiner, 1985). Based on this, it would be interesting, for example, to explore how audience members' own political partisanship affects the way they attribute responsibility for the Hill incident in light of ESPN's handling of the Schilling incident. Crisis communication literature, including Image Repair Theory has examined cases in which corporations attracted the negative attention of politicians (Blaney, Benoit,

& Brazeal, 2002; Cooley & Cooley, 2011; Harlow, Brantley, & Harlow, 2011; Hearit, 2018), and while some research has been conducted on crisis communication in the sports realm (i.e., Brown, Brown, & Billings, 2015; Glantz, 2010; Sanderson, 2008). Such a study could be a valuable contribution to the literature, as both sports and politics remain inextricably linked (Strenk, 1979).

References

Blaney, J. R., Benoit, W. L., & Brazeal, L. M. (2002). Blowout! Firestone's image restoration campaign. *Public Relations Review*, *28*(4), 379–392. doi.org/10/1016/S0363-8111 (02)00163=7

Brady, J. (2017, April 13). Like it or not, ESPN isn't sticking to sports. *ESPN*. Retrieved from http://www.espn.com/blog/ombudsman/post/_/id/831/not-sticking-to-sports-the-right-move-for-espn

Brown, N. A., Brown, K. A., & Billings, A. C. (2015). "May no act of ours bring shame" Fan-enacted crisis communication surrounding the Penn State sex abuse scandal. *Communication & Sport*, *3*(3), 288–311. doi.org/10/1177216779517739835

Brüggemann, M. (2014). Between frame setting and frame sending: How journalists contribute to news frames. *Communication Theory, 24*(1), 61–82.

Burke, T. (2018, May 24). There is no evidence whatsoever that ESPN is losing subscribers due to its "politics." *Deadspin*. Retrieved from https://deadspin.com/there-is-no-evidence-whatsoever-that-espn-is-losing-sub-1826305140

Clavio, G., & Vooris, R. (2017). ESPN and the Hostile Media Effect. *Communication & Sport, 6*(6), 728–744. Advance online publication. doi.org/10.1177/21674795177 39835

Coleman, R., & Thorson, E. (2002). The effects of news stories that put crime and violence into context: Testing the public health model of reporting. *Journal of Health Communication, 7*(5), 401–425. doi.org/10.1080/10810730290001783

Cooley, S. C., & Cooley, A. B. (2011). An examination of the situational crisis communication theory through the General Motors bankruptcy. *Journal of Media and Communication Studies, 3*(6), 203–211.

Coombs, W. T. (2007). Protecting organization reputations during a crisis: The development and application of situational crisis communication theory. *Corporate Reputation Review, 10*(3), 163–176. doi.org/10.1057/palgrave.crr.1550049

Crouch, I. (2017, September 12). ESPN can't win in Trump's rowdy America. *The New Yorker*. Retrieved from https://www.newyorker.com/culture/cultural-comment/espn-cant-win-in-trumps-rowdy-america

De Swert, K. (2012). Calculating inter-coder reliability in media content analysis using Krippendorff's Alpha. *Center for Politics and Communication*, 1–15.

De Vreese, C. H., Banducci, S. A., Semetko, H. A., & Boomgaarden, H. G. (2006). The news coverage of the 2004 European Parliamentary election campaign in 25 countries. *European Union Politics, 7*(4), 477–504. doi.org/10.1177/1465116506069440

Eastman, S. T., & Billings, A. C. (2000). Sportscasting and sports reporting: The power of gender bias. *Journal of Sport and Social Issues, 24*(2), 192–213. doi.org/10.1177/0193723500242006

Entman, R. M. (1993). Framing: Toward clarification of a fractured paradigm. *Journal of Communication, 43*(4), 51–58. doi.org/10.1111/j.1460-2466.1993.tb01304.x

Eshbaugh-Soha, M. (2014). The tone of Spanish-language presidential news coverage. *Social Science Quarterly, 95*(5), 1278–1294. doi.org/10.1111/ssqu.12101

Fogarty, B. J. (2005). Determining economic news coverage. *International Journal of Public Opinion Research, 17*(2), 149–172. doi.org/10.1093/ijpor/edh051

Gaines, C. (2017, September 13). The simple explanation for why ESPN did not fire Jemele Hill, but did fire Curt Schilling. *Business Insider.* Retrieved from http://www.businessinsider.com/espn-jemele-hill-curt-schilling-perceived-liberal-bias-2017-9

Gift, T., & Miner, A. (2017). "DROPPING THE BALL": The understudied nexus of sports and politics. *World Affairs, 180*(1), 127–161. doi.org/10.1177/0043820017715569

Gitlin, T. (1980). *The whole world is watching: Mass media in the making & unmaking of the New Left.* Berkeley, CA: University of California Press.

Glantz, M. (2010). The Floyd Landis doping scandal: Implications for image repair discourse. *Public Relations Review, 36*(2), 157–163. doi.org/10.1016/j.pubrev.2009.09.002

Goffman, E. (1974). *Frame analysis: An essay on the organization of experience.* Boston, MA: Harvard University Press.

Grautski, A. (2016, April 22). Curt Schilling goes on social media bender days after being fired by ESPN. *New York Daily News.* Retrieved from http://www.nydailynews.com/sports/baseball/curt-schilling-social-media-bender-espn-firing-article-1.2611099#

Harlow, W. F., Brantley, B. C., & Harlow, R. M. (2011). BP initial image repair strategies after the Deepwater Horizon spill. *Public Relations Review, 37*(1), 80–83. doi.org/10.1016/j.pubrev.2010.11.005

Hearit, L. B. (2018). JP Morgan Chase, Bank of America, Wells Fargo, and the Financial Crisis of 2008. *International Journal of Business Communication, 55*(2), 237–260. doi.org/10.1177/2329488417753952

Heck, J. (2016, May 9). Curt Schilling blasts "outwardly bigoted and intolerant" ESPN after firing. *Sporting News.* Retrieved from http://www.sportingnews.com/mlb/news/curt-schilling-facebook-meme-espn-fired-dan-patrick-show/1m9eqx6cfl-2ga19lv4jnt49bzc

Hester, J. B., & Gibson, R. (2003). The economy and second-level agenda setting: A time-series analysis of economic news and public opinion about the economy. *Journalism & Mass Communication Quarterly, 80*(1), 73–90. doi.org/10.1177/107769900308000106

Hill, J. [JemeleHill]. (2017, September 11). Donald Trump is a white supremacist who has largely surrounded himself w/other white supremacists. [*Tweet*]. Retrieved from https://twitter.com/jemelehill/status/907391978194849793

Hong, S. C. (2013). Scare sells? A framing analysis of news coverage of recalled Chinese products. *Asian Journal of Communication, 23*(1), 86–106. doi.org/10.1080/0129 2986.2012.717090

Hookstead, D. (2016, April 20). ESPN fires Curt Schilling for conservative views. *Daily Caller.* Retrieved from http://dailycaller.com/2016/04/20/espn-fires-curt-schilling-for-conservative-views/

Hopmann, D. N., Vliegenthart, R., De Vreese, C., & Albæk, E. (2010). Effects of election news coverage: How visibility and tone influence party choice. *Political Communication, 27*(4), 389–405. doi.org/10.1080/10584609.2010.516798

Hove, T., Paek, H. J., Isaacson, T., & Cole, R. T. (2013). Newspaper portrayals of child abuse: Frequency of coverage and frames of the issue. *Mass Communication and Society, 16*(1), 89–108. doi.org/10.1080/15205436.2011.632105

Iyengar, S. (1990). Framing responsibility for political issues: The case of poverty. *Political Behavior, 12*(1), 19–40. doi.org/10.1007/BF00992330

Iyengar, S. (1991). *Is anyone responsible? How television frames political issues.* Chicago, IL: University of Chicago Press.

Iyengar, S. (1996). Framing responsibility for political issues. *The Annals of the American Academy of Political and Social Science, 546*(1), 59–70.

Kahneman, D., & Tversky, A. (1979). Prospect theory: An analysis of decision under risk. In L. C. McLean & W. T. Ziemba (Eds.), *Handbook of the fundamentals of financial decision making, Part 2* (pp. 263–291). Hackensack, NJ: Word Scientific Press.

Kahneman, D., & Tversky, A. (2013). Choices, values, and frames. *American Psychologist, 39*(4), 341–350.

Kim, K., & McCombs, M. (2007). News story descriptions and the public's opinions of political candidates. *Journalism & Mass Communication Quarterly, 84*(2), 299–314. doi.org/10.1177/107769900708400207

Kopan, T., & Scott, E. (2016, March 23). North Carolina governor signs controversial transgender bill. *CNN.* Retrieved from https://www.cnn.com/2016/03/23/politics/north-carolina-gender-bathrooms-bill/index.html

Lee, S., Kim, S., & Love, A. (2014). Coverage of the Gay Games from 1980–2012 in U.S. newspapers: An analysis of newspaper article framing. *Journal of Sport Management, 28*(2), 176–188. doi.org/10.1123/jsm.2012-0243

Li, X., & Liu, X. (2010). Framing and coverage of same-sex marriage in U.S. newspapers. *The Howard Journal of Communications, 21*(1), 72–91. doi.org/10.1080/1064 6170903501161

Lombard, M., Snyder-Duch, J., & Bracken, C. C. (2002). Content analysis in mass communication: Assessment and reporting of intercoder reliability. *Human Communication Research, 28*(4), 587–604.

Marston, S. (2017). The Revival of Athlete Activism(s): Divergent black politics in the 2016 presidential election engagements of LeBron James and Colin Kaepernick. *Fair Play, Revista de Filo Sofia, Utica y Derecho del Deportee, 10*, 45–68.

Mastin, T., Choi, J., Barboza, G. E., & Post, L. (2007). Newspapers' framing of elder abuse: It's not a family affair. *Journalism & Mass Communication Quarterly, 84*(4), 777–794. doi.org/10.1177/107769900708400408

Messner, M. A., Duncan, M. C., & Cooky, C. (2003). Silence, sports bras, and wrestling porn: Women in televised sports news and highlights shows. *Journal of Sport and Social Issues, 27*(1), 38–51. doi.org/10.1177/0193732502239583

Nakamura, D. (2017, September 13). White House: ESPN's Jemele Hill should be fired for calling Trump a "white supremacist." *Washington Post*. Retrieved from https://www.washingtonpost.com/news/post-politics/wp/2017/09/13/white-house-espns-jemele-hill-should-be-fired-for-calling-trump-a-white-supremacist/?utm_term=.5cfab60f66e4

Pepin, M. (2016, April 28). Curt Schilling accuses ESPN commentators of racism. *Boston Globe*. Retrieved from https://www.bostonglobe.com/sports/redsox/2016/04/28/curt-schilling-accuses-espn-commentators-racism/fcyAOwNyBZvBMxrd5oYfZO/story.html

Purcell, K., Buchanan, J., & Friedrich, L. (2013, July 16). The impact of digital tools on student writing and how writing is taught in schools. *Pewinternet.org*. Retrieved from http://www.pewinternet.org/2013/07/16/the-impact-of-digital-tools-on-student-writing-and-how-writing-is-taught-in-schools/

Rowe, D. (2007). Sports journalism: Still the toy department of the news media? *Journalism, 8*(4), 385–405. doi.org/10.1177/1464884907078657

Saltzis, K. (2012). Breaking news online: How news stories are updated and maintained around-the-clock. *Journalism Practice, 6*(5–6), 702–710.

Sanderson, J. (2008). "How do you prove a negative?" Roger Clemens's image-repair strategies in response to the Mitchell Report. *International Journal of Sport Communication, 1*(2), 246–262. doi.org/10.1123/ijsc.1.2.246

Shoemaker, P. J., & Reese, S. D. (1996). *Mediating the message*. White Plains, NY: Longman.

Soroka, S. N. (2006). Good news and bad news: Asymmetric responses to economic information. *Journal of Politics, 68*(2), 372–385. doi.org/10.1111/j.1468-2508.2006.00413.x

Stelter, B. (2017, September 15). ESPN chief Skipper to staff: "ESPN is not a political organization." *CNN Money*. Retrieved from https://money.cnn.com/2017/09/15/media/john-skipper-espn-staff-memo/index.html

Strenk, A. (1979). What price victory? The world of international sports and politics. *The ANNALS of the American Academy of Political and Social Science, 445*(1), 128–140. doi.org/10.1177/000271627944500114

Swan, A. (2017, Oct. 11). ESPN's politics are killing its brand. *Forbes*. Retrieved from https://www.forbes.com/sites/andyswan/2017/10/11/espns-politics-are-killing-its-brand/#6edc575c1429

Thiel, A., Villanova, A., Toms, M., Friis Thing, L., & Dolan, P. (2016). Can sport be "un-political"? *European Journal for Sport and Society, 13*(4), 253–255.

Thrush, G., & Haberman, M. (2017, August 12). Trump is criticized for not calling out white supremacists. *New York Times.* Retrieved from https://www.nytimes.com/2017/08/12/ us/trump-charlottesville-protest-nationalist-riot.html

Tuchman, G. (1972). Objectivity as strategic ritual: An examination of newsmen's notions of objectivity. *American Journal of Sociology, 77*(4), 660–679.

Tuchman, G. (1973). Making news by doing work: Routinizing the unexpected. *American Journal of Sociology, 79*(1), 110–131.

Tversky, A., & Kahneman, D. (1985). The framing of decisions and the psychology of choice. In V. T. Covello, J. L. Mumpower, P. J. M. Stallen, & V. R. R. Uppuluri (Eds.), *Environmental impact assessment, technology assessment, and risk analysis: Contributions from the psychological and decision sciences* (pp. 107–129). Berlin: Spring-Verleg.

Vasilogambros, M. (2016, July 12). When athletes take political stands. *The Atlantic.* Retrieved from https://www.theatlantic.com/news/archive/2016/07/when-athletes-take-political-stands/490967/

Wastler, A. (2013, Aug. 10). Newspaper bane: Nobody reads the stories. *CNBC.* Retrieved from https://www.cnbc.com/id/100952247

Weiner, B. (1985). An attributional theory of achievement motivation and emotion. *Psychological Review, 92*(4), 548–573. dx.doi.org/10.1037/0033-295X.92.4.548

Zhang, Y., Jin, Y., & Tang, Y. (2015). Framing depression: Cultural and organizational influences on coverage of a public health threat and attribution of responsibilities in Chinese news media, 2000–2012. *Journalism & Mass Communication Quarterly, 92*(1), 99–120. doi.org/10.1177/1077699014558553

8. A "Fireable Offense?": Jemele Hill and the Rhetoric of Public Correction

Katherine L. Lavelle

In fall 2017, Jemele Hill (one of the few women of color who is a prominent sports opinion journalist) wrote two sets of tweets that became national news stories (Brady, 2017b). One tweet called President Donald Trump "a white supremacist who has largely surrounded himself with other white supremacist" (Loggins, 2017a, para.1). It was posted one month after alt-right groups protested the removal of a Confederate statue in Charlottesville, VA (Lopez, 2017). On October 9, 2017, Hill hypothesized how Dallas Cowboys fans could express disagreement with owner Jerry Jones' comments about National Football League (NFL) player protests (Brady, 2017b). Almost immediately, Hill was suspended for violating ESPN's social media policy[1] (Draper & Belson, 2017).

Historically, ESPN has suspended employees for controversial comments. Former ESPN columnist Bill Simmons was disciplined for criticizing the NFL's handling of the Deflategate scandal in 2014 (Deitsch, 2014). Baseball color commentator Curt Schilling, in comparing Muslims to Nazis, posted transphobic tweets, and was eventually fired in 2016 (Sandomir, 2016). Additionally, ESPN is perceived as politically liberal (Brady, 2017a). It awarded retired Olympic decathlon champion Caitlyn Jenner the Arthur Ashe Courage award after coming out as a transgender woman in 2015 (Moyer, 2015). More of ESPN's front facing talent is female, people of color, or openly gay or lesbian (McCarthy, 2015), a shift from when it was mostly heterosexual white men (Turner, 2013).

ESPN has attempted to balance its politics. They briefly employed conservative commentator Rush Limbaugh (Hartmann, 2007), they awkwardly covered Michael Sam's short NFL career (Kahn, 2015), and deferentially covered the Joe Paterno scandal in 2011 (Ott, 2012). The reaction to Hill's criticisms of Trump and Jerry Jones is an example of public correction, an expansion of Kenneth Burke's Terms of Order (Milford, 2015). This framework helps evaluate how a community deals with disruption. In this case, ESPN's response was complicated because of Hill's social location and Trump's discourse. This chapter will examine the context surrounding Hill's comments, Twitter scholarship, application of public correction to this situation, and discuss implications.

Context

The Charlottesville protests were violent. Groups of young white men were shouting racist slogans, and Trump's response demonstrated his unwillingness to disassociate from extremist groups (Lopez, 2017). Their actions were broadcast worldwide and offered a chilling reminder of racism in the United States (Reid, 2017). On August 12, 2017, a counter protestor was killed by a car driven into a crowd (Holmes, 2017). Despite bipartisan calls for condemnation, Trump blamed "both sides" for violence (Lopez, 2017). When Hill tweeted on September 11th, Trump's public position was unchanged. The following week, White House Press Secretary Sarah Sanders criticized Hill's comments, calling them a "fireable offense" (Lopez, 2017).

The next week at a political rally, Trump called NFL players involved in ongoing protests of systematic racism "son[s] of a bitch[es]" who should be fired (Schwartz, Braziller, & Golding, 2017, para 4). That weekend, over 200 NFL players protested in response to Trump (Schwartz et al., 2017). While NFL owners were initially supportive, stories emerged about upset owners. Dallas Cowboys owner Jerry Jones, one of the longest tenured and most forthright owners (Finley, 2017), wanted to "bench" any player "caught 'disrespecting the flag'" (Ley, 2017, para. 3). After Hill tweeted about Jones, she was suspended.

Twitter Scholarship

To understand this situation, it is critical to contextualize Twitter. Only 24% of social media users use Twitter, while 68% use Facebook ("Social Media Fact," 2017). Communication and sport scholars have cautioned against overanalyzing Twitter because of this disparity (Billings, 2014). However, studying Twitter is important. Twitter is an "enhanced platform far more influential" than these numbers suggest (Foote, Butterworth, & Sanderson, 2017, p. 281). It allows direct communication between fans and with public figures and has replaced the "quote" in traditional new sources (van Dijck, 2013, p. 77). van Dijck (2013) argued: "The tweet's effectiveness lies in having a personalized public message enter a customized online social environment" (p. 77). Additionally, social media discourse can be archived. "Utterances previously expressed offhandedly are now released into a public domain where they can have far-reaching and long-lasting effects" (van Dijk, 2013, p. 7). For popular users, tweeting is a more efficient way to communicate than traditional media sources. Consequently, Foote et al. (2017) encouraged scholars to examine the "cultural and political implications of Twitter" (p. 281).

Emerging Scholarship on Twitter

Considering this scholarship, there are three critical issues which emerge when evaluating Twitter. First, it is assumed that Twitter operates as a town hall, where all participate equally (van Dijck, 2013). However, algorithms manage Twitter posts, not ideas (Noble, 2013). Twitter does not "operate as a mere amplifier of individual voices as well as collective opinions" (van Dijk, 2013, p. 74). Twitter produced new relationships based on personal interaction (Noble, 2013), such as parasocial interaction with public figures (Frederick, Lim, Clavio, Pedersen, & Burch, 2014).

Despite these restrictions, Twitter can be welcoming for Black people, a group often underrepresented in other media spaces (Jackson & Banaszczyk, 2016; Maragh, 2016). "Black Twitter" is a place to discuss culture and experiences often ignored by mainstream media (Brock, 2009, 2012; Florini, 2014), such as #OscarsSoWhite, a campaign criticizing the Academy Awards lack of nominations for people of color (Schulman, 2018). As explained by Billings, Moscowitz, Rae, and Brown-Devlin (2015) in their study of public discussion about NBA player Jason Collins' coming out announcement in 2013, social media discussion often deviates from established media frames.

Finally, communication and sport scholars study Twitter (Billings et al., 2015; Rodriguez, 2017; Sauder & Blaszka, 2016). In the sports sphere, journalists use Twitter to promote their stories (Billings, 2014). Sports media personas (including athletes), use it to actively promote dialogue (Frederick et al., 2014), engage with fans during competitions (Sauder & Blaszka, 2016), and operate as a second screen during live games (Billings, 2014).

Despite the status of sports Twitter, ESPN faces unique challenges balancing "embrace the debate" with serious journalism. "ESPN's most successful and enduring shows (such as *Pardon the Interruption* and *First Take)*. … are designed to be the sports equivalent of 'the McLaughlin Group'"

(Farhi, 2017, para. 8). ESPN also supports serious journalism, especially on its program *Outside the Lines* (Deitsch, 2017a). However, Twitter has magnified ESPN's difficulties maintaining this balance between being provocative and serious. In his profile of Hill, The Ringer's Bryan Curtis (2017c) characterized Twitter as "the de facto coordinating producer of ESPN's daytime lineup" (para. 41). ESPN relies on Twitter engagement for content, but when one of their highest profile personalities was the subject of a Trump Twitter controversy, ESPN struggled to defend Hill without alienating Trump voters (Lopez, 2017).

Public Correction

As a sports network, ESPN's approach to politics must appear balanced. The reaction to Hill's Twitter comments disrupted hierarchy from a Burkean perspective because when hierarchy is disrupted, corrective action is required because the scapegoat poisons the community (Carlson & Hocking, 1988). In corrective action, a scapegoat can be identified and removed or punished through mortification to resolve conflict (Carlson & Hocking, 1988). In Major League Baseball, Rafael Palmeiro was successfully framed as a "foreign other" because of alleged use of PEDs and Cuban identity (Butterworth, 2008). In the National Basketball Association (NBA), former Los Angeles Clippers' owner Donald Sterling's racist comments about Black fans and NBA legend Magic Johnson forced Sterling out to demonstrate the league's stance against overt racism (Lavelle, 2016). In these communication and sport studies, the scapegoat was removed in order to restore order.

However, scapegoating can fail when involving larger community issues (Turnage, 2009). Milford (2015) analyzed a University of Miami football booster who provided unsanctioned gifts to the team and players, which are banned (Nocera, 2017). Instead of removing the scapegoat, the correction focused on the cultural lag[2] or mortification (Milford, 2015). In similar situations, ESPN had relied on suspensions and removals. But ESPN could not remove Hill because the President made racist comments. In fact, Disney (parent company of ESPN) President Bob Iger noted Hill was not suspended in September because Iger had never experienced racism (Simmons, 2017).

In this situation, there were two issues exposed by this cultural lag. First, prior to the Trump administration, U.S. Presidents had positive public interactions with athletes. For decades, championship teams were invited to the White House, a tradition regularized during the Reagan administration in the 1980s (Neumann, 2016). Presidents Bush and Obama expanded these interactions. Bush, a former part-owner of the Texas Rangers (Baker, 2011), hosted annual ceremonies for all National Collegiate Athletic Association Division I Championship teams as President (Neumann, 2016). In addition to hosting teams, Obama participated in public partnerships with athletes and sports personalities (Neumann, 2016).

ESPN partnered with Bush and Obama on high profile projects. In 2015, a *30 for 30* film *First Pitch* examined Bush's first pitch during the New York Yankees' World Series, weeks after the September 11, 2001 attacks (Ley, 2015). Obama annually filled out NCAA men's and women's basketball bracket in taped segments aired on ESPN (Curtis, 2017a). In 2016, Obama participated in a conversation about race in America hosted by The Undefeated, ESPN's race and culture site (Fletcher, 2016). Like *First Pitch*, these collaborations were not critical of Obama's presidency and promoted affirmative interactions.

Second, until recently, high profile athletes were not public advocates. From a scholarly perspective, sport is political (Butterworth, 2013; Leonard, 2017). There has been a lull of high profile active athletes engaged in substantive and sustained social justice work since the 1970s (Butterworth, 2013). However, in the past six years, this has changed. Both Women's National Basketball Association players and high-profile NBA players (e.g., LeBron James, Dwyane Wade, and Carmelo Anthony) have been actively involved in public discussions about police brutality and gun violence (Lavelle, 2019). In fact, WNBA players were briefly fined in 2016 for on-court demonstrations (wearing #Dallas5 #BlackLivesMatter t-shirts while on the court for pre-game activities) after several high-profile shootings of police officers and Black men (Lavelle, 2019). Started by Colin Kaepernick in 2016, some NFL players have used their platform to discuss institutionalized racism in the United States (Bishop, 2016). Specific political discussions have been a part of sports in ways they had not been previously.

Unlike his predecessors, Trump has criticized activist athletes and they have responded. In September 2017, Trump called NFL protests during the National Anthem "disrespecting our Flag & Country" (Held, 2017, para. 14). In response, Golden State Warriors star Steph Curry said he would not go to the White House championship celebration, leading Trump to revoke his invitation via Twitter (Rovell, 2017). In 2018, the Philadelphia Eagles ceremony was cancelled due to the misperception that the team participated in on-field protests (Shear, 2018). Instead, many opted not to go in response to a 2018 NFL policy which prohibited these protests, a policy enacted in wake of Trump's NFL criticisms (Shear, 2018). When asked about the Eagles' ceremony, 2018 NBA finalists LeBron James (Cleveland Cavaliers) and Steph Curry announced that neither team would visit the White House if their teams won the championship (Spears, 2018).

This marked shift in interaction between the White House and athletes meant that ESPN's previous treatment of presidential partnerships as apolitical became controversial because of Trump's combative interactions (Lopez, 2017). To some degree, some viewers already perceived ESPN as politically liberal because it reported on activist athletes (Kay, 2017). Despite ESPN's data that many viewers thought the network appropriately balanced political issues (Curtis, 2017b), when Trump was elected in 2016, individuals who felt that ESPN was too liberal had an influential ally (Kay, 2017).

In this situation, the cultural lag was exposed by the increased profile of activist athletes, a sitting U.S. President critical of them, and one of the highest profile ESPN anchors calling the President a white supremacist on Twitter. How does ESPN respond? In public correction, scholars identify priests and prophets to help correct orientation (Milford, 2015). For Milford, priests "function to uphold a given orientation towards ritual such as scapegoating" (p. 47) who both enforce and endorse the orientation of a given community. These individuals help maintain hierarchies and determine blame when order is disrupted (Milford, 2015). Priests criticize community members who violate order. In this situation, ESPN management and some personnel, such as Ombudsperson Jim Brady, and ESPN CEO John Skipper function as priests. In contrast, prophets "come outside the governing structure and work to revise these community's orientation "(Milford, 2015, p. 47). These individuals help articulate redemptive action and criticize the priests (Milford, 2015). In this situation, the prophets were supportive sports writers, Bill Simmons and other writers outside of ESPN, and Trump (who functions as both a priest and a prophet). In this situation, Trump wants ESPN to "stick to sports," but is also an outsider critical of ESPN. In this situation, I argue that Hill's social location expanded community orientation and protected her. Instead of removing Hill, the discussion shifted to ESPN's failure to manage Twitter and provide space for talent to discuss politics, as opposed to focusing on Hill's specific comments.

To study this phenomenon, I analyzed news articles from September 11, 2017 until February 1, 2018 to study how these priests and prophets redefined the orientation of ESPN in the wake of Hill's Tweets. The texts were selected from a Nexis Uni search (formerly LexisNexis Academic Universe), a search of individual news sites covering this story (e.g., *New York Times, Washington Post*, & National Public Radio), as well as national sports news sites (The Ringer, SI.com, ESPN.com). While the Hill story was a national story, the sources included in this study provided in-depth analysis, which focused on examining how Hill's actions fit into a larger narrative about how ESPN navigates political speech. The time frame (September 11-November 15, 2017) included both sets of Hill tweets characterized as violating ESPN's social media policy), the response from ESPN and Trump, and ESPN's revisions of its social media policy.

Analysis

Priests, ESPN Management

ESPN management was critical of Hill's tweets, evident in several internal documents. For instance, in a lengthy employee email from September 15, 2017, CEO John Skipper "remind[ed employees] about fundamental principles at ESPN," emphasizing that "ESPN is not a political organization," and that when employees use media platforms, "at a minimum, comments should not be inflammatory or personal" (Brady, 2017a, para. 1–5). Hill concurred. She cried in a meeting with him, not as a reaction to the personal attacks, but because she was "turn[ing] the network into a 'punching bag'" (Flood, 2017, para. 9). In a first-person essay on The Undefeated when discussing the implications of her comments, she noted, "[it] felt [like] I had let him [John Skipper] and my colleagues down" (Hill, 2017, para. 9). Additionally, *Sports Business Daily* reporter John Ourand reported "they [ESPN decision-makers] want to see Jemele suspended, and as more of a statement to the rest of the company … you can talk about sports' social issues, but let's remember why you are working for ESPN" (Deitsch, 2017b, para. 2). For these individuals, Hill's Trump tweets violated ESPN's mission and operated as "sin."

Additionally, in internal ESPN electronic communication, employees noted that colleagues (e.g., Britt McHenry, Bill Simmons, and Stephen A. Smith, among others) had been suspended for making less controversial comments on social media than Hill (Redford, 2017). Several cited the employee handbook, which suggests avoiding "sensitive or inflammatory subjects that are not related to work, such as politics or religion" (Redford, 2017, para. 8), as justification for more severe punishment for Hill. ESPN's suspension statement noted Tweets "that negatively reflect [on ESPN]" will have "consequences" (Brady, 2017b, para.17). After her suspension, Hill expressed her "regret" was "that my comments and the public way I made them painted ESPN in an unfair light" (as cited in Wemple, 2017, para.18). These comments suggest that even though Hill was not initially punished, her Trump tweets were justification for future punishment.

Priest, Public Editor Jim Brady

ESPN's Public Editor, Jim Brady, wrote columns justifying the suspension. The Public Editor is ESPN's Ombudsperson, who provides "independent communication, critique, and analysis of ESPN's programming and news coverage"

(Hall, 2015, para. 2). Operating as a priest, Brady published a series of lengthy analyses after the Trump tweets in September and again after Hill was suspended in October. Brady made two related arguments about this situation.

First, in September, Brady (2017a) promoted the value of objective journalism, even with Trump. He posited that Hill "erred in her judgment" with personal attacks against Trump (para. 20) and referred to Hill's comments as the "nuclear example" of the problems ESPN had discussing politics (para. 2). He characterized her tweets as a "doozy" because of the "highly combustible mix of race, politics, freedom of speech and corporate policy" (para. 18). What is not included in this column is the Twitter disagreement he was drawn into defending his position. Kalaf (2017, September 18) described Brady's behavior as a "sustained public meltdown" which contradicted Brady's call to avoid using Twitter for these types of debates (para. 16). When Hill was suspended in October, Brady (2017b) opened his column describing the relationship between Hill and ESPN as "uneasy" (para. 2). He said Hill was wrong for "poking the bear, again" (para. 19). Even though Brady discussed the larger problems ESPN had in this political environment, he still blamed Hill.

Second, when arguing that Hill must be objective, Brady (2017b) described the conflict of interest ESPN had if it suspended Hill for criticizing the NFL (a significant financial partner) as opposed to a specific second social media violation. Brady argued that journalists should "let consumers (as opposed to readers) come to their own conclusion" (para. 11). Brady wanted journalists to retain their values and "put our heads down and do what journalists do" (para. 7). He conceded that Trump was difficult, but journalists must be objective. In this situation, Brady operates as a priest with his role of "explainer" for controversies and issues related to ESPN journalism (Hall, 2015, para. 4). As Public Editor, it gives Brady latitude to speak from his own perspective, but also represent ESPN by publishing on their website.

Priests, Supportive ESPN Colleagues

Other priests emphasized the importance of objectivity in journalism, including T. J. Quinn and Bob Ley of *Outside the Lines*. Ley, a highly respected ESPN journalist, stated "You can love the sinner and hate the sin," arguing that Hill misused her "company-provided megaphone" with her Tweets, which represented ESPN (as cited in Deitsch, 2017, October 9, para. 11). Quinn argued that for him, journalistic objectivity was critical, and he kept his political opinions private (Deitsch, 2017, October 9). Both reporters emphasized their personal and professional relationships with Hill. Ley stated that he "loves[s] Jemele" and Quinn was angered by the "racist and misogynist backlash that [Hill dealt with]" (Deitsch, 2017d, para. 11). Quinn posted a supportive tweet for her as the "bare minimum" he could do (Deitsch, 2017d, para. 11). Both Quinn and Ley have credibility that other ESPN personalities might not have. Quinn and Ley are both reporters and friends of Hill. Still, they function as priests by promoting objectivity, even when responding to racism.

Priests, SportsCenter's *Legacy*

The objectivity standard is related to Hill's position as co-host of *SC6*, which ran from February 2017 to February 2018 (Withiam, 2018). *SportsCenter* is the flagship ESPN show and was appointment television for sports fans in the 1990s (Fahri, 2017). Traditionally, *SportsCenter* covered a narrow representation of (mostly) male sports (Cooky, Messner, & Musto, 2015; Turner, 2013). Turner (2013) found that *SportsCenter* highlighted stories about white athletes, rarely covered female athletes, and featured white males who "dominate positions of authority" (p. 321). Turner characterized *SportsCenter* as "a leader in the sports media's perpetuation and reinforcement of hegemonic (white) masculinity" (p. 322). Because of this history, Hill felt the tension of being herself and "honoring the legacy of a venerable franchise" as the host of the flagship ESPN show (Curtis, 2017c, para. 22). After the Trump comments, *Think Progress* reported that ESPN tried to pull Hill from the September 13, 2017 broadcast (Kay, 2017). It did not happen. Michael Smith refused to host without Hill, and two potential replacement hosts had prior commitments (Kay, 2017). But this attempt demonstrated how *SportsCenter* is expected to be apolitical. The presence of Hill frames her as political even when she made these comments off air.

Prophets, *Twitter's Fault*

Twitter is a problematic space to express controversial views. Operating as a priest, Hill conceded that "Twitter wasn't the place to vent my frustrations" and "isn't a great place to have nuanced, complicated discussions, especially when it involves race" (Hill, 2017, para. 18). Popular ESPN personality Dan LeBatard noted that ESPN was concerned about what people said on Twitter as opposed to making controversial comments on an ESPN program (Brady, 2017b). This observation makes sense; ESPN updated their social media policy in November 2017 with a new requirement for employees to receive supervisor permission before posting political content on social media (Gartland, 2017), a rule that could have prevented Hill from posting about Trump.

Prophets outside of ESPN made similar arguments. In a round table discussion about Hill's Trump comments, Danielle Belton, the Editor-in-chief of *The Root*, warned, "don't tweet anything that you're not going to be comfortable with if it's up on a billboard on the highway the next day" (Martin, 2017, para. 9). Former ESPN columnist and The Ringer founder, Bill Simmons (2017) noted, "everybody battles 'bad judgment' on Twitter?" in part because Twitter is "too comfortable," to post whatever thought might cross one's mind (as opposed to going through an editorial process) (para. 7). These prophets contextualize the problems inherent in using Twitter to have discussions about controversial issues.

The appropriateness of Twitter is significant when discussing Trump's place in this situation. In a Burkean sense, Trump is a prophet because he is an outsider critical of ESPN. When it was clear Hill would not be suspended, Trump tweeted, demanding ESPN "apologize for untruth [*sic*]" and criticizing its politics (Farhi, 2017, para. 6). Echoing some of the ESPN priests, Trump argued Hill should have been punished. When Hill was suspended for the Dallas Cowboys comments, Trump tweeted, "with Jemele Hill at the mike, it is not wonder [*sic*] ESPN ratings have 'tanked,' [*sic*] in fact, tanked so badly it is the talk of the industry!" (Held, 2017, para. 1). Here, he acts as a priest, wanting to preserve an apolitical version of ESPN.

Prophets, ESPN's Political Space

Prophets questioned ESPN's ability to avoid politics and were critical of ESPN's ability to deftly handle Hill's comments (Wemple, 2017). National Public Radio's David Folkenflik (2017), described ESPN as "freezing" when Hill tweeted about Trump. James Andrew Miller, co-author of ESPN's oral history, noted that many employees "don't want politics to enter the equation at all" (Farhi, 2017, para. 17). Bill Simmons described politics at ESPN "as the invisible third rail" explaining that when ESPN bought Nate Silver's FiveThirtyEight.com (a site named for the number of US Congressional districts) "they wanted to be an analytics site, not a political site" (Simmons, 2017, para. 32). Others observed that despite extensive social media guidelines, "ESPN handles everything on a case-by-case basis" (Simmons, 2017, para. 29).

Prophets were critical of this approach. Color of Change, an advocacy group focused on social justice campaigns to support people of color, encouraged Hill supporters to call ESPN to express their solidarity with her (Finley, 2017). Many prophets criticized ESPN for punishing Hill after including her in several social justice forums (Deitsch, 2017b). Clarence Hill Jr., a Dallas Cowboys beat writer, argued that ESPN had encouraged "socially conscious" discussions with Hill, noting that Hill "is passionate about telling the truth in the face of hate on a daily basis" (Deitsch, 2017b, para. 6). Simmons (2017) argued that ESPN did not seem to know how to handle diverse personalities, wondering if these individuals were hired to demonstrate diversity as opposed to bringing different perspectives to the network. Simmons described Hill's opinions as valuable ones, "just about impossible to find in the television landscape" (para. 39). David Leonard (2017) chronicled Hill's commitment to social justice issues in 2010, when she criticized the NFL's handling of two sexual assault charges against Pittsburgh Steelers Quarterback Ben Roethlisberger. Based on Hill's previous work, it was not surprising that she had an opinion about Trump's discourse (Simmons, 2017). These prophets wanted ESPN to be more consistent in the network's mission, as opposed to punishing Hill for her clearly established views.

Prophets, Jemele Hill Was Right

Prophets made three primary arguments to defend Hill's arguments. First, they argued Hill was right. Jeff Pearlman, who wrote a book about the USFL (a short-lived professional football team in the late 1990s which had Trump as an owner), argued that "Trump is as vile and disgusting as she wrote. There was nothing in her Tweets that rang untrue" (Deitsch, 2017b, para. 11). Mike Freeman concurred, nothing that after Charlottesville, the covers of *the New Yorker* and *the Economist* depicted Trump as a Ku Klux Klan member (Deitsch, 2017b). Trump had instituted discriminatory policies and frequently criticized people of color (Deitsch, 2017b). Jim Trotter, a longtime ESPN NFL journalist, posited that if a person was black and conscious of the United States' racial history, Hill's comments made sense. For Trotter, "it is time we stop pretending it is not true" (Deitsch, 2017d, para. 17). Prior to the events of fall 2017, Hill explained why she posted about racism, making the distinction that "racism isn't politics. Racism is an issue of right and wrong" (Deitsch, 2017d, para. 9). In her mea culpa essay on The Undefeated, Hill (2017) maintained this position. "I can't pretend as if the tone and behavior of this presidential administration is normal. And I certainly can't pretend that racism and white supremacy aren't real and that marginalized people don't feel threatened and vulnerable" (para. 14). For these reporters, Trump's discourse and racially divisive comments are radically different than other modern U.S. Presidents (Deitsch, 2017b).

Second, prophets argued it was unacceptable for the Trump administration to pressure ESPN to fire Hill (Deitsch, 2017b). Sarah Westbrook criticized Trump for using the bully pulpit to "try to crush a private individual for criticizing the President," which Westerbrook noted was not something that Richard Nixon would have done (who took vindictive actions against his enemies) (Martin, 2017, para.17). Even though Hill is a public figure, it is an unusual step for the President to attack a non-politician in such a potentially damaging way. Additionally, the National Association of Black Journalists released a support statement for Hill (Deitsch, 2017b). Many prominent Black sports journalists changed their social media avatars to pictures of Hill to support her (Deitsch, 2017b). Jeff Perlman, who self identifies as a Jewish white man recognized the importance of allies standing up for Hill (Deitsch, 2017b). Three of her fellow front-facing female colleagues sent supportive tweets in the wake of her suspension, including Josina Anderson, Cari Champion (Traina, 2017), and former *SportsCenter* anchor Lindsay Czarniak (Deitsch, 2017d). These prophets focus on Hill as a person and her rights as a journalist and a citizen.

Third, several prophets noted Hill's unique social location as a justification for ESPN to minimize her punishment. Hill's ESPN colleague Bomani Jones recognized that being a man who talks about sports for a living "is a level of privilege afforded to me" not shared by Hill and his other female colleagues (as cited in Curtis, 2017c, para. 70). Jones concluded that "As a woman, she [Hill] has to shake off people who have convinced themselves they watch sports to escape their wives or girlfriends. She's catching it worse than anybody else" (Curtis, 2017c). These prophets push back against ESPN for ignoring the unique position of Hill, and the importance of the network taking a stand for her from attacks from the White House.

Implications

By examining Hill's Tweets about Trump and the Dallas Cowboys' response to on-field protests, it demonstrates that ESPN continues to struggle with political conversations and is inconsistent when supporting its talent involved in controversy. In this case, public correction allowed ESPN to distance itself from Hill's position and consequently, avoided critical discussions about racism and the economic relationship between ESPN and the NFL. This public correction operates in two ways. First, ESPN's revised social media policy explicitly prohibits political discussion outside of sports news (Gartland, 2017). These revisions represent ESPN's attempts to correct its cultural lag—journalists speaking freely about politics. Second, SC6 was cancelled (Withiam, 2018, March 8). Hill is now a feature writer for The Undefeated and Michael Smith left SC6 soon after Hill (Withiam, 2018). Hill requested a termination of her contract in summer of 2018 and now writes for the Atlantic, focusing on sports, race, politics, and culture (Garcia, 2018).

ESPN wants to avoid inflammatory statements, yet in other cases from the same time period, they supported personalities who engaged in controversy. For instance, Sam Ponder's critical Tweets led to the cancellation of ESPN's *Barstool Sports* program (Ramos, 2017). Ponder, the newly installed host of ESPN's Sunday NFL show, had been the target of misogynistic and personal criticisms from the site, and after her posts, John Skipper personally cancelled the program after one broadcast (Ramos, 2017). In January 2018, Katie Nolan called Trump a "fucking idiot" on Viceland in January 2018 and was not publicly reprimanded (Masisak, 2018). While it is impossible to know why Hill was punished and reprimanded and others were not, this reorientation could be explained by considering the history of negative treatment towards Black women in the United States when they speak out for social justice issues (Loggins, 2017b). In the case of Hill, Loggins argued that when "angry Black wom[e]n" speak out, they are frequently "silence[d]" and "discredit[ed]," especially by those who want to "render them invisible and effort to mute their individual and collective voices" (para. 5–9). Brittney Cooper (2017) noted in an op-ed that reactions to Hill's comments are "cultural equivocation about who is at fault for racism that makes it hard to dismantle" (para. 8). By focusing on the inappropriateness of the use of Twitter as opposed to the substance of Hill's comments, it provides examples for ESPN's critics that the network is unable to manage what it stands for in terms of the latitude it grants its employees.

In the short term, ESPN attempted to resolve the crisis by suspending Hill, revising their social media policy, and Hill moving to a different position at the network. This incident demonstrates that ESPN and other media entities will be faced with increasingly complicated challenges when embracing social media and attempting to maintaining their identity in a world where media narratives are often shaped by outside forces. Future scholars should continue to explore issues, especially in a world where revising orientation might be more applicable than removing a scapegoat from a situation.

Notes

1. In a media release announcing the suspension, ESPN characterized Hill's tweets about the Dallas Cowboys as a "second violation of the company's social media guidelines" ("ESPN suspends anchor," 2017, October 10, para. 1), which meant that the Trump tweets were the first violation of these guidelines.
2. A cultural lag is an issue which becomes problematic when a disruption reorients the community (Jack, 2008). For instance, police brutality against people of color has taken place in the United States for decades, but until Black Lives Matter framed it as systematic racism, it was ignored in the dominant culture (Harris, 2015).

References

Baker, R. (2011, October 24). The Texas Rangers ... and how they made George W. Bush presidential. *Business Insider*. Retrieved from http://www.businessinsider.com/the-texas-rangersand-how-they-made-george-bush-presidential-2011-11

Billings, A. (2014). Power in the reverberation: Why Twitter matters, but not the way most believe. *Communication & Sport, 2*(2), 107–112. doi: 10.1177/2167479514527427

Billings, A. C., Moscowitz, L. M., Rae, C., & Brown-Devlin, N. (2015). The art of coming out: Traditional and social media frames surrounding the NBA's Jason Collins. *Journalism & Mass Communication Quarterly, 92*, 142–160. doi: 10.1177/1077699014560516

Bishop. G. (2016, December 15). And now what? *SI.com*. Retrieved from http://www.si.com/nfl/2016/12/15/doug-baldwin-social-activism-movement-colin-kaepernick-carmelo-anthony

Brady, J. (2017a, September 16). ESPN awash in rising political tide. *ESPN.com*. Retrieved from http://www.espn.com/blog/ombudsman/post/_/id/871/espn-awash-in-rising-political-tide-2

Brady, J. (2017b, October 11). ESPN navigating uncharted political, social and controversial waters. *ESPN.com*. Retrieved from http://www.espn.com/blog/ombudsman/post/_/id/887/espn-navigating-unchartered-political-social-and-controversial-waters

Brock, A. (2009). "Who do you think you are?": Race, representation, and cultural rhetorics in online spaces. *Poroi, 6*(1), 15–35. doi: 10.13008/2151-2957.1013

Brock, A. (2012). From the Blackhand side: Twitter as a cultural conversation. *Journal of Broadcasting & Electronic Media, 56*(4), 529–549. doi: 10.1080/08838151.2012.732147

Butterworth, M. L. (2008). Purifying the body politic: Steroids, Rafael Palmeiro, and the rhetorical cleansing of Major League Baseball. *Western Journal of Communication, 72*(2), 145–161. doi: 10.1080/10570310802038713

Butterworth, M. L. (2013). The athlete as citizen: Judgment and rhetorical invention in sport. *Sport in Society: Cultures, Commerce, Media, Politics, 17*(7), 867–883. doi: 10.1080/17430437.2013.806033

Carlson, A. C., & Hocking, J. E. (1988). Strategies of redemption at the Vietnam Veterans' Memorial. *Western Journal of Speech Communication, 52*(3), 203–215.

Cooky, C., Messner, M. A., & Musto, M. (2015). It's Dude Time! A quarter century of excluding women's sports in televised news and highlight shows. *Communication & Sport, 3*(3), 261–287. doi: 10.1177/2167479515588761

Cooper, B. (2017, September 15). Jemele Hill called Donald Trump a white supremacist. Where's the lie? *Cosmopolitan*. Retrieved from https://www.cosmopolitan.com/politics/a12242564/jemele-hill-espn-trump-white-supremacist/

Curtis, C. (2017a, February 15). ESPN should hire Barack Obama as bracketologist. *ForTheWin*. Retrieved from https://www.usatoday.com/story/sports/ftw/2017/02/15/

espn-should-hire-barack-obama-to-make-us-feel-good-about-our-march-madness-brackets/97962430/

Curtis, C. (2017b, June 5). ESPN study finds 64 percent of viewers agree with network's sports-politics mix. *For the Win*. Retrieved from https://ftw.usatoday.com/2017/06/espn-politics-too-liberal-poll-results-viewers-conservative-research

Curtis, B. (2017c, September 13). Jemele Hill and the fight for the future of ESPN. *The Ringer.com*. Retrieved from https://www.theringer.com/2017/9/13/16299136/jemele-hill-espn-michael-smith-sportscenter-the-six

Deitsch, R (2014, September 24). ESPN suspends Bill Simmons for criticism of Roger Goodell. *SI.com*. Retrieved from https://www.si.com/nfl/2014/09/24/espn-bill-simmons-roger-goodell-suspension

Deitsch, R. (2017a, September 13). ESPN employees respond to Jemele Hill controversy over Trump comments. *SI.com*. Retrieved from https://www.si.com/tech-media/2017/09/13/jemele-hill-espn-colleagues-respond-trump-twitter-comments

Deitsch, R. (2017b, September 17). Media circus: Jemele Hill finds support among media Twitter users; Tony Romo's second game. *SI.com*. Retrieved from https://www.si.com/tech-media/2017/09/17/jemele-hill-donald-trump-twitter-tony-romo-jim-nantz-cbs-beth-mowins

Deitsch, R. (2017c, September 21). SI Media Podcast: Addressing ESPN's recent missteps, what's next for the Network. *SI.com*. Retrieved from https://www.si.com/tech-media/2017/09/21/si-media-podcast-roundtable-jemele-hill-espn-public-editor-position

Deitsch, R. (2017d, October 9). ESPN suspends Jemele Hill two weeks for violating social media policy. *SI.com*. Retrieved from https://www.si.com/tech-media/2017/10/09/jemele-hill-suspend-espn

Draper, K., & Belson, K. (2017, October 9). Jemele Hill suspended by ESPN after response to Jerry Jones. *The New York Times*. Retrieved from https://www.nytimes.com/2017/10/09/sports/football/jemele-hill-suspended-espn.html

ESPN suspends anchor Jemele Hill for violating social media rules. (2017, October 10). *ESPN*. Retrieved from http://www.espn.com/espn/story/_/id/20971317/espn-anchor-jemele-hill-suspended-2-weeks-second-violation-social-media-rules

Farhi, P. (2017, September 20). ESPN likes opinionated personalities. Until it doesn't. Just ask Jemele Hill. *Washington Post Blogs*. Retrieved from https://www.lexisnexis.com

Finley, T. (2017, October 10). Celebs are showing their support for Jemele Hill on social media. *HuffPost*. Retrieved from https://www.huffingtonpost.com/entry/support-for-jemele-hill_us_59dcc946e4b00377980bc1fd

Fletcher, M. A. (2016, October 11). President Obama talks race, sports, and being undefeated. *The Undefeated*. Retrieved from http://theundefeated.com/features/president-obama-talks-race-sports-and-being-undefeated/

Flood, B. (2017, October 4). Disney CEO Iger says he didn't fire ESPN's Jemele Hill because he hasn't experienced racism himself. *FoxNews.com* Retrieved from http://

www.foxnews.com/entertainment/2017/10/04/disney-ceo-iger-says-didnt-fire-es-pns-jemele-hill-because-hasnt-experienced-racism-himself.html

Florini, S. (2014). Tweets, tweeps, and signifyin': Communication and cultural performance on "Black Twitter." *Television & New Media, 15*(3), 223–237. doi: 10.1177/1527476413480247

Folkenflik, D. (2017, October 10). ESPN suspends host Jemele Hill over controversial Tweet. *NPR.org*. Retrieved from https://www.npr.org/2017/10/10/556962376/espn-suspends-host-jemele-hill-over-controversial-tweet

Foote, J. G., Butterworth, M. L., & Sanderson, J. (2017). Adrian Peterson and the "Wussification of America": Football and myths of masculinity. *Communication Quarterly, 65*(3), 268–284. doi: 10.1080/01463373.2016.1227347

Frederick, E., Lim, C. H., Clavio, G., Pedersen, P. M., & Burch, L. M. (2014). Choosing between the one-way or two-way street: An exploration of relationship promotion by professional athletes on Twitter. *Communication & Sport, 2,* 80–99. doi: 10.1177/2167479512466387

Garcia, S. E. (2018, October 1). Jemele Hill Is joining The Atlantic and ready to talk politics. Retrieved from https://www.nytimes.com/2018/10/01/sports/jemele-hill-the-atlantic-.html

Gartland, D. (2017, November 2). ESPN lays out new social media guidelines for employees. *SI.com*. Retrieved from https://www.si.com/tech-media/2017/11/02/espn-employees-social-media-policy

Hall, A. (2015, November 6). Digital new veteran Jim Brady named ESPN Public Editor. *ESPNMedia Zone*. Retrieved from https://espnmediazone.com/us/press-releases/2015/11/digital-news-veteran-jim-brady-named-espn-public-editor/

Harris, F. C. (2015). The next Civil Rights Movement? *Dissent Magazine*. Retrieved from https://www.dissentmagazine.org/article/black-lives-matter-new-civil-rights-movement-fredrick-harris

Hartmann, D. (2007). Rush Limbaugh, Donovan McNabb, and "a little social concern": Reflections on the problems of Whiteness in contemporary American sport. *Journal of Sport & Social Issues, 31,* 45–60. doi: 10.1177/0193723506296831

Held, A. (2017, October 10). Trump slams NFL and Jemele Hill following suspensions. *NPR.org*. Retrieved from https://www.npr.org/sections/the two-way/2017/10/10/556817655/trump-slams-nfl-and-jemele-hill-following-espn-suspension

Hill, J. (2017, September 27). Jemele Hill on doing the right thing: A lesson from her grandmother: Be better. No matter what. *The Undefeated*. Retrieved from https://theundefeated.com/features/jemele-hill-on-doing-the-right-thing/

Holmes, O. (2017, August 18). *New Yorker* and *Economist* covers slam Trump's defense of white supremacists. *The Guardian*. Retrieved from https://www.theguardian.com/us-news/2017/aug/18/new-yorker-and-economist-covers-slam-trumps-defence-of-white-supremacists

Jack, J. (2008). Kenneth Burke's constabulary rhetoric: Sociorhetorical critique in *Attitudes toward History*. *Rhetorical Society Quarterly, 38*, 66–81. doi: 10.2139/ssrn.1525898

Jackson, S. J., & Banaszczyk, S. (2016). Digital standpoints: Debating gendered violence and racial exclusions in the Feminist counterpublic. *Journal of Communication Inquiry, 40*(4), 391–407. doi: 10.1177/0196859916667731

Kahn, A. I. (2015). Michael Sam, Jackie Robinson, and the politics of respectability. *Communication & Sport, 5*(3), 331–351. doi: 10.1177/2167479515616407

Kalaf, S. (2017, September 18). ESPN's public editor is mad online. *Deadspin*. Retrieved from https://deadspin.com/espns-public-editor-is-mad-online-1818524304

Kay, S. (2017, September 15). President Trump demands ESPN "apologize for untruth." *SI.com*. Retrieved from https://www.si.com/tech-media/2017/09/15/president-donald-trump-espn-twitter

Lavelle, K. L. (2016). No room for racism: Restoration of order in the NBA. *Communication & Sport, 4*(4), 424–441. doi: 10.1177/2167479515584046

Lavelle, K. L. (2019). "Change starts with us": Intersectionality and citizenship in the 2016 WNBA. In D. A. Grano & M. L. Butterworth (Eds.), *Sport, rhetoric, and political struggle* (pp. 39–54) . New York, NY: Peter Lang.

Ley, T. (2015, September 11). Why is ESPN doing George W. Bush's dirty work for him? *Deadspin*. Retrieved from https://deadspin.com/why-is-espn-doing-george-w-bushs-dirty-work-for-him-1730067091

Ley, T. (2017, October 9). ESPN suspends Jemele Hill two weeks for no good reason. *Deadspin*. Retrieved from https://deadspin.com/espn-suspends-jemele-hill-two-weeks-for-no-good-reason-1819290405

Leonard, D. J. (2017). *Playing while White: Privilege and power on and off the field*. Seattle, WA: University of Washington Press.

Loggins, A. H. (2017a, September 16). It is wrong to call Trump a white supremacist? *The Guardian*. Retrieved from https://www.theguardian.com/commentisfree/2017/sep/16/donald-trump-jemele-hill-espn-white-supremacist

Loggins, A. H. (2017b, October 12). ESPN's Jemele Hill is being reduced to an "angry black woman." *The Guardian*. Retrieved from https://www.theguardian.com/commentisfree/2017/oct/12/espn-jemele-hill-angry-black-woman-suspension-nfl

Lopez, G. (2017, September 15). Donald Trump's war with ESPN and Jemele Hill, explained. *Vox.com*. Retrieved from https://www.vox.com/identities/2017/9/15/16313800/trump-jemele-hill-espn-white-supremacist

Maragh, R. S. (2016). "Our struggles are unequal": Black Women's affective labor between television and Twitter. *Journal of Communication Inquiry, 40*(4), 351–369. doi: 10.1177/0196859916664082

Martin, M. (2017, September 16). Barbershop: Conservative free speech on college campuses. *All Things Considered*. Retrieved from https://www.npr.org/2017/09/16/551544785/barbershop-conservative-free-speech-on-college-campuses

Masisak, C. (2018, January 5). Katie Nolan rips "stupid" Donald Trump despite ESPN's policy. *NY Post.* Retrieved from https://nypost.com/2018/01/05/katie-nolan-rips-stupid-donald-trump-despite-espns-policy/

McCarthy, M. (2015, December 8). Future of ESPN will be more diverse than frat house of past. *Sporting News.* Retrieved from https://www.sportingnews.com/us/other-sports/news/espn-future-anchors-diversity-stephen-a-smith-skip-bayless-first-take-terry-bradshaw-fox/73wez2xt5n7hz4es5pphzjw1Milford, M. (2015). Kenneth Burke's punitive priests and the redeeming prophets: The NCAA, the college sports media, and the University of Miami scandal. *Communication Studies, 66,* 45–62. doi: 10.1080/10510974.2013.856806

Moyer, J. W. (2015, July 16). Why some critics don't think Caitlyn Jenner deserved the Arthur Ashe Courage Award. *The Washington Post.* Retrieved from https://www.washingtonpost.com/news/morning-mix/wp/2015/07/16/why-some-critics-dont-think-caitlyn-jenner-deserved-the-arthur-ashe-courage-award/?utm_term=.a4aa9b594d1d

Neumann, T. (2016, March 1). Why White House visits by champions are a U.S. tradition. *ESPN.com.* Retrieved from http://www.espn.com/college-football/story/_/id/14870667/how-white-house-visits-championship-teams-became-american-tradition

Noble, S. U. (2013). Google search: Hyper-visibility as a means of rendering Black women and girls invisible. *InVisible Culture: An Electronic Journal for Visual Culture, 19,* 1–35. Retrieved from ivc.lib.rochester.edu/

Nocera, J. (2017, October 13). It's business, NCAA. Pay the players. *Bloomberg News.* Retrieved from https://www.bloomberg.com/view/articles/2017-10-13/it-s-business-ncaa-pay-the-players

Ott, B. L. (2012). Unnecessary roughness: ESPN's construction of hypermasculine citizenship in the Penn State sex abuse scandal. *Cultural Studies ↔ Critical Methodologies, 12*(4), 330–332. doi: 10.1177/1532708612446433

Ramos, D. R. (2017, October 23). ESPN pulls "Barstool Van Talk" after one episode. *Deadline.* Retrieved from https://deadline.com/2017/10/espn-cancels-barstool-van-talk-pardon-my-take-sam-ponder-1202193330/

Redford, P. (2017, September 15). Here's what ESPN employees are saying about the Jemele Hill situation on their private message board. *Deadspin.* Retrieved from https://deadspin.com/heres-what-espn-employees-are-saying-about-the-jemele-h-1816198451

Reid, J. A. (2017, October 20). The seeds of Trump's victory were sown the moment Obama won. *NBCNews.com.* Retrieved from https://www.nbcnews.com/think/opinion/seeds-trump-s-victory-were-sown-moment-obama-won-ncna811891

Rodriguez, N. S. (2017). #FIFAputos: A Twitter textual analysis over "Puto" at the 2014 World Cup. *Communication & Sport, 5*(6), 712–731. doi:10.1177/2167479516655429

Rovell, D. (2017, December 11). Donald Trump named most powerful person in sports. *ESPN.com.* Retrieved from http://www.espn.com/moresports/story/_/id/21739896/president-donald-trump-named-most-influential-person-sports-sportsbusiness-journal

Sandomir, R. (2016, April 21). Curt Schilling, ESPN Analyst, is fired over offensive social media post. *The New York Times*. Retrieved from https://www.nytimes.com/2016/04/21/sports/baseball/curt-schilling-is-fired-by-espn.html

Sauder, M. H., & Blaszka, M. (2016). 23 players, 23 voices: An examination of the U.S. Women's National Soccer Team on Twitter during the 2015 World Cup. *Communication & Sport*, 1–26. doi:10.1177/2167479516685579

Schulman, M. (2018, January 23). Is the Era of #OscarsSoWhite Over? *The New Yorker*. Retrieved from https://www.newyorker.com/culture/cultural-comment/is-the-era-of-oscarssowhite-over

Schwartz, P., Braziller, Z., & Golding, B. (2017, September 24). More than 200 protest racism in loud NFL statement. *NY Post*. Retrieved from https://nypost.com/2017/09/24/about-100-protest-national-anthem-in-loud-nfl-statement/

Shear, M. D. (2018, June 4). Trump abruptly calls off Philadelphia Eagles' visit to White House. *The New York Times*. Retrieved from https://www.nytimes.com/2018/06/04/sports/philadelphia-eagles-white-house.html

Simmons, B. (2017, October 13). ESPN can't stick to sports. But can it stick by its talent? *The Ringer*. Retrieved from https://www.theringer.com/bill-simmons/2017/10/13/16469520/espn-jemele-hill-suspension-week-6-nfl-picks

Social media fact sheet. (2018, February 5). *Pew Research Center: Internet and Technology*. Retrieved from http://www.pewinternet.org/fact-sheet/social-media/

Spears, M. (2018, June 6). LeBron James, Stephen Curry agree that next NBA champs won't visit White House. Retrieved from http://www.espn.com/nba/story/_/id/23706091/lebron-james-cleveland-cavaliers-stephen-curry-golden-state-warriors-says-nba-champion-want-white-house-invite

Traina, J. (2017, September 15). White House doubles down on saying Jemele Hill's Tweets were fireable offense. *SI.com*. Retrieved from https://www.si.com/tech-media/2017/09/15/white-house-espn-jemele-hill-fireable-offense-linda-cohn

Turnage, A. K. (2009). Scene, act and the tragic frame in the Duke rape case. *Southern Communication Journal, 74*(2), 141–156. doi: 10.1080/10417940802335946

Turner, J. S. (2013). A longitudinal content analysis of gender and ethnicity portrayals on ESPN's *SportsCenter* from 1999 to 2009. *Communication and Sport, 2*(4), 303–327. doi: 10.1177/2167479513496222

van Dijck, J. (2013). *The cultural of connectivity: A critical history of social media*. New York, NY: Oxford University Press.

Wemple, E. (2017, October 17). ESPN doesn't deserve Jemele Hill. *The Washington Post Blogs*. Retrieved from https://www.washingtonpost.com/blogs/erik-wemple/wp/2017/10/09/espn-doesnt-deserve-jemele-hill/?utm_term=.5a8a25465d76

Withiam, H. (2018, March 8). Michael Smith's exit brings an end to ESPN's "SC6" experiment. *NY Post*. Retrieved from https://nypost.com/2018/03/08/michael-smiths-exit-brings-an-end-to-espns-sc6-experiment/

9. Jemele Hill, Twitter, and ESPN: Thinking Inside the (Potter) Box

Davíd Staton

This above all: to thine own self be true ...

—Hamlet act 1, scene 3

ESPN traverses a news-entertainment tightrope. It has outspoken strong personalities with opinionated takes on the issues of the day, a commitment to high quality sports journalism, as well as the straight ahead 24/7 business of box scores. As a $28 billion business ("Trefis Team," 2018), it also has an equally strong commitment to the financial bottom line. However, in the age of social networks and digital immediacy—an anytime, anywhere atmosphere—the "Worldwide Leader" appears to be struggling to find its balance. The colliding worlds of sports, culture, politics, and ethics have proven to be a sticky entanglement for the network and a few highly visible instances played out on social media have garnered some raised eyebrows in recent years.

Perhaps none of these incidents has been as visible as when the White House entered into the fray regarding Jemele Hill's use of social media, particularly her Twitter posts. When the ESPN personality described Trump as a white supremacist in a tweet on September 11, 2017 (a "fireable offense," said White House spokesperson Sarah Huckabee Sanders) a firestorm of attention erupted and Hill was reprimanded by the network, which distanced itself from her remarks (Nakamura, 2017, para. 2). Less than a month later, Hill took Dallas Cowboys' owner Jerry Jones to task on Twitter for his public position on National Football League (NFL) players kneeling during the National Anthem. In that particular series of tweets, noted below, she called for viewers to stop watching the Cowboys and cease patronizing the team's advertisers. In this instance, following a public rebuke of Hill via a company tweet, ESPN suspended her for a two-week period, as she had violated the network's social media policy (Amatulli, 2017). This chapter will interrogate the ethical implications and dimensions of this situation—did Hill, ESPN, and the audience behave within ethical norms?—by using an ethical decision-making framework known as the Potter Box (Potter, 1969).

Jemele Hill and the Twitter Storm

When Hill came to work for ESPN in 2006, she did so as a national columnist for the network's website, ESPN.com. Prior to her employment with ESPN, she was a beat writer at the *Detroit Free Press* as well as the *Orlando Sentinel*, where she was a sports columnist; columnists differ journalistically from a reporter in that they offer opinions or editorialize, whereas journalists hold steadfast to the ideal of objectivity. In a 2006 interview with the *Columbia Journalism Review*, the publication noted that Hill, then 30 years old, was the sole female African-American working as a sports columnist in the United States (Barrett, 2006). The insights she offered in her role of opinion sharer/shaper were often provocative. For instance, in a description of the ice dancing at the 2006 Winter Olympic games, she wrote "I know ice skating requires coordination, skill and timing, but so does picking your nose and that ain't a sport" (Barrett, 2006, para. 9). When WNBA player Sheryl Swoopes came out, Hill wrote "Lesbians don't pose a threat and have a certain appreciation in a male-dominated culture" (para. 9). ESPN hired Hill with awareness of her ability to be at minimum thought provoking and at most to be controversial.

Writing commentary pieces for the website's "Page 2" column and *ESPN The Magazine*, she retained those qualities as provocateur. In her debut column (November 14, 2006), in which she interviewed herself, she wrote "I also would ask: If former Miami Hurricanes announcer Lamar Thomas were white, would he have ever been given a broadcast job in the first place? His criminal sheet is so long he could have been a foot soldier for Tony Soprano" (Hill, 2006, para. 30). In the same column she noted, "as a columnist, I hope to make you think, piss you off, make you laugh, make you reach for Advil, and make you cry. Mostly, though, I hope to make you read" (Hill, 2006, para. 31). Five years later (December 28, 2011), she began an *ESPN The Magazine* column with this opening salvo, "I don't know why I keep hoping that one day Michael Jordan will grow a conscience" (Hill, 2011, para. 1). Her role with ESPN began to expand to include TV appearances and in 2013 she joined Michael Smith as co-host of *Numbers Never Lie* later rebranded as *His and Hers*. In a press release dated October 27, 2014, ESPN touted the duo and the show's new title:

Since the entertainment world and social dialogue are a passion of the duo, the revised format will be adjusted to allow for the organic inclusion of related topics. The change from *Numbers Never Lie* to *His & Hers* is truly a natural evolution for the program as it has grown over time to showcase more of their opinions while moving away from a focus on data. (Christie, 2014, para. 2)

On September 11, 2017, Hill, who by this time was co-host of the network's *SC6*, offered up some of these opinions. In the late afternoon that day, Hill took to her Twitter account to share this tweet with her 1.02 million followers: "Donald Trump is a white supremacist who has largely surrounded himself w/other white supremacists" (Hill, 2017a).

She followed this tweet almost immediately with "The height of white privilege is being able to ignore his white supremacy, because it's of no threat to you. Well, it's a threat to me" (Hill, 2017b). Four minutes later she tweeted: "Trump is the most ignorant, offensive president of my lifetime. His rise is a direct result of white supremacy. Period" (Hill, 2017c). Within the next two minutes, as detailed in an article in Uproxx (Kalland, 2017), she responded to interjections by various other Twitter account holders, noting:

- "No the media doesn't make it a threat. It IS a threat. He has empowered white supremacists (see: Charlottesville)."
- "He is unqualified to be president. He is not a leader. And if were not white, he never would have been elected."
- "Donald Trump is a bigot. Glad you could live with voting for him. I couldn't, because I cared about more than just myself."
- "And it's funny how you cling to Benghazi but I bet you didn't give one thought to what Trump said about the Central Park 5." (para. 4)

By the next afternoon, ESPN responded via Twitter: "The comments from Hill regarding the President do not represent the position of ESPN. We have addressed this with Jemele and she recognizes her actions were inappropriate" ("ESPN Public Relations," 2017a).

On Wednesday, September 13th during an afternoon news conference, White House Press Secretary Sarah Huckabee Sanders called Hill's tweets, "a fireable offense" (Nakamura, 2017, para. 2). Later that same day, Hill offered up a *mea culpa* via a message to Twitter followers, which reads in part: "My comments on Twitter expressed my personal beliefs. My regret is that my comments and the public way I made them painted ESPN in an unfair light. My respect for the company and my colleagues remains unconditional" (2017d).

All remained well for about a month, then the Hill controversy began in earnest. The uproar from her tweets about Trump had barely subsided when Hill again took to Twitter to opine. This time her target was Dallas Cowboys owner Jerry Jones, who had made statements to the press concerning NFL players kneeling during the playing of the National Anthem. Hill took to Twitter to respond to Jones' remarks as detailed by Amatulli (2017):

- "Don't ask Dak, Dez & other Cowboy players to protest. A more powerful statement is if you stop watching and buying their merchandise" (para. 9).
- "This play always work (sic). Change happens when advertisers are impacted. If you feel strongly about JJ's statement, boycott his advertisers" (para. 16).
- "Just so we're clear: I'm not advocating an NFL boycott. But an unfair burden has been put on players in Dallas & Miami w/anthem directives" (para. 19).

Here, Hill referenced edicts by both Cowboys owner Jones and Dolphins owner Steve Ross that players stand for the National Anthem. Hours later, ESPN announced the two-week suspension of Hill in a tweet:

Jemele Hill has been suspended for two weeks for a second violation of our social media guidelines. She previously acknowledged letting her colleagues and company down with an impulsive tweet. In the aftermath, all employees were reminded of how individual tweets may reflect negatively on ESPN and that such actions would have consequences. Hence this decision. ("ESPN Public Relations," 2017b)

Contextually, it is important to remember that when the calendar on the NFL season had flipped to week four, NFL players kneeling during the National Anthem controversy was in full blossom. During that weekend's (September 24, 2017) slate of games, there were protests league-wide by professional football players prior to taking the field. Members of the 32 teams kneeled and/or linked arms in a show of solidarity; some simply did not take the field during the playing of the anthem. Trump, who had previously weighed in with his sentiment concerning such protests, pronouncing during a September 22nd political rally: "Wouldn't you love to see one of these NFL owners, when somebody disrespects our flag, to say, 'Get that son of a bitch off the field right now. Out! He's fired. He's fired!'" (Jenkins, 2017, para. 4). Two days later Trump took to Twitter to echo his sentiment: "Sports fans should never condone players that do not stand during the National Anthem of their Country. NFL should change policy" (Trump, 2017).

For his part, Dallas Cowboys' owner Jerry Jones shared his opinion a few weeks later in widely-shared post game remarks. On October 8, 2017 Jones told journalists that the league "can't in any way give the implication that we tolerate disrespecting the flag" ("Jerry Jones," 2017, para. 8). Of his own players, he added, "If we are disrespecting the flag, then we won't play. Period" (para 8).

How and why ESPN came to the decision to suspend Hill was not made transparent. However, precedent for such action had previously been established with suspensions of ESPN personalities Curt Schilling and Linda Cohn for speaking out in ways the network considered ill- advised. The Hill suspension raises a slew of research questions with ethical dimensions.

1. If Hill was ostensibly hired to be a provocative host, why would the network publicly censure her for doing what she was being paid to do?
2. If she was doing what she was hired for, did she owe her company an apology for posting tweets to a Twitter account bearing her name?
3. Was Hill acting in the official capacity of a journalist and thereby bound by ethical considerations of the profession when she tweeted?

A framework for ethical decision making may lead to answers to these thorny questions.

The Potter Box

Black and Roberts (2011) offer a number of frameworks for making ethical decisions. They note, "Moral philosophy and normative ethics involves going beyond rules and codes, and utilizing *justification models*" (p. 49). These are ethical formulas or decision-making matrices that can be followed to logical ends. They point to the rotary four-way test, Bok's test of veracity, the TARES test, and particular to the case at hand, the Society of Professional Journalists Model among other justification methods. Stevenson and Peck (2011) suggest a version of Cavanaugh's Double-Effect reasoning model based on the norms of doing good and avoiding evil. Jones (1991) calls for a framework that supplements, but does not replace, other similar models. He dubs this structure the "issue-contingent" model and it explicitly "includes characteristics of the moral issue itself as either an independent variable or a moderating variable" (p. 371). This variable considers the moral intensity of the dilemma; a "construct that captures the extent of issue-related moral imperative in a situation" (p. 372).

While Christians, Fackler, Richardson, Kreshel, and Woods (2016) point out no single ethical perspective or decision-making tool is universal or even transnational. He and other scholars who *do ethics* note the Potter Box's use can "steer media practitioners toward socially responsible decisions that are justified ethically" (p. 31). Watley (2013) champions the Potter Box because its application does not require any advanced formal training in ethical philosophy. As one of the most frequently cited justification models it provides a clear and concise way to examine (and re-examine) ethical issues such as the Hill-ESPN situation (Black & Roberts, 2011).

The Potter Box was designed by Dr. Ralph Potter of Harvard Divinity School between 1958–1963 when the then-PhD candidate was writing his dissertation (Parsons, 2008). The topic of his work concerned how Christians should view nuclear weapons and, via his examination, he created four categories for ethical evaluation. The categories he considered universal to all ethical decisions. For example, imagine two sets of two boxes stacked atop one another side by side forming a quadrant (see Figure 9.1). These are the four boxes, or steps, one navigates while working their way through ethical quandaries. First, the ethical dilemma must be objectively defined in detail. This box is called *definitions*. The second box requires the values related to the situation be identified. What values are in operation that drive the situation? This box is called *values*. Next, a moral principle must be prescribed. Are the values guided by the principles of utilitarianism? The Golden Mean? A professional code of ethics? Some other guiding code? This box is called *principles*. Finally, the definition of loyalties and responsibilities must be addressed. What loyalties exist and why should they be adhered to? This box is called *loyalties*. Following this, a decision can be made as to whether an agent behaved ethically. Given feedback, the decision may be re-evaluated and, once again, the Potter Box may be navigated to refine one's position (Parsons, 2008)

When Potter designed this tool, he proposed that users could mix these steps in order to further fine-tune their decision-making process (Potter, 1969). For instance, one might consider defining the situation whilst identifying the moral principle(s) involved. Or, conversely, one might consider the moral principle(s) involved then define the situation. This sort of cross-examination of the issue might also find one using this framework identifying the values inherent in the ethical dilemma then choosing loyalties or, in reverse order, choosing loyalties to assist in identifying the values of the case (Potter, 1969). An application of the Potter Box to an actual ethical dilemma the researcher has dubbed *The Hill Affair* might clarify the particular fashion in which this decision-making tool might be applied.

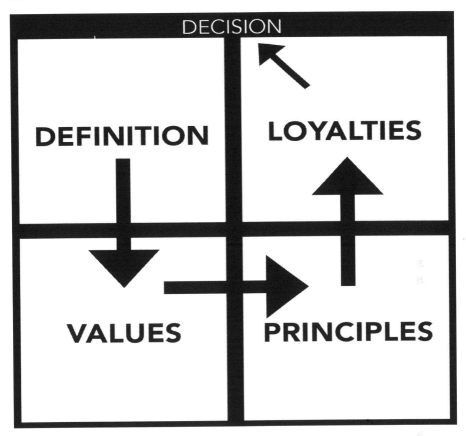

Figure 9.1: The Potter Box.
Source: Kathleen M. Ryan.

One of the significant features of the Potter Box is that it allows for consideration and reconsideration of the ethical dilemma from varying vantages (Parsons, 2008). In this examination, the researcher viewed the situation through a variety of lenses while moving through the quadrants of the framework and interrogate the ethics from the perspective of ESPN, Hill, and the audience.

Ethical situations often demand the sort of multi-faceted approach available by using the Potter Box, which despite the rigid formula or geometry its name might imply, is quite fluid allowing for cross-pollination. A change in ethical principles for instance—moving from the utilitarianism perspective that considers the greatest good for the greatest number of people to consider the same situation from Aristotle's Golden Mean (the balance between extremes)—might shape, reshape, or otherwise inform values or loyalties. Similarly, a change in values can have a bearing on one's loyalties (Parsons, 2008). In the case of *The Hill Affair*, the definition of facts (Hill fired off a series of tweets) that surround the situation remains fairly constant as does the applied principle (an ESPN policy regarding social media use by its employees). What remains in flux in this particular case are the values, loyalties, and ultimately the ethical outcome. What follows are several passes through the Potter Box from the aforementioned stakeholder positions (Parsons, 2008).

The Potter Box and the Hill Affair

The Potter Box begins by establishing the *definition* of the case. These facts remain largely undisputed from the perspective of multiple stakeholders. Hill was an employee of ESPN. Her tweets concerning President Trump and the NFL kneeling controversy resulted in a large public outcry, both in favor and in opposition. She was initially reprimanded by the network after a series of tweets about the President, and then later suspended for two weeks after a second series of tweets concerning NFL players kneeling during the playing of the National Anthem.

The Potter Box next asks for *values* to be determined and evaluated. For the first pass, I consider this from the perspective of ESPN, the self-described "Worldwide Leader in Sports." Because of its reportorial content, ESPN holds among its values those of professional journalistic codes. The network, in fact, has a social media policy, which serves to function as the *principles* section of the Potter Box. At the time Hill made the tweets, she was governed by a policy established in August 2011 with slight revisions made in 2012. ESPN again revisited its social media policy in November 2017 (Steinberg, 2017).

The language of the earlier code, the one that Hill was prescribed to follow, addressed to "talent and reporters," begins:

> ESPN regards social networks such as Twitter, Facebook, message boards, conversation pages and other social sites as important venues for content distribution, user engagement, newsgathering, transparency and the amplification of talent voices. As such, we will hold all talent who participate in social networking to the same standards we hold for interaction with our audiences across TV, radio and our digital platforms. ("Social networking," para. 1)

These guidelines apply to all ESPN talent, anchors, play-by-play, hosts, and analysts. The policy continues:

> Think before your tweet. Understand that at all times you are representing ESPN, and Twitter (as with other social sites) offers the equivalent of a live microphone.

> Simple rule: If you wouldn't say it on the air or write it in a column, don't post it on any social network. ("Social networking," 2011, para. 2)

The guidelines concluding admonition is; "We realize this is a fast moving space and these guidelines will be amended as warranted. Any violation of these guidelines could result in a range of consequences, including, but not limited to, suspension or dismissal" ("Social networking," 2011, para. 12). This stated policy will be revisited as it remains a guiding principle governing the various stakeholders in this scenario. It, along with the definition category, largely remain constants in this particular application of the Potter Box.

There is an intangible here in that employees and employer alike may apply or interpret the principle from a varying ethical perspective (e.g., it does not apply to me or the policy is in effect in this instance). Because of this variant factor I will examine that perspective through the lens of ethical egoism. Ethical egoism calls for a moral agent to do what is in their own self-interest. Ethical egoism claims that the promotion of one's own interests is always in accordance with reason. According to the *Oxford Companion to Philosophy* (Nagel, 1995):

> Egoism can seem true on the basis of a general argument which shows that all these apparently distinct motives, if properly analyzed, are really examples of self-interest after all—that any motive must be. The argument is that every voluntary act is something the person on balance wants to do, something he does because he desires to do it; therefore, he does it in order to satisfy his desire to do it; therefore the act is really self-interested. (p. 220)

Rand (1964) may be the most well-known and outspoken proponent of ethical, or rational, egoism. In the introduction to *The Virtues of Selfishness*, Rand notes, "To redeem both man and morality it is the concept of *'selfishness'* that one has to redeem" (p. X).

This Potter Box then has one remaining box in its quadrant, *loyalties*. ESPN's loyalties in this instance were to its viewers/readers and its parent companies, The Walt Disney Company and Hearst Communications. As an employer, ESPN also must consider loyalty to its employees. In this instance, by disassociating itself from Hill's tweets through public admonishment and suspension, the network acted to protect and preserve its loyalties to viewers and its financial bottom line. ESPNs social media policy clearly contains a section that explains violations may result in consequences including suspension or dismissal. Having navigated one pass of the Potter Box, ESPN—acting within its own self-interest or from a vantage of ethical egoism—seems to have acted ethically in accordance to its values, principles, and loyalties.

Hill and the Potter Box

Taking a second pass through the Potter Box—considering Hill as a stake-holder—may result in a different perspective. The definition of the case remains the same: Hill was an employee of ESPN. Her tweets concerning the NFL kneeling controversy resulted in a public outcry, both in favor and in opposition. She was initially reprimanded by the network after one series of tweets and later suspended for two weeks after the second series of tweets.

The values portion of the Potter Box might now be considered. Hill was an employee of ESPN. Ostensibly she was hired as a journalist by the company and should, accordingly, abide by its social media policy for "talent and reporters." Hill's role as an employee of ESPN fits into the definition (but not clearly or cleanly) of "talent and reporters." There is, after all, a difference in editorial scope of a reporter and one who travels in (thought-provoking) opinion or commentary as Hill demonstrably did. She was hired for her outsized personality and had a journalistic record of having strong takes on sports, politics, and culture. In a "be your brand" social media mindset, Hill was often outspoken and this was known by her reading and viewing audiences and her employer alike. Hill had worth to the network as an outspoken person. Herein, obviously, lies a tension that underscores ESPN's market position as both journalistic and entertainment enterprise. Toward serving her audience and being true to herself, Hill appears to have acted ethically:

> When do my duties to my job end and my rights as a person begin? I honestly don't know the answer to that. I do know that we're clearly living in a time of blurred lines. The president's recent inflammatory attacks on NFL players, his choice to disinvite the Golden State Warriors to the White House are just the latest examples of silence being impossible. This is not a time for retreating comfortably to a corner. (Hill, 2017e, para. 15)

ESPN's social media policy does not expressly forbid the voicing of opinion; it merely asks the employee to think before they tweet and not tweet what they would not say into a microphone. Her utterance, in this case a series of tweets, appears in harmony with the network's social media policy, which advocates for the use of social media for "the amplification of talent voices" (para. 1). As well, it appears congruent with her identity at ESPN as an outspoken personality. The principle, as previously stated, remains the same in this instance: The company had a social media policy implemented as a guideline for employee conduct. Loyalties, along with this change in stakeholder position from network to Hill, vary accordingly. Hill was loyal to her public by being loyal to self. Was she loyal to the social media policy? To this extent it allows for "amplification" of her voice, yes she was. As such, Hill acted ethically, particularly within the parameters of ethical egoism, in which self-interest is the dominant decision-making factor.

Audiences and the Potter Box

Taking a third pass through the Potter Box—considering the audience as a stakeholder—may, again, offer a different perspective. The definition portion of the Potter Box remains the same as previously stated, but is augmented by the audience's broader sense of history. It collectively recalls ESPN's handling of previous, high profile employee suspensions.

To wit, Major League Baseball analyst Curt Schilling was suspended in 2015 from the network for posts on social media comparing Muslims and Nazis. The former Big League pitcher was later fired for a Facebook post viewed as transphobic. Longtime ESPN *SportsCenter* host, Linda Cohn, was suspended for remarks made on *The Bernie and Sid* radio program in April, 2017, which included comments about the network overpaying for sports TV rights and its perception as left-leaning (McCarthy, 2017). Naturally, there was a segment of the audience that decried Cohn's reprimand when it became public and offered it as further proof the network was, indeed, left-leaning.

Given Hill was not suspended following her politically-oriented tweets, Fox News declared ESPN maintained a double standard when it came to the Hill and Cohn transgressions (see Flood, 2017). Days later, Schilling, in an interview with CNN's Michael Smerconish claimed, "I wasn't fired for speaking my mind. I was fired for being a conservative" (Delk, 2017, para. 1). And, in such fashion, the worlds of politics and sports collide. It is nothing new noted the network's Public Editor, or Ombudsman, Jim Brady (2017b) who wrote, "The desire to draw a boundary between sports, culture and politics is a fool's errand. Sport has always intersected with culture and politics. It isn't a recent phenomenon" (para. 4). Rather, what is new is the "perilous" intersection of traditional and social media (Brady, 2017a, para 1). This sticky situation informs the values portion of the Potter Box.

Particular values are expected by the ESPN audience. There is an expectation of the news value of the profession or some adherence to journalistic or objective codes when the network is presenting news-oriented programming. Here again, there are tensions between expectations of the value and its realization. ESPN offers hybrid programming of news and sports, often delivered by employees with opinions, and those opinions may be at variance with those of the audience. As such: is it necessary to be rigidly governed by a journalistic code of ethics such as that offered by the Society of Professional Journalists? Is it necessary to be apolitical? Or, in a crowded marketplace, is it necessary to have a strong take so that one's voice is heard above the din of competing voices? Again, ESPN's Ombudsman Brady weighed in with a relevant column.

> The world—and journalism—continues to evolve rapidly. The classic media model of objectivity has taken significant body blows in the digital age, accelerated in recent years by social media. And with an increasing number of athletes taking political stances, journalists are increasingly finding themselves wading into political waters. (Brady, 2016, para. 19)

There is also an audience expectation of logical values of consistency and competency. In the Hill Affair, this value would apply to the audience's view of her treatment by ESPN officials. The first series of controversial Trump tweets did not result in a suspension whereas the second, which raised the potential of a boycott of advertisers did. This does not seem consistent with ESPN's suspension of Schilling and Cohen, who were each suspended upon their first offense. It is worth noting ESPN is a major broadcast partner of the NFL. With a contract worth $1.9 billion, it is in the network's best interest if the relationship runs smoothly. Hill's tweets may have been interpreted as not acting in the best self-interest of the company's bottom line.

The principle, as with previous stakeholders, remains the same. ESPN had a social media policy in effect that governed "talent and reporters." The specifics of this policy are likely not widely known by the public. However, this did not stop audience members and members of the press from weighing in, both pro and con, once Hill was suspended. Everyone seemed to have a take on her take and this leads to the loyalties quadrant of the Potter Box. The audience's loyalties are driven by individual loyalties. There are those who have an allegiance to the network and, in their eyes, ESPN can do little wrong. Others have taken exception to what they see as the network's lean to the left of the political spectrum. As such, the audience acted neither ethically nor unethically. Rather, the audience acted in its own self-interest.

Sticky Situations and the Hill Affair

Though many viewers, readers, and journalists weighed in on the Hill Affair by referencing the Schilling and Cohn precedents, this is not an apples to apples comparison. Schilling's social media gaffe resulted in his firing; Hill was suspended. Cohn's remarks were made on air (she was interviewed for a radio program). Hill was suspended for her posts on social media. It is worth noting this was, in fact, Hill's second suspension. The other suspension, in 2008, garnered far less fanfare and controversy. In that incident, Hill wrote in a *Page 2* column, "rooting for the Celtics is like saying Hitler was a victim"

(Hill, 2008, para. 9). She was suspended for a week and her offending words were scrubbed from the column. So, along with Cohn, there was precedent for a one strike and you are out type of suspension. The viewing and reading public as well as a White House employee, who claimed a double standard existed for Hill when she was not initially suspended (or fired), largely ignored news of her prior suspension.

Although Schilling's suspension and firing focused on his airing of opinion concerning hot button issues, it appears the Cohn and Hill suspensions do hold in common a reason—they talked about financial decisions made by ESPN. In Cohn's case, she mentioned during the radio interview that she felt the network had overpaid for its licensing contracts including those of the NBA, the Pac-12 Network, and the SEC Network. In the Hill Affair, the tweets she posted concerned viewers tuning out commercial sponsors associated with the NFL. So, fewer eyes on the games could mean fewer advertising dollars. Hill and Cohn's comments directly dealt with the company's financial bottom line. This appears to be a sensitive subject for the network, which has seen its fortunes decline in recent years via a decrease in viewership and advertising sales along with an increase in expenditures for programming (Trefis Team, 2017). For his part, ESPN President John Skipper weighed in with a memo released four days after Hill's Trump tweets that is revealing. After reminding employees there existed social media guidelines, he continued, "We had a violation of those standards in recent days and our handling of this is a private matter. As always, in each circumstance we look to do what is *best for our business*" [emphasis added] (Holloway, 2017, para. 4).

Decidedly, what is not good for business is having employees question what is best for business as both Cohn and Hill did using public channels, radio and social media respectively. However, suspending the two was compatible with ESPNs social media guidelines and ethical egoism, in which self, or business, comes first. The action was neither deserved nor undeserved; it was self-serving. Further, Hill acted in her own self-interest, taking and giving voice to an ethical stance, whilst not specifically violating any of the company's social media codes that were in existence at the time. The audience members for her tweets, naturally, included both critics, those who considered Hill out of line and fans, those who thought Hill's assessment was correct. They spoke their minds and this too is ethically compatible with self-interest, which is at the core of ethical egoism.

The Potter Box offers a way to negotiate ethical meaning(s) and outcomes from a variety of perspectives until a decision regarding those ethics can be arrived upon. In this instance, the outcomes appear to justify the behavior of various stakeholders. Ethical behavior appears to have been observed by all parties. ESPN retained its appearance of being in control of its employees while protecting its own assets. Hill, in a testament of being true to self, stood by what she said, telling TMZ Sports in late October, 2017: "I put [ESPN] in a bad spot the truth of it is I regret the position [I put] the people I work with in, the position I put the show in. I put them in a bad spot. That's the truth. I will never take back what I said" (Callahan, 2017 para. 6). Finally, the audience was able to voice its opinion of vested self-interests.

With a different application of an ethical interpretation of the principle, say a utilitarianism perspective in which the greater good is central, the Potter Box findings might turn out differently. If the guiding principle was the revised social media policy—as noted, it has been reworded since the Hill suspension—the outcome might change. If one were to adopt an ethical perspective differing from the ethical egoism offered here, again, a different outcome might unfold. However, what likely is not going to change is the public's watchfulness and handling of ESPN's next *Hill Affair*. Will ESPN take bold, decisive steps when the next offender of its social media policy becomes a public controversy? Self-interest, or the bottom line, likely will dictate how it reacts. However, if it navigates the Potter Box to inform its decision, ESPN may well come up with a reasoned response. For example, the network might examine its own social media policy, which lies at the heart of the issue herein, as an ethical test case. In a hypothetical situation utilizing the Potter Box, the initial step requires that the definition must be set forth. In this imaginary case, an ESPN on-air personality has posted an item to a social media platform that invites public controversy. The facts, or definition, of the case can be simply established. It is the next steps in the Potter Box where things become more complicated. In identifying the values that define its social media policy, the network seeks to impose a unilateral policy applicable to a variety of journalists. The values of a color commentator are not those of a host of ESPN's *SportsCenter* and those values differ again for an employee such as Hill, who is, effectively, paid to be a provocateur and paid to have an active public, social media presence as such. In short, ESPN might question whether a one-size-fits-all policy is really on brand. Different social media platforms carry with them different expectations.

There are further complications moving on to the next step in the Potter Box, principles. The social media policy, as written, allows for only the self-interest of the network and, thereby, could curb or cripple personally held beliefs or moral positions held by its employees. The final step in the Potter Box, loyalties, poses nearly identical problems as encountered in principles. Loyalty to whom and by whom? The ultimate loyalty–to oneself–may be compromised by these guidelines. And, what of loyalty to an audience that expects a certain tone and angle from a specific personality? They, too, are due a loyalty that again may clash with the stated social media policy

In order for ESPN to remain a dominate force in sports network programming the social media policy needs to be revisited. The hyper competitive tone set by the 24/7 news cycle requires the social media policy to be more fluid and less rigid. It also should allow for its personalities to retain their personality.

References

Amatulli, J. (2017, October 9). Jemele Hill suspended from ESPN for 2 weeks after social media "violation." *HuffPost*. Retrieved from https://www.huffingtonpost.com/entry/jemele-hill-suspended-from-espn-for-two-weeks-after-social-media-violation_us_59dbccb6e4b0208970ceeaf2

Barrett, L. (2006, July 7). Jemele Hill on being black, female, young—and on the sports page. *Columbia Journalism Review*. Retrieved from https://archives.cjr.org/behind_the_news/jemele_hill_on_being_black_fem.php

Black, J., & Roberts, C. (2011). *Doing ethics in media: Theories and practical applications*. New York, NY: Taylor & Francis.

Brady, J. (2016, December 1). Inside and out, ESPN dealing with changing political dynamics. *Espn.com*. Retrieved from http://www.espn.com/blog/ombudsman/post/_/id/767/inside-and-out-espn-dealing-with-changing-political-dynamics

Brady, J. (2017a, February 13). The common sense approach to social media. *Espn.com*. Retrieved from http://www.espn.com/blog/ombudsman/post/_/id/805/the-common-sense-approach-to-social-media

Brady, J. (2017b, April 12). Like it or not, ESPN isn't sticking to sports. *Espn.com*. Retrieved from http://www.espn.com/blog/ombudsman/post/_/id/831/not-sticking-to-sports-the-right-move-for-espn

Callahan, Y. (2017, October 21). Jemele Hill on ESPN suspension: "I put ESPN in a bad spot." *TheRoot*. Retrieved from https://www.theroot.com/jemele-hill-on-espn-suspension-i-put-espn-in-a-bad-spo-1819741779

Christians, C., Fackler, M., Richardson, B., Kreshel, P., & Woods, R. (2016). *Media ethics: Cases and moral reasoning*. New York, NY: Routledge.

Christie, J. (2014, October 27). ESPN's numbers never lie will change to his & hers with Michael Smith and Jemele Hill on November 3. Retrieved from https://espnmediazone.com/us/press-releases/2014/10/espn2s-numbers-never-lie-will-change-to-his-hers-with-michael-smith-and-jemele-hill-on-november-3/

Delk, J. (2017, September 16). Curt Schilling says it's frustrating ESPN fired him and not Jemele Hill. *The Hill*. Retrieved from http://thehill.com/blogs/blog-briefing-room/351009-curt-schilling-cnn-host-spar-over-political-correctnes

ESPN Public Relations [ESPNR]. (2017a, September 12). The comments from Hill regarding the President do not represent the position of ESPN. We have addressed this with Jemele and she recognizes her actions were inappropriate. [*Tweet*]. Retrieved from https://twitter.com/espnpr/status/917469637033512960?lang=en

ESPN Public Relations [ESPNPR]. (2017b, October 9). Jemele Hill has been suspended for two weeks for a second violation of our social media guidelines. She previously acknowledged letting her colleagues and company down with an impulsive tweet. In the aftermath, all employees were reminded of how individual tweets may reflect negatively on ESPN and that such actions would have consequences. Hence this decision [*Twitter* Post]. Retrieved from https://twitter.com/ESPNPR/status/917469637033512960/photo/1?ref_src=twsrc%5Etfw&ref_url=https%3A%2F%

Flood, B. (2017). ESPN's double standard shows when hosts speak out. *Foxnews.com*. Retrieved from http://www.foxnews.com/entertainment/2017/09/13/espns-double-standard-shows-when-hosts-speak-out.html

Hill, J. (2006). I'm hearing voices. *ESPN.com Page 2*. Retrieved from http://webcache.googleusercontent.com/search?q=cache:9v1w_ZGFL4YJ:www.espncom/espn/page2/story%3Fpage%3Dhill/061115%26lpos%3Dspotlight%26lid%3Dtab-2pos1+&cd=1&hl=en&ct=clnk&gl=us&client=firefox-b-1-ab

Hill, J. (2007, December). The Celtics' rise fuels feelings of old times. *ESPN.com Page 2*. Retrieved from http://www.espn.com/espn/page2/story?page=hill/071226&sportCat=nba

Hill, J. (2008, June 15). Deserving or not, I still hate the Celtics. *ESPN.com Page 2*. Retrieved from http://www.espn.com/espn/page2/story?page=hill/080614

Hill, J. (2011, December, 28). Jordan, Nike need to stem violence. *ESPN, The Magazine*. Retrieved from http://www.espn.com/espncommentary/story/_/id/7393317/michael-jordan-nike-do-more-stem-violence

Hill, J. [JemeleHill]. (2017a, September 11). Donald Trump is a white supremacist who has largely surrounded himself w/other white supremacists. [*Tweet*]. Retrieved from https://twitter.com/jemelehill/status/907391978194849793

Hill, J. [JemeleHill]. (2017b, September 11). The height of white privilege is being able to ignore his white supremacy, because it's of no threat to you. Well, it's a threat to me. [*Tweet*]. Retrieved from https://twitter.com/jemelehill/status/907392229290934272

Hill, J. [JemeleHill]. (2017c, September 11). Trump is the most ignorant, offensive president of my lifetime. His rise is a direct result of white supremacy. Period. [*Tweet*]. Retrieved from https://twitter.com/jemelehill/status/907392229290934272

Hill, J. [JemeleHill]. (2017d, September 13). My comments on Twitter expressed my personal beliefs. My regret is that my comments and the public way I made them painted ESPN in an unfair light. My respect for the company and my colleagues remains unconditional. [*Tweet*] Retrieved from https://twitter.com/jemelehill/status/908173152370520064/photo/1?ref_src=twsrc%5Etfw&ref_url=https%3A%2F%2Fwww

Hill, J. (2017e, September 27). Jemele Hill on doing the right thing: A lesson from her grandmother; Be better. No matter what. *The Undefeated*. Retrieved from https://theundefeated.com/features/jemele-hill-on-doing-the-right-thing/

Holloway, D. (2017, September 15). ESPN's John Skipper says Jemele Hill violated social-media policy with Trump tweets. *Variety.* Retrieved from https://variety.com/2017/tv/news/john-skipper-jemele-hill-1202560723/

Jenkins, A. (2017, September 23). Read President Trump's NFL speech on national anthem protests. Retrieved from http://time.com/4954684/donald-trump-nfl-speech-anthem-protests/

Jerry Jones: Cowboys "will not play" if they disrespect flag . (2017, October 8). *USA Today.* Retrieved from https://www.usatoday.com/story/sports/nfl/2017/10/08/jerry-jones-nfl-cant-tolerate-players-disrespecting-flag/106456604/

Jones, T. (1991). Ethical decision making by individuals in organizations: An issue-contingent model. *Academy of Management Review, 16*(2), 231–248. doi: 10.2307/258867

Kalland, R. (2017, September 12). ESPN released a statement following Jemele Hill's Twitter tirade about "bigot" Donald Trump. *Uproxx.* Retrieved from https://uproxx.com/sports/espn-jemele-hill-twitter-donald-trump-white-supremacist-statement/

McCarthy, M. (2017, April 28). "SportsCenter" anchor Linda Cohen: Politics hurting ESPN. *SportingNews.com.* Retrieved from http://www.sportingnews.com/us/other-sports/news/linda-cohn-sportscenter-espn-layoffs-new-york-post-the-bernie-and-sid-show-wabc/xti6exskx6wp19v8pegqu7quz

Nagel, T. (1995). Egoism, psychological. In T. Honderich (Ed.), *The Oxford companion to philosophy* (p. 220). New York, NY: Oxford University Press.

Nakamura, D. (2017, September 13). White House: ESPN's Jemele Hill should be suspended for calling Trump "a white supremacist." *The Washington Post.* Retrieved from https://www.washingtonpost.com/news/post-politics/wp/2017/09/13/white-house-espns-jemele-hill-should-be-fired-for-calling-trump-a-white-supremacist/?noredirect=on&utm_term=.e0ff736f0de9

Parsons, P. J. (2008). *Ethics in public relations: A guide to best practices.* Philadelphia, PA: Kogan Page.

Potter, R. (1969). *War and moral discourse.* Louisville, KY: John Knox Press.

Rand, A. (1964). *The virtue of selfishness.* New York, NY: Signet Press.

Social networking for talent and reporters. (2011, August). *ESPN Front Row.* Retrieved from http://www.espnfrontrow.com/wp-content/uploads/2011/08/social-networking-v2-2011.pdf

Steinberg, B. (2017 November 3). ESPN unveils new social media guidelines for staff after Jemele Hill controversy. *Variety.* Retrieved from https://variety.com/2017/tv/news/espn-social-media-guidelines-jemele-hill-1202606411/

Stevenson, S., & Peck, L. (2011). "I am eating a sandwich now": Intent and foresight in the twitter age. *Journal of Mass Media Ethics, 26*(1), 56–65. doi.org/10.1080/08900523.2010.512823

Trefis Team. (2017, November 10). ESPN remains a drag on Disney. *Forbes.* Retrieved from https://www.forbes.com/sites/greatspeculations/2017/11/10/espn-remains-a-drag-on-disney/#71f361f62f79

Trefis Team. (2018, March 15). With subscriber declines continuing, how much is ESPN worth? *Forbes*. Retrieved from https://www.forbes.com/sites/greatspeculations/2018/03/15/with-subscriber-declines-continuing-how-much-is-espn-worth/#7ec-9cfabe3c9

Trump, D. [realDonaldTrump]. (2017, September 24). Sports fans should never condone players that do not stand during the National Anthem of their Country. NFL should change policy! [*Tweet*] Retrieved from https://twitter.com/realDonaldTrump/status/912080538755846144

Watley, L. (2013, Dec. 9). Training in ethical judgement with a modified Potter Box. *Business Ethics: A European Review, 23*(1), 1–14. doi:10.1111/beer/12034

10. *Adapting to the Digital Age: ESPN's Crisis Communication During the 2015 and 2017 Layoffs*

J. SCOTT SMITH

ESPN spent the 1990s and 2000s creating a cable juggernaut, reaching its peak of more than 100 million households subscribing in 2011 (Gaines & Nudelman, 2017). Since 2011, the number of households with ESPN has drastically dwindled each year (down to 86 million subscribers in 2018) as rising cable and satellite costs along with cheaper digital alternatives have led people to disconnecting their service, often referred to as cord-cutting (Draper, 2016; Littleton, 2018). 2013 would represent a turning point for the cable industry as the number of people dropping cable each year has out-numbered the amount of people purchasing cable TV services ("Cutting the Cord," 2016). In response to the changing media marketplace and declin-ing subscriber numbers, ESPN held two significant layoffs in October 2015 (Sandomir, 2015) and in April 2017 (Drape & Barnes, 2017), demonstrating the once-seemingly invulnerable sports cable giant now faced a questionable future as digital media were changing the landscape.

This analysis examines crisis communication strategies engaged in by ESPN to explain the layoffs as the cable company adapted to the chang-ing economic realities of the digital age. The 2015 and 2017 layoffs were prompted by Disney, ESPN's parent company, calling for the sports cable network to trim $100 million in operational costs in 2016 and another $250 million in 2017 (McIntyre, 2015). No longer the media juggernaut of the 1990s and 2000s, the layoffs, including some high-priced talent, illustrated that ESPN acknowledged the cable network would not retain the same profit margins in the digital age. To better understand how ESPN communicated these changes with the public, this analysis employs Benoit's

(2015) image repair theory to examine the crisis communication strategies ESPN engaged in 2015 and again in 2017 to reassure stakeholders and returning employees. After determining what image repair strategies ESPN employed, this analysis will evaluate if ESPN's discourse satisfied Brinson and Benoit's (1999) conditions needed for a successful use of a separation strategy.

Sports Image Repair

Scholars have identified sports crisis communication as a legitimate area of inquiry, which has primarily focused on attacks against individual athletes (Benoit & Hanczor, 1994; Blaney, Lippert, & Smith, 2013; Brazeal, 2008; Brown, Dickhaus, & Long, 2012; Frederick, Burch, Sanderson, & Hambrick, 2014; Glantz, 2010; Jerome, 2008; Nelson, 1984; Walsh & McAllister-Spooner, 2011). Recently, scholarship has turned its attention to sports organizational crisis communication. Present research on sports organizations' crisis communication efforts has examined Indy Car's image repair after a series of driver deaths (Pfahl & Bates, 2008), labor relations between Major League Baseball and the players union (Meyer & Cutbirth, 2013), the National Hockey League's apologetic discourse during the 2004–2005 lockout (DiSanza, Legge, Allen, & Wilde, 2013), FIFA's response to their 2015 corruption scandal (Onwumechili & Bedeau, 2016), the NFL's response to the Ray Rice domestic violence scandal (Smith & Keeven, 2018), and Duke University's response to the men's lacrosse team scandal (Barnett, 2008; Fortunato, 2008; Len-Rios, 2010). These studies reveal that organizations responding to a crisis in a timely manner and that relied on corrective action were more likely to be successful in their image repair efforts.

Separation Strategy

In addition, sports organizations also relied on separation strategies that distanced the organization from the accused actor or group, which has been extensively studied in organizational crisis communication. In the midst of crisis and scandal, organizations have a history of trying to distance the actions of a single person or group from the organization (Benoit & Lindsey, 1987; Benson, 1988; Brinson & Benoit, 1999; Coombs & Schmidt, 2000; Holtzhausen & Roberts, 2009; Snyder & Foster, 1983; Tyler, 1997). A separation image repair strategy uses a combination of bolstering, shift the blame, and corrective action (see Table 10.1) to demonstrate that the acts of particular employees do not represent the attitudes, thoughts, or actions of the organization (Brinson & Benoit, 1999). Brinson & Benoit identified three conditions needed for a successful use of a separation strategy: "The organization should show that the offensive action violated company policy, the scapegoats must be physically and symbolically separated from the organization, and corrective action must be instituted to prevent future violations of company policy" (p. 507). In the sports context, Len-Rios (2010) detailed the Duke University's successful use of a separation strategy that attacked both the media and the district attorney, bolstered the university's commitment to learning and diversity, and suspended the lacrosse team for the entire season. Fortunato (2008) also found that responding to a crisis in a timely manner demonstrated the organization understood the magnitude of the crisis, the importance the crisis would hold to the general public and stakeholders, and that the organization needed to attend to allegations promptly. In all, scholarship has found organizations that successfully employed a separation strategy identified and disassociated deviant members from the organization.

Given ESPN's unique circumstances that the crisis was derived from the changing media landscape and not from deviant employees, this chapter aims to expand on current separation scholarship to include an organization attempting to mitigate the crisis by arguing the separation of employees is the result of changing organizational circumstances. Commonly, an organization shifts the blame of a crisis to the actions of an employee or employees (Brinson & Benoit, 1999; Len-Rios, 2010; Tyler, 1997), which would attempt to separate the organization from the crisis and protect its image. In contrast, ESPN explained the crisis was a result of a changing media context (transcendence) and not a result of employee error or malice, which meant shifting the blame was not a viable image repair strategy to employ. Some ESPN anchors proactively asked to renegotiate their contracts and take less money to stay at ESPN (McCarthy, 2017b). Even though anchors sought to salvage their careers at ESPN by taking less money, the layoffs were also seen as symbolic for investors. A TV insider stated, "[ESPN's] not growing. So the only way to show fiscal responsibility is to lay people off. This is all Wall Street-driven. This is all about Disney ordering a Code Red" (as cited in McCarthy, 2017b, para. 13). Given that ESPN's layoffs were driven by their profit margins and not misdeeds committed by their employees, this article explores the effectiveness of ESPN's attempt to incorporate the image repair strategy transcendence (placing the deed in a larger or different context) within its separation strategy.

Method

This article examines ESPN's discourse in two ways. First, this study utilizes Benoit's (2015) image repair theory to determine what image repair strategies used in conjunction with the October 2015 and April 2017 layoffs. The strategies are denial (simple denial, shifting the blame), evasion of responsibility (provocation, defeasibility, accident, good intentions), reducing offensiveness of the event (bolstering, minimization, differentiation, transcendence, attack accuser, compensation), corrective action, and mortification (see Table 10.1). Second, after determining what strategies ESPN used, this analysis will evaluate if their efforts satisfied Brinson and Benoit's (1999) conditions needed for a successful use of a separation strategy. To mitigate the damage from the layoffs, ESPN would need to bolster its credentials as an innovative media organization, employ corrective action to prevent future layoffs, and in ESPN's case, demonstrate the crisis emanated from the changing media landscape and not executive incompetence.

Table 10.1: Image restoration strategies.

Strategy	Characteristic	Example
Denial Simple denial	Did not perform the act or act is not harmful	Weiner: I did not send that illicit photo
Shift the blame	Another performed the offensive act	A madman poisoned Tylenol capsules
Evasion of Responsibility Provocation	Offense was a response to the bad act of another	Gave tax breaks to prevent another state from luring business away.
Defeasibility	Lack of information or ability to prevent offense	W Bush: Bad intelligence to blame for justification for War in Iraq.
Accident	Mishap	Could not see your car when I hit it.
Good Intentions	Meant well	Reagan (I-C): My heart and best intentions tell me I did not trade arms for hostages

Strategy	Characteristic	Example
Reducing the Offensiveness Bolstering	Stress good traits and deeds	Clinton (Drug Record): We've asked for more money and treatment to stop drug abuse.
Minimization	Portray offense as less serious than it appears	Clinton (WW): Happened years ago
Differentiation	Portray offense as less offensive than similar acts	I borrowed your car, I didn't steal it
Transcendence	More important values	Clinton (Lewinsky): I need to go back to work for the American people.
Attack Accuser	Reduce credibility of accuser	Limbaugh (Sandra Fluke): This woman is a useful idiot.
Compensation	Reimburse victim	BP reimburses victims of Deep Water Horizon spill
Corrective action	Plan to solve/prevent offense from reoccurring	Reagan (I-C): New CIA director, new national security advisor, new procedure
Mortification	Apologize and express remorse	Hugh Grant apologizes to Elizabeth Hurley

Note. Adopted from: Benoit (2015) p. 28.

Analysis

Driven by ESPN President John Skipper's comments in October 2015 and April 2017, ESPN adapted a separation strategy that relied on the image repair strategy transcendence as opposed to shifting the blame to explain ESPN's layoffs. This strategy was consistently used throughout statements and questions about the layoffs in October 2015 and April 2017. This analysis focuses on Skipper's October 21, 2015, memo to employees ("Message from John Skipper," 2015), his January 20, 2016, interview with the *Wall Street Journal* (Amol & Ramachandran, 2016), his April 26, 2017 memo to employees ("John Skipper message," 2017), and an April 26, 2017, "content evolution strategy" authored by seven ESPN executives.[1] In these statements, Skipper and ESPN executives used an adapted separation strategy that included bolstering, transcendence, and corrective action.

Bolstering

Skipper and ESPN executives used bolstering in four ways. First, ESPN thanked the employees losing their jobs for their service. Skipper stated in his October 2015 memo:

> The people who will be leaving us have been part of ESPN's success, and they have our respect and appreciation for their contributions. We will be as support-ive as we can during this transition, including providing a minimum of 60-days notice, a severance package reflective of their years of service, and outplacement benefits to help them find future employment. ("Message from John Skipper," 2015, para. 4)

During the announcements of the April 2017 layoffs, Skipper also thanked employees for their contributions but did not discuss severance packages or any other statements of support for ex-employees.[2] Skipper stated in his April 2017 memo, "These decisions impact talented people who have done great work for our company. I would like to thank all of them for their efforts and their many contributions to ESPN" ("John Skipper mes-sage," 2017, para. 1). Skipper's statements sought to bolster ESPN and his leadership by acknowledging the contributions employees made to the most successful sports cable channel in history. This appeal was most likely aimed at returning employees, as Skipper noted, "There is no question that it [layoffs] creates issues of morale" (as cited in Amol & Ramachandran, 2016, p. B1).

Second, ESPN bolstered its image by arguing that adapting to change has been a hallmark of ESPN's historical success. Yet, ESPN's appeals were inconsistent between his October 2015 memo and his January 2016 inter-view with the *Wall Street Journal*. Skipper stated in his 2015 memo, "Our 36 years of continuous growth and success has been driven by our consistent willingness to reimagine our future, to embrace change and make the right choices for our business" ("Message from John Skipper," 2015, para. 2). In contrast, Skipper told the *Wall Street Journal*, "We are still engaged in the most successful business model in the history of media, and see no reason to abandon it" (as cited in Amol & Ramachandran, 2016, p. B1). These incon-sistencies in statements illustrates that Skipper believed ESPN only needed tweaks to its business model and not wholesale changes given his steadfast belief the organization would remain successful through its traditional deliv-ery systems.

Third, ESPN bolstered its image by highlighting the organization's ability to deliver content through various media. Skipper told the *Wall Street Journal*, "We're going to be delivering our content through the traditional cable bundle, through a lighter bundle, through Dish's Sling TV, through new over-the-top distributors, and through some content that is direct-to-consumer" (as cited in Amol & Ramachandran, 2016, p. B1). In 2017, ESPN executives also lauded the company's ability to provide sports content to viewers. The executives' memo stated, "Our goal continues to be to maximize our unparalleled scale in every medium with storytelling that stands out and makes a difference. We are well-equipped to thrive going forward by embracing these themes" (Donoghue et al., 2017, para. 8). In each statement, Skipper bolstered his network's image by suggesting the company possessed the resources and the wherewithal to adapt to the shifting media marketplace.

Fourth, Skipper argued that ESPN executives took the decision to dismiss employees seriously and that the future plans of the organization were transparent to returning employees, thus bolstering the organization. Skipper stated in his October 2015 memo, "We carefully considered and deliberated alternatives before making each decision … I realize this process will be difficult—for everyone—but we believe the steps we are taking will ultimately create important competitive advantages for our business over the long term" ("Message from John Skipper," 2015, para. 9–10). Skipper expanded on the decision-making process in his interview with the *Wall Street Journal*. In response to a question about the loss of subscribers, Skipper stated,

> We stayed pretty calm. [The loss of subscribers] didn't come as a bolt out of the blue to us. We had been thinking about this. We had a big town hall meeting in December. We had a priorities meeting earlier where we gathered everybody together to try to ground ourselves in our business. People want pragmatic, optimistic leadership. They want to hear you have a plan. They want to hear that particularly in light of layoffs. A little sturm und drang in the environment doesn't matter relative to our performance—it matters to our investor relations guys. It doesn't have to matter to me. (as cited in Amol & Ramachandran, 2016, p. B1)

If accepted by audiences, particularly returning employees, Skipper's statements about the seriousness with which ESPN's leadership took with regards to the layoffs and the future of the company might mitigate the damage of the crisis.

Transcendence

Along with bolstering, Skipper used transcendence to contextualize the layoffs for audiences. To reduce the offensiveness of the crisis, Skipper sought to characterize the layoffs as collateral damage from the changing media market. He stated in his October 2015 memo, "The demand for sports remains undiminished, though the landscape we operate in has never been more complex" ("Message from John Skipper," 2015, para. 1). Skipper continued to echo these remarks in his January 2016 interview with the *Wall Street Journal*, stating,

> You have to kind of look every so often at how you're organized and do you need Job Y that you have had for 22 years. At a certain point you need people who do new things, so you've got to be straight with people … Those issues tend to be pretty transient because we continue to grow and continue to be in a good position. (as cited in Amol & Ramachandran, 2016, p. B1)

Skipper's statements in response to the October 2015 layoffs demonstrated ESPN understood cord-cutting represented a threat to their business model and that emerging context, and not mismanagement by ESPN, represented the cause of the layoffs.

In April 2017, Skipper and ESPN executives further relied on transcendence to explain the layoffs through the changing media marketplace. Skipper provided an expansive response in his April 2017 memo, stating,

> Our objective in all we do is to best serve fans and their changing consumption habits while still maintaining an unparalleled and diverse talent roster that resonates with fans across all our platforms. We will continue to foster creativity and investment in the products and resources necessary to embrace the opportunities that lie ahead. ("John Skipper message," 2017, para. 2)

ESPN executives affirmed Skipper's statements by also focusing on how audiences are receiving content through various mediums. The executives' memo stated, "In short, given how fans' habits are changing, our focus continues to be providing high-quality, distinctive content at any minute of the day on any screen" (Donoghue et al., 2017, para. 2). The focus on audiences' evolving consumption habits in the 2017 memos illustrated that ESPN had a stronger grasp of the issues stemming from the declining desire for cable/satellite services, resulting in greater levels of cord-cutting.

Corrective Action

Skipper and ESPN executives paired their use of transcendence with corrective action to better position the organization for the future. Skipper stated in his October 2015 memo, "Beginning today, we will be enacting a number of organizational changes at ESPN to better support our future goals—a process that will include the elimination of a number of positions, impacting friends and colleagues across the organization" ("Message from John Skipper," 2015, para. 3). Skipper added in his 2015 memo, "These changes are part of a broad strategy to ensure we're in position to make the most of new opportunities to build the future of ESPN" ("Message from John Skipper," 2015, para. 5).[3] When asked by the *Wall Street Journal* how ESPN could cope with changes in the industry, Skipper stated, "You can do games with fixed cameras and robotic cameras. You send fewer people to do production of a game now, because you can do a lot more back here [in Bristol]" (as cited in Amol & Ramachandran, 2016, p. B1). These statements illustrated that ESPN was committed to allocating fewer resources and using more remote technology in the future to balance the losses from fleeing subscribers. The removal of production elements placed greater emphasis on on-air talent providing premium and unique content for audiences.

In 2017, Skipper frankly discussed the changes ESPN would be making with regards to on-air talent. He stated in the 2017 memo:

> Dynamic change demands an increased focus on versatility and value, and as a result, we have been engaged in the challenging process of determining the talent—anchors, analysts, reporters, writers and those who handle play-by-play—necessary to meet those demands. We will implement changes in our talent lineup this week. ("John Skipper message," 2017, para. 1)

In addition to addressing on-air talent, Skipper discussed content changes in the 2010s and called for continued innovation. He stated in his 2017 memo, "Our content strategy—primarily illustrated in recent months by melding distinct, personality-driven *SportsCenter* TV editions and digital-only efforts with our biggest sub-brand—still needs to go further, faster ... and as always, must be efficient and nimble" ("John Skipper message," 2017, para. 1). Skipper's April 2017 statements illustrated that the changes ESPN made after the 2015 layoffs were not as successful as desired. His contention that the content "needs to go further, faster" that ESPN was still searching for the right shows and on-air talent to return to the prominence of the late 1990s and early 2000s (para. 1).

Echoing Skipper's comments, ESPN executives also used corrective action to detail how the company is changing its content and its delivery systems to compete with the changing media market. The executives' memo stated,

> Perhaps the most noted example of this strategy is our recent approach to our flagship program, *SportsCenter*. *SportsCenter with Scott Van Pelt*, the launch of *SC6 with Michael Smith and Jemele Hill*, and the debut of more digital-only content socially and on our App means *SportsCenter* in its many forms is easily accessible, informative and primed with personality. (Donoghue et al., 2017, para. 3)

In addition to changing content, ESPN executives described how the delivery of that content was evolving as well. The executives' memo stated, "Our evolving ESPN App is the best mobile destination for sports fans ... and on the horizon is more live news video and enhanced video and audio streaming" (para. 4). The executives discussed various improvements in ESPN's delivery content which included ESPN's "multi-screen approach around big events,"[4] providing greater access to sideline reporters and analysts during telecasts,[5] add more coverage and behind-the-scenes focus on their premiere shows,[6] and a renewed focus on investigative journalism shows.[7] The executives' focus on "personality" illustrated that ESPN leadership was still trying to find the right combination of on-air talent to content format to reconnect with audiences that are cutting the cord.

Evaluation

This section evaluates ESPN's image repair discourse with regards to the plausibility and of the strategies used and external data. First, this section will determine if ESPN's adapted separation strategy satisfies Brinson and Benoit's (1999) three conditions required of a successful separation strategy. In addition, polling data will be used to assist in evaluating ESPN's separation strategy in October 2015 and April 2017.

An argument can be made that ESPN's adapted use of a separation strategy was an appropriate strategy in 2015, but lost credibility when ESPN had two subsequent rounds of layoffs in 2017. Rather than shifting the blame to employees that "violated company policy" (Brinson & Benoit, 1999, p. 507), ESPN used transcendence to argue the changing media context, not poor leadership, was the reason for the layoffs in 2015 and 2017. ESPN explained the physical separation of employees from the company was a difficult, yet necessary component of ESPN's future. ESPN's use of bolstering suggests the network was "driven by our consistent willingness to reimagine our future" was appropriately paired with corrective action that mapped a new future with regards to content and delivery ("Message from John Skipper," 2015, para. 2). Yet, these initial cuts would be panned by critics that saw ESPN's corrective action as a shameless move that focused on profitability above content. Robert Silverman (2015) of The Daily Beast opined:

> ESPN's going to ride or die with "Stick to Sports," a dismissive shorthand for anyone who might suggest a connection between the sports world and economics or politics or any social racial or gender issues, that it's not just box scores and harrumphing about Tom Brady's "legacy." But in ESPN's mind, that's the winning formula. The rest of us have lost. (para. 19–21)

Silverman's criticism was derived from the layoffs and Skipper's decision to end Grantland, ESPN's highbrow sports and culture website created by Bill Simmons. Ironically, ESPN's decision-making after the 2015 layoffs did not match the "Stick to Sports" ethos as demonstrated by Caitlyn Jenner winning the Arthur Ashe Courage Award at the 2015 ESPYs, Curt Schilling being fired for posting controversial comments about Muslims and transgendered individuals on social media in 2016 (Hiebert, 2017), and *SportsCenter* host Jemele Hill calling President Donald Trump a "white supremacist" on social media (Gaines & Nudelman, 2017). As *National Review* columnist Dan McLaughlin (2017) concluded, "This is why 'stick to sports' is not just good manners for sports journalism, it's good business advice" (para. 7).

After the April 2017 layoffs, *New York Daily News* columnist Bob Raissman (2017) also criticized ESPN's talent decisions and overall leadership. He quoted an anonymous industry executive who stated, "Face it, you couldn't pick any of the current (*SportsCenter*) anchors out of a police lineup" (Raissman, 2017, p. 48). Raissman argued the leadership at ESPN could not be introspective when facing declining subscribers, concluding, "When the whip eventually came down at ESPN, and comes down again, those running the joint don't publicly self-examine and call their own lousy decisions into question" (p. 48). The criticism of Skipper and ESPN executives illustrates that while they may have been successful in mitigating the damage of the layoffs through bolstering and transcendence, they failed to deliver on-air talent that would connect with audiences across mediums as promised.

Polling data supported media criticism that on-air talent and ESPN's TV shows underwhelmed audiences. A March 7–14, 2017 Barrett Sports Media scientific poll found that only 34% of respondents thought ESPN's on-air talent was "solid" with 40% describing the talent as "underwhelming," and 19% describing on-air talent as "terrible" (McCarthy, 2017a). Respondents were also disappointed with the current state of ESPN TV shows with 52% of respondents stating the shows were "weak" and only 3% stated they "loved" their programming. Additionally, a May 2, 2017, YouGov scientific poll revealed that respondents' positive perception of ESPN has continually dropped since April 2013 (Heibert, 2017). Based on an impression measure that asks respondents to range their positive or negative impression (scores ranging from –100 to 100) of ESPN, the poll found that in April 2013 ESPN had an impression number of 60, which dropped to 41 by July 2017. When separated for partisanship, Republicans (32 impression rating in April 2013; 16 rating in April 2017) have moved away from ESPN and Democrats have declined in their support of ESPN as well (28 rating in April 2013; 24 in April 2017). Additionally, 25% of the respondents polled stated they were considering canceling their service to ESPN in the future. YouGov data journalist Paul Hiebert (2017) concluded, "Whether ESPN's programming has become more liberal in recent year or not is beside the point; the figures suggest that enough Republicans believe it has, and this belief has ostensibly contributed to their diminished view of the sports network" (para. 9). This polling data revealed that ESPN was unable to return to a "Stick to Sports" model, which inevitably alienated some audiences and had inhibited ESPN's ability to successfully adapt to the changing media landscape.

Implications

After examining ESPN's crisis communication discourse, this chapter offers two implications with regards to sports organizational crisis communication. First, organizations can adapt a separation strategy when the organization must reduce its labor force due to changing market forces. Brinson and Benoit (1999) noted that successful uses of a separation strategy depend on three conditions. First, the organization should establish that the employee violated corporate policy; second, the offenders should be symbolically and physically separated from the organization; and third, the company should take corrective action to avoid similar violations in the future. As opposed to traditional uses of a separation strategy, ESPN relied on bolstering, transcendence, and corrective action in response to their 2015 and 2017 layoffs. Rather than shifting the blame to deviant employees, ESPN used transcendence to explain the layoffs were in response to the changing media marketplace, suggested ESPN needed to replace some of its current labor force with employees that could adapt to emerging technology, and suggested on-air talent, content, and delivery changes in response to declining subscribers. By placing the layoffs in a broader context, ESPN visualized future success for stakeholders and returning employees that would be undoubtedly concerned about the layoffs.

Second, this chapter supports previous research (Fortunato, 2008; Meyer & Cutbirth, 2013; Pfahl & Bates, 2008) that sports organizations that respond to a crisis in a timely manner and rely on corrective action are more successful in their image repair efforts. Skipper's initial use of corrective action detailed a specific and transparent plan for how the organization was going to be successful in the future. This strategy may have been more successful if the content and talent decisions after the 2015 layoffs presented a more successful "Stick to Sports" ethos that ESPN championed in the 1990s. Consistent with Furgerson and Benoit (2013), Skipper's image repair was effective for primary stakeholders (Disney executives) but would not repair ESPN's image with conservative audiences that perceived ESPN as promoting a liberal bias (Hiebert, 2017). Polling data (McCarthy, 2017a) and sagging TV ratings (McLaughlin, 2017) revealed that ESPN misfired on their content and talent decisions as they adapted slowly to the digital age, which may have deepened ESPN's subscriber crisis. Skipper's assertion in 2015 that ESPN was successful at change was undermined when the company had two more rounds of significant layoffs in 2017. Even though corrective action was the appropriate strategy and delivered well by Skipper, ESPN subsequently made poor talent and content decisions that weakened the effectiveness of Skipper's 2015 use of corrective action.

In the immediate future, ESPN will remain the "Worldwide Leader in Sports" due to its extensive television rights deals with various college and professional leagues, but its hallmark in the 1990s and 2000s was its ability to find talent and provide formats for that talent to flourish. If ESPN's responses to the October 2015 and April 2017 layoffs portends its future, its days of dominance in providing premium content from on-air talent are far less certain.

Notes

1. Not included in this analysis is Skipper's (2017) November 29, 2017, perfunctory memo to employees about further layoffs. The memo reads: "Today we are informing approximately 150 people at ESPN that their jobs are being eliminated. We appreciate their contributions, and will assist them as much as possible in this difficult moment with severance, a 2017 bonus, the continuation of health benefits and outplacement services. They will also appreciate your support. The majority of the jobs eliminated are in studio production, digital content, and technology and they generally reflect decisions to do less in certain instances and re-direct resources. We will continue to invest in ways which will best position us to serve the modern sports fan and support the success of our business."

2. ESPN executives' statement mirrored Skipper's use of bolstering. The April 2017 ESPN executive memo stated, "Tied to the news ESPN President John Skipper shared with ESPN employees this morning, we first wanted to thank our colleagues for their collective contributions" (Donoghue et al., 2017, para. 1).

3. Skipper bullet-pointed the initiatives in the memo, which included: "Constant and relentless innovation, including integrating emerging technology into all aspects of our business. Enhancing our sales and marketing efforts with new tools and techniques that generate greater data, personalization and customization for our advertisers. Integrating our distribution efforts to better serve current and future distribution partners with our industry leading networks and services" ("Message from John Skipper," 2015, para. 6–8).

4. "There are numerous examples this year of ESPN's multi-screen approach around big events, ranging from the College Football Playoff Championship Megacast, the NBA Sidecast, the Tournament Challenge and Fantasy Football Marathons, and the Women's Final Four" (para. 5).

5. The executives' memo stated, "And at the start of NFL free agency, ESPN3's show featured 'Schefter Cam' while ESPN.com and the App were providing extensive clips featuring our NFL reporters and analysts, and ESPN2 wrapped it up with a comprehensive show" (para. 5).

6. The executives' memo stated, "And on the immediate horizon, three days of NFL Draft TV coverage will be complemented with even more online (which can be personalized to match a fan's favorite team), the cover package of *ESPN The Magazine*, *Mike & Mike*, and *First Take* on location, behind-the-scenes coverage on Instagram stories and more" (para. 6).

7. The executives' memo stated, "In May, two of our biggest journalism brands— *Outside the Lines* and *E:60* — will relaunch with an emphasis on increased collaboration and a larger presence digitally, socially, and across all our screens" (para. 6).

References

Amol, S., & Ramachandran, S. (2016, January 20). Boss talk: ESPN executive goes on offense—President John Skipper delves into cable cord-cutting, Grantland and leading through layoffs. *Wall Street Journal*, B1.

Barnett, B. (2008). Framing rape: An examination of public relations strategies in the Duke University lacrosse case. *Communication, Culture, & Critique*, *1*(2), 179–202. doi:10.1111/j.1753-9137.2008.00018.x

Benoit, W. L. (2015). *Accounts, excuses, and apologies: A theory of image repair theory and research* (2nd ed.). Albany, NY: State University of New York Press.

Benoit, W. L., & Hanczor, R. S. (1994). The Tonya Harding controversy: An analysis of image restoration strategies. *Communication Quarterly*, *42*(4), 416–433. doi:10.1080/01463379409369947

Benoit, W. L., & Lindsey, J. J. (1987). Argument strategies: Antidote to Tylenol's poisoned image. *Journal of the American Forensic Association*, *23*(3), 136–146.

Benson, J. A. (1988). Crisis revisited: An analysis of strategies used by Tylenol in the second tampering episode. *Central States Speech Journal*, *39*, 49–66. doi:10.1080/10510978809363234

Blaney, J. R., Lippert, L. R., & Smith, J. S. (Eds.). (2013). *Repairing the athlete's image: Studies in sports image restoration*. Lanham, MD: Rowman & Littlefield.

Brazeal, L. M. (2008). The image repair strategies of Terrell Owens. *Public Relations Review*, *34*, 145–150. doi:10.1016/j.pubrev.2008.03.021

Brinson, S. L., & Benoit, W. L. (1999). The tarnished star: Restoring Texaco's damaged public image. *Management Communication Quarterly*, *12*(4), 483–510. doi:10.1177/0893318999124001

Brown, K., Dickhaus, J., & Long, M. (2012). LeBron James and "the decision": An empirical examination of image repair in sports. *Journal of Sports Media*, *7*, 149–175. doi: 10.1353/jsm.2012.0010

Coombs, W. T., & Schmidt, L. (2000). An empirical analysis of image restoration: Texaco's racism crisis. *Journal of Public Relations Research*, *12*(2), 163–178. doi: 10.1207/S1532754XJPRR1202_2

Cutting the cord: Television is at last having its digital-revolution moment. (2016, July 16). *The Economist.* Retrieved from https://www.economist.com/news/business/21702177-television-last-having-its-digital-revolution-moment-cutting-cord

DiSanza, J. R., Legge, N. J., Allen, H. R., & Wilde, J. T. (2013). The puck stops here: The NHL's image repair strategies during the 2004–2005 lockout. In J. R. Blaney, L. R. Lippert, & J. S. Smith (Eds.), *Repairing the athlete's image: Studies in sports image restoration* (pp. 319–358). Lanham, MD: Lexington Books.

Donoghue, M., Druley, S., King, R., Kosner, J., Magnus, B., Schell, C., & Williamson, N. (2017, April 26). ESPN's content evolution strategy. *EspnFrontRow.* Retrieved from https://www.espnfrontrow.com/2017/04/espns-content-evolution-strategy/

Drape, J., & Barnes, B. (2017, April 27). ESPN, its brand lagging, sheds several big names. *New York Times,* B8.

Draper, K. (2016, November 8). ESPN is hemorrhaging subscribers and pretending it doesn't matter. *Deadspin.* Retrieved from https://deadspin.com/espn-is-hemorrhaging-subscribers-and-pretending-it-does-1788618362

Fortunato, J. (2008). Restoring a reputation: The Duke University lacrosse scandal. *Public Relations Review, 34,* 116–123. doi: 10.1016/j.pubrev.2008.03.006

Frederick, E. L., Burch, L. M., Sanderson, J., & Hambrick, M. E. (2014). To invest in the invisible: A case study of Manti Te'o's image repair strategies during the Katie Couric interview. *Public Relations Review, 40,* 780–788. doi:10.1016/j.pubrev.2014.05.003

Furgerson, J. L., & Benoit, W. L. (2013). Limbaugh's loose lips: Rush Limbaugh's image repair after the Sandra Fluke controversy. *Journal of Radio & Audio Media, 20*(2), 273–291. doi:10.1080/19376529.2013.823971

Gaines, C., & Nudelman, M. (2017, September 16). ESPN has lost nearly 13 million subscribers in 6 years, but it is not as bad as it sounds. *Business Insider.* Retrieved from: http://www.businessinsider.com/espn-losing-subscribers-not-ratings-viewers-2017-9

Glantz, M. (2010). The Floyd Landis doping scandal: Implications for image repair discourse. *Public Relations Review, 36*(2), 157–163. doi:10.1016/j.pubrev.2009.09.002

Hiebert, P. (2017, May 3). Conservatives seem to be turning away from ESPN. Retrieved from https://today.yougov.com/news/2017/05/03/Conservatives-seem-to-be-turning-away-from-ESPN/

Holtzhausen, D. R., & Roberts, G. F. (2009). An investigation into the role of image repair theory in strategic conflict management. *Journal of Public Relations Research, 21*(2), 165–186. doi:10.1080/10627260802557431

Jerome, A. M. (2008). Toward prescription: Testing the rhetoric of atonement's applicability in the athletic arena. *Public Relations Review, 34*(2), 124–134. doi: 10.1016/j.pubrev.2008.03.007

John Skipper message to ESPN employees. (2017, April 26). Retrieved from https://espnmediazone.com/us/john-skipper-message-espn-employees/

Len-Rios, M. E. (2010). Image repair strategies, local news portrayals and crisis stage: A case study of Duke University's lacrosse team crisis. *International Journal of Strategic Communication, 4,* 267–287. doi:10.1080/1553118X.2010.515534

Littleton, C. (2018, November 21). ESPN loses 2 million subscribers in fiscal 2018. *Variety*. Retrieved from https://variety.com/2018/biz/news/espn-disney-channel-subscriber-losses-2018-1203035003/

McCarthy, M. (2017a, March 31). Is ESPN too liberal? New poll finds 60 percent think network leans left. *Sporting News*. Retrieved from http://www.sporting-news.com/other-sports/news/espn-liberal-bias-bob-iger-disney-jason-barrett-bar-rett-sports-media/1vkiau005ud0i135hcxdg6wxat

McCarthy, M. (2017b, April 26). "Bloodbath" in Bristol: ESPN could cut 70 people. *Sporting News*. Retrieved from http://www.sportingnews.com/other-sports/news/espn-layoffs-espn2-mike-greenberg-mike-golic-sportscenter-am-katie-nolan-charis-sa-thompson-fs1-jamie-horowitz-john-skipper/1qyp55nrppaub1omvedncxtmfg

McIntyre, J. (2015, September 21). Layoffs are coming to ESPN. *USA Today Sports*. Retrieved from https://thebiglead.com/2015/09/21/layoffs-are-coming-to-espn/

McLaughlin, D. (2017, April 26). ESPN layoffs should be a wake-up call about politi-cizing sports. *National Review*. Retrieved from https://www.nationalreview.com/corner/espn-layoffs-stick-sports/

Message from John Skipper to ESPN employees. (2015, October 21). Retrieved from https://espnmediazone.com/us/174517-2/

Meyer, K. R., & Cutbirth, C. W. (2013). No pepper: Apologia and image repair in the 2002 labor negotiations between major league baseball and the players association. In J. R. Blaney, L. R. Lippert, & J. S. Smith (Eds.), *Repairing the athlete's image: Studies in sports image restoration* (pp. 267–282). Lanham, MD: Lexington.

Nelson, J. (1984). The defense of Billie Jean King. *Western Journal of Speech Communica-tion, 48*, 92–102. doi:10.1080/10570318409374144

Onwumechili, C., & Bedeau, K. (2016). Analysis of FIFA's attempt at image repair. *Com-munication and Sport, 5*, 407–427. doi:10.1177/2167479516633843

Pfahl, M. E., & Bates, B. R. (2008). This is not a race, this is a farce: Formula One and the Indianapolis Motor Speedway tire crisis. *Public Relations Review, 34*, 135–144. doi:10.1016/j.pubrev.2008.03.019

Raissman, B. (2017, April 17). Leader no more: After cuts, ESPN just like the rest in media world. *New York Daily News*, 48.

Sandomir, R. (2015, October 21). ESPN to lay off 300 workers, reacting to shifts in sports viewing. *New York Times*. Retrieved from: https://www.nytimes.com/2015/10/22/business/media/espn-to-lay-off-300-workers-reacting-to-shifts-in-sports-viewing.html

Skipper, J. (2017, November 29). John Skipper's memo to ESPN employees. Retrieved from https://www.espnfrontrow.com/2017/11/john-skippers-memo-espn-employees/

Smith, J. S., & Keeven, D. (2018). Creating separation from the on-field product: Roger Goodell's image repair discourse during the Ray Rice domestic violence case. *Com-munication & Sport, 20*, 1–18. doi:10.1177/2167479518769896

Snyder, L., & Foster, L. G. (1983). An anniversary review and critique: The Tylenol crisis. *Public Relations Review, 9*, 24–34. doi:10.1016/S0363-8111(83)80182-9

Tyler, L. (1997). Liability means never being able to say you're sorry. *Management Communication Quarterly, 11*, 51–73. doi:10.1177/0893318997111003

Walsh, J., & McAllister-Spooner, S. M. (2011). Analysis of the image repair discourse in the Michael Phelps controversy. *Public Relations Review, 37*(2), 157–162. doi:10.1016/j.pubrev.2011.01.001

Section Three

Changes and Challenges in the Sports Media Programming Environment

11. The Present (But Not Future) ESPN Ombudsman: Levying Accountability Through the Inception of the Digital Age

Xavier Ramon, José Luis Rojas Torrijos, and Andrew C. Billings

Ombudsman (*n*): an official appointed to investigate individuals' complaints against maladministration, especially that of public authorities.

"Candor and responsibility in a democracy is very important. Hypocrisy has no place."

—Alan Dershowitz

For the longest time, the moniker for journalism was quite simple: If one wished to succeed, one must be first, be best, or be different. Structures for advancing in the labor force were much more apparent; strong work would rise. Then the Internet laid all those assumptions bare, inequivalently monetizing (and, hence, valuing) the first, from the best, from the different. Even in the sports world, breaking a story became being a minute ahead of the competition, rather than a day and the "increasingly complex digital media landscape" (Boyle & Haynes, 2014, p. 85), became increasingly difficult to decipher (Hutchins & Boyle, 2017). In this context of "digital plenitude" (Hutchins & Rowe, 2009), sports journalists faced severe challenges, including "commercial and economic restrictions" (English, 2017, p. 534), "greater demands in terms of publishing platforms, technology, content and workloads" (English, 2016, p. 1002) and "growing competition from content aggregators and 'social' news specialists" (Hutchins & Boyle, 2017, p. 499).

In the process, sports not only became big business, sports became the only business that truly resonated in a mass way. Ratings for television shows were cut by more than half; newspaper circulations plummeted—and yet, ratings for the World Cup, Super Bowl, and Olympics continued to climb. And, there was one media company that rose above all others: ESPN, fairly dubbed the "Worldwide Leader in Sports" if for no other reason than no other entity could ably levy a counterclaim. ESPN knew it was the behemoth and also knew it was much more than an entertainment company, breaking news that frequently had hard news elements and doing so to a mass audience. In 2005, acknowledging that with great power comes great responsibility, ESPN assigned George Solomon the title of first "Ombudsman," functioning much like a referee: Decreeing things fair or foul with little focus on the economic, social, or political ramifications embedded in such judgments.

Because the sports newsroom has been argued to contain "cheerleaders, hero worshippers, fans, homers and sycophants" that are "biased and responsible for boosterism of athletes, teams, organizations and the sports industry" (English, 2017, p. 532), the role of the Ombudsman was deemed exceedingly important. The dissolution of the frontiers between facts and comments was regarded as commonplace at this point (Boyle, 2006), and this was before the advent of social media options that blurred such divisions even further. Interplay between media and the sport industry led to questions as to whether sports journalists were properly covering the "problems, issues and topics that permeate the social world to which sport is intimately connected" (Rowe, 2007, p. 400). To maintain credibility, ESPN wished to fill that potential void with an Ombudsman whose role would be demonstrably different from any other ESPN employee.

ESPN's "status as a cultural icon and ultimate authority on sports" (Banagan, 2011, p. 159) seems undisputable. However, even ESPN concurs that this does not mean the organization, its content, and its journalistic and managerial practices should be exempt from critical scrutiny. Given the role ESPN plays in conveying messages about social issues (Coche, 2013; Kian, Mondello, & Vincent, 2009) and yet often could be accused of having conflicts of interests (Ott, 2012; Vogan, 2015) where athletes, leagues, and other sports entities become "inextricably intertwined, for they operate under the same set of governing philosophies" (Banagan, 2011, p. 157).

Hence, there was the need for accountability. Lest ESPN become the embodiment of the fear of sports journalism, namely it become a "bastion of easy living, sloppy journalism and 'soft' news" (Boyle, 2006, p. 1), the Ombudsman served the role of ensuring that sports journalism exhibited the standard of being "accountable to the professional norms that advance the entire profession's credibility" (Hardin & Zhong, 2010, p. 6).

According to McQuail (2003), "accountable communication exists where authors (originators, sources, or gatekeepers) take responsibility for the quality and consequences of their publication, orient themselves to audiences and others affected, and respond to their expectations and those of the wider society" (p. 19). For 13 years, six ESPN Ombudsmen collectively served in this role. However, on May 9, 2018 the company decided to discontinue this position, stating that "the position had outlived its usefulness, largely because of the rise of real-time feedback of all kinds" (Merida, 2018, para. 2). If video killed the radio star, social media appeared to have effectively killed the need for an ESPN Ombudsman. With the role of Ombudsman discontinued, this chapter will reflect on its value to examine how it fostered both criticism and transparency while helping fans understand ESPN's journalistic culture and the editorial criteria behind the content. The body of material on which our qualitative analysis rests refers to all the columns (N = 153) written by the representatives in the post between 2005 and 2018 (George Solomon, Le Anne Schreiber, Don Ohlmeyer, The Poynter Institute, Robert Lipsyte, and Jim Brady). The articles composing the sample were systematically collected from the ESPN website and then examined through qualitative content analysis (Bryman, 2016). Doing so provided insight into the range of issues covered by Ombudsman representatives and evaluate the ways in which they handled users' "complaints, questions or remarks about the content" (van Dalen & Deuze, 2006, p. 461) of the network.

The Ombudsmen/Public Editors

George Solomon

George Solomon is a former Sports Editor and Columnist at *The Washington Post* (1975–2003) and was the first Ombudsman for ESPN for two years (2005–2007). During his tenure, he wrote 17 columns on ESPN's website.

Solomon placed a heavy emphasis on issues of ethics, often linking reporting with commentary. He criticized the network for airing *Bonds on Bonds*, a reality series on baseball star Barry Bonds, for not making clear the difference between information and opinion. As Solomon argued, "an impending business relationship between ESPN Original Entertainment and San Francisco Giants slugger Barry Bonds seems to be pushing the envelope for what's an acceptable practice for a network that prides itself on newsgathering, reporting, commentary and analysis" (Solomon, 2006a, para. 1). Solomon (2006b) also argued the network was too driven by ratings, stating "ESPN needs more journalism, less sensationalism" (para. 1).

Moreover, in response to the repeated refrain from some that ESPN should "stick-to-sports," Solomon contended ESPN should give ample time to racial remarks and social and political issues when they are noteworthy. He also analyzed readers' complaints with regard to ESPN's bias when selecting games from Eastern teams and covering athletes accused of using performance-enhancing drugs. He contended there could be more investigation on cases like NFL wide receiver Terrell Owens's suspension and cycling's Lance Armstrong's doping case (Solomon, 2005). In his last column, Solomon (2007) wrote:

> ESPN's impact, breadth and reach in the sports world–on television, radio, the Internet and in print with its magazine and book division–is, of course, huge. The innovative technical skills, ability, intelligence and journalistic efforts of so many ESPN staffers never stopped amazing me. Their work often sets the agenda for sports media around the country and the world. But, on occasion, those attributes were offset by company decisions and ego-driven actions that ignored and violated basic journalistic standards and ethics, angering many ESPN viewers, listeners and readers. Not to mention the ombudsman. (para. 3–4)

Le Anne Schreiber

Le Anne Schreiber was a former sports editor for *Time* magazine and Editor-in-chief of *Women Sport's Magazine*. She then joined *The New York Times* sports department and, in 1980, became Deputy Editor of the newspaper's book review. In 2007, she became the new Ombudsman for ESPN. She wrote 26 columns until March 2009.

Since the beginning of her tenure, Schreiber called out ESPN for its conflicts of interests and the demoralizing effect of too much self- and cross-promotion. As Schreiber (2007a) commented:

> I wish ESPN would consider adding to its lineup a crisp, half-hour, nightly news version of *SportsCenter*—just news and highlights, without gimmicks or sponsored segments or recaps, without self- or cross-promotion, with a consistent anchor team accountable for a consistent tone, with spare to no use of instant commentary. A prime-time island of clean, clear, straightforward news on which ESPN's journalistic credibility could securely rest. (para. 31)

She also observed too much opinion and speculation, arguing that "factuality has been devalued in 24/7 sports media" (Schreiber, 2007b, para. 10). As she highlighted, "if you look at the proportion of airtime and cyberspace devoted to reporting fact versus delivering opinion on ESPN, ESPN.com and ESPN Radio, it is clear that the main function of sports news is to serve as the molehill on which mountains of opinion are built" (para. 10). This advanced her ultimate thesis that "we don't have news cycles anymore. We have opinion cycles" (para. 10).

Ultimately, she led the case for advancing ESPN's standards and practices, using the warrant that:

> ESPN's many layers of editors and producers are not all on the same page, not even about some basic principles that define the nature of a journalistic enterprise. Without a formal, written handbook of guidance and policy, there is not much chance they ever will be, and the price for that will be paid in avoidable suspensions, apologies and erosion of credibility. (Schreiber, 2008a, para. 41)

ESPN soon answered her call. As Schreiber (2008b) explained, John Walsh, ESPN's Senior Vice President and Executive Editor, formed a committee, headed by Patrick Stiegman, Vice President and Executive Editor/Executive Producer of ESPN.com, to create a standards and practices guidebook, addressing such topics as sourcing, attribution of credit in reporting, editorial/advertising relationships and conflicts of interest. There was a second committee, headed by Gary Hoenig, Editorial Director of ESPN Publishing, establishing commentary guidelines.

Finally, Schreiber (2008c) echoed the sentiments of Solomon regarding ESPN's ideal role on issues of social justice, claiming that "ESPN is right to engage, not avoid, racial matters in sports." However, she used her last column to warn of inherent biases within the company, claiming that "overcoverage of the favored few teams and players not only kills joy through its sheer tedium, it is also the root of fan grievances about bias, about cross-promotion, and about corporate conflict of interest" (Schreiber, 2009, para. 20).

Don Ohlmeyer

Don Ohlmeyer (1945–2017) began his career in 1967 with ABC Sports, where he produced and directed three Olympics broadcasts, including the Munich 1972 Olympics. Later, he moved to NBC as Executive Producer of the sports division. He served as ESPN Ombudsman for 18 months (2009–2011), writing 14 columns. In his first article, Ohlmeyer (2009) defined the Ombudsman as "a person who investigates complaints," (para. 1) firmly establishing that the biggest challenge for ESPN was respecting, serving, and listening to the audience. This was a consistent theme throughout his tenure.

The most complex issue he had to address was perceived conflicts of interest hosting *The Decision*, ESPN's LeBron James primetime special in which he announced his decision to leave Cleveland Cavaliers and sign with the Miami Heat. Ohlmeyer discussed the internal conflict between the network's business side and the newsgathering side. He noted two big mistakes made by

ESPN: Allowing James to designate Jim Gray as the interviewer and the fact that the program could have been handled in five minutes instead of delaying the announcement until 28 minutes into the show (Ohlmeyer, 2010a).

Beyond this case, Ohlmeyer (2010b) challenged sportscasters to be more accountable and egoless when reporting. Unequivocally, he specifically delineated guidelines for on-air commentary, arguing functions should be:

> Identifying the competitors, giving enhanced background information, pointing out key turning points in the contest, creating and adjusting the storyline of the competition, providing the analysis of why things are happening on the field, providing proper context, and folding in informative elements that enhance the viewing experience. (para. 11)

Linking to the work of his predecessors, he also demanded that journalists to avoid malpractices such as conflicts of interest, advertising on violent movies/video games, or reporting using anonymous sources (Ohlmeyer, 2010c).

Finally, Ohlmeyer (2010d) commended the formal establishment of ESPN's editorial guidelines, dubbing them "an important effort to address transparency, integrity, fairness, propriety and responsibility" (para. 53).

The Poynter Review Project Blog

The Poynter Institute for Media Studies is a non-profit school for journalism founded in 1975 located in St. Petersburg, Florida. They agreed with ESPN to create a panel of faculty called the Poynter Review Project, who wrote 38 columns between 2011 and 2012. The panel's contributors were Kelly McBride, Regina McCombs, and Jason Fry.

Early in the tenure of the Poynter Review Project, ESPN issued a revised *Standards and Practices* manual, addressing many contemporary issues, including social media protocols and guidelines for avoiding conflicts of interests. Those guidelines were received with mixed feelings by the panel, as they argued they were "an important step forward and will go a long way toward bolstering the network's image as an organization concerned with integrity and credibility ... there is too much wiggle room carved out to accommodate big stars" (McBride & McCombs, 2011, para. 4).

From the beginning, the Poynter Review focused on the need to give more exposure to women's sport. They praised ESPN's Women's Soccer World Cup coverage (McBride, 2011a) and positively reflected on the launch of espnW. However, they also reminded readers that "in spite of efforts to hire and promote women on air and behind the scenes," ESPN was "branded as a men's network," composed by "male-dominated shows and culture" (McBride, 2011b, para. 29).

Beyond gender, the Poynter Review Project highlighted the unnecessary self-involvement of journalists in their stories. As they unequivocally explained, "journalists and other ESPN employees sit on a perch of influence. So they have an enormous reach. They should take that role seriously. When you become part of the story, you lose your ability to tell an independent story" (McBride, 2012a, para. 12).

The Poynter Review Project also considered how social media—especially Twitter—was changing the way ESPN broke news and connected to fans, urging the network to revise their policies in these respects (Fry, 2012a). Likewise, the Poynter Review Project underlined the need to revise the standards for linking to other organizations' stories. As Fry (2012b) argued:

> Links are intrinsic to responsible aggregation, simultaneously serving as sound journalism ethics and good customer service. They aren't just a courtesy but a way to show your work, whether it's giving credit in a news story or linking to an opposing viewpoint so readers can judge whether an opinion piece was fair. (para. 28)

Finally, McBride (2012b) critically commented on ESPN's attitude towards rumors: Claiming ESPN was seeking to find a common ground between a "high-minded organization" and a "tabloid," concluding "ESPN straddles the line, serving up a serious helping of rumors, yet staying away from the most shaky, most sordid whispers" (para. 7).

Robert Lipsyte

Robert Lipsyte is an American sports journalist who started his career in 1957 as an editorial assistant for *The New York Times*. Throughout his career, he has written for *The New York Post* and *USA Today* and has been a correspondent for CBS and NBC. In 2013, he was appointed as ESPN Ombudsman, months after the Poynter Review project ended. In the 25 columns he wrote during his appointment, Lipsyte promoted thoughtful discussion on a myriad of issues, focusing particularly on two main areas: conflicts of interest and diversity.

Regarding conflicts of interest, Lipsyte reflected on ESPN's "dueling journalism and profit motives" (Lipsyte, 2013a, para. 17), in covering football concussion investigations. Particularly, he focused on the fact that ESPN had removed its brand from a two-part documentary by *Frontline* (PBS) titled *League of Denial: The NFL's Concussion Crisis*. Lipsyte argued that ESPN could be proud of its contributions to the program, but posed the following question: "How far can ESPN go reporting on the NFL, the network's most important sports partner?" (Lipsyte, 2013e, para. 4).

Lipsyte also commented on "ESPN's ambivalence toward its role as the putative leader of sports journalism" (Lipsyte, 2014a, para. 19) in covering many other competitions in which the company has business interests. As Lipsyte (2014a) highlighted:

> College football and basketball, for example, are important revenue producers for the company. Extensive investigative reporting into the exploitation of college athletes, and the legal battles around that, would seem to conflict with ESPN's business model. How do you turn over the rocks in the Southeastern Conference, for instance, while owning the SEC Network? (para. 4)

Regarding diversity, Lipsyte urged ESPN "to make a greater effort on more platforms to report and explain, finding voices within and outside the company to offer perspective and context" (Lipsyte, 2014c, para. 23). Lipsyte (2013b) criticized the network's coverage of professional basketball player Jason Collins's announcement coming out as gay, believing discussion between commentators on personal religious beliefs became a distraction from the news and wondering "why ESPN did not do more to advance the Collins story or at least connect more dots to other sports stories, perhaps even link to the gay struggle for equal rights" (para. 24). In addition, Lipsyte (2013c) stimulated the discussion on racism, reflecting on the use of the Washington Redskins team name. He also advocated to tackle sexist comments within the company (Lipsyte, 2013d).

Enhancing readers' understanding of the company's assets was another of Lipsyte's core concerns. He reflected on ESPN's relationship with affinity sites, including FiveThirtyEight, Grantland, ESPN Films, ESPNFC.com, and espnW. Regarding the news desk organization, he explained to readers that ESPN would need "better trained and empowered production staff" (Lipsyte, 2014d, para. 61) and "a senior staff willing to stand up to pressure groups and a standards-and-practices editor, sort of a pre-Ombudsman, alerting, coaching and needling the pack to be smarter, less entitled and more sensitive" (para. 61).

Jim Brady

Jim Brady is a former sports and executive editor at WashingtonPost.com and Editor-in-chief of Digital First Media, who joined the ESPN Ombudsman post on November 2015. At this point, the network updated its title to "Public Editor" to "better reflect the goal of transparency and advocacy for fans, especially in this increasingly multimedia world" (Hall, 2015, para. 4).

Throughout his appointment, which ended in March 2018, Brady published 33 articles. He pursued a much more wider approach than his predecessors, both in the range of topics covered and the inclusion of further voices from readers and representatives within the company. In his first two columns (Brady, 2015, 2016a), he encouraged readers to send their views and questions through email and brand-new social media handles on Twitter and Facebook. He later answered those queries through columns such as, "Your Questions Answered: How *30 for 30* films, *SportsCenter* anchors are chosen" (Brady, 2016b), where he reflected on this shift of focus: "I wanted to make sure readers were active participants in the discussion around ESPN, its journalism and its future … You deserve more than insight into how ESPN produces journalism—though the role of internal critic still rightfully stands" (para. 3). In order to "facilitate communication between the audience and the network's senior executives" (Brady, 2016c, para. 2), a Question & Answer was held with Connor Schell, ESPN's Senior Vice President (Brady, 2016d).

One of the main issues of debate during Jim Brady's appointment was ESPN's perceived shift toward infusing political stories into coverage. Despite recognizing "the separation of sports and politics has always been a fantasy" he highlighted that, "if ESPN continues to let its personalities debate the issues of the day but finds a way to better balance those conversations, it will be richer for it" (Brady, 2016e, para. 65).

The discussion on politics and ESPN's perceived leaning towards the political left came to the forefront after Jemele Hill's tweets on Donald Trump calling him a white supremacist. As the Public Editor emphasized: "In journalism, we're expected to be cautious, thorough and thoughtful. And even though she is a commentator and not a news reporter, she's still a journalist, and I don't think she met that standard here" (Brady, 2017a, para. 18). After Hill's suspension over a second controversy, Brady (2017b) reminded readers that "it's not the job of journalists to skip past facts and go straight to inflammatory labels" (para. 29). Afterwards, he commented on the revised social media guidelines for ESPN reporters launched after the case (Brady, 2017c).

In his mission to explain readers the strategic decisions behind the company, Brady closely examined the issues that led to Grantland's demise, commenting on the progress and challenges regarding sportswomen at ESPN (Brady, 2016f, 2017d). He also provided insight on the creation of The Undefeated (Brady, 2016g) and the rationale behind ESPN's investment in esports (Brady, 2016h). Arguing that a loosening of standards had taken place with the treatment of *The Body Issue* photographs, Brady (2016i) argued that "it's not just nudity where ESPN has relaxed a bit" (para. 13). As he pointed out, "the use of profanity—while far from common—is used in higher frequency on ESPN's sites, in The Mag and even on air" (para. 13). He praised ESPN's "willingness to experiment on the digital front" (Brady, 2018a, para. 1) and argued that *SportsCenter* would be helped by being seen in more plat-forms (2018b).

That being said, Brady (2016j) was also critical with some of the new avenues taken by ESPN, such as the expanded coverage of WWE: "pro wrestling is simply well-performed fiction. For a news organization, I think this is a poor fit, and one that comes with real risk" (para. 5). In terms of transparency, as Brady (2018c) highlighted in his last column, "no one expects the network to openly discuss everything inside its walls, but there are times when ESPN has hurt itself publicly by not explaining decisions or failing to make important corrections in a timely manner" (para. 47). Other suggestions provided by Brady in his last column include: engaging better with consumers, staying away from "easy clicks," focusing on storytelling and talking "publicly about how it manages the intersection of its business relationships and its journalism" (para. 56).

Conclusion

As Brady (2018a) argued, "when you're the biggest player in the space, it's up to you to set the rules of proper behavior. If you won't lead, you can't ask others to follow" (para. 21). The ESPN Public Editor represented a unique practice in terms of media accountability in sports journalism. Throughout this 13-year period, its representatives acted as internal critics and audiences' advocates. Through the reflection on core ethical concerns (conflicts of interest, the separation between reporting and commentary, sensationalism, sourcing, transparency, diversity, and the coverage of issues behind the play), all set very high standards about what ESPN should be and what audiences should expect from the organization in its myriad platforms. ESPN Ombudsmen have shown independence, not shying away from expressing their criticism towards the organization. Beyond representing an opportunity to advance conversations in many ethical areas, their columns have revealed ESPN's strategic decisions behind the content, something especially relevant for a company in constant transition in the contemporary "fluid and commercially volatile context" (Hutchins & Boyle, 2017, p. 496).

However, as mentioned above, in May 2018, ESPN announced it discontinued the Public Editor position. The company stated that "in the recent years both *The Washington Post* and *The New York Times* eliminated their Ombudsman role in recognition that the position had outlived its usefulness, largely because of the rise of real-time feedback of all kinds" (Merida, 2018, para. 2). ESPN argued that "access to the Internet and its social platforms has created a horde of watchdogs who communicate directly with us to share observations and questions" (para. 3). The company added that beyond its users, their "multi-faceted newsgathering operation is made up of a diverse collection of seasoned journalists who engage in spirited discussion and respectful disagreement to land in the best possible place" (para. 3). ESPN ended its statement welcoming "the continued scrutiny" its fans and critics offer.

Such conclusions are undoubtedly contentious, as social media vitriol could be argued to be less purposeful and informed than the Ombudsman/ Public Editor. One could ably question whether a "horde of watchdogs" can substitute for such critical analysis. Jim Brady argued in an interview to *Columbia Journalism Review* that "the public can only report on what it sees, and there are things going on inside a company that someone in that role is more able to get at" (Vernon, 2018, para. 9). As he highlighted, "even if the public doesn't automatically see the value in the position, that doesn't mean it's not worthwhile" (Vernon, 2018, para. 28). This chapter has revealed the value that this unique post delivered. It is yet to be seen whether new forms of accountability will be able to challenge "the rules of the game" within the world's largest sports media empire in the ways the Public Editor did.

References

Banagan, R. (2011). The decision, a case study: LeBron James, ESPN and questions about US sports journalism losing its way. *Media International Australia, 140*(1), 157–167. https://doi.org/10.1177/1329878X1114000119

Boyle, R. (2006). *Sports journalism: Context and issues.* London: Sage.

Boyle, R., & Haynes, R. (2014). Watching the games. In V. Girginov (Ed.), *Handbook of the London 2012 Olympic and Paralympic Games. Volume Two: Celebrating the Games* (pp. 84–95). Abingdon, Oxon: Routledge.

Brady, J. (2015, November 25). Public Editor: ESPN not "monolithic" but still deserving of scrutiny. Retrieved from http://www.espn.com/blog/ombudsman/print?id=503

Brady, J. (2016a, January 4). Questions about ESPN's journalism? Let the public editor know. *Espn.com.* Retrieved from http://www.espn.com/blog/ombudsman/print?id=536

Brady, J. (2016b, January 28). Your Questions Answered: How 30 for 30 films, SportsCenter anchors are chosen. *Espn.com.* Retrieved from http://www.espn.com/blog/ombudsman/print?id=573

Brady, J. (2016c, May 27). Public Editor Q&A: Questions for ESPN's Connor Schell. *Espn.com.* Retrieved from http://www.espn.com/blog/ombudsman/print?id=665

Brady, J. (2016d, July 24). Public Editor Q&A: ESPN's Connor Schell on films, debate shows. *Espn.com* Retrieved from http://www.espn.com/blog/ombudsman/print?id=710

Brady, J. (2016e, November 8). Inside and out, ESPN dealing with changing political dynamics. *Espn.com*. Retrieved from http://www.espn.com/blog/ombudsman/print?id=767

Brady, J (2016f, February 8). Looking back at Grantland, ESPN decision sad, not necessarily wrong. *Espn.com*. Retrieved from http://www.espn.com/blog/ombudsman/print?id=604

Brady, J. (2016g, May 16). ESPN finally ready to unleash The Undefeated. *Espn.com*. Retrieved from http://www.espn.com/blog/ombudsman/print?id=656

Brady, J. (2016h, May 13). Investment in esports smart play for ESPN. *Espn.com*. Retrieved from http://www.espn.com/blog/ombudsman/print?id=649

Brady, J. (2016i, August 30). ESPN loosens standards with treatment of Body Issue photos. *Espn.com*. Retrieved from http://www.espn.com/blog/ombudsman/print?id=723

Brady, J. (2016j, September 7). ESPN wrestling with fiction/non-fiction in deciding to "cover" WWE. *Espn.com*. Retrieved from http://www.espn.com/blog/ombudsman/print?id=743

Brady, J. (2017a, September 15). ESPN awash in rising political tide. *Espn.com*. Retrieved from http://www.espn.com/blog/ombudsman/print?id=871

Brady, J. (2017b, October 11). ESPN navigating uncharted political, social and controversial waters. *Espn.com*. Retrieved from http://www.espn.com/blog/ombudsman/print?id=887

Brady, J. (2017c, November 2). ESPN's new social guidelines show right instincts. *Espn.com*. Retrieved from http://www.espn.com/blog/ombudsman/print?id=896

Brady, J. (2017d, December 20). ESPN shows progress, faces challenges, regarding women in sports. *Espn.com*. Retrieved from http://www.espn.com/blog/ombudsman/print?id=906

Brady, J. (2018a, January 18). ESPN's evolution: Snapchat, esports and attribution guidelines. *Espn.com*. Retrieved from http://www.espn.com/blog/ombudsman/print?id=912

Brady, J. (2018b, February 7). While evolving, SportsCenter remains sun in ESPN's solar system. *Espn.com*. Retrieved from http://www.espn.com/blog/ombudsman/print?id=921

Brady, J. (2018c, March 15). Taking on the oh-so-simple subject of ESPN's future. *Espn.com*. Retrieved from http://www.espn.com/blog/ombudsman/print?id=929

Bryman, A. (2016). *Social research methods* (5th ed.). Oxford: Oxford University Press.

Coche, R. (2013). Is ESPN really the women's sports network? A content analysis of ESPN's internet coverage of the Australian Open. *Electronic News*, 7(2), 72–88. https://doi.org/10.1177/1931243113491574

English, P. (2016). Mapping the sports journalism field: Bourdieu and broadsheet newsrooms. *Journalism*, 17(8), 1001–1017. https://doi.org/10.1177/1464884915576728

English, P. (2017). Cheerleaders or critics? Australian and Indian sports journalists in the contemporary age. *Digital Journalism*, 5(5), 532–548. doi:10.1080/21670811.2016.1209082

Fry, J. (2012a, July 6). ESPN faces challenges in Twitter Era. *Espn.com*. Retrieved from http://www.espn.com/blog/poynterreview/print?id=373

Fry, J. (2012b, October 3). Making the case for standardized policies. *Espn.com*. Retrieved from http://www.espn.com/blog/poynterreview/print?id=482

Hall, A. (2015, November 6). Digital news veteran Jim Brady named ESPN public editor. *ESPN Front Row*. Retrieved from https://espnmediazone.com/us/press-releases/2015/11/digital-news-veteran-jim-brady-named-espn-public-editor/

Hardin, M., & Zhong, B. (2010). Sports reporters' attitudes about ethics vary based on beat, *Newspaper Research Journal, 31*(2), 6–19. https://doi.org/10.1177/073953291003100202

Hutchins, B., & Boyle, R. (2017). A community of practice: Sport journalism, mobile media and institutional change. *Digital Journalism, 5*(5), 496–512. doi:10.1080/21670811.2016.1234147

Hutchins, B., & Rowe, D. (2009). From broadcast scarcity to digital plenitude: The changing dynamics of the media sport content economy. *Television & New Media, 10*(4), 354–370. doi:10.1177/1527476409334016

Kian, E. M., Mondello, M., & Vincent, J. (2009). ESPN—The women's sports network? A content analysis of internet coverage of march madness. *Journal of Broadcasting & Electronic Media, 53*(3), 477–495. doi:10.1080/08838150903102519

Lipsyte, R. (2013a, August 25). Was ESPN sloppy, naive or compromised? *Espn. com*. Retrieved from http://www.espn.com/blog/ombudsman/print?id=96

Lipsyte, R. (2013b, June 28). What are commentary boundaries at ESPN? *Espn.com*. Retrieved from http://www.espn.com/blog/ombudsman/print?id=7

Lipsyte, R. (2013c, September 6). So what if ESPN refused to use the Rword? *Espn. com*. Retrieved from http://www.espn.com/blog/ombudsman/print?id=119

Lipsyte, R. (2013d, October 24). Pollack, Peterson offer teachable moments. *Espn.com*. Retrieved from http://www.espn.com/blog/ombudsman/print?id=192

Lipsyte, R. (2013e, October 15). Winning ugly: ESPN journalism prevails. *Espn. com*. Retrieved from http://www.espn.com/blog/ombudsman/print?id=176

Lipsyte, R. (2014a, December 3). Serving sports fans through Journalism. *Espn.com*. Retrieved from http://www.espn.com/blog/ombudsman/print?id=501

Lipsyte, R. (2014b, November 4). Probing the gray areas of ESPN's journalism. *Espn. com*. Retrieved from http://www.espn.com/blog/ombudsman/print?id=477

Lipsyte, R. (2014c, March 18). Give fans what they want, or should have? *Espn.com*. Retrieved from http://www.espn.com/blog/ombudsman/print?id=321

Lipsyte, R. (2014d, September 9). Content "crimes" and punishment at ESPN. *Espn. com*. Retrieved from http://www.espn.com/blog/ombudsman/print?id=440

McBride, K. (2011a, May 1). ESPN resources pay off at World Cup. *Espn.com*. Retrieved from http://www.espn.com/blog/poynterreview/print?id=80

McBride, K. (2011b, December 22). Letter of intent. *Espn.com*. Retrieved from http://www.espn.com/espn/print?id=7379853

McBride, K. (2012a, May 1). To cover a story, or be part of it? *Espn.com*. Retrieved from http://www.espn.com/blog/poynterreview/print?id=284

McBride, K. (2012b, November 5). ESPN straddles the line on rumors. *Espn.com*. Retrieved from http://www.espn.com/blog/poynterreview/print?id=500

McBride, K., & McCombs, R. (2011, April 20). So close, yet so far. *Espn.com*. Retrieved from http://www.espn.com/espn/print?id=6399130

McQuail, D. (2003). *Media accountability and freedom of publication*. New York, NY: Oxford University Press.

Merida, K. (2018). ESPN discontinues public editor position. *ESPN Front Row*. Retrieved from https://www.espnfrontrow.com/2018/05/espn-discontinues-public-editor-position/

Ohlmeyer, D. (2009, August 18). Serve the audience. *Espn.com*. Retrieved from http://www.espn.com/espn/print?id=4405442&type=Columnist&imagesPrint=off#

Ohlmeyer, D. (2010a, July 21). The "Decision" dilemma. *Espn.com*. Retrieved from http://www.espn.com/espn/print?id=5397113

Ohlmeyer, D. (2010b, April 20). Soothing the irritation. *Espn.com*. Retrieved from http://www.espn.com/espn/print?id=5120107

Ohlmeyer, D. (2010c, May 25). Root of all evil? *Espn.com*. Retrieved from http://www.espn.com/espn/print?id=5220492

Ohlmeyer, D. (2010d, October 21). Evolution or Devolution? *Espn.com*. Retrieved from http://www.espn.com/espn/print?id=5710213

Ohlmeyer, D. (2011, January, 26). Can you hear me now? *Espn.com*. Retrieved from http://www.espn.com/espn/print?id=6063051

Ott, B. L. (2012). Unnecessary roughness: ESPN's Construction of hypermasculine citizenship in the Penn State sex abuse scandal. *Cultural Studies ↔ Critical Methodologies, 12*(4), 330–332. https://doi.org/10.1177/1532708612446433

Rowe, D. (2007). Sports journalism: Still the "toy department" of the news media? *Journalism, 8*(4), 385–405. https://doi.org/10.1177/1464884907078657

Schreiber, L. A. (2007a, August 7). After "Who's Now," question for ESPN is "What's Next?" *Espn.com*. Retrieved from http://www.espn.com/espn/print?id=2965515

Schreiber, L. A. (2007b, October 5). Fed fast food of opinion, ESPN audience starves for reported fact. *Espn.com*. Retrieved from http://www.espn.com/espn/print?id=3050882

Schreiber, L. A. (2008a, July 13). Written guidance necessary to establish boundaries of comment. *Espn.com*. Retrieved from http://www.espn.com/espn/print?id=3485712

Schreiber, L. A. (2008b, December 15). ESPN can define boundaries and keep its edge, too. *Espn.com*. Retrieved from http://www.espn.com/espn/print?id=3772091

Schreiber, L. A. (2008c, April 13). ESPN is right to engage, not avoid, racial matters in sports. *Espn.com*. Retrieved from http://www.espn.com/espn/print?id=3345832

Schreiber, L. A. (2009, March 15). ESPN's excess root of fan frustration. *Espn.com*. Retrieved from http://www.espn.com/espn/print?id=3983722

Solomon, G. (2005, September 9). Network puts sports in perspective after Katrina. *Espn. com*. Retrieved from http://www.espn.com/espn/print?id=2156485

Solomon, G. (2006a, January 26). Plan for Bonds reality show "boggles the mind." *Espn. com*. Retrieved from http://www.espn.com/espn/print?id=2307658

Solomon, G. (2006b, May 26). ESPN needs more journalism, less sensationalism. *Espn. com*. Retrieved from http://www.espn.com/espn/print?id=2459811

Solomon, G. (2007, March 28). ESPN reflections: The good, the bad and the Boo-Yah. *Espn.com*. Retrieved from http://www.espn.com/espn/print?id=2816724

van Dalen, A., & Deuze, M. (2006). Readers' advocates or newspapers' ambassadors? *European Journal of Communication*, *21*(4), 457–475. https://doi.org/10.1177/0267323106070011

Vernon, P. (2018). ESPN's final public editor on the "unfortunate" decision to eliminate the position. *Columbia Journalism Review*. Retrieved from https://www.cjr.org/q_and_a/espn-public-editor.php

Vogan, T. (2015). *ESPN: The making of a sports media empire*. Urbana, IL: University of Illinois Press.

12. SportsCenter *at 40: Evolving With the Times*

JOHN MCGUIRE

While content has come and gone in the history of ESPN, one program has been omnipresent since the network's first minutes on air: *SportsCenter*. The concept was simple enough: A daily program that recapped the day in sports. ESPN's founders envisioned *SportsCenter* becoming the program of record in reporting on the world of sports, just as the nightly network newscasts served that function for decades.

For two generations, *SportsCenter* has been a place to find not only scores and highlights, but also expert opinions and colorful personalities. In the beginning, anchors like Bob Ley, Chris Berman, and Tom Mees started building a loyal following, especially among Baby Boomers that were into sports. Gayle Gardner and Sharon Smith blazed a path at ESPN for female anchors who followed like Linda Cohn and Suzy Kolber. As *SportsCenter* matured as a program and expanded to hour-long broadcasts, ESPN was creating a slew of popular (and sometimes outspoken) hosts who attracted attention in popular culture as well as the sports world. Keith Olbermann and Dan Patrick called their 11 p.m. *SportsCenter* "The Big Show." Others like Greg Gumbel, Rich Eisen, Mike Tirico, and Robin Roberts made their marks at the network before going onto other, more prominent jobs. Younger talent like Craig Kilborn and Kenny Mayne brought a David Lettermanesque-quality to delivering highlights. In the 2000s, Stuart Scott created his unique niche with his portfolio of phrases appealing to second generation ESPN viewers. In the 2010s, anchors like John Anderson, John Buccigross, Sage Steele, Steve Levy, Scott Van Pelt, Neil Everett, and Stan Verrett have carried on the tradition of colorful and entertaining anchors.

SportsCenter would give birth to similar shows around the globe. In England, *Sky Sports News* would come on the air in the 1990s, using many of the conventions that its American counterpart had established since going on the air. In Canada, TSN (in which ESPN has an ownership stake) used the name and similar looking sets and graphics. A Spanish-language version of *SportsCenter* was part of ESPN Deportes when it came on the air in the 2000s. As ESPN expanded internationally, *SportsCenter* became an ingrained part of the lives of people in countries like Australia, Brazil, and the Philippines. But as *SportsCenter* approaches its 40th anniversary in September 2019, the network's flagship program is having something akin to a midlife crisis. From evolving show formats to how content is presented, *SportsCenter* and other shows like it around the globe are faced with figuring out its place in the sports media world in an era when sports news and highlights are available almost anytime and anywhere on a person's smartphone.

This chapter offers a look at four decades of *SportsCenter* and factors influencing its ongoing evolution. The past will be represented by an examination of *SportsCenter* episodes aired from 1985 to 2004. The present involves examining shows from the summer of 2018, some that are personality-driven while others are more traditional highlight-driven programs. Finally, this chapter discusses what may be part of *SportsCenter*'s future: *SC* on Snapchat episodes. The author will also discuss the production of *SportsCenter* through DeFleur and Ball-Rokeach's "media as social system" perspective and the show's evolution through the idea of media ecology: Specifically, the chapter considers Scolari's idea of evolutionary ecology (2012).

A Brief History of SportsCenter

One of the first images of ESPN's debut night of September 7, 1979, was anchor George Grande sitting at the inaugural *SportsCenter* set. Grande invited sports fans in that night for what was seen as an experiment in television: "From this desk in the coming weeks and months, we'll be filling you in on the pulse of sporting activity, not only from around the country, but around the world as well" ("ESPN," 1979, para. 6). Ironically, the initial *SportsCenter* broadcasts had a different name in television schedules for that first week (*Sports Recap*). Company founder Bill Rasmussen said *SportsCenter* was only used in television listings for the first time four days later (Rasmussen, 2010).

Since that opening night, the program has become a fixture in the lives of young and old alike: ESPN estimated more than 115 million people in the U.S. still tune in to *SportsCenter* at least once a month ("ESPN Inc.," 2018). During its long run, the show has been able to deliver demographics similar to that of the whole network—mostly male, mostly college-educated, and higher than average income ("ESPN: Network Profile," n.d.).

The original *SportsCenter* programs ran 30 minutes and were repeated through overnight and morning hours. The early years saw an absence of highlights because of technology or lack of rights to show them. As a result, banter among the anchors became common to fill time. Lee Leonard did a segment called *Lee's Lip* in the early days: "Sometimes it had to do with sports and sometimes it was just whatever I could think of that day, like a little editorial" (Miller & Shales, 2011, p. 66). The early morning shows at 2 a.m. Eastern gave carte blanche to young anchors to talk about the sports news of the day among themselves, most notably Tom Mees and Chris Berman. One ESPN director noted the two men had a chemistry that made them one of the best ESPN anchor teams of all time (Miller & Shales).

As ESPN figured out it indeed had an audience for 24-hour sports, *SportsCenter* began expanding with more live editions airing in more day-parts. The content and structure of the show, however, was still very similar to its main cable competitor of the day, Cable News Network's (CNN) *Sports Tonight*, which often out performed *SportsCenter* in head-to-head ratings (Vogan, 2015). ESPN President Steve Bornstein said the *SportsCenter* franchise was valuable, "but that it had no direction … the inmates are running the asylum" (Miller & Shales, 2011, pp. 157–158). An industry expert commented "*SportsCenter* was undervalued by people within ESPN … there was a new executive producer every 18 months" (Miller & Shales, 2011, pp. 159–160). The editorial aspect of *SportsCenter* began changing in the late 1980s with the arrival of John Walsh, first as a consultant, but installed in 1989 as overseer of the network's flagship show. Walsh, who came from a print background, wanted the first block of each program to focus on all the top stories, much like a newspaper's front page (Miller & Shales). *SportsCenter*'s bona fides as a journalistic entity was cemented later in 1989, when an earthquake struck moments before the start of Game 3 of the World Series in Oakland. ESPN was able to stay on the air from the game site, helping sister network ABC get the first footage of damage that struck the Bay area (Vogan, 2015). ESPN's journalistic image and quality of content would also be supported by *Outside the Lines*, a hard news program covering sports debuting in 1990.

The 1990s saw *SportsCenter* come into its own, with top-flight anchors, more highlights, more reporters, and a greater focus under Walsh's leadership. The most notable *SportsCenter* team of the decade was the team of Keith Olbermann and Dan Patrick, seen during much of the '90s on the 11 p.m. Eastern show. The earlier 6 p.m. edition featured a trio of heavyweights: Charley Steiner, Bob Ley, and Robin Roberts. The 11 p.m. show was more edgy with Olbermann and Patrick coming across with an attitude targeting a sophisticated audience. The 6 p.m. show was seen as more traditional, focusing on news of the day (Miller & Shales, 2011). Perhaps even more important to the show was the marketing campaign developed in the mid '90s. The *This is SportsCenter* campaign, showing athletes and mascots working alongside the ESPN personalities, created a cultural sensation. One ESPN executive summed up the importance of the campaign this way: "*SportsCenter* was good when we came, but it wasn't hip. Now it became hip" (Miller & Shales, 2011, p. 237). By 2000, nearly a third of all content on ESPN was its *SportsCenter* franchise. As Brady (2018) noted, *SportsCenter* at its height "didn't just reflect the conversations happening in sports, it drove them" (para.3).

SportsCenter hit 25,000 episodes in 2002 (Hogan, 2002), but troubling trends were emerging regarding viewership. The 6 p.m. Eastern show had shown a steady decline in viewership from 1999 through 2002 (Sandomir, 2002). Overall viewership for live sporting events was also declining on the network, especially for the Male 18–34 age group. Another viewership decline was reported in 2005 among Men 18–34 as well as Men 18–49 ("ESPN Sees," 2006). Executives gave reasons for decline ranging from the impact of 9/11 to young people dealing with tough economic times (Bernstein, 2002). Another factor being cited for declines was the emergence of the Internet. Although sports websites were coming into vogue as of the late 1990s (ESPN had its website operating in 1995), available technology still limited its potential. As Internet speeds improved and people could stream video content at a higher quality later in the 2000s, the network had a new challenger (Brady, 2018).

The end of the 2000s also saw ESPN relying more upon sports debate shows, particularly in morning and afternoon dayparts. *Pardon the Interruption* was the first of this genre, followed by *Around the Horn*. The most significant of these shows, however, was *First Take*. First seen on ESPN2 in 2007, the show spun off controversial commentator Skip Bayless from *Cold Pizza* and was later paired up with another opinionated commentator, Stephen A. Smith (Miller & Shales, 2011). *First Take* and simulcasts of ESPN Radio programs began filling time slots that *SportsCenter* once occupied on the various ESPN networks (e.g., ESPN, ESPN2).

As the 2010s unfolded, *SportsCenter* continued struggling with stagnant ratings, despite the show's ever-improving production and journalistic quality. Longtime viewers had become unhappy with the show as it began emphasizing talk and debate over highlights (Ourand, 2017; Putterman, 2018). At the same time, the younger segment of ESPN's audience was turning to mobile media, thanks to smartphones, for sports highlights (Ourand, 2013). Even Keith Olbermann, one of *SportsCenter*'s most famous alumnus, predicted *SportsCenter*'s days might be numbered because of all the competition the network faced online and from league networks (e.g., MLB TV, NFL Network) (Glasspiegel, 2016). As Crupi (2017) noted: "… in some ways, the classic *SportsCenter* formula is in danger of becoming as antiquated as the show's original synth-happy theme song" (para. 3).

Solving the conundrum of satisfying two distinct, but important, audience demographics became a priority for ESPN decision-makers. Roberts (2017) said company officials had two themes to the changes they were making: having *SportsCenter* become more digital and tying the show to a much greater extent to the hosts. One of the biggest changes was reformatting some versions of *SportsCenter*. One of the major changes in 2015 involved the Midnight Eastern edition, which became *SportsCenter with Scott Van Pelt*. The popular anchor, who had also been an ESPN radio host, changed the television program to make it more like his radio show (e.g., continuing his *One Big Thing* segment), but with game highlights. Van Pelt engaged in more question-and-answer (Q-and-A) segments with athletes and ESPN commentators, playing off the night's prime-time ESPN lineup of games. In a way, Van Pelt's show was returning to *SportsCenter*'s roots back in the 1980s and 1990s when shows featured dominant personalities talking about sports. After its first two years, the network saw growth in the Van Pelt daypart, particularly with the 18–34 demographic, the one that had been so difficult for ESPN to capture during the decade (Brady, 2018; Crupi, 2017). *SportsCenter Los Angeles* and *SportsCenter at Night* were more highlight-driven, but the network tried to keep the same anchors on week in and week out. One personality-driven *SportsCenter* hour that did not work out so well: *SC at 6* with Jemele Hill and Michael Smith met with early audience interest, but was eventually canceled after Hill, and then Smith left the show. (Hill's story is addressed in other chapters of this text).

Fall of 2017 saw another significant moment for *SportsCenter* as the company laid out a multiplatform strategy for the show. On television fewer episodes of *SportsCenter* would be seen (no editions on any of ESPN's networks between 10 a.m. and 6 p.m. Eastern) (Brady, 2018). During the various morning debate and talk shows, a segment called *SportsCenter Right Now* would be run as 2-to-3 minute updates on the day's latest sports news with shorter videos (the segments were also placed on the Web) (Roberts, 2017). On the Internet, ESPN would launch mini-episodes of *SportsCenter* on Snapchat as a way to reach the third generation of ESPN users (Putterman, 2018). This multipronged approach was trying the address changing audience habits that had occurred in the new century. One ESPN executive called what was happening as evolution: "I don't think we're doing this in a way that we're throwing out everything else we've been doing" (Roberts, 2017, para. 42).

But by late 2018, and under new leadership at the network, *SportsCenter* reversed course again, returning to an emphasis on news and highlights, particularly its 6 p.m. Eastern edition (Strauss, 2018). Norby Williamson, a long-time ESPN executive who was placed in charge of *SportsCenter*, suggested "they had miscalculated a little bit," devaluing highlights even in an era of smartphones and instantaneous highlights (Strauss, 2018).

Scholarly Research on SportsCenter

One of the interesting aspects when reviewing research about ESPN's primary news and information program is that *SportsCenter* was virtually ignored by scholars during the first 15 years it was on the air. The first article focusing on *SportsCenter* in *Journal of Broadcasting and Electronic Media* was not published until 1997 (Tuggle's study on gender representation). With the emergence of more sports-oriented scholarly journals in the 2000s, the level of scholarship on *SportsCenter* has gone up dramatically.

The vast majority of research about *SportsCenter* has focused on gender; specifically, the lack of representation of women athletes in the broadcasts. Tuggle (1997) examined the two daily cable sports news shows on at the time: *SportsCenter* and CNN's *Sports Tonight*. Using episodes recorded over a four-week period, Tuggle coded stories for several conditions (e.g., type of sport, length of story) in addition to gender. Tuggle's study showed stories featuring male athletes on all episodes studied were significantly more in number (95%) than stories about females (5%). Furthermore, stories on female athletes focused on those in individual sports (i.e., tennis) versus females in team competition (i.e., WNBA). Tuggle concluded, "In nearly every measurable way, the two programs portrayed women's sports as less important than men's athletic program" (p. 22).

Lack of coverage of female athletes and sports leagues on *SportsCenter* has been documented in numerous other scholarly articles (Adams & Tuggle, 2004; Billings & Young, 2015; Coche, 2012; Eastman & Billings, 2000). Other studies examining the lack of coverage for female sports were done from a longitudinal perspective. Turner (2014) examined *SportsCenter* episodes 10 years apart (1999 & 2009). Turner found female athletes were covered less on *SportsCenter* during 2009 than in 1999, noting an absence of female anchors on *SportsCenter* episodes coded in the two samples (77 male anchors versus only 7 female anchors). Cooky, Messner, and Musto (2015) examined coverage of female athletes on *SportsCenter*, starting from 1999 and repeating the study every five years through 2014 (the same researchers had studied local television sportscasts in Los Angeles on the same topic since 1989). The study marking 15 years of studying *SportsCenter* found a downward decline in coverage of female sports, with the show favoring the big three male sports of football, baseball, and basketball (Cooky et al., 2015).

SportsCenter has been analyzed from other perspectives. Johnson and Romney (2017) examined self-promotion on *SportsCenter* using the show's content to promote other ESPN programming (most often live sports events). The authors found *SportsCenter* leaned significantly toward high-lighting leagues the network had partnerships with such as the National Football League (NFL). The same authors examined *SportsCenter* for geographic bias regarding the show's content. They found teams in the Eastern United States tended to get more attention on *SportsCenter* compared to teams based on the West Coast, despite having some *SportsCenter* episodes televised from Los Angeles (Johnson & Romney, 2018).

Other *SportsCenter* research has included Fareed's (2000) study that examined how Stuart Scott and other ESPN anchors had influenced popular culture and the sports lexicon through language (e.g., Scott's description of a player being as "cool as the other side pillow"). Language was also at the heart of Park's study (2014) about how the media (including ESPN) represented the ethnic background of basketball player Jeremy Lin during his breakout National Basketball Association (NBA) 2011–12 season.

New and Social Media Impact on Sports News Shows

While there are no specific examples of research examining how *SportsCenter* content has been impacted by new and social media, there are studies that speak to issues facing the program in this new information environment. Hull and Lewis (2014) discussed how Twitter was seen as a threat to displace broadcast sports media because of the platform's immediacy and number of sources available to instantaneously deliver scores, and in many cases, high-lights. The authors cited the growth of smartphones and tablets for exacer-bating mobile media's impact upon traditional media. This research syncs up with a Gantz and Lewis (2014) study about fanship differences between traditional and new media. While the authors suggested that there will still be some reliance on traditional sports sources like *SportsCenter*, the new gener-ation of sports fans "will seek out media content wherever available" (Gantz & Lewis, 2014, p. 19). The author's study also discussed what types of plat-forms sports fans are using and what factors impact that usage, including: (a) level of interactivity; (b) temporal constraints on when fans can access desired sports information; (c) fidelity, or quality, of picture; (d) screen size impacting immersion in the sporting experience, and (e) accessibility.

In looking ahead to the future, Hull and Lewis (2014) suggested local sports segments needed to change to emphasize (a) brevity in storytelling;

(b) creating parasocial interaction for fans with teams and athletes; (c) creating community among users; and (d) merging the private and public in its coverage, showing the athlete both on the field and their everyday life. It is suggested that Hull and Lewis's research is applicable to regional and national sports news programs as well. This study also suggests it is why ESPN is looking to platforms like Snapchat to present *SportsCenter* in new formats.

SportsCenter, *System Theory, and Media Ecology*

One way to understand how *SportsCenter* has survived as one of the longest-running network news and information programs in U.S. history is by analyzing its production through a media system theory perspective (DeFleur & Ball-Rokeach, 1989). The researchers posited all media content being generated through systems that identified the interaction of critical components (e.g., distribution, production, financing) in a system with permeable boundaries (allowing back-and-forth interaction with elements outside the system) (DeFleur & Ball-Rokeach, 1989). Certain repetitive actions can be identified as functions in any media system, including: (a) generating content attracting audiences; (b) earning revenue from advertising within popular content; (c) avoiding actions bringing about regulation (either mandatory or voluntary); and (d) maintaining the equilibrium of the system so the first three functions can go on (DeFleur & Ball-Rokeach, 1989). Kast and Rosenzweig (1974) have suggested systems need to achieve *dynamic equilibrium*, requiring them to be adaptable to forces and threats both inside and outside of the media system. Kast and Rosenzweig also argued dynamic equilibrium is essential for avoiding system entropy, which could render such systems from being able to adapt to changes within and outside the system. For this study, Kast and Rosenzweig's idea of dynamic equilibrium seems most appropriate for discussing ESPN's experiences, as the company has long tried to keep up with both audience demand and technological changes over its history, from establishing one of the first major U.S. sports websites to experimenting with 3D telecasts ("ESPN to," 2010).

By identifying ESPN's generation of content through a system perspective, one can also consider *SportsCenter*'s place in the media ecology. The study of media ecology has attracted significant scholars, from Postman to McLuhan and is suggested to be something akin to creating environments; or as Nystrom defined it, "the study of complex communication systems as environments" (as cited in Scolari, 2012, p. 206).

Considering the changes that have unfolded, the *SportsCenter* franchise can be classified by Scolari (2012) as *evolutionary ecology* [Scolari's emphasis]. In this case, not only is the individual media content (*SportsCenter*) evolving, it is also evolving with the rest of the media system that surrounds and interacts with the show. A network like ESPN and its programming like *SportsCenter* must be responsive to influences in order to continue functioning. Specifically, Scolari argued "media can cooperate with each other" in advancing the self-interests of each within the system (2012, p. 214). An examination of *SportsCenter* episodes from television and Snapchat can offer a better understanding of the ongoing evolution.

Methodology

To better understand *SportsCenter*'s evolution, the researcher undertook an analysis of three sets of *SportsCenter*s: The first set included eight episodes from 1985 to 2004, 2 from each 5-year period starting from 1985–1989. This was a purposeful sample, as the researcher used the only available full episodes of *SportsCenter*, retrieved from YouTube, for coding. The second set of *SportsCenter* episodes available were randomly recorded during June and July of 2018. Four of the episodes were episodes of *SportsCenter with Scott Van Pelt* (personality-driven) and the other four *SportsCenters* were from other dayparts more content-driven. Content analysis was used to examine both (a) format of story and (b) type of story. Five sub-categories are being used here for classifying story format:

Voice-Overs (VOs)

VOs involve the anchor talking over video on screen, such as an anchor narrating highlights of a baseball or football game. On these stories, the sound of the game commentators is played at a low level (sometimes mixed with music). Such stories may end with a full-screen graphic, where statistical information takes up the entire screen.

Voice-Over/Sound-On-Tape (VO/SOT)

VO/SOTs are stories that feature video as well as audio with a newsmaker, such as a coach or player. Like VOs, game commentary and/or music is heard under the VO portion of the story and will occasionally utilize full screen graphics at the end.

Packages

These stories are self-contained, featuring a reporter narrating over video and using sound-on-tape. These are typically longer stories than VOs and VO/SOTs.

Readers

These are stories utilizing only written scripts narrated by the anchor and typically use a full-screen graphic.

Question-and-Answer (Q-and-A)

This story type for this study is classified as (a) where the anchor is interviewing an athlete or coach or (b) the anchor talking with a reporter or commentator for analysis.

The second area for examining structure involved the type of story, again using five sub-categories:

Pregame Stories

These are classified as stories that will preview a sporting event before it takes place, such as a report about the final warm-up round before the U.S. Open golf tournament.

Postgame Stories

These are classified as stories featuring results of games either in progress or having concluded. Stories can have highlights or summarizing results using full screen graphics.

Profiles

These are defined as packages that are done about a sports team, sports figure, or historical event. These stories would typically be about the length of Q-and-A stories.

Straight News

These are stories where no game result is given; rather, it reports details on newsworthy topics such as athlete injuries, athletes facing legal problems, or business issues in the world of sports. The stories may occasionally feature VOs and/or full-screen graphics.

Question-and-Answer (Q-and-A)

As stated above, this is classified as (a) where the anchor is interviewing an athlete or coach or (b) the anchor talking with a reporter or commentator for analysis.

Finally, eight randomly selected episodes of *SportsCenter* on Snapchat from July of 2018 were examined. Because the online segments bear no resemblance to its television counterpart, the author focused on descriptive analyses.

Results

Televised SportsCenters: *Story Format*

Content analysis of the 16 *SportsCenters* on television examined for this study showed VOs were used for more than half of all stories (n = 230, 54.8%) (see Table 12.1). Most of these VOs were used for in-game or postgame highlight stories, as the anchor narrated over the video of the game or match. VOs were also used in many cases for general news stories, such as showing past footage of an athlete performing in their sport while reporting on a trade or a contract signing. Readers represented one-fifth of all stories examined in the sample (n = 84, 20%). Readers were most often used for in-game updates or reporting general sports news. These stories were typically accompanied by full-screen graphics that provided more story facts. Q-and-A segments, including one-on-one interviews and analyst segments, represented the third most-used story format (n = 52, 12.4%), followed by VO/SOTs (n = 36, 8.6%) and television packages represented (n = 18, 4.3%).

Table 12.1: SportsCenter story format.

	VO	VO/SOT	PACKAGE	Q&A	READER
1985–2004	105 (49.3%)	18 (8.5%)	12 (5.6%)	6 (2.8%)	72 (33.8%)
2018	125 (60.4%)	18 (8.7%)	6 (2.9%)	46 (22.2%)	12 (5.8%)
TOTAL	230 (54.8%)	36 (8.6%)	18 (4.3%)	52 (12.4%)	84 (20%)

Source: Author.

1985–2004 vs. 2018

Of the eight *SportsCenters* examined from 1985 through 2004, 213 total stories were coded. The most common story format was VOs (n = 105, 49.3%). Readers were the second most common story format (n = 72, 33.8%). VO/SOTs (n = 18, 8.5%), packages (n = 12, 5.6%), and Q&A's (n = 6, 2.8%) were few in number on these *SportsCenters*.

The 2018 sample had 207 coded stories, with VOs making up more than half of the total sample (n = 125, 60.4%), even more than in the sample examining earlier *SportsCenters*. The major differences between the sets of televised *SportsCenters* emerge from use of Q-and-A stories and the use of readers. In 2018, Q-and-As made for more than one out of every five *SportsCenter* stories (n = 46, 22.2%), nearly eight times more than *SportsCenters* studied from 1985–2004. On the other hand, the use of readers in 2018 declined dramatically (n = 12, 5.8%) compared to sample of earlier *SportsCenters* (72). Use of VO/SOTs (n = 18, 8.7%) and packages (n = 6, 2.9%) in the 2018 *SportsCenters* had about the same usage as those shows from the past. A 2×5 chi-square was completed, and the researcher found a significant difference between the *SportsCenters* examined from 1985 through 2004 and those from 2018: $x^2(4) = 77.3$, $p < .001$.

Personality vs. Content-Driven SportsCenters

A breakdown of the 2018 *SportsCenters* was performed to determine if differences existed between the personality-driven version of the show (in this case, hosted by Scott Van Pelt) versus more content-driven *SportsCenters* (shows seen at 6 and 11 p.m. and 1 a.m. Eastern) regarding type of story (see Table 12.2). The four Van Pelt programs relied heavily on VOs, with nearly two out of every three stories having that format (n = 64, 63.3%). Q-and-A segments made up more than one-fifth of all stories (n = 22, 21.8%) of the stories. VO/SOTs (n = 8, 7.9%), readers (n = 5, 5%), and packages (n = 2, 2%) were rarely seen on Van Pelt's shows. The four other content-driven *SportsCenter* shows from 2018 had a similar reliance on VOs (n = 61, 57.6%) and Q-and-As (n = 24, 22.7%). These programs relied slightly more on VO/SOTs (n = 10, 9.4%), readers (n = 7, 6.6%) and packages (n = 4, 3.8%) than Van Pelt's *SportsCenters*. After dropping the package category for lack of cases, the researcher ran a 2 × 4 chi square, but found no significant difference regarding story format between the *SportsCenters* in the personality versus content driven shows in 2018 ($x^2(3) = .67$, $p<.88$).

Table 12.2: 2018 personality vs. content-driven *SportsCenter* (story format).

	VO	VO/SOT	Package	Q&A	Reader
SportsCenter w/Van Pelt	64 (63.3%)	8 (7.9%)	2 (2%)	22 (21.8%)	5 (5%)
Other *SportsCenters*	61 (57.6%)	10 (9.4%)	4 (3.8%)	24 (22.7%)	7 (6.6%)
TOTAL	125 (60.3%)	18 (8.7%)	6 (2.9%)	46 (22.2%)	12 (5.8%)

Source: Author.

Televised SportsCenters*: Story Type*

Exploring types of stories appearing on *SportsCenter* during the two time periods being examined (see Table 12.3), more than half of all stories (n = 233, 55.5%) were postgame stories or game updates while more than a quarter of all stories covered general sports news (n = 110, 26.2%). Q-and-As (n = 52, 12.4%) made up the third-most common story type, followed by pregame stories (n = 15, 3.6%) and profiles (n = 10, 2.4%)

Table 12.3: *SportsCenter* story type.

	Pre-Game	Post-Game	Profile	News	Q&A
1985–2004	2 (.9%)	145 (68.1%)	6 (2.8%)	54 (25.4%)	6 (2.8%)
2018	13 (6.3%)	88 (42.5%)	4 (1.9%)	56 (27%)	46 (22.2%)
TOTAL	**15 (3.6%)**	**233 (55.5%)**	**10 (2.4%)**	**110 (26.2%)**	**52 (12.4%)**

Source: Author.

1985–2004 vs. 2018

One of the interesting differences found between the time periods examined regarded the amount of postgame (or in-progress) stories. The 1985–2004 sample had 68.1% (n = 145) of all its stories focusing on games in progress or completed, far more than *SportsCenters* seen in 2018 (n = 88, 42.5%). But the *SportsCenters* of 2018 made far greater use of Q-and-A segments (n = 46, 22.2%) versus the period covering 1985 through 2004 (n = 6, 2.8%). The use of general sports news was about the same in both periods (n = 56, 27% for 2018 compared to n = 54, 25.4% for 1985–2004). The same is true for use of profiles (n = 6, 2.8% in 1985–2004 compared to n = 4, 1.9% in 2018). Pregame stories were limited in both samples, but used to a greater extent in 2018 (n = 13, 6.3%) versus 1985 through 2004 (n = 2, .9%). After dropping the profile category for lack of cases, the researcher ran a 2×4 chi square and found a significant difference regarding story type between the *SportsCenters* in 1985–2004 and 2018 ($x^2(3) = 52.8$, p < .001).

Personality vs. Content-Driven SportsCenters

Episodes of *SportsCenter with Scott Van Pelt* episodes compared to *SportsCenters* from other dayparts in 2018 suggest they have more in common than one might think. Postgame stories appeared most frequently, but slightly more on Van Pelt's show (n = 46, 45.6%) than the other *SportsCenters* (n = 42, 39.7%). Q-and-A segments appeared slightly more often on the content-driven *SportsCenters* (n = 26, 24.5%) than on Van Pelt's shows (n = 20, 19.8%). General sports news stories were also seen slightly more often on content-driven *SportsCenters* (n = 30, 28.3%) versus Van Pelt's shows (n = 26, 25.7%).

Use of pregame stories (n = 7, 7% on the personality-driven Van Pelt shows versus n = 6, 5.7% on the other *SportsCenters*) and profiles (n = 2, 1.9% for both) also had about the same usage rate. After dropping the profile category for lack of cases, the author ran a 2x4 chi square, the researcher found no significant difference regarding story type between the personality and content versions of *SportsCenter* from 2018 ($x^2(3) = 1.2$, p<.75).

Table 12.4: 2018 personality vs. content-driven *SportsCenter* (story type).

	Pre-Game	Post-Game	Profile	News	Q&A
SportsCenter w/Van Pelt	7 (7%)	46 (45.6%)	2 (1.9%)	26 (25.7%)	20 (19.8%)
Other *SportsCenters*	6 (5.7%)	42 (39.7%)	2 (1.9%)	30 (28.3%)	26 (24.5%)
TOTAL	**13 (6.2%)**	**88 (42.5%)**	**4 (1.9%)**	**56 (27%)**	**46 (22.2%)**

Source: Author.

SportsCenter *on Snapchat*

The discussion above has no relevance to the discussion of *SportsCenter* (*SC*) on Snapchat because the online episodes are so distinct in format and appearance. From the eight episodes from July 2018 examined (averaging between five and seven minutes in length), it is obvious *SC* Snapchat is more about entertainment than sports news of the day. Instead of game highlights, the focus is on finding memorable sports video of some kind, often taken from social media as much as televised games. Instead of giving more time for the most important sports stories, the longest segments were often those played for laughs.

A good example of this comes from the July 4, 2018 afternoon edition (new *SC* episodes are put on Snapchat at 5 a.m. and 5 p.m. Eastern weekdays). There were multiple afternoon baseball games on the holiday, yet not one score or highlight was provided. Instead, the episode started with highlights from the Nathan's Hot Dog eating contest, followed by a nearly three-minute video about the worst-ever renditions of The National Anthem (e.g., Roseanne Barr and Carl Lewis). The Snapchat episode finished with an appearance by the most recent *Bachelorette* (a show seen on ESPN's sister network, ABC). Other afternoon segments were generally formatted the same way: little attention to the day's sporting events (an exception over this period was World Cup and some Wimbledon results), but greater attention on visually interesting video. On an afternoon episode from July 13, 2018, host Katie Nolan gave 30 seconds to a Wimbledon semifinal result, but more than two minutes for a charity football game between a boy's midget team and sports mascots.

One of the interesting aspects of the *SC* on Snapchat was the sometimes-coarse nature of language used by the anchors. More than half of all the segments analyzed had at least one case where the anchor's language was censored. Some segments also featured what could be charitably described as bathroom humor. A July 11, 2018, story discussed what to do with the statue for former Carolina Panthers owner Jerry Richardson in front of the team's stadium. Richardson had been disgraced and forced to sell the team because of workplace misconduct. The sale terms required, as the host explained, that Richardson's statue had to remain in place. Among the visual suggestions from the *SC* host was to place portable toilets around Richardson's statue—the photo-shopped image of that was accompanied by the sound effect of farting.

The morning Snapchat segments were more straightforward regarding information delivery, but game coverage was limited. Baseball highlights shown typically featured only one play (usually a home run) and a score via on-screen graphic. The longest story on the July 3, 2018, morning edition highlighted an on-court fight at an international basketball tournament game between players from Australia and the Philippines, including slow-motion shots of people kicking each other and chairs being thrown. Almost all morning segments included (more than 80%) included a Top-Five plays segment (versus Top 10 on television). Some segments also featured five-second ads interspersed within the Snapchat *SC* without introduction.

Discussion

The limited content analysis used for this study points to *SportsCenter*'s evolution on television. Television episodes examined in the study showed a heavy reliance on game reports, both games underway and completed (68.1%) for the *SportsCenters* between 1985 and 2004. In the 2018 *SportsCenters* examined, reliance on postgame stories declined sharply, accounting for only 42.5%

of all stories. There are myriad reasons likely impacting these numbers: From the dayparts when the *SportsCenters* occurred and the time of season on the sports calendar to mobile social media taking root in the 2000s.

The result is that consumers' need or desire to watch *SportsCenter* to catch a particular game's highlights has become less important to certain audience segments. In the 2010s, the sports consumer (particularly the 18–34 demographic) has the ability to program his or her own sports news: selecting the game highlights or statistical recaps he or she wants to view while ignoring other content. As a result, *SportsCenter* on television has to offer something more to its viewers. ESPN's answer has been to utilize its roster of experts to provide content and more context to the day's sporting news. This is demonstrated in the number of Q-and-A segments (interviews, athlete profiles, and analytical discussion) appearing on the 2018 *SportsCenters* examined (22.2%). Only a handful of segments from the 1985–2004 *SportsCenters* (2.8%) involved any interviews or analytical segments. The longer and more numerous interview and analytical segments on *SportsCenter* in 2018 came mainly at the expense of postgame stories (only 88 in 2018 versus the 145 in *SportsCenters* from 1985 through 2004). This fit with the network's strategy of providing greater context behind the sports stories of the day as a way of competing with social media. Another difference with the 2018 *SportsCenters* not found in these numbers is the acknowledgment and incorporation of social media within the shows. For example, one of Scott Van Pelt's "Best Video I Saw Today" segment had nothing to do with sports: Instead, it was smartphone video of a bear in a glassed-in cage watching a little boy jump up and down—and then the bear joining in jumping. This sort of clip was rarely, if ever, found on *SportsCenters* from the 1980s and 1990s. *SportsCenter's Top 10* plays are now littered with clips from social media of astounding and outstanding feats from a wide variety of sporting events including little league to high school games. In this sense, the television version of *SportsCenter* is co-opting the multiple media platforms that are challenging its supremacy as the go to place for sports highlights.

The difficulty ESPN executives face going forward are the distinct audiences that the television version of *SportsCenter* is trying to serve. Longtime viewers want their father's *SportsCenter*: the one that was heavy on highlights (Ourand, 2017). Younger viewers, however, seemed to prefer the sort of *SportsCenter* that Scott Van Pelt is putting on, with a mix of highlights, lots of commentary, and social media content. In 2017, Van Pelt's show was performing better in drawing Men 18–34 than some of the terrestrial network's late-night talk shows (Guthrie, 2017). From a media systems perspective, the pressure of changing audience tastes has forced ESPN executives to re-tune its strategies in the 2010s.

SC on Snapchat is an altogether different program, only sharing the *SportsCenter* brand with its television counterpart. As the *SC* on Snapchat experiment is still in its infancy, the show is likely to undergo many modifications as its predecessor has on cable. In its current state, *SC* on Snapchat demonstrates the traits Hull and Lewis (2014) described as what the new generation of sports consumers are seeking; brevity in storytelling and creating community among users with the use of social media. Scolari's (2012) discussion of evolutionary ecology can also be appropriately applied here. The fact that there is an audience segment of sports fans that accept and consume the Snapchat program as *SportsCenter* (despite little resemblance to the television version) demonstrates how the *SportsCenter* brand is being disseminated across different platforms with a variety of formats. Perhaps the best comparison is to the evolution of radio after the emergence of television. Instead of disappearing from the media ecology, the medium transformed into a new form of communication where stations served smaller niche audiences based on content format (e.g., rock, country, sports talk, all-news). It is possible the future holds even be more forms of *SportsCenters* for all types of media platforms (e.g., YouTube, Twitter) as *SportsCenter* may become more audience centric. As technology and audience tastes continue evolving, the challenge of ESPN executives will by determining what the audience wants and how to deliver sports content.

So, what is to become of *SportsCenter*? It is worth remembering there were dire predictions close to three decades ago about network evening newscasts vanishing because of 24-hour cable television networks, yet they are still around ("Tough Times," 1991). Even Keith Olbermann, who predicted the eventual demise of *SportsCenter*, is back hosting *SportsCenter* for the first time in more than two decades (Perez, 2018). Perhaps George Grande ironically foreshadowed the show's future status at the end of the very first *SportsCenter* in September 1979: "We'll be filling you in on further updates as the broadcast progresses" ("ESPN," 1979, para. 8).

References

Adams, T., & Tuggle, C. A. (2004). ESPN's SportsCenter and coverage of women's athletics: "It's a boy's club." *Mass Communication & Society, 7*(2), 237–248. doi: 10.1207/s15327825mcs0702_6

Bernstein, A. (2002, May 20). Males 18 to 34 turning off sports. *Sports Business Journal*. Retrieved from https://www.sportsbusinessdaily.com/Journal/Issues/2002/05/20/This-Weeks-Issue/Males-18-To-34-Turning-Off-Sports.aspx

Billings, A. C., & Young, B. D. (2015). Comparing flagship news programs: Women's sport coverage in ESPN's *SportsCenter* and Fox Sports 1's *Fox Sports Live*. *Electronic News, 9*(1), 3–16. doi:10.1177/1931243115572824

Brady, J. (2018, February 7). While evolving, SportsCenter remains sun in ESPN's solar system. *ESPN.com*. Retrieve from www.espn.com/blog/ombudsan/print?id=921

Coche, R. (2012). Is ESPN really the women's sports network? A content analysis of ESPN's Internet coverage of the Australian Open. *Electronic News, 7*(2), 72–88. doi:10.1177/089124321776056

Cooky, C., Messner, M. A., & Musto, M. (2015). "It's dude time!": A quarter century of excluding women's sports in televised news and highlight shows. *Communication Sport, 3*(3), 261–287. doi: 10.1177/2167479515588761

Crupi, A. (2017, March 20). Now *this* is SportsCenter. *Adage.com*. Retrieved from http://adage.com/article/news/sportscenter/308448/

DeFleur, M. L., & Ball-Rokeach, S. J. (Eds.). (1989). *Theories of mass communication* (5th ed.). New York, NY: Longman.

Eastman, S. T., & Billings, A. C. (2000). Sportscasting and sports reporting: The power of gender bias. *Journal of Sport and Social Issues, 24*(2), 192–213. doi.org/10.1177/0193723500242006

ESPN. (1979, September 7). *1979-ESPN Commercials-First Day/3 months: SportsCenter, NCAA*. Retrieved from https://www.youtube.com/watch?v=v0ed1dkqHZY&t=8s

ESPN Inc. Fact Sheet. (2018). *Espnmediazone.com*. Retrieved from https://espnmedia-zone.com/us/ espn-inc-fact-sheet/

ESPN: Network profile. (n.d.). *National Media Spots*. Retrieved from http://www.nationalmediaspots.com/network-demographics/ESPN.pdf

ESPN to Launch First 3D Television Network, ESPN 3D. (2010, January 5). *Espnmediazone.com*. Retrieved from https://espnmediazone.com/us/press-releases/2010/01/espn-to-launch-first-3d-television-network-espn-3d/

ESPN sees overall ratings drop in 2005. (2006, January 9). *Sports Business Journal*. Retrieved from https://www.sportsbusinessdaily.com/Journal/Issues/2006/01/09/Media/ESPN-Sees-Overall-Ratings-Drop-In-2005.aspx

Farred, G. (2000). Cool as the other side of the pillow: How ESPN's SportsCenter has changed television sports talk. *Journal of Sport & Social Issues, 24*(2), 96–117. doi:10.1177/0193723500242002

Fisher, B. A. (1978). *Perspectives on human communication*. New York, NY: Macmillan.

Gantz, W., & Lewis, N. (2014). Fanship differences between traditional and newer media. In A. C. Billings, M. Hardin, & N. A. Brown (Eds.), *Routledge Handbook of sport and new media* (pp. 19–31). London, England: Routledge.

Glasspiegel, R. (2016, February 8). Keith Olbermann bearish on future of SportsCenter (and all generalist studio sports TV). *Thebiglead.com*. Retrieved from https://thebiglead.

com/2016/02/08/keith-olbermann-bearish-on-future-of-sportscenter-and-all-general-studio-sports-tv/ Guthrie, M (2017, November 14). ESPN signs Scott Van Pelt to new deal. *The Hollywood Reporter*. Retrieve from https://www.hollywoodreporter.com/news/espn-signs-scott-van-pelt-new-deal-1056545?utm_source=twitter

Hogan, M. (2002, July 14). ESPN celebrates milestone "SportsCenter." *Multichannel News*. Retrieved from https://www.multichannel.com/news/espn-celebrates-milestone-sportscenter-148448

Hull, K., & Lewis, N. P. (2014). Why Twitter displaces broadcast sports media: A model. *International Journal of Sport Communication, 7*, 16–33. doi: 10.1123/ISJC.2013–0093

Johnson, R. G., & Romney, M. (2017). Boosterism or audience interest? An examination of self-promotion on sports network highlight shows. *Journal of Sports Media, 12*(2), 1–23. doi: 10.1353/jsm.2017.0008

Johnson, R., & Romney, M. (2018). Howe the west was lost: Geographic bias on sports-network highlight shows. *Journal of Sports Media, 13*(1), 99–121. Retrieved from https://search.proquest.com/docview/2056814186?accountid=4117

Kast, F. E., & Rosenzweig, J. E. (1974). *Organization and management: A systems approach* (2nd ed.). New York, NY: McGraw-Hill.

Miller, J. A., & Shales, T. (2011). *Those guys have all the fun: Inside the World of ESPN*. New York, NY: Little, Brown.

Ourand, J. (2013, July 1). Ratings not living up to demand for highlights-heavy shows. *Sports Business Daily*. Retrieved from https://www.sportsbusinessdaily.com/Journal/Issues/2013/07/01/Media/Sports-Media.aspx

Ourand, J. (2016, April 25). ESPN pushes back on negative critiques of 'SportsCenter'. *Sports Business Journal*. Retrieved from https://www.sportsbusinessdaily.com/Journal/Issues/2016/04/25/Media/ESPN-response.aspx

Park, M. K. (2015). Race, hegemonic, masculinity, and the "Linpossible!": An analysis of media representations of Jeremy Lin. *Communication and Sport, 3*(4), 367–389. doi: 10.1177/2167479513516854

Perez, A. J. (2018, May 25). Keith Olbermann takes an expanded role at ESPN, including a return to "SportsCenter." *USA Today*. Retrieved from https://www.usatoday.com/story/sports/2018/05/25/keith-olbermann-back-sportscenter-expanded-espn-role/644277002/

Putterman, A. (2018, March 26). What is SportsCenter? In search of a 21st-century identity, ESPN's signature show has changed course once again. *AwfulAnnouncing.com*. Retrieved from http://awfulannouncing.com/?s=what+is+sportscenter

Rasmussen, B. (2010). *Sports junkies rejoice! The birth of ESPN*. United States of America: CreateSpace Independent Publishing Platform.

Roberts, D. (2017, May 15). Inside ESPN's plan to reinvent SportsCenter. *YahooFinance.com*. Retrieved from https://finance.yahoo.com/news/inside-espns-plan-reinvent-sportscenter-140002621.html

Sandomir, R. (2002, May 13). Sports news shows come and go, but "SportsCenter" keeps on rolling. *New York Times*. Retrieved from https://www.nytimes.com/2002/05/13/business/media-sports-news-shows-come-and-go-but-sportscenter-keeps-on-rolling.html

Scolari, C. A. (2012). Media ecology: Exploring the metaphor to expand the theory. *Communication Theory, 22*(2), 204–225. doi.org/10.1111/j.1468-2885.2012.01404.x

Strauss, B. (2018, December 5). ESPN returns 'SportsCenter' to its roots: 'I think we miscalculated a little bit.' *Chicago Tribune*. Retrieved from https://www.chicagotribune.com/sports/ct-spt-espn-sports-center-changes-20181205-story.html??dssReturn=true

Tough times for TV: Networks face trouble on nightly newscasts. (1991, September 19). *Christian Science Monitor*. Retrieved from https://search.proquest.com/docview/291197969/abstract/458E5AA0D3C54039PQ/1?accountid=4117

Tuggle, C. A. (1997). Differences in television sports reporting of men's and women's athletics: ESPN *SportsCenter* and CNN *Sports Tonight*. *Journal of Broadcasting and Electronic Media, 41*(1), 14–24. doi: 10.1080/08838159709364387

Turner, J. S. (2014). A longitudinal content analysis of gender and ethnicity portrayals on ESPN's SportsCenter from 1999 to 2009. *Communication and Sport, 2*(4), 303–327. doi: 10.1177/2167479513496222

Vogan, T. (2015). *ESPN: The making of a sports media empire*. Urbana, IL: University of Illinois Press.

13. ESPN's Evolving Mobile Motives: Development, Consumption, Competition

JAKE KUCEK, ZACH HUMPHREYS, ADAM C. EARNHEARDT,
AND GREG G. ARMFIELD

Sports fans have access to more news, information, entertainment, and live events than ever thanks in part to the seemingly endless options for sports mobile applications (apps) and social media platforms to complement their viewing experience. Although fans continue to follow their favorite sports, teams, and athletes through traditional media platforms, the new multiscreen, multiplatform, mobile format has forever changed the sports media landscape, how fans experience it, and what consumers expect from it. ESPN is leading these expectations along with the development of its ever-expanding multiscreen experiences, albeit with strong competition from professional leagues and other sports media outlets. This chapter addresses the rise of sports mobile apps by focusing on ESPN's domination of the sports app market and their ability to introduce new digital products to engage and retain a large but increasingly fragmented audience.

We address the history of apps, in general, and sport apps specifically, the motivation for mobile app use with respect to sports media consumption, key demographics, and app rankings, provide a timeline of previous, current, and future sports app developments—and address how ESPN has influenced those developments. The greatest need for exploration is the current landscape of ESPN's family of sports apps, how competitors have influenced or been influenced by that landscape, including the development of ESPN's all-encompassing app, and the addition of ESPN+ to said app. Understanding how ESPN utilizes social media in conjunction with the development of its mobile technology will also be emphasized. Lastly, we explore how the rise of smart devices for accessing information and the multiscreen behaviors of sports media fans and consumers impact future research and questions for academics, administrators, sports leagues, media outlets, and digital marketers and advertisers.

Sports App Market

It is important to understand historical advancements of mobile apps. In 1997, the Nokia 6110 mobile phone was first to introduce a simple game called Snake. But it was not until July 2008 when the first 500 apps were made publicly available in the Apple App Store for iPhone users (Strain, 2015). Statista (2018) claimed over 5 billion mobile phone users globally and approximately 237.6 million users located in the United States. eMarketer.com (2017) reported the average adult in the U.S. spent nearly two-and-a-half-hours a day using mobile apps in 2017, a 10% increase from 2016. Although there are a wide variety of apps across various categories (i.e., games, social networking, entertainment, productivity), the sport categories arguably have had a larger and more significant impact on the overall popularity in the mobile app marketplace.

According to Crook (2012), the number of apps downloaded through Apple's App Store rose from 3 billion in 2010 to 30 billion in 2012. Sports categories were among the top 15 most downloaded categories throughout this time period. This upward trend in general, and sport apps specifically, has continued. Evidence for this can be found in reports that show over 25 million iOS apps downloaded in 2016, and more than 197 million total app downloads in 2017 (Statista, 2017). The ESPN app easily dominates this marketplace as the number one most downloaded sports app in 2018 for iOS and Android platforms (Redbytes, 2019). Sports apps, especially those created by ESPN, have continued to see success in the digital age. To fully understand why ESPN's apps have enjoyed success, it is important to explore the key demographics related to these digital technologies, mobile apps, and media consumers.

Demographics

The ways in which we absorb content, information, and entertainment has experienced a revolutionary shift. This revolution was driven, in part, by critical mass, global adoption of smartphones and tablets that have empowered consumers, wherever they are, with more control over content (Martin, 2013). The trend for most media companies is to move content and other offerings toward mobile platforms. Martin (2013) stated mobile app penetration exceeded the entire population of 106 countries. Furthermore, worldwide mobile advertising passed $28 billion in 2016 and there is projected to be more than 10 billion mobile connections in the next decade. Content and advertisements are being created and tailored more for mobile devices and apps than traditional media like radio and newspapers.

According to Pew Research Center (2018), the vast majority of Americans (95%) own mobile phones of some kind. The portion of Americans that owns smartphones is 77%, up from just 35% from 2011. Most Americans now have smartphones and the ability to download apps, send, share, and receive content, and get instant access to information and entertainment. Furthermore, mobile devices and app adoption is not just for the young. Pew (2018) found seniors are maintaining more digitally connected lives. Four in ten (42%) adults age 65 and older report owning smartphones, up from 18% in 2013 (Pew Research, 2018). Internet use and home broadband adoption have risen substantially among this age group. Today, 67% of seniors use the Internet, a 55% increase in just under two decades (Anderson & Perrin, 2017). According to Anderson (2017), many lower-income Americans are relying more on smartphones. In 2016, one-fifth of adults living in households earning less than $30,000 a year were "smartphone-only" Internet users, and just over 70% of adults with household incomes below $30,000 a year own a smartphone.

These statistics are important to highlight when considering the rise in development and adoption of mobile-ready information and entertainment content and apps, including sports media information and entertainment from sources like ESPN. If a media outlet is not able to reach its audience through mobile search and display, or it is not providing a satisfactory mobile experience, it will lose subscribers to competitors. In many ways, ESPN has history, albeit short, of leading this eager group of sports-related content providers, even if it is not always the "worldwide leader."

Sports App Development

ESPN's attempt at becoming a wireless carrier through an ESPN-branded cellular service with ESPN-branded phones hints at the sports media leader's willingness to pursue new technological frontiers. Although the product and service ultimately failed, ESPN officials reportedly agree that the experience it gained in building mobile software and services proved invaluable in their development of smartphone apps and mobile-ready content (McCracken, 2016).

As apps became a useful tool for consumers to find information and entertainment, the demand for sports apps rose. Leading the way was the app rendition of ESPN's Internet-based content. At the peak of mobile devices in 2008, then President of ESPN and ABC Sports Customer Marketing and Sales, Ed Erhardt, said "we're seeing extraordinary usage with mobile devices," calling mobile "a big part of the future as it relates to how fans are going to consume sports" (Cuneo, 2008, para. 1). This led to the creation of the ESPN app in June of 2009. The ESPN app was the fifth sports-related app, lagging behind TheScore and Yahoo Sports, which were released almost a year earlier. Fox Sports and CBS Sports also beat ESPN to its app launch. Table 13.1 lists the original release date for the most highly used apps that provide scores, news, and updates for multiple sports. Specialized apps that only provide information on one sport (i.e., league-owned apps such as NFL Mobile or FIFA) were excluded from this list.

Table 13.1: App release dates.

App	Date
TheScore	July, 2008
Yahoo Sports	July, 2008
Fox Sports	November 2008
CBS Sports	March, 2009
ESPN	June, 2009
Bleacher Report	March, 2011
Watch ESPN	April, 2011
NBC Sports	July, 2012
Barstool Sports	April, 2013
Fox Sports Go	October, 2013
Bleacher Report	May, 2016

Source: iOsnoopes. (2019). Top 200 free iPad apps for sports. Retrieved from https://www.iosnoops.com/apps-charts/ipad/sports/free/sort-by-rank/

ESPN has consistently ranked in the top three most popular downloaded apps among the list of sports apps in both Google and Apple's app stores. As of January 2019, ESPN ranked second in terms of downloads among its competitors for IOS consumers and third among Android users. Table 13.2 shows the rankings of the most popular sports apps according to Google Play and iTunes.

Table 13.2: App rankings.

Apple Store Ranking (Sports)	Google Play Store Ranking (Sports)
CBS Sports	CBS Sports
ESPN	Yahoo Sports
Yahoo Sports	ESPN
Bleacher Report	NBC Sports
NBC Sports	WatchESPN
WatchESPN	Fox Sports Go
Fox Sports	TheScore
TheScore	Bleacher Report
Barstool Sports	Barstool Sports

Source: Google Play. (2019). Top free in sports. Retrieved from https://play.google.com/store/apps/category/SPORTS/collection/topselling_free
Source: iTunes. (2019) App store sports. Retrieved from https://itunes.apple.com/us/genre/id6004

ESPN may have been the fifth sports application created behind The-Score, Yahoo, and other competition, but they continue to rank among the highest downloaded apps. It is clear ESPN's contribution continues to dominate the app market influencing the way sports media deliver content. The ESPN app has become the most popular sports app on the market, setting the bar for other competing apps (Redbytes, 2019).

Motivation for Sport App Use

Motivations behind smartphone usage are important to consider for marketers and academics alike. Face-to-face communication has been shown to be positively associated with cell phone usage (Jin & Park, 2010). A 2016 study conducted by emarketer.com found 31% of the 3,005 U.S. smartphone users surveyed reported they installed a mobile application because a friend recommended it to them. It is clear interpersonal communication plays a role in which apps will be downloaded and which apps will not be. However, it is also necessary to explore personal motivations, which are often more consistent with individual consumers.

Remick (2011) argued apps are specifically designed for mobile devices to help users execute specific tasks. While users are utilizing mobile technology and apps for a variety of reasons, scholarship has only recently begun to explore the motivations behind app usage. The Technology Acceptance Model

(TAM) was developed to explain perceptions, intentions, and the actual usage of technologies (Kang, Ha, & Hambrick, 2015). TAM has been used to further understand mobile TV, mobile data usage, mobile games, and mobile Internet services. Overall, smartphones are being adopted faster than most mediums and their impact can be felt on consumer behavior and an increase in effective communication (Jieng, 2009; Liang & Yeh, 2011; Verkasalo, 2011). Additionally, Seo and Green (2008) developed the Motivation Scale for Sport Online Consumption (MSSOC) for understanding sport-specific consumer motivations, including: (a) fanship, (b) information, (c) entertainment, (d) economics, (e) interpersonal communication, (f) escape, (g) pass time, (h) team support, (i) fan expression, and (j) technological knowledge.

Sports apps also support sport involvement and psychological commitment as college students "primarily used smartphones and sport-related apps to consume and communicate about sports" (Kang et al., 2015, p. 285). Specifically, the group of college students studied by Kang et al. listed fanship, convenience, and information as the three motives for using sport apps. As sports apps and features continue to evolve, it will be important for research to continue exploring the unique motivations sports fans have for using sports apps.

Motivation and ESPN App Development

Sports media critics and industry leaders predict that as mobile-connection speeds continue to increase, there will be more interest in live game viewing on mobile devices (Cuneo, 2008). As ESPN became aware of consumers using mobile to receive their sports information, it began to adapt and focused on the development of its app market share. The media landscape dramatically shifted in the 2010s due to digital innovations, and many consumers have called on traditional news outlets to evolve with the technology. Along those lines, ESPN unveiled its ESPN Developer Center in 2012 in an effort to reinvent how its content is used and distributed (Strange, 2012). This center has revolutionized how viewers receive their sports content by dedicating an entire division to the creation and distribution of apps. Jason Guenther, Vice President of ESPN Digital Media Technology, said:

> The ESPN Developer Center allows us to scale more quickly and to reach more fans in new ways with the ESPN content they want … Making ESPN APIs available to innovative partners and independent developers helps ensure that we remain nimble, efficient and creative in our own product development, which translates to more and better ESPN products for fans. (Strange, 2012, p. 3)

As stated on the Center website, "Time to start coding. You know the code. We know sports. Let's build some cool stuff" (ESPN Development Center, 2018, para. 1).

As recently as 2017, ESPN Senior Vice President for Production and Multimedia Integration Tina Thornton led a push for the ESPN app to evolve. The marketing campaign focused on the message of telling viewers to download and stream the ESPN app to simulcast ESPN TV channels, making available archived material to authenticated cable subscribers (Ourand, 2017). The campaign started by replacing the ESPN brand on its microphone flags with the app's "E" logo. ESPN ran promos during *SportsCenter* and highlighted the app on the ticker. Advertisements ran on TV, radio, digital, and social media. ESPN also had its on-air talents mention the app in nearly every live-read and recorded promotion. The campaign is the result of ESPN trying to further revolutionize their app as a streaming service, in order to combat the issue of losing television subscribers due to cord-cutting.

ESPN has struggled in the last few years as a result of consumers leaving cable and satellite packages in favor of streaming services such as Netflix, Hulu, and Amazon (Owens, 2018). Online streaming platforms like Netflix changed contemporary viewing preferences (i.e., binge-watching), technologies (i.e., viewing on different platforms), choice-based environments and previous structures (i.e., channel structure and schedule) (Samuel, 2017). According to a study by *Variety* in 2017, a total of 22.2 million U.S. adults will have cut the cord on cable or satellite service, up 33% from 16.7 million in 2016. Consumers who have never subscribed to pay TV (cord-nevers) increased 5.8% in 2017, to 34.4 million. By 2021, the number of cord-cutters is predicted to nearly equal the number of cord-nevers; a total of 81 million U.S. adults. Meaning, approximately 30% of U.S. adults will not have traditional pay TV, per eMarketer's revised forecast (Spangler, 2017).

To combat the cord-cutting trend, ESPN revolutionized the sports app market again by adding a streaming service to their popular ESPN app. ESPN's parent company, Walt Disney, launched an ESPN-branded multisport video streaming service (ESPN+). The streaming service combines ESPN's two most popular apps, ESPN and WatchESPN. Robert Iger, chairman and chief executive of Disney said:

> The changes will be dramatic, with more compelling visuals as well as an easy, intuitive interface with exceptional video and sound quality. Users will be able to enjoy and increasingly personalized experience as the app blends explicit choices with implicit behavior to curate a unique mix of specific, relevant content tailored to the taste of each individual user. (Duberstein, 2018, para. 3)

As noted above, when ESPN app development started, developers created as much content as they could until it had more than 50 app offerings (e.g., ESPN "pinball" app). ESPN then refocused on only primary apps: the

ESPN app, WatchESPN (a video-centric app, which can authenticate paying cable or satellite subscribers and unlock entitled content), and ESPN's fantasy sports app. ESPN has revolutionized its app market by unifying ESPN and WatchESPN, focusing on artificial intelligence to give the user an adaptive and customized experience. ESPN's plan is to identify, create, and distribute highlights designed not to please everybody, but special audiences, such as NBA fans in Australia who follow local heroes such as Melbourne-born Dante Exum (McCracken, 2016). "There are no highlights on those guys," LaBerge says. "We're thinking we need to be able to cut highlights for players that we don't care about here, but that could instantly create an Australian NBA highlight clip for all the Australian players, and include that in product for Australia" (McCracken, 2016, p. 4). And that is exactly what ESPN plans to do. ESPN wants its app to deliver highlights in a quicker manner than the user having to rewind his or her DVR.

The new subscription-based streaming app ESPN+, embedded in the ESPN app, gives users access to more live sports, even content that is unavailable on ESPN's linear networks. This paid access includes boxing, golf, rugby, baseball, and cricket. For a Netflix-like experience, ESPN+ offers a library of ESPN Films, including the *30 for 30* series of documentary films (Leung, 2018). ESPN+ is an acknowledgment that the sports app game has changed for sports broadcasters. "We have to challenge ourselves on how we maintain relevance and connection at every point along the way, so that the ESPN brand continues to mean something special," said Justin Connolly, Executive Vice President of Affiliate Sales and Marketing for Disney/ESPN Media Networks (as cited in Steinberg, 2018, para. 3).

To that end, and with the addition of ESPN+, it is clear that the sports app market is saturated with an abundance of options. ESPN started the trend with its ESPN-branded cellular devices and then became the fifth sports app created. Since then, it has revolutionized the app market: ESPN once offered more than 50 apps, but has narrowed it's focus to three core apps. ESPN is taking the first leap into the future of apps becoming a fully fledged, monthly subscription-based streaming company. ESPN is devoted to spending its resources on the development of apps, which has resulted in its apps being consistently listed on top of both Apple and Google's top-ranked sports apps.

ESPN App Competition and Vulnerability

ESPN has paved the way for other sports media organizations to develop app technology and cater to the growing consumer who desires more information and entertainment at his or her fingertips. In 2017, fans averaged 2.9 million daily views of *SportsCenter* videos on ESPN digital platforms, (Hall, 2017); translating into more than one billion *SportsCenter* video views on ESPN platforms a year.

As ESPN continues its dominance in the sports media landscape, competitors will continue to make strides in the digital platform arena. For example, TheScore, a popular sports app, is the primary competitor for ESPN apps. First and foremost, its partnership with Facebook heavily influences the amount of attention the app receives from consumers. Olenski (2017) posits TheScore has utilized chatbot engagement strategies to encourage traffic and interest (i.e., quiz-based Super Bowl challenge). Moreover, large corporations like Subway, Mountain Dew, Sony Pictures, and Doritos have conducted campaigns aimed at engaging esports fans interested in information on competitive gaming (Olenski, 2017).

As of January 2016, TheScore esports had 750,000 monthly active users (Olenski, 2017), only a year after the company launched the application. In 2017, the app averaged 4.4 million monthly users, and has shown immense growth during its first three years. John Levy, the Founder and CEO of TheScore states "from the very start, we always treated mobile as its own unique product," and that this "independence also means we aren't afraid to aggregate and share news and content from multiple sources" (Olenski, 2017, p. 1). One unique feature TheScore's apps offer is that it allows the users to create their own content page where they can follow their favorite teams, players, scores, stats, and news that matters most to them.

While the ESPN app utilizes some of these same features, it does not allow the user to follow a specific player. Instead a user can select his or her favorite teams and follow news on only those teams. Olenski (2017) concluded that, "TheScore's approach and visionary understanding of the sports and gaming audience has put large media companies like ESPN on the defensive" (p. 2). The idea of player-only news, and news designed for a specific audience is something that ESPN hopes to incorporate into its mobile apps soon. For example, highlights targeted for NBA fans in Australia, who follow local players like Dante Exum, will be the future says ESPN CTO Aaron LaBerge (McCracken, 2016). ESPN better hurry though; TheScore is excelling at offering this feature to its users.

ESPN, while remaining a dominant force in the industry, faces challenges on other fronts. In December 2017, ESPN laid off 150, after 300 were let go in 2015 (Hruby, 2017), while digital competitors such as Barstool Sports have entered the arena and have been embraced by younger demographics, leading to a weakened market share for ESPN. Reporter Richard Deitsch said, "there was once a time when ESPN was a safe harbor, the destination job for people in sports media, but that's no longer the case. They're facing all sorts of headwinds, and facing them in an incredibly challenging media environment" (Hruby, 2017, p. 7). ESPN is facing this financial and competitive trouble, in part, because of cord-cutters and cord-nevers, but also because of shifts in content, platform, and style preferences (i.e., Barstool Sports has a less conservative approach than ESPN, and at times borders on a misogynistic tone). Additionally, the fight over broadcast rights in sports will be an interesting area to watch as streaming devices and cord-cutters become more prevalent.

ESPN App Future and Social Media

Sports media consumers have a need for instant gratification through quick highlights and interview clips, and ESPN has begun to combat this issue by developing additional mobile content that can be accessed through popular social media platforms. For example, *SportsCenter* is available on Snapchat. The first episode aired in November of 2017. This may be the future direction for ESPN's most popular show. *SportsCenter* on Snapchat features younger hosts, and content that is fast-paced (Leung, 2018). The show targets audience members between the ages of 13 and 24. Katie Nolan, who gained popularity as one a host of the Snapchat iteration of *SportsCenter* believes that it is geared toward kids and other millennials, and that "the reason they've named it *SportsCenter* is because they want it to mean something to a different generation of people" (p. 1). For a more indepth analysis of *SportsCenter* on Snapchat see chapter 12.

Social media and sport communication scholars can point to moments in social media and app development history to show how the relevance of platforms fade and give way to new mediums (i.e., MySpace). ESPN, and other competitors, will have to be at the forefront of emerging and declining social media and sports platforms as they continue to enhance their mobile content to reach the smartphone masses. While Snapchat is popular today, changes in technology—interface, content, accessibility—can quickly impact the number of active users on a specific platform. It will be important for sport communication scholars to continue to examine how ESPN and other sports media networks embed mobile content in and through those platforms as social media platforms like Twitter have the ability to stream NFL video, including a 30-minute digital show airing five nights per week (Perez, 2017).

Conclusion

Mobile applications have clearly forced media outlets like ESPN to focus on innovative ways for engaging consumers who actively seek sports information and entertainment—content consumers can access at times and places of their choosing. These innovations have led to ESPN's dominance of the sports app market. Watching an hour-plus-long cable TV shows like *SportsCenter* to fill a sports information-news-entertainment fix is quickly being replaced by a desire to watch content tailored for the consumer in shorter, fragmented news clips and highlights. The statistics regarding smartphone use, mobile app download data, and increased usage of sports apps for information and entertainment shows that consumers are enamored with mobile media forms and willing to embrace new technologies, so long as those new technologies come with an ease-of-use and desirable content. Understanding where ESPN ranks in the world of sports apps sheds some light on competition surrounding ESPN. Moreover, social media platforms will continue to be utilized by companies like ESPN to appeal to millennials and young demographics.

References

Anderson, M. (2017, March 22). Digital divide persists even as lower-income Americans make gains in tech adoption. *Pew Research Center.* Retrieved from http://www.pewresearch.org/fact-tank/2017/03/22/digital-divide-persists-even-as-lower-income-americans-make-gains-in-tech-adoption/

Anderson, M., & Perrin, A. (2017). Tech adoption climbs among older adults. *Pew Research Center.* Retrieved from http://www.pewinternet.org/2017/05/17/tech-adoption-climbs-among-older-adults/

Crook, J. (2012, June 11). Apple's App Store hits 30 billion downloaded apps, paid out $5 billion to developers. *Tech Crunch.* Retrieved from https://techcrunch.com/2012/06/11/apples-app-store-hits-30-billion-downloadedapps-paid-out-5-billion-to-developers/

Cuneo, A. (2008). More fans hit ESPN's mobile site than its PC pages. *AdAge.* Retrieved from https://adage.com/article/digital/football-fans-hit-espn-s-mobile-site-pc-pages/122885

Duberstein, B. (2018, Feb 13). 3 things Bob Iger wants you to know about Disney's future: The new Disney is direct to you. *The Motley Fool.* Retrieved from https://www.fool.com/investing/2018/02/13/3-things-bob-iger-wants-you-to-know-about-disneys.aspx

ESPN Development Center. (2018). Home of the ESPN API. *ESPN.* Retrieved from http://www.espn.com/static/apis/devcenter/overview.html

eMarketer. (2016, September 15). *What makes smartphone owners download an app?* Retrieved April 19, 2018, from https://www.emarketer.com/Article/What-Makes-Smartphone-Owners-Download-App/1014482

Google Play. (2019). Top free in sports. Retrieved from https://play.google.com/store/apps/category/SPORTS/collection/topselling_free

Hall, A. (2017, August 14). *SportsCenter* to increase digital emphasis, revise TV lineup. *ESPN Press Room*. Retrieved from https://espnmediazone.com/us/press-releases/2017/05/sportscenter-increase-digital-emphasis-revise-tv-lineup/

Hruby, P. (2017, December 07). ESPN: Can the worldwide leader in sports manage its own decline? *The Guardian*. Retrieved from https://www.theguardian.com/sport/2017/dec/07/espn-revenue-viewership-politics-layoffs

iOsnoopes. (2019). Top 200 free iPad apps for sports. Retrieved from https://www.iosnoops.com/apps-charts/ipad/sports/free/sort-by-rank/

iOsnoopes. (2019). Top 200 free iPhone apps for sports. Retrieved from https://www.iosnoops.com/apps-charts/iphone/sports/free/sort-by-rank/

iTunes. (2019) App store sports. Retrieved from https://itunes.apple.com/us/genre/id6004

Jin, B., & Park, N. (2010). In-person contact begets calling and texting: Interpersonal motives for cell phone use, face-to-face interaction, and loneliness. *Cyberpsychology, Behavior, and Social Networking, 13*(6), 611–618. doi.org/10.1089/cyber.2009.0314

Kang, S. J., Ha, J. P., & Hambrick, M. E. (2015). A mixed-method approach to exploring the motives of sport-related mobile applications among college students. *Journal of Sport Management, 29*(3), 272–290. doi.org/10.1123/jsm.2013-0065

Leung, D. (2018, February 7). Why ESPN is reimaging its app with a $4.99 ESPN+ streaming service. *SportTechie*. Retrieved from https://www.sporttechie.com/why-espn-reimagining-app-499-streaming-service-plus/

Liang, T., & Yeh, Y. (2011). Effect of use contexts on the continuous use of mobile services: The case of mobile games. *Personal and Ubiquitous Computing, 15*(2), 187–196. doi:10.1007/s00779-010-0300-1

Martin, C. (2013). *Mobile influence: The new power of the consumer*. New York, NY: Palgrave Macmillan.

McCracken, H. (2016, June 13). The technology behind ESPN'S digital transformation. *Fast Company*. Retrieved April 19, 2018, from https://www.fastcompany.com/3060717/the-technology-behind-espns-digital-transformation

Olenski, S. (2017, June 14). The brand that's giving ESPN its run for the mobile money. *Forbes*. Retrieved from https://www.forbes.com/sites/steveolenski/2017/06/14/the-brand-thats-giving-espn-its-run-for-the-mobile-money/#f000ffe1af95

Ourand, J. (2017, August 29). ESPN making stronger push for app with new promos, branding, ad campaign. *Sports Business Daily*. Retrieved from https://www.sportsbusinessdaily.com/Daily/Issues/2017/08/29/Media/ESPN-App.aspx

Owens, J. C. (2018). With Fox merger and ESPN streaming effort, Disney has a confusing mess to sort out. *Market Watch*. Retrieved from https://www.marketwatch.com/story/with-fox-merger-and-espn-streaming-effort-disney-has-confusing-mess-to-sort-out-2018-02-06

Perez, S. (2017, August 29). Twitter announces a new deal for year-round NFL content that includes live video, but no games. *Tech Crunch*. Retrieved from https://

techcrunch.com/2017/05/11/twitter-announces-a-new-deal-for-year-round-nfl-content-that-includes-live-video-but-no-games/

Pew Research Center. (2018, February 5). *Mobile fact sheet*. Received from http://www.pewinternet.org/fact-sheet/mobile/

Redbytes. (2019). Top 15 sports apps for iOS and Android 2018. Retrieved from https://www.redbytes.in/sports-apps-2018/

Remick, J. (2011). What is a web app? Here's our definition. *App Storm*. Retrieved from https://web.appstorm.net/general/opinion/what-is-a-web-app-heres-our-definition/

Samuel, M. (2017). Time wasting and the contemporary television-viewing experience. *University of Toronto Quarterly, 86*(4), 78–89. doi: 10.3138/utq.86.4.78

Seo, W. J., & Green, B. C. (2008). Development of the motivation scale for sport online consumption. *Journal of Sport Management, 22,* 82–109. doi.org/10.1123/jsm.22.1.82

Spangler, T. (2017, September 13). Cord-cutting explodes: 22 million U.S. adults will have canceled cable, satellite TV by end of 2017. *Variety.* Retrieved from http://variety.com/2017/biz/news/cord-cutting-2017-estimates-cancel-cable-satellite-tv-1202556594/

Statista. (2017). *Number of available apps in the iTunes App Store from 2008 to 2017.* Retrieved from https://www.statista.com/statistics/268251/number-of-apps-in-the-itunes-app-store-since-2008/

Statista. (2018). *Number of mobile phone users worldwide 2013–2019.* Retrieved from https://www.statista.com/statistics/274774/forecast-of-mobile-phone-users-worldwide/

Steinberg, B. (2018). Can a new president and streaming service help ESPN win again? *Variety.* Retrieved from http://variety.com/2018/tv/features/espn-trouble-jimmy-pitaro-streaming-service-ratings-disney-1202736283/

Strain, M. (2015, February 13). 1983 to today: A history of mobile apps. *The Guardian.* Retrieved from https://www.theguardian.com/media-network/2015/feb/13/history-mobile-apps-future-interactive-timeline

Strange, A. (2012). ESPN launches developer center for mobile sports apps. *PC Mag.* Retrieved from https://www.pcmag.com/article2/0,2817,2401170,00.asp

Verkasalo, H. (2011). An international study of smartphone usage. *International Journal of Electronic Business, 9*(1/2), 158–181. doi:10.1504/IJEB.2011.040360

14. Creation of The Longhorn Network: Shadow of a Dying Business Model

JARED JOHNSON

It was 2011 and college football was a prize sought after by television networks. The Bowl Championship Series (BCS) had increased interest in college football and schools were lining up to get in to a major conference with access to the BCS. Conferences were aware of the demand their product wielded. The Big Ten, which wanted a bigger share of the media rights pie, had successfully brokered its own network agreement with Fox Sports in 2004, forming the Big Ten Network with 24/7 programming of men's and women's sports (Smith & Ourand, 2017). The Big Ten Network launched in 2006 and boosted the revenue to each of its member teams to $22 million by 2011 (Smith & Ourand, 2017). That revenue (among other factors) successfully drew the interest of the University of Nebraska, luring it away from the Big-12 conference. But more importantly, the creation of the Big Ten Network changed the landscape of college football and its media rights, beginning a trend of conferences launching their own networks. Although the Pac-10 (later Pac-12) said initially it would not start its own network in 2008 (Smith & Ourand, 2017), the league changed its position by 2012, adding two schools (University of Utah and University of Colorado) and launching the Pac-12 Network (Miller, 2011). The Southeastern Conference (SEC)—a football powerhouse—followed suit and partnered with ESPN to start the SEC Network in 2014.

In the middle of all this scrambling for conference networks was the start of another network in 2011: The Longhorn Network (LHN). This network launch was different from the others. Rather than base the network around an athletic conference, it was launched around the athletics of a single school—The University of Texas at Austin (UT). The prominence of UT, the size of its athletic program and alumni base, and its success in athletics in the 2000s (e.g., a national football title, a Final Four trip for its men's basketball team) seemingly made its athletic program an ideal partner for ESPN and its sports business. Yet in its first five years of existence, media research firm SNL Kagan estimated LHN sustained estimated losses of $48 million (Selcraig, 2015). There is currently no public disclosure of LHN finances from 2016 or 2017.

This case history analyzes the creation of LHN within the framework of resource analysis as an attempt by ESPN and UT to gain a sustained competitive advantage (Barney, 1991). Although several media companies were investing in collegiate athletics media rights, nearly all were based around a conference. This case history suggests that despite putting massive resources into the success of LHN, the network (resource) value was simply not strong enough to gain the competitive advantage ESPN sought.

Literature Review

Firm resources (Barney, 1991) is a theoretical model that is designed to analyze companies attempting to achieve a sustained competitive advantage in a market system. Firm resources include all assets, firm attributes, information, knowledge, capabilities, and other attributes controlled by a firm that can be used to create a competitive advantage. ESPN (the firm in this case) brought its resources to bear in the creation of LHN in the hope that it could create that sustained advantage by purchasing exclusive rights and managing the content shown on the network. Generally, resources are classified into three categories: (a) physical capital resources (Williamson, 1975); (b) human capital resources (Becker, 1964); and (c) organizational capital resources (Tomer, 1987). These categories are appropriate to the case history involving ESPN's creation of LHN.

Sustained Competitive Advantage

In order for ESPN to gain a sustained competitive advantage through the creation of LHN, research says the resource (LHN in this case) must have four attributes (Barney, 1991): (a) it must be valuable in the sense that it exploits opportunities and/or neutralizes threats in the firm's environment; (b) it must be rare among the firm's current and potential competition; (c) it must be hard to imitate; and (d) there cannot be equivalent substitutes for this resource. In this case, competition would refer to any other sports network owned by companies outside of ESPN. Networks monopolize resources, in this case the rights to broadcast games in college sports. ESPN and others pay physical capital resources (money) in the form of contractual agreements with schools or conferences that give them exclusive rights to the broadcast of games. It is in the best interest of networks to tie up schools or conferences with highly desirable products into exclusivity arrangements to deny these resources to competitors. These attributes become resources only to the extent that they are valuable. Valuable can loosely be defined as desirability by audiences to view the product (Barney, 1991).

The framework of firm resources categorizes resources by their value. Rareness is required to produce a sustained competitive advantage (Barney, 1991). Networks diligently protect their broadcast rights exclusivity in order to maintain the rareness of their resource. If any competitor can imitate or duplicate resource, then the value diminishes such that a sustained competitive can no longer be achieved.

Creation of LHN

Following in the shadow of the successful launch of the Big Ten Network, ESPN launched LHN on August 26, 2011, just months after the initial announcement of the network's creation ("Texas, ESPN," 2011). It became a 24-hour television network dedicated to covering intercollegiate athletics, music, cultural arts and academic programs from UT. ESPN wanted to tap in to the lucrative media markets around the state of Texas and chose a school it felt had enough national appeal to draw in an audience. ESPN owns and operates the network and pays all its employees. It also established internships for UT students ("Longhorn Network Facts," 2012).

The basis for the formation of LHN was to acquire the third-tier media rights for the network. In college athletics, media rights are placed on three tiers. Initially, tier one was broadcast national networks, tier two was national cable, and tier three was syndication or local television either through the conference or through the local institutions (T. Odjakjian, personal communication, 2018). Over time, tiers one and two merged together with the media rights holders deciding where games were carried. Tier-one media rights are mainly for football and men's basketball games and are usually negotiated on a conference basis (e.g., ESPN networks and Fox networks hold the rights for Big-12 football games). In the case of the Big-12, the various networks rotate in regards to first selection of games (tier-one). The remaining, unselected games (tier-two) would then be distributed based on agreements between the Big-12 and its broadcast and cablecast partners. Third-tier media rights cover all other athletic events of the member schools that are not chosen by tier-one or tier-two rights holders (e.g., most men's and women's non-conference basketball games, women's soccer). In a Big-12 example, if UT is playing

Oklahoma State University (OSU) in football, ESPN would get the choice to broadcast that game if the network had the first-tier choice. If ESPN declined the game, it would fall into tier-two. If no national or regional partner picks up the game, then it falls to the third-tier media rights holder (Smith, 2012).

Third-tier media rights in the Big-12 and many other conferences are negotiated separately. At that time, the Big-12 allowed third tier rights to be held by individual schools, which were able to keep all revenue generated from that sale (T. Odjakjian, personal communication, 2018). So, in the case of UT, ESPN bought the third-tier media rights for LHN. As of 2018, LHN broadcast 175 sporting events per year, including live events from all 20 UT sports. The LHN schedule also includes hundreds of hours of original studio programming, including pre- and post-game shows with the *Texas Gameday* crew. LHN also does dozens of weekly coaches shows, live news conferences, features and documentary programs on current and former UT athletes, and behind the scenes access with UT teams ("Longhorn Network," 2018).

ESPN bore full responsibility of getting LHN carried on regional cable and national satellite systems, as well as distribution ("Texas, ESPN," 2011). IMG College (another UT media partner) was included in the contract and was responsible for advertising and sponsorships ("Longhorn Network Facts," 2012). UT had the responsibility in the contract to provide access to university players and coaches and content for LHN. The contract provided an annual payment to UT that started at $11 million in its first year and was set to grow by 3% annually for an average payment of just under $15 million per year over a 20-year period according to SNL Kagan. Based on the expected revenue, UT allocated 50% of its revenue from LHN/ESPN to go toward academics, funding endowed chair positions in several units ("Longhorn Network Facts," 2012).

One of the biggest barriers to the launch and success of LHN, however, was the initial lack of carriage by cable and satellite providers. ESPN did have the benefit of using its existing leverage (carriage fees for ESPN's other networks) with service providers to secure a channel position for LHN. Verizon FiOS was the first to carry LHN (Reynolds, 2018). Within a year, LHN had negotiated for carriage with AT&T U-verse, along with a slew of smaller cable providers around Texas. A little over a year later, in 2012, Cablevision, Cox and Charter Communications all agreed to carry LHN (Adler, 2012). One major holdout was Time-Warner Cable, which finally agreed to carry LHN in August of 2013—two years after its launch (Adler, 2013). Satellite providers were the biggest laggards. Dish Network agreed to carry LHN in 2014 (Adler, 2014), or more than three years after LHN's launch and DirecTV followed suit in 2015 (Vega, 2015).

Methodology

Research utilizing case history, a form of case study, allows for a focus on the evolution of a particular event or process (Denzin, 1989). Cases can be classified in such a manner to encompass a wide range of phenomena: From a single child to a classroom of children, even an incident such as the mobilization of professionals to study a childhood condition (Stake, 1995). Case history appears to be particularly applicable as a methodological approach regarding the examination of systems, as one seeks to evaluate the evolution of a given phenomenon (Fisher, 1978).

Several data collection methods were employed in this study, with in-depth interviews serving as the primary method. Four in-depth interviews were conducted. Interviews lasted between 20 and 50 minutes and were conducted both by phone and in person. Particular attention was given to individuals who were affiliated in some way with ESPN or LHN during the time of its creation to the present day. All interview participants were asked a standard set of questions, and then additional questions related to a participant's area of expert knowledge. Other materials, including documentary evidence, archival records, and published media reports were collected as part of the case history research process (see Yin, 1994). Credibility of the research was established through data triangulation (multiple sources to corroborate evidence) and member checks (Cresswell, 1997; Stake, 1995).

Case Results

Creation

The creation of LHN was a classic attempt to utilize firm resources to create a sustained competitive advantage over the competition. Following the success of the Big Ten Network with Fox, ESPN thought it could create something new around a single school with a large national following. ESPN was intrigued by the possibility of creating something different than a conference network. This was an attempt to create a unique resource. Initially, ESPN wanted another school as a partner to create a network around: "What ESPN really wanted was Notre Dame. Its large national following was attractive in the creation of a network" (M. Minor, personal communication, 2018). However, the Irish turned ESPN down and stuck with its TV contract with NBC for football and other networks through its affiliation with The Big East conference (the school moved to the Athletic Coast Conference in the 2013–14 sports season).

Once Notre Dame was no longer an option, ESPN looked for an alternative. The Big-12 had no network and UT had many favorable attributes, including its successful athletic teams. Its value was high at the time. Additionally, the state of Texas is a highly desirable location with several large media markets (Dallas and Houston are both top-10 U.S. television markets) and UT was the dominant school in the state at that time. ESPN felt that it could use those resources to its advantage. Another resource ESPN could bring to bear was human and technical capital. The creation of a new sports network was something the company had experience with (e.g., ESPN2, ESPNU). It had the people and knowledge to easily create a very professional-looking network. ESPN also had the connections to achieve the most difficult part of forming a network (distribution) and could use its connections to secure distribution to the audience on cable and satellite systems.

ESPN took this venture seriously from the beginning, committing some of its best human capital to the venture, sending employees from its headquarters in Bristol, Connecticut to Austin to staff the fledgling network. That human capital included talent, producers, and engineers. The process began with ESPN sending Dave Brown to oversee the LHN set-up out to Brigham Young University (BYU), a school that had recently invested in a multimillion dollar broadcast facility, including a 52-foot production expando-truck for live sports broadcasts (M. Minor, personal communication, 2018). BYU had just ramped up its production of televised sports content on the University's cable channel, after declaring its independence in Division-One football and joining the West Coast Conference in other sports as well as hiring senior producer Mikel Minor away from ESPN to run BYUtv sports programming. ESPN was familiar with what BYUtv had done and, in fact, regularly partnered with BYUtv on broadcasts. BYUtv was already included in nearly all major cable and satellite carriers and distributed to a nationwide audience (M. Minor, personal communication, 2018).

ESPN personnel toured the BYUtv facilities and met with BYUtv executives to get their insight on the creation and distribution of a network. This was an effort by ESPN to avoid any pitfalls and to assess the status of its own resources going in to this new venture (M. Minor, personal communication, 2018). BYUtv executives were able to discuss valuable strategies in getting cable/satellite services to add the service and, more importantly, reiterate the necessity of inclusion in those services to the success of the network. "We had been down that road long before. We have BYU fans all over the nation that wanted to see BYU games and the biggest hurdle was getting providers to include BYUtv in their package of service" (M. Minor, personal communication, 2018). BYUtv gave feedback regarding the importance of access to coaches and players for compelling content on the network, the use of state of the art graphics, and using prominent alums to give insight and drive viewer interest.

Initial Response

The initial response to LHN was expected. UT fans that could receive the channel loved the content as well as the fact their school was the only one with its own network. Other Big-12 conference schools were either envious, felt threatened, or were ambivalent to the network. Generally, any other schools in Texas, or nearby, such as the University of Oklahoma (OU), were unhappy about the network, feeling it gave the Longhorns an unfair advantage, both in money received and exposure ("Texas talks to rivals," 2011). Many also pointed to the potential damage it would do to the Big-12 (Tramel, 2016).

Also expected was the extreme pushback from cable companies to carry the network. This is something the Big Ten Network had also struggled with (Smith & Ourand, 2017). LHN struggled to gain carriage agreements with cable providers. Many UT fans—even those living in the state of Texas—were unable to get the channel, which led to several news articles and complaints to ESPN and UT athletics about not being able to see the games they wanted (Taliaferro, 2011).

Cable/satellite companies played the typical resistance game – not willing to foot the bill for distribution of LHN to audiences. ESPN fought back as Big Ten Network did by getting potential viewers to complain to their TV providers about carrying LHN. Over time, cable companies and eventually the satellite providers relented and network penetration grew. But the subscriber rates are not comparable to the rates conference networks command. By 2015, LHN received only 29-cents per month from 7.5 million subscribers compared to the Big Ten Network's $1 per month in home state subscribers and the $1.30 or more per month the SEC commands (Selcraig, 2015). Even in the state of Texas, subscribers pay more for the SEC Network than they do for the Longhorn Network (Selcraig, 2015).

Critics of LHN were abundant in the early days. Many accused LHN announcers of homerism during game broadcasts. Several blogs surfaced, (e.g., blatanthomerism.com) taking LHN to task. Several people interviewed for this research noted LHN executives frequently made a point to show how ESPN was running the UT operation just like the flagship in terms of on-air neutrality (A. Wall, personal communication, 2018; S. Druley, personal communication, 2018). Yet ESPN and LHN both maintained that critics must not truly be seeing the content: "The worst thing to me would be to produce TV only for Texas fans would want to see. Why would we do that?" (A.Wall, personal communication, 2018). Interviewees indicated there are standard professional practices that are implemented to make sure journalistic standards are met.

> When things happen we're going to report it. We have always done that and we have always asked the tough questions. We are journalists and consider it part of our job to do so. People would leave if they were ever asked to do things in a way that favors only Texas. (S. Druley, personal communication, 2018)

Interviewees like Druley expressed a significant level of frustration in the early days of LHN with criticisms about homerism. But most interviewees also indicated these criticisms faded significantly after the first five years. They indicated this is likely due to the fact that the product is more widely known and such criticisms simply don't stick (A. Wall, personal communication, 2018).

LHN's desire to carry high school football games also created pushback by other conference schools. ESPN and UT had counted on having high school football coverage as a potential resource to gain a sustained advantage for building interest and viewership (M. Minor, personal communication, 2018). Texas is one of the most fertile recruiting grounds for college prospects and UT has always had more name recognition in the state of Texas and a tradition of students wanting to attend UT as a life-long dream (S. Druley, personal communication, 2018; Hiestand, 2011). This controversy was at least partially responsible for the departure of Texas A&M to the SEC in 2012 (Staples, 2012). Other Big-12 schools felt this unfair advantage would be difficult to overcome in trying to recruit the top football players in the state. These schools appealed to the NCAA, which ruled in 2011 (after the launch of LHN had taken place) that high school sports cannot be covered by a university-branded network (Liebsohn, 2013). Doing so would be considered a sanctionable recruiting violation. The NCAA reinforced its position in January 2012, effectively putting an end to hopes of covering high school sports by university or conference-branded networks (Liebsohn, 2013).

Although ESPN and LHN initially indicated their desire to fight the NCAA ruling over high school football in court, nothing ever came to fruition. Several law reviews have indicated that a reversal of this ruling could only come via antitrust lawsuit. But all have said this would be a tricky argument, at best. In either case, a legal battle would tie up the network for years and not be guaranteed to garner a favorable result (Liebsohn, 2013).

This ruling was a setback to both ESPN and UT. For ESPN, this represented a devaluation of a firm resource it was attempting to make unique.

Although broadcasting high school sports is still an option for ESPN itself, doing so on a University-affiliated regional sports network with an avid audience—and being the first to do so—would be a unique and difficult to imitate resource. ESPN saw this as a resource during the planning phase of LHN (M. Minor, personal communication, 2018). It was especially concerning because a rival regional sports network (RSN), Fox Sports Southwest, had recently signed a deal in the state of Texas to broadcast all 10 of the state championship football games (Cantu, 2011).

For UT, this was less of a problem. It was still guaranteed to receive its annual payment from ESPN and still had its sports and university-related events covered in-depth. However, UT received the brunt of negative feedback because its brand was on the network. UT has always had the reputation in the Big-12 of being "the 800-pound gorilla" in the conference and throwing its weight around to get what it wanted—whether this perception was fair or not (S. Druley, personal communication, 2018). Many schools simply did not want to deal with this dynamic and giving UT a recruiting advantage with LHN. Certainly, there were some jealousies at play as well with the big payday UT was getting from ESPN that was not shared within the conference, as revenues from conference-branded networks are. The one exception was OU, which sold their third-tier media rights to Fox Sports for $58 million over 10 years (Staples, 2016). In 2019, the remaining eight conference schools agreed to sell its third-tier rights to ESPN's streaming service, ESPN+, with the transition taking place over a two-year period. The deal, however, fell well short of delivering these conference schools the sort of revenue enjoyed by UT through LHN (Carlton, 2019).

Another tactic LHN has taken to increase the value of its resources is to attempt to lock up games it sees as potentially important as a means to make sure distributors continue to offer LHN to viewers. Football is king and carries the most weight. The media rights deal with the Big-12 allows each school at least one home football game to be broadcast on its platform ("Texas Tech still not fans", 2011). Usually that means a non-conference game against a lesser opponent. But the truly anticipated games are against major opponents and especially conference foes. In order for LHN to be able to broadcast any conference home game, it must receive permission from the opposing school. In 2011, both Texas Tech and OSU rejected such a deal, with Tech's chancellor commenting that he did not want Tech fans to have to "give one dime to [LHN]" ("Texas Tech still not fans", 2011). But Iowa State (ISU) and Kansas (KU) both agreed ("Texas Tech still not fans", 2011; "Texas-Kansas," 2011). Both athletic directors said in press reports that they just wanted to act as a conference team and help each other out. They said the games aired on LHN felt like "just another game" to their fans. Interview subjects said LHN and ESPN arranged for a separate crew of announcers for those games in order to be neutral for an out-of-Texas audience (A. Wall, personal communication, 2018; S. Druley, personal communication, 2018).

In 2011, neither ISU (6–7) nor KU (2–10) were garnering national attention and both schools were just trying to build their brand. However, published media reports said that the deals struck with ESPN allowed for Jayhawk TV and Cyclones.TV to broadcast those games as well and helped grow the value of those school-based outlets ("Texas-Kansas football," 2011). The addition of those games to LHN brought the total in 2011 to three football games that aired live that year on LHN. That's roughly a quarter of the team's schedule and made negotiating with cable companies like Time Warner and DirecTV much easier. This is something interview subjects all said forms the current backbone of plans of LHN to remain competitive.

> The thing that draws the most eyeballs is football. If we can get three games broadcast live per year, that makes it possible to sustain all the other programming. Add in some men's basketball and, if UT is good, we can get more and more people watching. That's what we have to do going forward. (A. Wall, personal communication, 2018)

Another setback to ESPN and LHN has been the lack of competitiveness of the UT football team during the stretch that LHN has been in existence. In 2008 and 2009, UT was at the top of the football world, winning 25 of 27 games, culminating with a loss in the national title against Alabama in 2009. The first three seasons of LHN saw the football team turn in performances of 8-5 (2011), 9-4 (2012), and 8-5 (2013) with two bowl wins. The winning records were not enough to save Mack Brown's job as head coach and Charlie Strong was hired from Louisville in 2014 to end what was considered to be a string of mediocre performances (Volk, 2013). Things only got worse. In 2014 through 2016, UT finished with more losses than wins, never finishing higher than fifth in the Big-12 standings and making only one bowl appearance. Two straight years with no bowl appearance (2015 and 2016) were enough to prompt another coaching change and Tom Herman was brought in for the 2017 season to right the ship, as the football team finished 7-6. The issue with a less-than-stellar UT football team for ESPN was that on-field performance affected the value of the firm resource available to LHN. When UT teams win, the resource becomes more valuable. The value of winning is even greater in football and men's basketball than other UT sports.

It is clear in popular media reports and in-depth interviews for this study that ESPN has continually stated its commitment to the LHN venture. It felt like it had access to resources that would make it dominant in the region and that UT was the dominant program and would result in significant revenue during the length of the contract. Both the NCAA ruling on high school broadcasts, which negated one key resource, and the lack of competitiveness of UT teams since the 2011 launch, have rescinded the school's resource value to the point where LHN has sustained financial losses since its launch. One interviewee, who was at ESPN during the time the decision was being made to form LHN, said he thinks this is one instance where ESPN simply overestimated the value of a network based on a single school: "That was a decision I thought was strange to begin with, but ESPN was doing everything it could at that time to buy up as much college football as it could. In hindsight, I think they just overextended themselves" (M. Minor, personal communication, 2018).

The Future

It seems clear, including to the interview subjects in this study, that a network based around a single school (in this case, the UT) was not a valuable enough resource to propel a network to a sustained competitive advantage in the cable and satellite television market. The current trend in consumers ditching cable and satellite providers in favor of alternative methods of consuming media content (e.g., over-the-top services) has made predicting the industry's financial future even more difficult. Interviewees indicated we are in a time of transition when the sports broadcasting industry has to figure out where the revenue is coming from and how to best distribute college sports. ESPN agreed with the Atlantic Coast Conference (ACC) to help it form a conference network for fall 2019. ESPN has also announced that it will stream ACC games live in an effort to reach audiences who have cut cords already ("ACC, ESPN," 2016).

There have been efforts to get ESPN and UT to convert LHN into a network for the Big-12. But talks have stalled in those efforts with disagreements ranging from how the network would be named to compensation levels for UT (Carlton, 2016). At the time of this writing, neither the interview subjects, nor popular media, have given any hints of what is to come after the existing contract between UT and ESPN expires. Once the ACC Network launches in linear form, the Big-12 will be the only conference of the so-called "Power 5" conferences (Big Ten, SEC, ACC, and Pac-12) not to have a linear television network. Without such a network, most interview subjects and popular media analysts (e.g., Tramel, 2016) doubt the Big-12 can keep up with revenue per school handed out in other conferences. Most interview subjects also agreed that in order for a conference network to have sufficient content to be viable, it needed a conference membership of at least 12 schools, with 14 being the ideal number. The Big-12 currently has 10 schools and has had public disagreements on whether or not to expand and also who to add if expansion does occur (Carlton, 2016).

Most interview subjects for this study and many analysts in popular media still maintain that linear networks are not dead yet. They cite the monetary success of the Big Ten and SEC Networks as examples. Those people say that sports are the most valuable resources TV networks have because they are "the only thing you have to watch live" (M. Minor, personal communication, 2018).

Implications and Conclusion

This study has traced the history of the creation of the Longhorn Network by ESPN and UT as a case history within the framework of Barney's framework of firm resources analysis (1991). The analysis found that in engaging in strategic planning, ESPN identified the creation of a network around a single university to be valuable in several ways, including the attraction of a desirable regional audience. Upon announcing and creating the network, several setbacks to the value of the resource, as envisioned by ESPN, took place (e.g., the NCAA's denial of carrying high school football on LHN).

This study also found that the resources possessed by ESPN may have been overestimated as to their value and imitability during the planning process. Although ESPN and UT gave this initiative an honest effort, allocating valuable human capital and technological resources, the effort was not sufficient to gain the sustained competitive advantage it desired because the value of the resources were both overestimated and diminished by the market after creation. When considering the initial start-up years, strictly from a financial standpoint, the only beneficiary has been UT, still collecting its yearly payments for its third-tier rights. At the same time, LHN provides coverage of many non-athletic events on campus that might otherwise go unnoticed by the general public. ESPN, meanwhile, sustained financial losses in the first five years of the network (Selcraig, 2015). For a company that had been able to successfully get so many other networks off the ground, including the SEC Network, LHN was a drain on resources.

As with any case history research, there are limitations to the findings of one particular case. It can be useful to see that the creation of a network around a single school is risky, and likely not sufficient to generate sustained competitive advantage. But it is not sufficient to say that other schools that maintain their levels of success and with high marketability on a national scale would end up with the same result should a firm attempt to secure that resource (e.g., Notre Dame). Additionally, the field of sports broadcasting is very large. Case histories relating to other conference networks, including interviews with key people in those networks, would add to the value of this study greatly.

The future of sports broadcasting is a moving target. Although this study would appear to indicate that single-school networks are not viable in a for-profit market at a national level, it is unclear if other initiatives will appear that could change the value of that resource. However, analyzing these ventures in the long-establish framework of Firm Resources Analysis does have value in showing what variables increase or decrease the value of media rights as a resource.

References

ACC, ESPN partner for new conference channel. (2016, July 21). *ESPN.com*. Retrieved from espn.com/college-sports/story/_/id/17102933/acc-espn-agree-20-year-rights-deal-lead-2019-launch-acc-network

Adler, K. (2012, December 13). The Walt Disney Company and Cox Communications announce comprehensive distribution agreement. *ESPN Media Zone*. Retrieved from espnmediazone.com/us/press-releases/2012/12/the-walt-disney-company-and-cox-communications-announce-comprehensive-distribution-agreement/

Adler, K. (2013, August 30). Time Warner Cable Launches Longhorn Network. *ESPN Media Zone*. Retrieved from espnmediazone.com/us/press-releases/2013/08/time-warner-cable-launches-longhorn-network/

Adler, K. (2014, March 3). The Walt Disney Company and DISH Network sign groundbreaking long-term, wide-ranging agreement. *ESPN Media*. Retrieved from espnmediazone.com/us/press-releases/2014/03/walt-disney-company-dish-network-sign-groundbreaking-long-term-wide-ranging-agreement/

Barney, J. (1991). Firm resources and sustained advantage. *Journal of Management, 17*(1), 99–120. doi.org: 10.1177/014920639101700108

Becker, G. S. (1964). *Human Capital*. New York, NY: Columbia University Press.

Cantu, R. (2011, September 17). TV jumping as audience clamors for more preps. *Austin-American Statesman*, C1.

Carlton, C. (2016, May 12). What Texas needs from the Big 12 when it comes to expansion, The Longhorn Network. *Dallas Morning News*. Retrieved from https://sportsday.dallasnews.com/college-sports/texaslonghorns/2016/05/12/carlton-texas-needs-big-12-comes-expansion-longhorn-network

Carlton, C. (2019, April 10). Latest Big 12 media rights move will shift how fans watch favorite teams, and may cost extra for some viewers. *Dallas Morning News*. Retrieved from https://sportsday.dallasnews.com/college-sports/collegesports/2019/04/10/ latest-big-12-media-rights-move-will-shift-fans-watch-favorite-teams-may-cost-extra- viewers

Cresswell, J. W. (1997). *Qualitative inquiry and research design: Choosing among five Approaches*. Thousand Oaks, CA: Sage.

Denzin, N. K. (1989). *Interpretive biography*. Newbury Park, NJ: Sage.

Dosh, K. (2011, May 5). Television contract breakdown. *The Business of College Sports*. Retrieved from http://businessofcollegesports.com/2011/05/05/televison- contract-breakdown/

Fisher, B. A. (1978). *Perspectives on Human Communication*. New York, NY: MacMillan.

Hiestand, M. (2011, August 12). How Texas is steering College TV Sports. *USA Today*, 3C.

Leibsohn, B. (2013). Analysis of the NCAA rule prohibiting a school or conference-owned television network from televising high school sports events. *Marquette Sports Law Review, 23* (2), 435–454.

Longhorn Network Facts. (2012, March 5). *Texassports.com*. Retrieved from https://tex- assports.com/news/2012/3/5/030512aaa_240.aspx

Miller, T. (2011, July 27). Pac-12 announces deal for national, regional networks. *espn.com*. Retrieved from espn.com/blog/pac12/post/_/id/23602/pac-12- announces-deal-for-national-regional-networks

Reynolds, M. (2018, March 29). ESPN's Longhorn Network corrals Verizon FiOS as first announced affiliate. *Multichannel News*. Retrieved from https://www.multichan- nel.com/news/espns-longhorn-network-corrals-verizon-fios-first-announced-affili- ate-327394

Selcraig, B. (2015, December 26). Costliest college network in the country has lost mil- lions. *San Antonio Express News*. Retrieved from https://www.expressnews.com/ news/local/article/Costliest-college-network-in-the-country-has-lost-6721906.php

Smith, C. (2012, June 4). The ACC's third tier rights and why they're killing the conference. *Forbes*. Retrieved from https://www.forbes.com/sites/chrissmith/2012/06/04/ the-accs-third-tier-rights-and-why-theyre-killing-the-conference/#65ce0b906375

Smith, M., & Ourand, J. (2017, August 21). Big Ten Network's survival story. *Sports Business Journal*. Retrieved from https://www.sportsbusinessdaily.com/Journal/ Issues/2017/08/21/ In-Depth/BTN-main.aspx

Stake, R. E. (1995). Case studies. In N. K. Denzin & Y.S. Lincoln (Eds.), *Handbook of qualitative research*, 2nd edition (pp. 435–454). Thousand Oaks, CA: Sage.

Staples, A. (2012, July 5). TCU finally in Big 12. *Sports Illustrated*, 2.

Staples, A. (2016, March 28). The future of college sports media rights: How will deals evolve with the landscape? *Sports Illustrated*. Retrieved from https://www.si.com/ college-football/2016/03/28/how-are-college-sports-media-rights-deal-evolving

Taliaferro, T. (2011, August 31). If you want the Longhorn Network, call your cable provider now. *Alcalde*. Retrieved from https://alcalde.texasexes.org/2011/08/ if-you-want-the-longhorn-network-call-your-cable-provider-now/

Texas talks to rivals about TV network. (2011, July). ESPN.com. Retrieved from http://www.espn.com/college-sports/story/_/id/6787513/texas-seeks-calm-big-12-rivals-concerns-longhorn-network

Texas Tech still not fans of Longhorn Network. (2011, September). *Texammonthly. com*. Retrieved from https://www.texasmonthly.com/articles/texas-tech-still-not-fans-of-the-longhorn-network/

Texas-Kansas football game to air on Longhorn Network. (2011, September 2). *Texassports.com*. Retrieved from texassports.com/news/2011/9/2/090211aah_140.aspx

Tomer, J. F. (1987). *Organizational capital: The path to higher productivity and well-being*. New York, NY: Praeger.

Tramel, B. (2016, January 14). David Boren would like to end The Longhorn Network. *The Oklahoman*. Retrieved from newsok.com/article/5472488/david-boren-would-like-to-end-the-longhorn-network

Vega, J. (2015, January 22). Longhorn Network now on DirecTV. *kxan.com*. Retrieved from www.kxan.com/news/longhorn-network-now-on-directv/1049491423

Volk, P. (2013, December 14). Mack Brown officially resigns as head coach of Texas. *SBNation*. Retrieved from www.sbnation.com/college-football/2013/12/14/5203518/mack-brown-resigns-texas-head-coach

Williamson, O. (1975). *Markets and hierarchies*. New York: Free Press.

Yin, R. K. (1994). *Case study research: Design and methods* (2nd ed.). Thousand Oaks, CA: Sage.

15. National vs. Local: Fox Sports 1 and Fox Sports Networks in the 2010s

WILLIAM M. KUNZ

When Fox Sports 1 (FS1) launched in the summer of 2013, one of the network's slogans was "we are here to change the game." Rupert Murdoch no doubt dreamed of an influence commensurate with the impact the National Football League (NFL) on FOX had two decades earlier, when the deal News Corp. signed with the NFL in December 1993 and the affiliate swaps that followed transformed the television marketplace, turning the Big Three into the Big Four (Noglows, Flint & Lowry, 1994). The challenge for FS1 was perhaps even more daunting. Whereas the three major broadcast networks—ABC, CBS, and NBC—were showing signs of decline in the mid-1990s when the NFL arrived at FOX, ESPN began the head-to-head battle with FS1 with a considerable advantage, both in terms of prominent rights deals and lucrative carriage agreements with distributors. Murdoch had tried to dethrone ESPN once before, starting in the late 1990s, when News Corp. teamed first with Tele-Communications Inc. and then with Cablevision Systems Corp. in an attempt to link together regional sports networks to form a national challenger with Fox Sports Net. That bid failed, but it taught Fox executives a valuable lesson: there is a difference between national and local.

FS1 and Fox Sports Networks are different, but at the same time similar. One is a national service with a sister network, Fox Sports 2 (FS2), while the other is a collection of 22 regional sports networks (RSNs); one shares programming with the FOX broadcast network while the other focuses on the local television rights for professional baseball, basketball and hockey teams. The value of such contracts is also different. While the loss of a rights deal for a league or event can be a setback for a national network, it frees resources to pursue other deals; the loss of a rights deal for RSNs can be a death knell, since there are often limited programming alternatives in local markets. While the differences between the two might be significant, so too are the similarities. Both brandished the FOX logo and the Fox attitude. Fox Sports Media Group President Eric Shanks described the belief behind that combination: "Fans know when they see the Fox Sports shield that they are going to get something that is probably a little different, done a different way, with on-air talent you want to sit down and have a beer with, and you're going to have a little fun" (Block, 2013, p. 42). The business models for both are predicated on distribution on the most widely distributed tiers as opposed to sports tiers or as a premium service. That, in turn, makes carriage fees from cable, satellite and broadband distributors the most significant revenue stream, which makes cord-cutting and new distribution platforms a threat to their financial health.

The various holdings within Fox Sports contribute to critical debates around the ownership and regulation of television. Central to the evolution and growth of cable and satellite television were vertical integration, in which a company owns both distribution systems and content networks, and horizontal integration, in which a company owns multiple units of either distribution or content, and both combinations continue to raise anti-trust concerns. Vertical mergers generate the biggest headlines, evident in the combinations Comcast and NBC Universal in 2011 and AT&T and Time Warner in 2018. Horizontal integration, which allows companies to share resources and maximize economics of scale while consolidating and extending their control within a given media sector, is most critical to the discussion of Fox Sports. What was most interesting about the Fox holdings at the start of 2018 is that horizontal integration was seen at two different levels, the national and local level. Fox could share some resources across those levels, such as producers and announcers as well as management and even facilities, but there was one area in which it could not. At the heart of sports television are the rights to live event coverage, and while Twenty-First Century Fox could sign multi-billion-dollar national rights deals that included FOX, FS1 and FS2, the agreements it reached for its RSNs with individual teams were local ones and the content could not flow to FOX, FS1 or FS2. That difference proved to be significant as the future of the Fox Sports Media Group was negotiated over the course of 2018.

The Roots of Fox in Sports

It was a masterstroke that sent shockwaves through the world of sports television. On December 17, 1993, the National Football League accepted a pre-emptive bid from Rupert Murdoch for one of the crown jewels of sports television. For $1.58 billion over four years, the seven-year-old FOX

Television Network acquired the rights to the National Football Conference, a staple on CBS for close to four decades (Shapiro, 1993). Ten days earlier, Fox executives had made its pitch to the NFL television committee, trying to convince the league that the upstart network was worthy of its marquee package. Fox opened that presentation with a video entitled "Revolution" and the changes to the television landscape that flowed from that deal proved worthy of the title (Shapiro, 1993). In the months that followed, the Murdoch-controlled News Corp. acquired a 20% stake in New World Communication for $500 million and secured the shift of Fox affiliates in prominent markets from the UHF spectrum to the more powerful VHF spectrum, in many cases at the expense of CBS. News Corp. would acquire New World outright in 1997, but there is little question that the events of May 1994, called a "sweeping realignment of the television industry" in *The New York Times* and a "drive toward big network parity" in *The Washington Post*, changed the game (Carmody, 1994, A1; Carter, 1994, A1).

The evolution of Fox Sports Networks, and FS1, cannot be traced to such a singular moment and is better framed as an evolution than a revolution. In May 1996, News Corp. finalized a deal with cable operator Tele-Communications Inc. (TCI) to create a 50-50 joint venture, Fox/Liberty Networks (Flint & Peers, 1996). News Corp. contributed the FX basic cable channel and $350 million to the venture, while TCI added its financial interest in 15 RSNs, including the seven Prime Sports networks in which it held a majority interest and investments in three SportsChannel regional networks as well as SportSouth and Sunshine Network. Fox/Liberty added another service with the launch of Prime Sports Arizona in September 1996. That November, all the Prime Sports networks were relaunched under the Fox Sports Net (FSN) brand (Umstead, 1996). Then in January 1997, SportSouth relaunched as Fox Sports South after TCI acquired an additional 44% of the Atlanta-based regional network as part of the consent decree Time Warner Inc. signed with the Federal Trade Commission to complete its merger with Turner Broadcasting (Haddad, 1996). The same month, News Corp. launched a second RSN in Los Angeles, Fox Sport West 2, a sister network to the old Prime Network service in that market (Hettrick, 1996).

The size, and prominence, of Fox Sports Net grew soon thereafter. In June 1997, in a deal among media heavyweights, Fox reached agreement with Rainbow Media Holdings, a joint venture of Cablevision Systems Corp. and NBC, Inc. that created Regional Programming Partners. Rainbow contributed Madison Square Garden Network and its interest in seven RSNs for a 60% interest while the Fox group paid $850 million for a 40% interest in the new venture (Umstead, 1997). That deal gave Fox Sports Net access to the

New York market, with the addition of both Madison Square Garden Network and SportsChannel New York, but it did far more than that as the Rainbow group included SportsChannel networks in what were then three additional top six markets, Chicago, San Francisco, and Boston, and one more in the top 15, Cleveland. While Madison Square Garden Network maintained the MSG moniker, the five SportsChannel networks were relaunched under the Fox Sports Net banner in January 1998. The combination of the ten Fox/Liberty networks with the five rebranded Rainbow networks and seven affiliates gave Fox Sports Networks access to 58-million households (Reynolds, 1998).

There were predictions with the expansion of Fox Sports Net that it was positioned to be a "legitimate contender" to ESPN, but it was a very different breed of network. One of the challenges from the outset was to become more than a "loosely knitted confederation of regional sports networks" (Mansell, 1997). One of the pieces that was designed to bring the disparate parts together was *Fox Sports News,* which debuted in 1996. Following the expansion of the network in 1998, *Fox Sports News* distributed 2½ hours of programming per night, 30 minutes before evening game telecasts and 2 hours after (10:00 pm to midnight). The national program, however, struggled to gain traction. In October 1998, ESPN's 11:00 pm Eastern edition of *SportsCenter* averaged a 1.3 rating and 956,000 households, while the 10:00 pm Eastern edition of *Fox Sports News* averaged a 0.29 rating and 179,000 households (Donohue, 1998). The following month, Fox Sports Net announced that ESPN veterans Keith Olbermann and Chris Myers would join the network. While the arrival of Olbermann in January 1999 made headlines, it did not bring the ratings or stability Fox executives desired, and the national news program was shortened over time. In April 2000, the show relaunched as *National Sports Report,* but Olbermann was not long for the program. That summer, he shifted to a one-hour weekly show, *The Keith Olbermann Evening News,* but that too failed to build an audience and Olbermann left the network in May 2001 (Sporich, 2001). Fox Sports Net cancelled its national sports news shows, including the *National Sports Report,* in January 2002 (Sandomir, 2002).

There were various additions and subtractions to the Fox Sports portfolio over this period. In 1997, Fox/Liberty acquired the rights to first the Detroit Pistons of the NBA and then the Detroit Red Wings of the NHL. Securing the rights to the Red Wings for the 1997–98 season allowed Fox Sports Detroit to debut in September 1997. News Corp. was on the other end of similar move in Chicago, where Comcast struck a deal with the owners of the Cubs (Tribune Co.), White Sox and Bulls (Jerry Reinsdorf), and Blackhawks (Bill Wirtz) in December 2003, exchanging an ownership interest in a new regional network for the rights to those teams for the new Comcast SportsNet

Chicago, which debuted in October 2004. Fox Sports Chicago was part of the joint venture with Regional Programming Partners, but in February 2005, the two sides divided the assets, with News Corp. acquiring 100% ownership of FSN Florida and FSN Ohio and Cablevision gaining 100% ownership of Madison Square Garden Network, FSN New York and FSN Chicago, with the lattermost going dark in 2006 (Dempsey, 2005). Finally, in 2008, News Corp. sold FSN Northwest, FSN Rocky Mountains, and FSN Pittsburgh to Liberty Media in a complicated deal that also included DirecTV.

The path to FS1 was not quite as complicated but it was far from direct. In the 1990s, News Corp. invested in three new sports networks: Golf Channel, Speedvision and Outdoor Life Channel. In 1996, News Corp. acquired a one-third interest in Golf Channel for $50 million; in 1998, it acquired one-third interests in Speedvision and Outdoor Life Network for $90 million (Hettrick, 1998; Levin, 1996). Comcast was one of the other investors in all three services, a connection that became significant in 2001 when News Corp. acquired the two-thirds interest in Speedvision it did not control in a series of transactions that transferred its interest in Golf Channel and Outdoor Life Network to Comcast. Those moves created an important connection between FOX and Speedvision. In November 1999, Fox acquired the first 18 races of the NASCAR Cup Series starting with the Daytona 500 in 2001 in a deal valued at $1.4 billion (Schlosser, 2001). When that deal was announced, FX and Fox Sports Net were the services within News Corp. projected to create synergies with FOX around the NASCAR events, but control of Speedvision created a more natural partner. The name of the network was changed to Speed Channel in 2002 and just SPEED in 2005, but more significant was the influx of ancillary programming related to NASCAR, including practice sessions and pre-race qualifying, and the arrival of the NASCAR Truck Series in 2003. And while the name of the network changed to FS1 in 2013, the new television deal that started with the 2014 season included race coverage for the top two NASCAR series on FS1, a very important asset for the new network.

The Rise of Fox Sports 1

From the moment FS1 and FS2 debuted on August 17, 2013, when SPEED and Fuel ended their runs with the flip of a switch, their collective success was to be measured against ESPN and its collection of services. When Fox confirmed widespread speculation of a new multi-sport service the previous March, the headline in the *USA Today* read, "Fox throwing down challenge to ESPN" (Hiestand, 2013a, p. 1C). David Hill, the man who created Fox

Sports 20 years earlier, said, "We're not expecting to knock ESPN off in the first week or two. It's going to take two to three years. It will be a solid slog" (Deitsch, 2013, para. 2). While that prediction might have been offered somewhat in jest, by the time FS1 reached the three-year mark, the Aussie had left Fox Sports, most of the original lineup had been scuttled, and even the Murdoch-controlled *Wall Street Journal* said the network was experiencing a "personality crisis" (Flint, 2016, para. 3).

If there was to be a challenge to the supremacy of ESPN, FS1 began with a significant deficit in regard to event programming. In 2013, ESPN had contracts with the three most prominent professional leagues in the United States—Major League Baseball (MLB), National Basketball Association (NBA) and the NFL. In golf, it was home to early round coverage of The Masters and U.S. Open and exclusive home of the British Open. FS1 had few marque events when it launched, with college football and basketball from the Big-12 and Pac-12 conferences among the highlights, but added the NASCAR Cup Series, Big East basketball, and MLB in 2014 and United States Golf Association (USGA) tournaments in 2015 (Hiestand, 2013b; Sirak, 2013). What is significant about that collection of properties is that the contracts were part of broader deals with Fox.

The one area where Fox could compete, in theory, was with its studio programming. When the launch of FS1 was announced in March 2013, the press release discussed four programs: *Fox Sports Live, Rush Hour, Fox Football Daily,* and *Being,* the lattermost a documentary series that was to take a "deep dive into the lives of today's biggest athletes and sports personalities" (Schrager, 2013, para. 13). *Rush Hour,* scheduled for weekdays from 5:00–6:00 pm Eastern time, received considerable attention at the Times Square presentation of the network with former morning show host Regis Philbin slated as its host. The name of the show was changed to *Crowd Goes Wild* before it debuted that August, Philbin began limiting his appearances the following February, and the program was replaced in May. That show lasted slightly longer than *Fox Football Daily,* scheduled for weekdays from 6:00–7:00 pm Eastern, as it was replaced by *America's Pregame* a month earlier. Fox executive Scott Ackerson promised that *America's Pregame* would "put fans first more so than any show of its kind," but it was cancelled in September 2015 (Bacardi, 2014, para. 3).

No show exemplified the struggles of FS1 more than *Fox Sport Live,* with the challenges stemming from changes in both sports television and in leadership. That program debuted on the opening night of FS1, following a live *UFC Fight Night,* with Jay Onrait and Dan O'Toole as co-hosts. Onrait and O'Toole were imported from TSN in Canada and were viewed as personalities who shared a chemistry not seen since Keith Olbermann and Dan Patrick teamed on *SportsCenter* in the 1990s. In an interview prior to launch, Fox Sports Media Group President Eric Shanks joked that is was a "dark day for Canada" when the duo departed, but he also spoke of the investment made in a "24/7 news operation" and the audience expectations that accompany the "Fox Sports shield" in the delivery of information and highlights (Block, 2013, p. 42). Neither the Fox brand nor Fox resources, however, could address the dearth of high-quality live event programming as a lead-in to *Fox Sports Live* in its first year.

The addition of MLB and NASCAR Sprint Cup in 2014 helped and *Fox Sports Live* set an audience record that February with 2.272 million viewers following the NASCAR Dual 150 qualifying races from Daytona (Fox Sports, 2014). That mark was broken three months later with 2.584 million following the NASCAR Sprint All-Star Race, but such nights were few and far between and the absence of live primetime events was a recurring theme (Fox Sports, 2014). The week of the network's first anniversary in August 2014 was a case in point. A studio show, *MLB Whiparound*, was the lead-in to the 11:00 pm Eastern *Fox Sports Live* on Monday through Friday, with no live events on the primetime schedules on any of those evenings. For 2014, the average primetime television household delivery for FS1 was just 221,000 compared to 1.7 million for ESPN (SNL Kagan, 2018b). The soft ratings came at a time when the Internet and social media were starting to make sports news shows less relevant.

Fox Sports Live went through various iterations over its first 12 months and those that followed, most notably moving from a panel of five former athletes, including Donovan McNabb, Gary Payton and Andy Roddick, to a focus on extended blocks of highlights, but its ratings remained far behind *SportsCenter*. The ultimate death knell for the show can be traced to the arrival of Jamie Horowitz as President of Fox Sports National Networks in April 2015. Horowitz made his name at ESPN on opinion-based programs such as *First Take* and *SportsNation* and he promoted a similar approach with FS1. The "Embrace Debate" tagline attached to *First Take* was updated to "Embrace Debate 2.0" and in time ESPN alums Colin Cowherd, Skip Bayless, and Jason Whitlock would join Horowitz at Fox Sports (Maese, 2016). The changes reached *Fox Sports Live* in the first quarter of 2016 when the show was revamped, offering little news and highlights and featuring the humor and opinions of Onrait and O'Toole. That lasted for just a year, as the program was cancelled in February 2017 and the pair returned to Canada and TSN soon after (Bonesteel, 2017a). Horowitz was fired that summer amidst an investigation into sexual harassment.

The perceived battle between FS1 and ESPN, often debated through the head-to-head ratings of *Undisputed* with Bayless and Shannon Sharpe and the revised *First Take* with Stephen A. Smith and Max Kellerman, was somewhat misguided. That becomes clear when one examines the numbers behind the two networks (See Table 15.1 for average subscribers and revenue per subscriber for five multi-sport services). The number of subscribers for four of the networks—ESPN, ESPN2, FS1, and NBCSN—were more or less equal in 2017, averaging between 83.8 and 87.7-million, the result of modest increases for FS1 and NBCSN and significant declines for ESPN and ESPN2 (see Table 15.1). What was not equal is the average revenue per average subscriber the networks received from carriers. Fox was able to double the average carriage fee around the launch of FS1, from an average of 24-cents in 2013 to an average of 48-cents in 2015, with more modest increases after that. Even with the increases, the FS1 fees were miniscule compared to those of ESPN, which received an average of $7.54 per subscriber per month in 2017 and surpassed $8 a month in 2018 (see Table 15.1). And, that is where the notion of a head-to-head competition falters. ESPN generated a total of $8.3 billion in affiliate revenue in 2017 compared to just $684 million for FS1. That was three times more revenue for FS1 than SPEED generated in its final full year, but it did not give FS1 the resources to truly compete with ESPN for expensive sports rights packages.

Table 15.1: Average subscribers and average revenue per average subscriber per month for five multi-sports networks, ESPN, ESPN2, FS1, FS2 and NBCSN, 2012 though 2017.

	2012	2013	2014	2015	2016	2017
ESPN	98.8 million	97.8 million	95.8 million	93.0 million	89.9 million	87.7 million
	$5.04	$5.54	$6.10	$6.61	$7.04	$7.54
ESPN 2	98.7 million	97.7 million	95.8 million	92.9 million	89.8 million	87.5 million
	$0.67	$0.70	$0.77	$0.83	$0.87	$0.94
FS1	79.9 million	84.5 million	86.6 million	84.9 million	84.9 million	84.9 million
	$0.22	$0.24	$0.35	$0.48	$0.60	$0.64
FS2	36.4 million	36.2 million	40.3 million	47.8 million	50.7 million	51.3 million
	$0.15	$0.16	$0.16	$0.17	$0.19	$0.20
NBCSN	77.0 million	77.7 million	79.5 million	82.4 million	83.3 million	83.8 million
	$0.25	$0.26	$0.29	$0.30	$0.33	$0.34

Source: Kagan, a media research group within S&P Global Market Intelligence.

Competing with ESPN might not be the ultimate measure of FS1. The headline in *The New York Times* in March 2013 reporting on the planned launch of FS1 read "Seeing Riches in Sports TV, Fox Will Create New Network" (Sandomir & Chozick, 2013, B10). The article that followed discussed Rupert Murdoch's long-standing desire to challenge ESPN, but it also described a "companywide faith in sports as a DVR-proof way to attract viewers—especially young men" (Sandomir & Chozick, 2013, B12). A month earlier, News Corp. executive Chase Carey told investment analysts on a quarterly call, "We think sports is a really attractive arena that has room in it to build big businesses" (Bercovici. 2013, para. 3). While it is tempting to measure FS1 against ESPN, the building of a "DVR-proof" business that can withstand the changes in the television marketplace is the true measure of success within its corporate parent. As discussed, Fox was able to extract increased carriage fees from cable, satellite and broadband carriers prior to the launch of FS1, which positioned the network for higher profits down the road. Just as important, a multi-sport service provided the perfect partnership for the Fox broadcast network in the negotiation of sports rights deals. While the agreement with the NFL that give birth to Fox Sports remained focused on the terrestrial broadcast platform, rights deals in the 2010s benefited from a broadcast-cable partnership, including those with the USGA, NASCAR and FIFA.

Therein lies the true value of FS1 in the Murdoch empire, which was most evident in June of 2018. As the network moved towards the end of its fifth year, a collection of national and international events made FS1 more prominent in the lives of sports fans than ever before. Some were things that FS1 had grown accustomed to, such as a handful of national baseball games and NASCAR Cup Series races. There were others, however, that were more global and more cherished. In mid-June, FS1 featured the opening rounds of the 2018 U.S. Open. The true jewel was the 2018 FIFA World Cup from Russia, the first time the men's event was carried on FOX and FS1, even if the failure of the U.S. men's national team to qualify tempered the enthusiasm. FOX was home to the semifinals and final, but FS1 carried 21 group play matches live in the month of June as well as four matches in the knockout phase in July.

The Continued Dominance of Fox's Regional Networks

While FS1 might have struggled to find its personality over its first five years, there was not such angst for Fox regional networks over the same period. Their moment of discovery occurred two decades earlier during Murdoch's initial run at the ESPN throne, when he teamed with TCI and then with

Cablevision in an attempt to cobble together a national network from regional services. *Fox Sports News* was the thread that was supposed to pull those disparate services together when it launched in the mid-1990s, but it proved to be far too weak to do so. The failure of that endeavor was revisited in the lead-up to the launch of FS1. Long-time executive Randy Freer said that Fox learned a valuable lesson from that experiences, realizing that it is "hard to serve two masters" and at the regional sports level services had to be "as local as possible" (Block, 2013, p. 42).

The Fox RSNs might not have experienced an identity crisis on par with its corporate cousin, but a series of emotional break-ups framed its thinking in this period. News Corp. bought the Los Angeles Dodgers for $311 million in 1998, a connection that lasted until 2004 when News Corp. sold the team to Frank and Jamie McCourt for around $430 million, which included an extension of the Dodgers television rights through 2013 (Hammond, 2003). News Corp. and the Dodgers reached a new rights agreement in April 2011, but Commissioner Bud Selig blocked the deal that June. In time, McCourt sold the Dodgers to Guggenheim Baseball Management for $2 billion and the team reached agreement on a 25-year deal estimated at $8 billion with Time Warner Cable to launch a new cable network. The drama surrounding the Dodgers and Fox reinforced a desire for long-term contracts and Fox assumed a prominent role in that movement. In September 2010, Fox Sports Southwest agreed to a new 20-year, $1.6 billion deal with the Texas Rangers that began with the 2015 season (Barron, 2010). The deal was topped 14 months later, in December 2011, when Fox Sports West (FSW) agreed to a 20-year, $3 billion deal with the Los Angeles Angels of Anaheim (Shaikin & Baxter, 2011). Over the next five years, Fox inked deals for one of its RSNs with the Arizona Diamondbacks, Cincinnati Reds, San Diego Padres, and St. Louis, ranging between 15 and 20 years that extend into the 2030s.

While Fox's RSNs were working to extend their rights with existing partners, it pursued a relationship the New York Yankees and YES Network. In December 2012, News Corp. acquired a 49% interest in YES for $584 million and paid an additional $250 million of upfront costs for programming (News Corp, 2013). That agreement included an option for News Corp. to acquire an additional 31% interest, which was exercised in 2014 (Twenty-First Century Fox, 2015). An important aspect of the initial agreement was the extension of the rights deal between the Yankees and YES through 2042. The price paid to acquire a majority interest in YES was steep, but the profits that it generates are significant. In 2017, YES was in an average of 8.1 million households with average affiliate revenue per subscriber per month of $6.05, which generated $586.0 million in affiliate revenue (SNL Kagan, 2018a).

The drama that unfolded in Los Angeles in 2011, and continued after that, is a microcosm of the most prominent issues related to RSNs. In October 2012, Time Warner Cable launched SportsNet as part of a contract with the Los Angeles Lakers; and then in February 2014, SportsNet LA premiered. In a matter of 16 months, the number of RSNs in the Los Angeles market doubled, from two to four, without counting the Pac-12 Networks. Time Warner Cable struggled to gain carriage for SportsNet LA from multichannel video programming distributors, however, with DirecTV and Dish Network among those that refused to acquiesce to the asking price (Block, 2014). Charter Communications and Time Warner Cable announced a merger in May 2015, and Charter added SportsNet LA to its systems in the market two weeks later. The impact of the impasse over carriage was most evident in the spring of 2018, when FSW and Prime Ticker were in an estimated 6.0 million and 5.2 million households, respectively, and SportsNet LA was available in only 1.8 million.

Carriage for the Fox networks in the Los Angeles market might have remained high, but there were financial consequences from the loss of the Dodgers and Lakers. FSW and Prime Ticket retained the rights to four professional sports teams, the MLB Angels, NBA Clippers and NHL Ducks and Kings, but the average affiliate revenue saw significant losses after the Lakers and Dodgers left (See Table 15.2). The first reduction was seen on FSW between 2011 and 2012, when the per month average dropped from $2.50 to $1.95. That resulted in a loss of just under $50 million in affiliate revenue between 2011 and 2012 (see Table 15.2). The total might have been more, but FSW carried only Laker home games. The second reduction was seen on Prime Ticket between 2013 and 2014, when the per month average dropped from $2.71 in 2013 to $1.35 in 2014 (see Table 15.2). The loss of the Dodgers was far more significant for Prime Ticket since it carried 100 games in the 2013 season. The loss of affiliate revenue from 2013 to 2014 was just over $100 million.

Table 15.2: Estimated affiliate revenue per average subscriber per month for Los Angeles regional sports networks, 2010–2017.

	2010	2011	2012	2013	2014	2015	2016	2017
Fox Sports West	$2.44	$2.50	$1.95	$2.15	$2.28	$2.21	$2.50	$2.69
Prime Ticket	$2.39	$2.47	$2.56	$2.71	$1.35	$1.35	$1.51	$2.06
Spectrum SportsNet	–	–	$3.10	$3.29	$3.51	$3.74	$4.01	$4.28
Spectrum SportsNet LA	–	–	–	–	$3.79	$3.87	$3.89	$4.64
LOS ANGELES TOTALS	$	$	$	$	$	$	$	$

Source: Kagan, a media research group within S&P Global Market Intelligence.

While Fox may have taken a financial hit, cable consumers in the Los Angeles market were facing a dramatic increase in the total cost for all the RSNs. In 2011, the last full year before the launch of TWC SportsNet, the average per month cost for FSW and Prime Ticket was $4.97. The average cost per month increased to $7.61 in 2012, with three regional networks, and then topped $10 a month in 2014 with the addition of SportsNet LA, although many households in the Los Angeles market did not receive the Dodgers network. In 2017, that total reached an average of $13.67 per household per month (see Table 15.2). What is also significant about the Los Angeles market is that these new deals shifted almost all local telecasts to pay platforms with the elimination of games on free-to-air broadcast stations (e.g., all Laker games now on Spectrum SportsNet).

The horizontal integration of regional networks within Fox Sports is representative of a broader pattern among RSNs (see Table 15.3). Within MLB, 25 of 29 U.S.-based teams were carried on networks owned in whole or in part by Twenty-First Century Fox, Comcast/NBC or AT&T Inc. in 2018. A total of six teams were connected with NBC Sports Networks, including Comcast's minority interest in SportsNet NY, co-owned by the New York Mets. Four more were affiliated with AT&T, including the three ROOT Sports networks relaunched as AT&T SportsNet outlets in 2017 (AT&T still held a minority interest in ROOT Sports Northwest in a joint venture with the Seattle Mariners). The four teams outside that group were the Boston Red Sox (New England Sports Network), Los Angeles Dodgers (Spectrum SportsNet LA), and the Baltimore Orioles and Washington Nationals (Mid-Atlantic Sports Network). In each of those cases, the owners of the MLB teams launched their own RSNs, a form of vertical integration, with the Orioles and Nationals sharing ownership of MASN and the Red Sox and Boston Bruins sharing ownership of NESN. There was a similar relationship between the Toronto Blue Jays and SportsNet with the one team based in Canada, with common ownership under Rogers Communications.

The FSN share of local NBA teams was even higher in 2017–18, with 17 of 29 (58.6%) teams under contract to one of the Fox-owned regional networks. The percentage of teams connected with the three major ownership groups was also higher with the NBA, with 26 of 29 (89.7%) under contract with the Fox, Comcast/NBC or AT&T groups. The three U.S.-based teams outside those conglomerates were the Los Angeles Lakers with Spectrum SportsNet, New York Knicks with MSG Network and Denver Nuggets with Altitude Sports. In the case of the Knicks and Nuggets, ownership of team and RSN were in the same hands. Among NHL teams, the three major RSNs controlled the rights to 18 of the 24 U-S teams, with

Table 15.3: Dominant regional sports network groups with NBA and NHL contracts during the 2017–18 seasons and MLB contracts at start of 2018 season.

Network Group	Parent Corporation	Regional Sports Networks	Mlb Teams Under Contract	Nba Teams Under Contract	Nhl Teams Under Contract
Fox Sports Regional Networks	Twenty-First Century Fox	15/22[1]	15	17	12
NBC Sports Regional Networks	Comcast Corp.	8[2]	6	7	4
AT&T SportsNet	AT&T Inc.	4[3]	4	2	2
Totals[4]	—		25 of 29	26 of 29	18 of 24

Source: AT&T Inc. (2018), Comcast Corp. (2018), and Twenty-First Century Fox, Inc. (2017).
Source: AT&T Inc. (2018, February 20). Form 10-K: Annual Report. Retrieved from https://www.sec.gov/Archives/edgar/data/732717/000073271718000009/ye17_10k.htm
Source: Comcast Corp. (2018, January 31). Form 10-K: Annual Report.
Source: Twenty-First Century Fox, Inc. (2017, August 14). Form 10-K: Annual Report. Retrieved from https://www.sec.gov/Archives/edgar/data/1308161/000156459017017693/fox-10k_20170630.htm
In its Form 10-K, Twenty-First Century Fox states that it owns 15 RSNs and numerous sub-regional feeds and lists 22 different feeds in other corporate documents
[1]In its Form 10-K, Twenty-First Century Fox states that it owns 15 RSNs and numerous sub-regional feeds and lists 22 different feeds in other corporate documents.
[2]Includes the Comcast interest in SportsNet New York and the seven branded NBC Sports Regional Networks outlets formerly known as Comcast SportsNet.
[3]Includes the AT&T interest in ROOT Sports Northwest and the three rebranded AT&T SportsNet outlets, Houston, Pittsburgh, and Rocky Mountains formerly known as ROOT Sports.
[4]Totals are for U.S. based teams and do not include the one MLB and one NBA team and seven NHL teams in Canada.

three of six outside the group under common team and RSN control (Altitude and the Colorado Rockies, NESN and the Boston Bruins and MSG and the New York Rangers; MSG also owned media rights for the New York Islanders, New Jersey Devils, and Buffalo Sabres). Rights to the seven Canadian NHL teams are concentrated with two major media groups; Bell Media-owned TSN with four (Montreal, Ottawa, Toronto, and Winnipeg) and the Rogers Communications-owned SportsNet with three (Calgary, Edmonton and Vancouver).

Conclusion

The differences between FS1 and FSN was most evident in December 2017 when Twenty-First Century Fox Inc. and the Walt Disney Co. announced a $52.4 billion deal that would transfer some assets to Disney while leaving others behind. When the Department of Justice approved a potential Disney acquisition in June 2018, one of the conditions it imposed was requiring Disney to divest the 22 RSNs that were part of the deal (DOJ, 2018). The concern voiced in that decision was over the potential combination of the RSNs and ESPN networks. Market definition is an important consideration in antitrust review and while one could argue that ESPN and the RSNs compete in different markets for programming, the government focused on the carriage fees for sports networks, both national and local. The DOJ argued, "American consumers have benefited from head-to-head competition between Disney and Fox's cable sports programming that ultimately has prevented cable television subscription prices from rising even higher" (DOJ, 2018, para. 3).

An auction for the Fox RSNs in 2019 produced only a few interested parties and bids well below the $20 billion-plus sales price Disney originally set. A group led by Sinclair Broadcasting submitted the winning bid of $10.6 billion for 21 of the RSNs (the remaining RSN, the YES Network, was sold separately for nearly $3.5 billion to a group including the New York Yankees and Sinclair) (Adgate, 2019; Ozanian, 2019). Cord-cutting and its future impact on cable and satellite television revenues was seen as one reason for the lower than expected acquisition price. Yet media experts saw Sinclair's purchase as strategic for the company, as it would provide a way to leverage carriage fees for both its new RSNs and the company's 190-plus local television stations in 89 markets ("About," 2019). The RSNs also provided an opportunity to use programming from Sinclair's Stadium Sports operation (seen on digital cable and Internet).

Twenty-First Century Fox's decision to give up these RSNs provided insight into what Rupert Murdoch valued most. The focus would be on live news and sports and it would retain the FOX broadcast network and local stations as well as Fox News Channel, Fox Business Channel, and three sports channels: FS1, FS2 and Big Ten Network. One of the reasons Twenty-First Century Fox was willing to part with the regional networks but not the national networks is that RSN contracts made it difficult to share content with its parent network (FOX) while FS1 was a natural partner. The regional contracts also raised questions about streaming rights outside the local market. In 2018, Fox had a national contact for baseball that included both FOX and FS1, but it also had local contracts with 15 different teams, and while those contracts were all under the auspices of the Commissioner of Baseball, the rights received were quite different. Once again, the differences between national and local were clear.

Therein lies an area in which FS1 and the Fox regional networks share some common concerns, as both are reliant on carriage fees in an era of cord-cutting that has reduced penetration of many sports services. While the average fee per subscriber per month has continued to increase, and in turn offset some of the subscriber losses, the financial model remains under threat. For the Fox-owned YES Network, for example, average subscriber numbers have dropped from 9.4 million in 2010 to 8.1 million in 2017, with no significant changes in programming. Over the same time period, total revenue rose by almost $200 million thanks to an increase in average subscriber fees from $3.44 to $6.05. The question is whether such increases can continue to offset subscriber losses moving forward. A cause for concern with the Fox regional networks is that there is far greater long-term exposure. As discussed earlier, the YES agreement with the Yankees extends through 2042, and many other Fox regional deals with baseball teams continue into the 2030s.

When the initial deal between Fox and Disney was being negotiated, the value of the RSNs was placed at $22.4 billion, about one-third of the total value of the assets being acquired. One reason for that valuation is the loyalty to regional sports services in their respective local markets. In 2016, Nielsen completed a survey for Fox in which local RSNs ranked as the most-essential non-broadcast channel on the average cable system, ahead of ESPN and behind only the four major broadcast network stations (Bonesteel, 2017b). In St. Louis, Fox Sports Midwest ranked as the most essential network, ahead of the ABC, CBS, FOX, and NBC affiliates in that market; in Detroit, Fox Sports Detroit ranked as the second most essential. The question, however, was whether such loyalty was enough to offset the other challenges that linear services face, including cord-cutting and young viewers who were raised on streaming services. The willingness of the Murdoch family to include the regional networks in the deal with Disney suggested that a point might be reached when it is no longer possible to charge such high carriage fees for such services (Crupi, 2017). That would send shock waves through the industry and alter the business model forever.

References

About (2019). *Sinclair Broadcast Group*. Retrieved from sbgi.net.

Adgate, B (2019, May 3). 4 takeaways from Sinclair's acquisition of Fox regional sports networks from Disney. *Forbes.com*. Retrieved from https://www.forbes.com/sites/

bradadgate/2019/05/03/some-takeaways-from-sinclairs-acquisition-of-fox-regional-sports-networks/#7f03a0432596

AT&T Inc. (2018, February 20). Form 10-K: Annual Report. Retrieved from https://www.sec.gov/Archives/edgar/data/732717/000073271718000009/ye17_10k.htm

Bacardi, F. (2014, March 17). Fox Sports 1 Adds Nightly "America's Pregame" Telecast. *Variety.* Accessed at https://variety.com/2014/tv/news/fox-sports-1-cues-nightly-americas-pregame-telecast-1201136421/

Barron, D. (2010, September 27). Rangers, Fox Sports Southwest agree to $1.6 billion deal. *Houston Chronicle.* Retrieved from https://www.chron.com/sports/astros/article/Rangers-Fox-Sports-Southwest-agree-to-1-6-1603662.php

Bercovici, J. (2013, February 6). News Corp. Admits 'World's Worst-Kept Secret': It's Planning ESPN Clone. *Forbes.* Retrieved from https://www.forbes.com/sites/jeffbercovici/2013/02/06/news-corp-admits-it-plans-espn-clone-coo-calls-it-worlds-worst-kept-secret/#3e533d077c9d

Block, A. B. (2013, July 24). Fox Sports 1 Execs reveal strategy to take in ESPN (Q&A). *Hollywood Reporter*, 42.

Block, A. B. (2014, July 29). FCC chairman threatens to intervene over Dodgers pay TV standoff. *HollywoodReporter.com.* Retrieved from Nexis Uni database.

Bonesteel, M. (2017a, February 23). FS1 blows up late night: 'Fox Sports Live' canceled, Katie Nolan in Limbo; "Garbage Time" as we know it is no more. *Washington Post Blogs.* Retrieved from Nexis Uni database.

Bonesteel, M. (2017b, December 14). Disney-Fox deal gives ESPN a local strategy to combat its financial woes. *Washington Post Blogs.* Retrieved from Nexis Uni database.

Carmody, J. (1994, May 24). Fox nabs 12 affiliates from rivals; Deal boosts network in major markets; CBS is hit hardest. *The Washington Post,* A1.

Carter, B. (1994, May 24). Fox will sign up 12 new stations; Takes 8 from CBS. *The New York Times,* A1.

Comcast Corp. (2018, January 31). Form 10-K: Annual Report.

Crupi, A. (2017, December 5). Fox regional sports networks would be a game-changer for ESPN. *AdAge.* Retrieved from http://adage.com/article/media/espn--acquisition-fox-regional-game-changer-streaming/311537/

Deitsch, R. (2013, March 18). A shot at the champ: Fox promises to come out swinging with a new 24/7 sports channel, but can FS1 really challenge ESPN? *Sports Illustrated.* Retrieved from https://www.si.com/vault/2013/03/18/106298086/a-shot-at-the-champ

Dempsey, J. (2005, February 23). Rupe swaps regional networks with cablevision. *Daily Variety.* Retrieved from Nexis Uni.

Department of Justice (DOJ). (2018, June 27). The Walt Disney company required to divest twenty-two regional sports networks in order to complete acquisition of certain assets from twenty-first century fox. Press Release. Retrieved from https://www.justice.gov/opa/pr/walt-disney-company-required-divest-twenty-two-regional-sports-networks-order-complete

Donohue, S. (1998, November 16). Fox Sports gets EPSN veterans on its side. *Electronic Media*. Retrieved from Nexis Uni database.

Flint, J. (2016, April 13). Fox Sports 1 looks to Fox News for inspiration. *The Wall Street Journal*. Retrieved from https://www.wsj.com/articles/fox-sports-1-attempts-makeover-of-its-talk-shows-1460576052

Flint, J., & Peers, M. (1996, May 10). News Corp. firms sports alliance with TCI-Liberty. *Daily Variety*, 1.

Fox Sports Media Group. (2014, May 20). *Fox Sports 1 thunders to big viewership weekend* [Press Release]. Retrieved from https://foxsports-wordpress-www-prsupports-prod.s3.amazonaws.com/uploads/sites/2/2016/12/nc10-Days-of-Thunder-Weekend-1-Ratings.pdf

Haddad, C. (1996, September 13). Assembling a $20 billion company. *Atlanta Journal and Constitution*, F8.

Hammond, R. (2003, October 11). Dodger sold; Boston developer scores with $430 million deal. *Los Angeles Daily News*, N1.

Hettrick, S. (1996, November 1). Fox Sports is casting wide Net. *Hollywood Reporter*, p. 1. Retrieved from Nexis Uni database.

Hettrick, S. (1998, March 27). Fox/Liberty speeding to speedvision, Outdoor net. *Hollywood Reporter*. Retrieved from Nexis Uni database.

Hiestand, M. (2013a, March 6). Fox Sports launches direct challenge to ESPN dominance. *USA Today*, p. C1.

Hiestand, M. (2013b, March 6). Fox looks to bolster coverage; FS1 expected to air bit of everything. *USA Today*, p. C3.

Levin, G. (1996, August 5). Fox chips in $50 mil for Golf cut. *Daily Variety*. Retrieved from Nexis Uni database.

Maese, R. (2016, June 13). Listen up: Cowherd has plenty to say. *The Washington Post*, D1.

Mansell, J. (1997, December 1). Rough stuff: All-sports nets play a new brand of ball. *Cable World*. Retrieved from Nexis Uni database.

News Corp. (2013, August 19). Form 10-K: Annual Report. Retrieved from https://www.sec.gov/Archives/edgar/data/1308161/000119312513338522/d578800d10k.htm

Noglows, P., Flint, J., & Lowry, B. (1994, May 24). Fox places new world order; $500 mill delivers 12 affils. *Daily Variety*, 1. Retrieved from Nexis Uni database.

Ozanian, M. (2019, March 8). New York Yankees buy back YES Network for $3.47 billion. *Forbes.com*. https://www.forbes.com/sites/mikeozanian/2019/03/08/new-york-yankees-buy-back-yes-network-for-3-47-billion/#2a84e15d483c

Reynolds, M. (1998, February 2). Fox Sports reemerged as big national player. *Cable World*. Retrieved from Nexis Uni database.

Sandomir, R. (2002, May 13). Sports News shows come and go, but "SportsCenter" keeps on rolling. *The New York Times*, 9.

Sandomir, R., & Chozick, A. (2013, March 5). Seeing riches in Sports TV, Fox to create new network. *The New York Times*, B10.

Schlosser, J. (2001, February 12). Revved up for NASCAR. *Broadcasting and Cable*. Retrieved from Nexis Uni database.

Schrager, P. (2013, March 5). *FOX Sports 1 announcer Aug. launch*. [Press Release]. Retrieved from https://www.foxsports.com/other/story/fox-sports-1-launch-in-august-will-feature-live-events-news-original-programming-030513

Shaikin, B., & Baxter, K. (2011, December 9). Angeles double play: Pujols and Wilson; Money from TV allows team to acquire stars. *Los Angeles Times*, C1.

Shapiro, L. (1993, December 26). And the fourth shall be first: How Fox stalked the NFL and bagged TV deal. *The Washington Post*, D1.

Sirak, R. (2013, August 19). Changing channels. *Golf World*. Retrieved from Nexis Uni database.

SNL Kagan. (2018a). Network profile—Yes Network, SNL Kagan database. Accessed May 30, 2018. Retrieved from https://platform.mi.spglobal.com/web/client?auth=inherit #tvnetwork/networkprofile?id=527

SNL Kagan. (2018b). TV Network Summary—Average Prime Time TVHH Delivery. Accessed May 26, 2018. Retrieved from https://platform.mi.spglobal.com/web/client?auth=inherit#industry/tv_NetworksSummary

Sporich, B. (2001, May 16). Olbermann cut from lineup at Fox Sports Net. *Hollywood Reporter*. Retrieved from Nexis Uni database.

Twenty-First Century Fox, Inc. (2015, August 12). Form 10-K: Annual Report. Retrieved from https://www.sec.gov/Archives/edgar/data/1308161/000156459015007133/fox-10k_20150630.htm

Twenty-First Century Fox, Inc. (2017, August 14). Form 10-K: Annual Report. Retrieved from https://www.sec.gov/Archives/edgar/data/1308161/000156459017017693/fox-10k_20170630.htm

Umstead, R. T. (1996, October 16). Fox Sports will try to capture local market. *Multichannel News*. Retrieved from Nexis Uni database.

Umstead, R. T. (1997, June 23). Fox builds sports empire. *Multichannel News*. Retrieved from Nexis Uni database.

16. "Seeking a Storybook Ending": Examining the Future Distribution of Women's Sporting Events

Anji L. Phillips and Dunja Antunovic

From its beginning, ESPN was an organization led by men, focused on men's sports, and targeting male audiences, with limited attention to women's sport or women viewers (Vogan, 2015). Even today, scholars critique ESPN for systematically omitting women's sports from coverage. For instance, *SportsCenter*, ESPN's flagship program dedicates only 2% of its coverage to women's sports (Cooky, Messner, & Musto, 2015). More recently, ESPN made a substantial effort to create programming specifically about women, but this content is relegated to separate sites (Wolter, 2015a).

ESPN, however, is not the sole network that has the ability to promote and broadcast women's sports. Fox Sports 1, NBC Sports Network, and CBS Sports Network, among others, are sports broadcasting channels that are part of larger companies with multiple broadcast outlets. Lifetime television broadcasted WNBA games from 1997–2000, with programming later shifting to ESPN2 (Brockington, 2000; Johnson, 1997; Langdon, 2000). Hearst Communications and The Walt Disney Company both have a joint stake in ESPN and A+E Networks (De La Merced, 2012; "Disney," 2009; "About the Walt," n.d.).

Additionally, A+E Networks is the parent company of Lifetime ("About A+E Networks," n.d.). In February of 2017, A+E secured the rights to air National Women's Soccer League (NWSL) on Lifetime, and A+E also secured an equity stake in the NWSL (Hipes, 2017; Schwindt, 2017). Therefore, Lifetime retains a role as not only sponsor and broadcaster of weekly games, but also retains some control of NWSL because A+E has a 25% ownership in

NWSL (Hagey, 2017). Shared ownership would likely prevent other broadcasters from garnering broadcast rights, and may also be motivation for A+E to find the NWSL a broadcast home regardless of ratings.

Alternately, some organizations are taking broadcasting into their own hands. The Women's Tennis Association (WTA), for example, allowed their broadcast rights to lapse at the end of 2016 with the Tennis Channel (Rothenberg, 2017). The WTA has since launched their own streaming service in partnership with Perform Media, called WTA TV that provides live matches, and behind the scenes coverage of women's tennis players ("WTA media," n.d.; "WTA staff," 2017). In short, women's sports organizations are looking to market options for both their broadcast and digital rights to increase reach to their fan base.

Scholars have conducted a variety of studies on ESPN's treatment of women's sport in several segments of programming such as ESPN's *SportsCenter* (Cooky et al., 2015), espnW webpage content (e.g., Roessner & Whiteside, 2016; Wolter 2015a; Wolter, 2015b), and *Nine for IX* films (e.g., Hartman, 2015; Heinecken, 2018). These analyses of content certainly document contemporary patterns in coverage of women's sports. Beyond merely capturing content, this body of work has created new conceptual frameworks on the representation of women's sports (Cooky et al., 2015; Wolter, 2015b). Studies on ESPN have, thus, advanced the study of gender, sport, and media.

That said, the changing landscape of women's sports coverage in multiple distribution platforms (e.g., traditional broadcast, cable, and Internet), the financial potential of broadcast rights retained by women's sports organization, including the ability of women's organizations to become their own broadcaster to overcome the lack of women's sports content, calls for further research. Additionally, while there are plenty of studies that interrogate gender ideologies in media content, there is surprisingly little discussion about the structural and long-term implications of ESPN's women-centered initiatives. It is unclear how these initiatives have changed the position of women's sports—if at all—beyond these platforms and channels. Considering that much of ESPN's coverage of women's sport is constrained to separate spaces, Roessner and Whiteside (2016) suggest "it is worth considering the transformative potential such narratives may have on the overall sporting landscape" (p. 595). Great opportunity exists in situating ESPN's women's sports-related content within the broader media landscape.

This chapter provides a theoretical foundation for future research on women's sports broadcasts and ancillary women's sport initiatives in the following ways:

- Evaluates existing research on ESPN's women-centered initiatives.
- Positions ESPN's broadcasts of women's sports within the broader media landscape.
- Proposes future areas of research to better understand the implications of ESPN's women's sports coverage within the current media landscape.

As such, this chapter contributes to the vibrant research in the area of sport, media, and gender.

Literature Review: ESPN and Women's Sports

ESPN's coverage of women athletes has received a plethora of scholarly attention. United States-based scholarship on gender representations on television typically focuses either on NBC's Olympic broadcasts (e.g., Billings & Eastman, 2003), solely on ESPN content (e.g., Cooky et al., 2015), and/or compares *SportsCenter* to other networks' sports highlight shows (e.g., Billings & Young, 2015). Considering ESPN's products extend beyond television, scholars also examined ESPN's films, online platforms, and magazine. The overarching conclusion about ESPN is that the network marginalizes women's sports across a variety of initiatives, including *SportsCenter* (e.g., Adams & Tuggle, 2004; Cooky et al., 2015; Tuggle, 1997; Turner, 2014), Division I NCAA Men's and Women's basketball tournament coverage (Billings, Halone, & Denham, 2002; Kian, Mondello, & Vincent, 2009), *30 for 30* films (Billings & Blackistone, 2015; Lavelle, 2015; Vogan, 2015), and *ESPN The Magazine* (Clavio & Pedersen, 2007; Cranmer, Brann, & Bowman, 2014; Kian, Smith, Lee, & Sweeney, 2015). However, scholars also point out the "lack of women's coverage is not an ESPN-specific phenomenon" (Billings & Young, 2015, p. 12), but a wider problem in sports media where hierarchies between sports continue to deepen, leaving women's sports perpetually marginalized.

In the United States, women's sports participation has grown on the interscholastic, professional, and international levels. Yet, over the last few decades, *SportsCenter*'s coverage of women's sports between 1995 and 2014 oscillated between a low of 1.3% to a high of 5% (e.g., Adams & Tuggle, 2004; Cooky et al., 2015; see also Cooky, Messner, & Hextrum, 2013; Messner, Dunbar, & Hunt, 2000; Messner, Duncan, & Cooky, 2003; Tuggle, 1997; Turner, 2014). *SportsCenter* dedicated 2.0% of its coverage to women's sports in the most recent dataset from 2014 (Cooky et al., 2015). Several of these studies also found that stories about men are on average longer than stories about women (e.g., Billings & Young, 2015; Cooky et al., 2015; Tuggle, 1997). Billings and Young (2015) took the emergence of new sports networks into consideration and examined how ESPN's news coverage of women's sports compares to Fox Sports 1's *Fox Sports Live*. Billings and Young (2015) found these programs dedicated less than 2% of airtime to women's sports, even with the increase during the 2014 Winter Olympic Games. Billings and Young (2015) noted the *Fox Sports Live* coverage mirrors existing gender hierarchies, and "the introduction of Fox Sports 1 is more entrenchment than revolution" (p. 14). In sum, news/highlight programs remain male-dominated across networks.

ESPN has been critiqued for its treatment of women's sports in a variety of other initiatives. For instance, in ESPN's *30 for 30* films Volume I of the series, which features 43 films, only three (*Marion Jones: Press Pause*, 2010; *Rene*, 2011; *Unmatched*, 2010) focused on women. The series is up to 96 films and the only additional film, *The Price of Gold* (Tonya Harding and Nancy Kerrigan), is about women. These three films reinforce conventional notions of femininity and set narrow gender expectations (Lavelle, 2015). The omission of women illustrates ESPN's version of sporting past is a male-dominated endeavor (Vogan, 2015). A platform that has occupied a center of scholarly and popular debate is *ESPN The Magazine*'s *The Body Issue*. Once a year, this issue features photos of naked or half-naked athletes with short explanations of how the athletes developed a particular body shape, attained injury marks, and/or accomplished their sport-related feats. *The Body Issue* appears to portray male and female athletes in similar ways, and subsequently recognizes them as athletes (Kian et al., 2015), but images of female athletes still "de-emphasize their athleticism and sexualize them" (Cranmer et al., 2014, p. 159). In short, ESPN's depiction of women athletes is ambivalent at best.

Over the years, ESPN has taken several significant steps to create spaces for women's sport, most of which are implemented through espnW. espnW has been positioned as a platform for women fans, often by women, and about women's sports. espnW initiatives include not just the online site, but also podcasts (e.g., *The Trifecta*), *Nine for IX* films (the women-focused, shorter equivalent of *30 for 30*), a Title IX commemoration website, the espnW + Sports Summit, Campus Conversations for female athletes, and more recently a Women, Sports and Media conference co-organized with the University of Maryland. Wolter (2014, 2015a, 2015b, 2015c) and others (e.g., Hartman, 2015; Heinecken, 2018; Roessner & Whiteside, 2016; Whiteside & Roessner, 2018) found espnW-related content counters the absence of women's sport from media coverage—although, it does so through problematic representation strategies. espnW does not, however, broadcast any games.

The literature reviewed above indicates ESPN's multi-platform coverage of women's sports (or lack thereof) has received significant scholarly attention. Hartman (2015) argued "ESPN serves as the leading broadcaster of sport to millions of people globally, thereby indicating its ability to influence and frame sport for its viewers" (p. 98). At the same time, scholars should move beyond ESPN and contextualize women's sports coverage within the broader broadcasting landscape to identify other spaces where coverage—specifically broadcasting—of women's sports occurs.

Theoretical Frameworks

In order to propose future directions for research on ESPN's role in women's sports coverage, we first must briefly identify the most commonly employed theoretical frameworks, methodological approaches, and sites of analyses. Scholars draw upon a variety of theories from cultural studies, gender studies, and mass communication to conduct quantitative content analysis, and qualitative textual or discourse analysis to study representation issues. We focus on three primary areas: (a) gender ideologies in coverage; (b) framing of content, and (c) agenda-setting.

In terms of gender ideologies, scholars have observed a shift in representation strategies over the years and subsequently further the conceptual frameworks that inform their work. Hegemonic masculinity is perhaps the most commonly used concept in this area of research. Hegemonic masculinity is the gender-related process through which sports media culture centralizes and elevates men, while positioning female athletes in gender stereotypical ways (Kian et al., 2009; Kian, Vincent, & Mondello, 2008; Wolter, 2015b). Musto, Cooky and Messner (2017) have also coined new, more precise concept of "gender-bland sexism" to explain the less overt forms of sexist televised commentary whereby sports commentators "render women athletes visible in ways that makes women's athletic accomplishments appear lackluster compared to men's" (p. 578). Scholars have expanded the conceptual frameworks to better understand new articulations of femininity on legacy and digital media platforms as women now take an active role in producing media content through new platforms (e.g., Thorpe, Toffoletti, & Bruce, 2017).

Another body of research on women's sports draws upon framing theory. Framing has been useful in identifying the ways in which media select which sporting events to cover (Adams & Tuggle, 2004; Billings & Eastman, 2003; Cranmer et al., 2014; Turner, 2014). Adams and Tuggle (2004) argued framing theory can have useful implications for sports coverage, suggesting "ESPN could help frame the WNBA as a prominent league and an important part of sports" (p. 246). Framing is the idea a particular issue, or in this case, coverage of men's sports is given focus or precedence to the exclusion of other information (i.e., women's sports) (Borah, 2011; Price & Tewksbury, 1997). This could mean, for example, the lack of news coverage and distribution platforms (e.g., traditional broadcast, cable, and social media via the Internet) of women's sports may lead heavy viewers of ESPN and its contemporaries to conclude women's sports are unpopular, unimportant, or both.

Agenda setting (McCombs & Shaw, 1972) has also been used as a key theoretical framework to explain the selection function of sports media outlets and programs. For instance, in a study on *ESPN The Magazine*, Clavio and Pedersen (2007) argued "An increase of coverage and hype for leagues with a television contract with ESPN would hypothetically increase interest in the leagues being televised" (p. 97). The authors found agenda setting did not appear to have affected the decisions at the magazine, which—for women's sports—raises the question of whether leagues such as the WNBA could expect cross promotion across ESPN's many platforms. Billings and Young (2015) suggested agenda setting should be expanded in order to capture the current media environment, and "because of the growth of ancillary networks and particularly the Internet, such debates change to whether a sport receives primacy (shown on ESPN's main channel rather than ESPNU) and the ease in which content can be found" (p. 6). In fact, as we are writing this chapter, we are seeking out the 2018 NCAA Women's Basketball tournament games on ESPN2 and on ESPN's streaming services, and the 2018 NWHL Isobel Cup Final on Twitter—a common and often tedious task fans complete in order to locate women's sports coverage. While we can expect future studies to utilize these frameworks in relation to coverage of ESPN, we propose a few additional areas of research that could help scholars better understand the relationship between ESPN, its contemporaries, and women's sports.

Future Directions: Beyond ESPN's Coverage of Women's Sports

Based on this research, we identify two potential areas of research to examine aftereffects of ESPN upon women's sports: Sports league's contracts with various broadcast mediums and sports industry publications. Both of these require we situate ESPN within the broader sport media landscape.

Women's Sports Organizations and Broadcast Mediums

Although ESPN has been the primary carrier of sports content in the United States, it is not the only one. In fact, women's sports leagues and teams have turned to other cable networks and web-based platforms to broadcast content. Thus, research on women's sports would greatly benefit from looking beyond ESPN and examining the ways in which women's sports organizations essentially *go around* ESPN to ensure visibility for their contests. We briefly identify the state of these broadcasts as of April 2018.

National Women's Hockey League (NWHL)
Women's professional hockey in the U.S. began its inaugural season in 2015 with the first Isobel Cup hosted in 2016 ("NWHL about," n.d.). A game of the week was streamed live on both Twitter and YouTube.

Women's Football Alliance (WFA)
Women's professional U.S. football began as a nonprofit organization in 2007 with play starting in 2009 ("About WFA," n.d.). The WFA maintains traditional Facebook, Twitter, and YouTube accounts to engage fans with highlights, however, the postings are sporadic at best. The WFA have had bowl games on ESPN3 in 2016 presented by Go Live Sports Cast ("W Bowl 2016," n.d.). Score Sports carried a live game on YouTube in March of 2018, however, there are no links from the main WFA website to find a broadcast schedule of games ("Atlanta Phoenix," 2018). A separate Twitter and Facebook account started in March of 2018, called "Watch the WFA," which has links to live WFA games around the country.

National Pro Fastpitch (NPF)
Women's professional softball broadcast their regular season games on a paid subscription television platform. The previous streaming service was in existence since 2016 ("NPF announces," 2017). Some previous seasons offered one free game of the week ("NPF announces," 2017). FloSports has exclusive access to all 134 regular season games for digital broadcast since spring of 2019. NFP's 16th season is the first time "the league's content is streamed in its entirety by a third-party platform" ("Flosports adds," 2019, para. 2). NPF has a social media presence on Facebook, YouTube, and with only a couple of post-season games posted for free via "View Broadcasts" on Twitter. NPF began in their current form in 2004 with Major League Baseball (MLB) as an official development partner ("MLB shows support," 2004; "NPF to celebrate," 2018). Prior incarnations of NPF were "in operation since 1997 under the names Women's Pro Fastpitch (WPF) and Women's Pro Softball League (WPSL)" ("MLB shows support," 2004, para. 3).

National Women's Soccer League (NWSL)
Women's soccer is regularly featured on the cable channel Lifetime ("Five things to know," 2018). Women's professional soccer made its Lifetime

television debut in 2017, and the channel features a game of the week for each of the NWSL's 24-game regular season. Additionally, games could be streamed live on go90, a free ad-supported streaming service from Verizon with games featured on the NWSL website after a waiting period (Tannenwald, 2017). In June 2018, Verizon announced that it was discontinuing go90, so the NSWL streamed the majority of the games on its website (Goldberg, 2018). Highlights of games and fan interaction are found on Facebook, YouTube, and Twitter. The women's national team (WNT) shares a website with the men's national team (MNT), and provides a unified platform for soccer fans while both teams receive limited one or two game television coverage on Fox Sports 1, FOX, and ESPN2 in the United States ("WNT," 2018, "MNT," 2018).

Women's Tennis Association (WTA)

Women's professional tennis signed a deal with iQIYI in China for digital rights to run 2017–2027 ("WTA signs digital," n.d.). Previous contracts from 2013–2017 with Perform, MCS TV Group, and IEC in Sports and media group increased the televised and digital reach of the WTA, which included parts of Europe, Asia, and Africa ("WTA signs rights deal," n.d.). WTA also negotiated a 10-year extension of their contract with Perform in 2014, which resulted "in the creation of WTA Media" (Jessop, 2014, para. 2). The deal with Perform is also considered the "largest media rights agreement in the history of women's sports" (Jessop, 2014, para. 1). WTA also has a social media presence on Facebook and Twitter, and notably is the creation of a free-to-fans fantasy tennis league in 2018 that has gained popularity (Gillies, 2016; "WTA launches new," 2018).

Women's National Basketball Association (WNBA)

Women's basketball is the only professional women's team to have regular season games featured on an ESPN platform. Specifically, the WNBA's 2018 season featured up to 33 games on ESPN2, which also stream live on the ESPN app ("2018 WNBA national," 2018). Additional WNBA games air on both Twitter, and NBA TV. Twitter live streamed 20 games per season for 2017, 2018, and 2019 (Casey, 2017). The WNBA also has a presence on Facebook and YouTube featuring highlights from various games and players. Full WNBA games are posted on YouTube, but games are not posted by the official WNBA organization.

Based on this overview, it is clear ESPN and other cable and terrestrial networks are far from the only potential avenue for women's sport coverage. The patterns above prompt several questions. For instance, how does women's professional leagues' relationship to the equivalent men's leagues shape the availability and access of broadcasts? How do men's professional teams cross-promote women's teams? Where can fans find women's sports content, and do they have to pay for that content? Studies on fandom could also examine how fans of women's sports access content, how they make decisions about watching women's sports, and which factors shape their decisions to follow and invest money (e.g., tickets, merchandise, subscriptions) in women's sports. All of these factors have significant implications for the status of women's sports coverage.

Women's Sports and Sports Industry Analytics

The landscape of women's sports broadcasts is partially illustrated through an examination of sports industry analytics regarding the monetization potential of women athletes compared to their male counterparts and celebrities ("Women and sport," 2015). Repucom, acquired by Nielsen Sports in 2016, collect and analyze data regarding "media, sponsorship, communication and experiential platforms" including the popularity of sports channels and platforms ("Nielsen completes acquisition," 2016, para. 7). Nielsen, most known for capturing viewership and listenership numbers in television and radio, along with sports media data from Repucom, publish an annual review of broadcast ratings and social media metrics by medium, channel, and demographics (e.g., Master, 2017; Stainer & Master, 2018). Nielsen's Year in Sports reports average almost 27 pages in length with a low of 13, and a high of 40. In these reports, women's sports are barely, if at all, mentioned over the years.

2009
No women's sports were listed out of 10 sports covered. Four women's tennis finals were mentioned; and while NASCAR is not specific to gender, women drivers are few to none (Master, 2010).

2010
No women's sports were listed out of nine sports covered, except the "Olympics" listed in general. Tennis (for men or women) was not mentioned at all. Nielsen introduced an "endorsement score" for companies to "evaluate how effective a sports figure will be when endorsing their products" (Master, 2011, p. 2). Top five women were included in this list featuring Venus and Serena Williams. Lindsey Vonn was second highest for an endorsement score, and was listed third as a top endorser for Winter Olympic athletes overall. Danica Patrick received the third highest endorsement score in NASCAR (Master, 2011).

2011

No women's sports were listed out of nine sports covered including "international," and while "Motor Sports" is not gender specific, again, few women participate. Danica Patrick was the only female mentioned. Serena and Venus Williams were mentioned as the top two endorsement scores among African-American athletes. The LPGA Championship and Women's U.S. Open viewers were included with the men's number of viewers. Danica Patrick's endorsement score was third among the top five listed. Hope Solo, Abby Wambach, and Megan Rapinoe had the top three endorsement scores for soccer. Women's World Cup European viewer numbers were included. Data for the year includes ratings and shares for select European games for women's soccer (Master, 2012).

2012

No women's sports were listed out of the 12 sports covered except "Summer Olympics." Gabby Douglas had the highest female endorsement score for those over 65. Viewership numbers included the LPGA Championship, and U.S. Women's Open. Hope Solo's endorsement score for soccer and one non-Olympic U.S. women's soccer game viewership numbers were mentioned. Two of Serena Williams matches are mentioned in other marquee events. U.S. Swimmer, Rebecca Soni, was declared the funniest athlete compared to all other Olympians. A majority of the "buzz" surrounding the U.S. "Female" Women's Gymnastics team was found to be on Twitter (Master, 2013).

2013

No women's sports were listed out of eleven sports covered. Danica Patrick was discussed in "Motor Sports," and was the top tweeted driver at the Daytona 500. The LPGA, and the U.S. Women's Open was included in viewership and season highlights. The Wimbledon Women's Final was mentioned in other marquee sports programming (Master, 2014).

2014

No women's sports were listed out of 13 sports covered. Women were mentioned, in general, regarding viewers of ice skating, a soccer final, and a soccer semi-final in the Olympics. Danica Patrick was mentioned as a NASCAR fan favorite for being good looking and stylish. The U.S. Women's Open including Michelle Wie, and the LPGA Championship were mentioned in golf's season highlights for total number of viewers. NCAA Women's Basketball was mentioned by name for the first time in comparison to NCAA Men's Basketball demographics, although, there was no mention of the WNBA alongside the NBA. Around the world, the World Figure Skating

Championships Women's Free Skate was mentioned for a large television audience in Japan (Kanto region). The Women's Wimbledon Final and the U.S. Open Women's Final viewers are mentioned as part of "other sports programming" (Master, 2015).

2015

One women's sport was listed out of 13 sports covered. The separate heading for Women's World Cup for U.S. Soccer was the first time one page of highlights were dedicated to a single game of women's competition. "The 2015 Women's World Cup Final was not only the most-watched English language soccer match in U.S. history, but it was also the third most viewed non-football sporting event of 2015" (Master, 2016, p. 8). However, only Major League Soccer (MLS) was listed under the heading "Soccer," while the NWSL was not mentioned. The LPGA Tour, LPGA Championship, and U.S. Women's Open was mentioned along with women's golf top two athletes Lydia Ko and Inbee Park. The section on the UFC included a picture of Ronda Rousey, and Rousey's endorsement score compared to Holly Holm, and three of Rousey's matches were mentioned. The women's NCAA final game total viewers received a mention. Serena Williams, including her performance at all four Grand Slam tournaments was listed under other sports programming (Master, 2016).

2016

No women's sports were listed out of 13 sports covered. U.S. women's gymnastics were mentioned along with Katie Ledecky and Simone Biles for top endorsement scores. The Women's PGA Championship and the U.S. Women's Open were mentioned with winners alongside the men's viewership highlights (Master, 2017).

2017

No women's sports were listed out of 13 sports covered, and included "esports" for the first time. MLS was listed separate from soccer. The NWSL gets a mention due to their first season televised on Lifetime. The remaining page on Soccer is dedicated to men's soccer. The Women's PGA Championship is mentioned along with LPGA popularity around the world. The UFC Women's Bantamweight viewership was mentioned. Venus and Serena Williams' head-to-head match viewership numbers were mentioned for the Australian Open Women's Final. Serena's Twitter shout outs to Madison Keys and Sloane Stephens were also noted, along with the Williams sisters considered as the "most marketable pro athletes of 2017" (Stainer & Master, 2018, p. 23). Top advertisers were mentioned by sport, but only tennis included similar coverage of women, and golf included a mention of the Women's PGA Tournament (Stainer & Master, 2018).

The exclusionary positioning of women's sports in industry publications is alarming considering these reports may impact programming choices, promotional choices, sponsorship, and advertising. Future studies could draw on the previously outlined theoretical frameworks—and expand into others—to systematically assess how women's sports are situated in these reports and to identify gender ideologies that permeate these reports. Advertisers utilize industry publications to understand metrics, and subsequently women may receive fewer sponsorships because their sports are invisible in the publications targeted toward the advertising world.

Conclusion

Over the last decade, sports media networks including ESPN have been critiqued for marginalizing women's sports, but ESPN has also created platforms and content specifically about women. As the self-declared "Worldwide Leader in Sports," ESPN has positioned itself as a go-to space for sports fans. It is understandable, then, that women's sports advocates problematize ESPN's treatment of women's sports and argue for a more nuanced representations. ESPN certainly does, can, and should play a role in creating an empowering place for women's sports. ESPN has hired women in key leadership positions (e.g., Alison Overholt as the first female Editor-in-chief for *The Body Issue*) and has significantly expanded its women-focused content online providing live coverage of women's college sports through ESPN3 but does not stream any women's games on espnW or ESPN+. The coverage and promotion of the 2018 WNBA's Final Four can be a standalone case study in terms of hours of coverage, broadcast commentary, cross-promotion on other platforms and accompanying promotional materials. Scholarship would certainly benefit from further engagement with ESPN, their sports broadcast contemporaries of women's sports content including regular season games, in addition to, tournaments in order to track how gender ideologies change across various sports and broadcast outlets both terrestrial and online.

At the same time, we must recognize in the current media environment, ESPN is only one among the many choices for sports promoters and sports leagues. Broadcasts of women's regular season games are limited, which restricts the fan base for tournament games, which may lead to lower television ratings. Based on our review of literature, we would also argue scholars of gender and sports media have inadvertently positioned ESPN as the "Worldwide Leader" for women's sports news coverage and broadcasts. The sheer amount of studies on ESPN and the dearth of studies on women's sports content on other platforms serve as evidence.

The two areas of research we suggest are by no means exclusive, but we hope our brief overview sparks new questions and new areas of engagement for scholars who are invested in changing the treatment of women in sports media. There are theoretical, practical, and educational benefits to situating women's sports beyond ESPN. On a theoretical level, identifying media outlets that do provide coverage of women's sports would contribute to theorizing on gender ideologies. On a practical level, scholars could offer examples to media practitioners of platforms and/or networks that promote women's sports. As educators, we could also use this scholarship to expand students' view of sports media beyond ESPN's coverage—a task that has been challenging in the environment where ESPN is the ideal potential employer for many students. Perhaps we will ultimately conclude the marginalization of women's sports is entrenched across the media landscape, but searching out spaces of interruption is an important step in the quest towards women's sports "storybook ending."[1]

Note

1. We recognize "storybook ending" as a gendered trope for happily ever after. The Hays (2017) article from espnW was originally titled, "Seeking a storybook ending: Stanford's Andi Sullivan, South Carolina's Savannah McCaskill aiming for the same ending" (para. 1). See also Clarey (2018).

References

2018 WNBA national TV schedule. (2018, February 20). *WNBA*. Retrieved from http://www.wnba.com/news/2018-wnba-national-tv-schedule/

About A+E Networks. (n.d.). *A+E Networks*. Retrieved from http://www.aenetworks.com/about

About The Walt Disney Company. (n.d.). *The Walt Disney Company*. Retrieved from https://thewaltdisneycompany.com/about/

About WFA. (n.d.). Women's Football Alliance: The world's top professional league. *Women's Football Alliance*. Retrieved from http://www.wfaprofootball.com/about/

Adams, T., & Tuggle, C. A. (2004). ESPN's SportsCenter and coverage of women's athletics: "It's a boys' club." *Mass Communication and Society, 7*(2) 237–248. doi: 10.1207/s15327825mcs0702_6

Atlanta Phoenix vs Tampa Bay Inferno WFA week 1. (2018, March 31). Score Sports Bat Idea, LLC. Retrieved from https://www.youtube.com/watch?v=PwUuHafbJko&feature=youtu.be

Billings, A. C., & Blackistone, K. B. (2015). Sprawling hagiography: ESPN's 30 for 30 series and the untangling of sports memories. In J. McGuire, G. G. Armfield, & A. Earnheardt (Eds.), *The ESPN effect: Exploring the worldwide leader in sports* (157–169). New York, NY: Peter Lang.

Billings, A. C., & Eastman, S. T. (2003). Framing identities: Gender, ethnic, and national parity in network announcing of the 2002 Winter Olympics. *Journal of Communication, 53*(4), 569–586. doi: 10.1111/j.1460-2466.2003.tb02911.x

Billings, A. C., Halone, K. K., & Denham, B. E. (2002). "Man, that was a pretty shot": An analysis of gendered broadcast commentary surrounding the 2000 men's and women's NCAA Final Four basketball championships. *Mass Communication & Society, 5*(3), 295–315. doi: 10.1207/S15327825MCS0503_4

Billings, A. C., & Young, B. D. (2015). Comparing flagship news programs: Women's sport coverage in ESPN's *SportsCenter* and FOX Sports 1's *FOX Sports Live*. *Electronic News, 9*(1), 3–16. doi: 10.1177/1931243115572824

Borah, P. (2011). Conceptual issues in framing theory: A systematic examination of a decade's literature. *Journal of Communication, 61*(2), 246–263. doi: 10.1111/j.1460-2466.2011.01539.x

Brockington, L. (2000, December 18). Lifetime shifts its WNBA games to ESPN2. *Sports Business Journal*. Retrieved from https://www.sportsbusinessdaily.com/Journal/Issues/2000/12/18/No-Topic-Name/Lifetime-Shifts-Its-WNBA-Games-To-ESPN2.aspx

Casey, T. (2017, May 1). Twitter signs a deal to stream regular-season W.N.B.A. Games. *The New York Times*. Retrieved from https://www.nytimes.com/2017/05/01/sports/basketball/wnba-twitter-streaming.html

Clarey, C. (2018, July 14). No storybook ending for Serena Williams. Instead, a Wimbledon title for Angelique Kerber. *The New York Times*. Retrieved from https://www.nytimes.com/2018/07/14/sports/serena-williams-angelique-kerber-wimbledon.html

Clavio, G., & Pedersen, P. M. (2007). Print and broadcast connections of ESPN: An investigation of the alignment of editorial coverage in ESPN The Magazine with ESPN's broadcasting rights [ISBN 978-089641-442-6]. *International Journal of Sport Management, 8*(1), 95–114. Retrieved from https://www.americanpresspublishers.com/IJSMContents2007.html

Cooky, C., Messner, M. A., & Hextrum, R. H. (2013). Women play sport, but not on TV: A longitudinal study of televised news media. *Communication & Sport, 1*(3), 203–230. doi: 10.1177/2167479513476947

Cooky, C., Messner, M. A., & Musto, M. (2015). "It's dude time!": A quarter century of excluding women's sports in televised news and highlight shows. *Communication & Sport, 3*(3), 261–287. doi: 10.1177/2167479515588761

Cranmer, G. A., Brann, M., & Bowman, N. D. (2014). Male athletes, female aesthetics: The continued ambivalence toward female athletes in ESPN's *The Body Issue*. *International Journal of Sport Communication, 7*(2), 145–165. doi: 10.1123/IJSC.2014-0021

De La Merced, M. J. (2012, July 10). Comcast to sell back its stake in A+E for $3 billion. *The New York Times.* Retrieved from https://dealbook.nytimes.com/2012/07/10/comcast-to-sell-back-its-stake-in-ae-for-3-billion/

Disney- ABC Television Group, Hearst Corporation & NBC Universal announce joining of A&E television networks and Lifetime Entertainment Services. (2009, August 27). *The Walt Disney Company.* Retrieved from https://thewaltdisneycompany.com/disney-abc-television-group-hearst-corporation-nbc-universal-announce-joining-of-ae-television-networks-and-lifetime-entertainment-services/

Five things to know about the 2018 NWSL season. (2018, March 23). *U.S. Soccer.* Retrieved from https://www.ussoccer.com/stories/2018/03/23/19/55/20180323-feat-wnt-five-things-about-the-2018-nwsl-season

Flosports adds professional softball coverage, announces partnership with National Pro Fastpitch. (2019, May 1). *National Pro Fastpitch.* Retrieved from https://pro-fastpitch.com/flosports-adds-professional-softball-coverage-announces-partnership-with-national-pro-fastpitch/

Gillies, T. (2016, February 7). Fantasy sports: The lucrative market that may be legal. *CNBC.* Retrieved from https://www.cnbc.com/2016/02/05/fantasy-sports-the-lucrative-market-that-may-be-legal.html

Goldberg, J. (2018, July 2). NWSL will stream games on website in August and September after go90 shuts down. *The Oregonian.* Retrieved from https://www.oregonlive.com/portland-thorns/2018/07/nwsl_will_stream_games_on_webs.html

Hartman, K. L. (2015). ESPN's mythological rhetoric of Title IX. In J. McGuire, G. G. Armfield, & A. Earnheardt (Eds.), *The ESPN effect: Exploring the worldwide leader in sports* (97–110). New York, NY: Peter Lang.

Hagey, K. (2017, February 2). A+E Networks buys stake in National Women's Soccer League. Retrieved from https://www.wsj.com/articles/a-e-networks-buys-stake-in-national-womens-soccer-league-1486048177

Hays, G. (2017, November 30). Stanford's Andi Sullivan, South Carolina's Savannah McCaskill aiming for the same ending. *espnW.* Retrieved from http://www.espn.com/espnw/sports/article/21610866/stanford-cardinal-andi-sullivan-south-carolina-gamecocks-savannah-mccaskill-aiming-same-ending-college-cup

Heinecken, D. (2018). For us all? Nine for IX and the representation of women in sport. *Women in Sport and Physical Activity Journal, 26*(1), 23–32. doi: 10.1123/wspaj.2017-0005

Hipes, P. (2017, February 2). Lifetime to air National Women's Soccer League games as A+E Networks kicks in for equity stake. *Deadline.* Retrieved from https://deadline.com/2017/02/lifetime-national-womens-soccer-league-tv-deal-ae-networks-stake-1201900415/

Jessop, A. (2014, December 9). The WTA signs the largest media rights contract in the history of women's sports. *Forbes.* Retrieved from https://www.forbes.com/sites/aliciajessop/2014/12/09/the-wta-signs-the-largest-media-rights-contract-in-the-history-of-womens-sports/#1675f3d86d3a

Johnson, S. (1997, July 11). WNBA coverage on Lifetime: Women's professional basketball? … *Chicago Tribune*. Retrieved from http://articles.chicagotribune.com/1997-07-11/features/9707110348_1_wnba-lifetime-game

Kian, E. M., Mondello, M., & Vincent, J. (2009). ESPN—The women's sports network? A content analysis of Internet coverage of March Madness. *Journal of Broadcasting & Electronic Media, 53*(3), 477–495. doi: 10.1080/08838150903102519.

Kian, E. M., Smith, L. R., Lee, J. W., & Sweeney, K. (2015). *ESPN The Magazine* "Body Issue": Challenging yet reinforcing traditional images of masculinity and femininity in sport. In J. McGuire, G. G. Armfield, & A. Earnheardt (Eds.), *The ESPN effect: Exploring the worldwide leader in sports* (139–154). New York: Peter Lang.

Kian, E. M., Vincent, J., & Mondello, M. (2008). Masculine hegemonic hoops: An Analysis of media coverage of March madness. *Sociology of Sport Journal, 25*(2), 223–242. doi: 10.1123/ssj.25.2.223

Langdon, B. (2000, December 18). Lifetime shifts its WNBA games to ESPN2. *Sports Business Journal*. Retrieved from http://www.sportsbusinessdaily.com/Daily.aspx

Lavelle, K. L. (2015). The ESPN effect: Representation of women in 30 for 30 films. In J. McGuire, G. G. Armfield, & A. Earnheardt (Eds.), *The ESPN effect: Exploring the worldwide leader in sports* (127–138). New York: Peter Lang.

Master, S. (2010). The changing face of sports media: January 2010. *The Nielsen Company*. Retrieved from http://www.nielsen.com/us/en/insights/reports/2010/The-Changing-Face-of-Sports-Media-Jan2010.html

Master, S. (2011). State of the media: Year in sports 2010. *The Nielsen Company*. Retrieved from http://www.nielsen.com/us/en/insights/reports/2011/year-in-sports-2010.html

Master, S. (2012). State of the media: 2011 year in sports. *The Nielsen Company*. Retrieved from http://www.nielsen.com/us/en/insights/reports/2012/state-of-the-media--2011-year-in-sports.html

Master, S. (2013). State of the media: 2012 year in sports. *The Nielsen Company*. Retrieved from http://www.nielsen.com/us/en/insights/reports/2013/state-of-the-media--2012-year-in-sports.html

Master, S. (2014). Year in sports media report: 2013. *The Nielsen Company*. Retrieved from http://www.nielsen.com/content/dam/corporate/us/en/reports-downloads/2014%20Reports/year-in-sports-media-report-2013.pdf

Master, S. (2015). Year in sports media report: 2014. *The Nielsen Company*. Retrieved from http://www.nielsen.com/us/en/insights/reports/2015/the-year-in-sports-media-report-2014.html

Master, S. (2016). Year in sports media report: 2015. *The Nielsen Company*. Retrieved from http://www.nielsen.com/us/en/insights/reports/2016/the-year-in-sports-media-report-2015.html

Master, S. (2017). Year in sports media report: 2016. *The Nielsen Company*. Retrieved from http://www.nielsen.com/us/en/insights/reports/2017/the-year-in-sports-media-report-2016.html

McCombs, M. E., & Shaw, D. L. (1972). The agenda-setting function of the mass media. *Public Opinion Quarterly, 36*(2), 176–187. doi: 10.1086/267990

Messner, M. A., Dunbar, M., & Hunt, D. (2000). The televised sports manhood formula. *Journal of Sport and Social Issues, 24*(4), 380–394. doi: 10.1177/0193723500244006

Messner, M. A., Duncan, M. C., & Cooky, C. (2003). Silence, sports bras, and wrestling porn: Women in televised sports news and highlights shows. *Journal of Sport and Social Issues, 27*(1), 38–51. doi: 10.1177/0193732502239583

MLB shows support for NPF. (2004). *National Pro Fastpitch.* Retrieved from http://www.profastpitch.com/news/index.html?article_id=262

MNT Schedule & Tickets. (2018). *U.S. Soccer.* Retrieved from https://www.ussoccer.com/mens-national-team/schedule-tickets

Musto, M., Cooky, C., & Messner, M. A. (2017). "From fizzle to sizzle!" Televised sports news and the production of gender-bland sexism. *Gender & Society, 31*(5), 573–596. doi: 10.1177/0891243217726056

Nielsen completes acquisition of Repucom. (2016, June 21). *Nielsen.* Retrieved from http://www.nielsen.com/us/en/press-room/2016/nielsen-completes-acquisition-of-repucom.html

NPF announces 2017 season coverage on NPFTV. (2017, April 12). *National Pro Fastpitch.* Retrieved from285 http://www.profastpitch.com/news/news/index.html?article_id=2773

NPF to celebrate 15th season with season-long initiatives. (2018, January 16). *National Fastpitch Coaches Association.* Retrieved from https://nfca.org/index.php?option=com_content&view=article&id=7641:npf-to-celebrate-15th-season-with-season-long-initiatives&catid=116&Itemid=149

NWHL about. (n.d.). About the National Women's Hockey League. *NWHL.* Retrieved from https://www.nwhl.zone/about-the-nwhl

Price, V., & Tewksbury, D. (1997). News values and public opinion: A theoretical account of media priming and framing. In G. A. Barnett & F. J. Boster (Eds.), *Progress in communication sciences: Advances in persuasion* (Vol. 13, pp. 173–212). Greenwich, CT: Ablex Publishing.

Roessner, A., & Whiteside, E. (2016). Unmasking Title IX on its 40th birthday: The operation of women's voices, women's spaces, and sporting mythnarratives in the commemorative coverage of Title IX. *Journalism, 17*(5), 583–599. doi: 10.1177/1464884915572868

Rothenberg, B. (2017, January 11). Looking to watch women's tennis? For now, good luck. *The New York Times.* Retrieved from https://www.nytimes.com/2017/01/11/sports/tennis/womens-tennis-tv-coverage.html

Schwindt, O. (2017, February 2). A+E Networks, National Women's Soccer League ink major deal. *Variety.* Retrieved from https://variety.com/2017/tv/news/womens-soccer-lifetime-1201975617/

Stainer, J., & Master, S. (2018). Nielsen sports: Year in sports media report: U.S. 2017. *The Nielsen Company.* Retrieved from http://www.nielsen.com/us/en/insights/reports/2018/2017-year-in-sports-media.html

Tannenwald, J. (2017, April 15). How to watch NWSL games on the go90 streaming platform, and how the rights deal got done. *The Inquirer*. Retrieved from http://www.philly.com/philly/blogs/thegoalkeeper/NWSL-go90-streaming-Verizon-rights-fee-Lifetime-television.html

Thorpe, H., Toffoletti, K., & Bruce, K. (2017). Sportswomen and social media: Bringing third-wave feminism, postfeminism, and neoliberal feminism into conversation. *Journal of Sport and Social Issues, 41*(5), 359–383. doi: 10.1177/0193723517730808

Tuggle, C. A. (1997). Differences in television sports reporting of men's and women's athletics: ESPN SportsCenter and CNN Sports Tonight. *Journal of Broadcasting & Electronic Media, 41*(1), 14–24. doi: 10.1080/08838159709364387

Turner, J. S. (2014). A longitudinal content analysis of gender and ethnicity portrayals on ESPN's SportsCenter from 1999–2009. *Communication & Sport, 2*(4), 303–327. doi: 10.1177/2167479513496222

Vogan, T. (2015). *ESPN: The making of a sports media empire*. Urbana, IL: University of Illinois Press.

W Bowl 2016 on GLSC and ESPN Women's National Football Championship watch live. (n.d.). *Go Live Sports Cast*. Retrieved from http://golivesportscast.com/2016/07/w-bowl-2016-on-glsc-and-espn-womens-national-football-championship-watch-live/

Whiteside, E., & Roessner, A. (2018). Forgotten and left behind: Political apathy and privilege at Title IX's 40th anniversary. *Communication & Sport, 6*(1), 3–24. doi: 10.1177/2167479516676577

WNT Schedule & Tickets. (2018). *U.S. Soccer*. Retrieved from https://www.ussoccer.com/womens-national-team/schedule-tickets

Wolter, S. (2014). "It just makes good business sense": A media political economy analysis of *espnW*. *Journal of Sports Media, 9*(2), 73–96. doi: 10.1353/jsm.2014.0011

Wolter, S. (2015a). A critical discourse analysis of espnW: Divergent dialogues and post-feminist conceptions of female fans and female athletes. *International Journal of Sport Communication, 8*(3), 345–370. doi: 10.1123/IJSC.2015-0040

Wolter, S. (2015b). A quantitative analysis of photographs and articles on espnW: Positive progress for female athletes. *Communication & Sport, 3*(2), 168–195. doi: 10.1177/2167479513509368

Wolter, S. (2015c). espnW: Catering to a new audience. In J. McGuire, G. G. Armfield, & A. Earnheardt (Eds.), *The ESPN effect: Exploring the worldwide leader in sports* (111–126). New York: Peter Lang.

Women and sport: Insights into the growing rise and importance of female fans and female athletes. (2015). *Repucom*. Retrieved from http://nielsensports.com/women-sport/

WTA launches new free-to-play WTA fantasy tennis. (2018, January 23). *WTA Tennis*. Retrieved from http://www.wtatennis.com/news/wta-launches-new-free-play-wta-fantasy-tennis

WTA media: The most significant women's sport partnership. (n.d.). *Perform Group*. Retrieved from http://www.performgroup.com/brands/wta-media/

WTA signs digital rights deal with iQIYI. (n.d.). *WTA Tennis.* Retrieved from http://www.wtatennis.com/content/wta-signs-digital-rights-deal-iqiyi-0

WTA signs rights deal with MCS TV Group. (n.d.). *WTA Tennis.* Retrieved from http://www.wtatennis.com/news/wta-signs-rights-deal-mcs-tv-group

WTA staff. (2017). The WTA will launch a unique WTA Livestreaming subscription service in 2017 where tennis fans can view every WTA singles and many doubles semifinals and finals matches. *Women's Tennis Association.* Retrieved from http://www.wtatennis.com/news/wta-launch-unique-all-new-women%E2%80%99s-tennis-livestreaming-service-2017

Section Four

The Changing Sports
Media Landscape

17. "Tying the Brand to Something a Little Bit Bigger": A Political Economy Analysis of espnW

Sarah Wolter

espnW was founded in 2010 and serves as the primary multiplatform business of ESPN. The site is "dedicated to engaging and inspiring women through sports" and "offers total access to female athletes and the sports they play, takes fans inside the biggest events, and captures the biggest trends in sports life/style" by focusing on the "crossroads of sports and culture" and "stories that matter most to women" (ESPN Media Zone, n.d., para. 1). This happens primarily through digital content and events, though the site also produces content for television, radio, films, educational platforms, and social media (ESPN Media Zone, n.d.). espnW forayed internationally into Australia and Brazil in 2016. The site consistently presents female athletes as serious competitors (Wolter, 2014; Wolter, 2015a), something that mainstream media has often neglected (Tucker Center for Girls & Women in Sport, 2013).

The purpose of this analysis is to investigate how ESPN positions espnW as the company wrestles with intersections between sports, politics, and culture. Player protests and ESPN employees discussing "political" issues via social media have prompted a discussion about how much politics should infiltrate the company's sports media. Past actions show that ESPN tries to relegate political content to sites with a "broader editorial mission" like espnW so they can focus on apolitical sports news on their mainstream networks. ESPN is one of the most powerful sports organizations in the world, so analyzing espnW from a political economy perspective reveals how the company shapes larger cultural discourse about women's sports (Davidson, 2017).

Political economy analysis of espnW reveals its initiatives empower female athletes in a context where women's issues are at the forefront of U.S. culture. The site first staked a claim in women's issues by establishing a "Women's Initiatives" focus in 2015. As part of this initiative, they employ authors and executives who make sure issues related to women are covered on the site. Additionally, content is potentially influenced by corporate partnerships that fulfill profit imperatives of ESPN.

Review of Literature

Research on espnW is mixed. Wolter (2015a, 2015b) conducted quantitative analysis of photographs and articles on espnW for three time periods: 2011, 2013–14, and 2015–16 and found exceptional positive presentation of athletes, especially female athletes. For photographs, in all three time periods, female athletes are covered (68%, 87.5%, and 85.6%, respectively) more than male athletes (12.4%, 12.5%, 12.0%, respectively). Athletes in uniform, on the playing surface, and in action are indicators of the site presenting serious athleticism in these studies. Total athletes are in uniform 87.1%, 83.0%, and 81.8%, respectively, and female athletes are in uniform 92.3%, 84.3%, and 84.1%, respectively. Athletes are on the playing surface of their respective sports 83.2%, 74.4%, and 76.8%, respectively, and female athletes are on the playing surface 88.6%, 72.7%, and 78.8% of the time, respectively, as a percentage of total female athlete photographs. Athletes are in action 53.2%, 47.9%, and 46.3%, respectively, and female athletes are in action 58.2%, 48.1%, and 51.0% of the time, respectively as a percentage of total female athlete photographs. Article presentation mirrors photographs, favoring female athletes in 68.2%, 89.9%, and 86.3%, respectively of articles. Other indicators of positive portrayals like positive skill levels/accomplishments, reference to prowess/strength, and reference to psychological/emotional strengths are high for all athletes as well as female athletes. Content analysis of articles in these studies shows unprecedented positive portrayals of female athletes.

Critical discourse analysis and political economy analysis of espnW show less favorable outcomes from the site (Wolter, 2015a, 2015b). Analysis of almost 500 articles in 2011 shows two major themes for discourse in espnW articles. First, espnW authors use divergent dialogues like descriptive language for female athletes, mention of nonsporting topics, and direct references to physical appearance or personality attributes. Second, espnW was geared toward female fans as *additive content* to ESPN, which excludes women if traditional sports journalism is upheld by masculine ideals in the institution of sport. Political economy analysis of the site in 2014 shows that ESPN appropriates interest in women's sports as a means to garner profit through elements like planning retreats and leadership structure. The study found that ESPN's history of discrimination exploits women and that could have an influence on espnW.

Method

Political economy analysis is the most appropriate approach to examine how ESPN uses espnW to secure dividends for The Walt Disney Company at a time where the company is wrestling with intersections between sports, politics, and culture. The definition of political economy employed for this study is,

> the study of how values of all kinds are produced, distributed, exchanged, and consumed (the economic); how power is produced, distributed and exercised (the political); and how these aspects of the social world are related at any given place and time. (Graham, 2006, p. 494)

A political economy analysis reveals relationships between audiences, how they engage with media, initiatives advanced by corporations, and how these initiatives have the power to develop, maintain, and change both social and political structures (Graham, 2006; Wasko, 2014).

The first element of political economy analysis is economic. Information as a commodity is an essential point of analysis as the United States has transitioned from an industrial based economy to an information-based economy. Power derived from the production, distribution, and use of information in commodity form constitutes a "political economy of information" (Mosco, 1988). Traditional conceptions of "corporatization, commercialization, commodification, and concentration" (Wasko, 2014, p. 260) characterize information that is shaped into marketable forms (Mosco, 1988). Additionally, a theme of the political economy of information is that audiences are commodities sold to advertisers (Graham, 2006). An economic study of espnW encompasses how The Walt Disney Company garners power from the production, distribution, and use of information on espnW in a commodity form.

The second element of political economy analysis is political. Entities who have the power to shape information and technology set patterns for how citizens think about and act on issues in culture (Mosco, 1988). Information and media/communication systems affect political and social power, especially in ways they enable or limit citizens' self-government (McChesney, 2013). Political economy of information examines who creates, distributes, and consumes information in broader cultural contexts to see who wields power in shaping discourse and interaction patterns with information (Wasko, 2014). A political analysis of espnW looks at how ESPN exerts power in shaping discourse on the site.

The third element of political economy analysis is how values and power come together in a particular context such as the institution of sport. Political economy centers relationships between people, who control production, how people engage mediated content, and how that intersection shapes or has the potential to shape social and political structures that socialize people into sets of acceptable values (Graham, 2006; Mosco, 1988). An analysis of espnW from this perspective pulls economic and political perspectives together in the context of the institution of sport, especially the commercialization of sport, to determine the site's potential influence.

The research question for this study is, "How does ESPN position espnW as the company wrestles with intersections between sports, politics, and culture?" The sample for this analysis is the espnW website, specifically the editorial mission of espnW, the Sales Media Kit, and major initiatives presented on the main menu of the site. For example, under the "Culture" tab, I looked at content that described espnW initiatives, such as, "Evolution of Title IX," "LGBTQ Inclusion," "IMPACT25," "espnW Summit," "Campus Conversations," "Everyday Heroes," "Global Sports Mentoring Program," "espnW Australia," and "espnW Brazil." I then conducted an Internet search to find additional supporting documents posted on ESPN. Investor Relations site and media interviews with espnW leadership to further explain and supplement the purpose of and history behind the initiatives. I did not analyze content of articles written about sports on the site, only those that covered espnW's initiatives.

The theoretical framework for this study is feminist theory and commercialization of sports. The goal of feminist theory is to deconstruct the social, relational, and power aspects of systems of knowledge to figure out how language and context frame masculine bias and women's experience (Ritzer & Stepinsky, 2018). Feminist ideals are invoked in a sense of *moral justice* to articulate how women are positioned in sport media (Pringle, 2018). Examining espnW through a feminist lens means analyzing the construction of gender in espnW initiatives and explaining how those constructions help entities yield power (Dow, 2006; Foss, 2004).

A second theoretical framework is looking at espnW through the lens of a commercial sports media landscape where sports and initiatives that are highlighted are also those granted cultural significance (Coakley, 2009). A sports media landscape centered on commercial sports favors a heroic orientation, which emphasizes mastery of style, winning, and danger/exciting movements

(Coakley, 2009). The purpose is to get audiences to attend or watch events based on the performance aspects of the sport and then those audiences are sold to sponsors who pay to have their brands associated with events. In addition, the sports media landscape is also affected by consumers moving away from television and toward more digital mediums to watch sports (Jason, 2017). This analysis of espnW looks at the degree to which initiatives on the site promote a commercial orientation.

Results

ESPN straddles a traditional narrative that has brought them success in the past and a progressive narrative prompted by a more blatantly political sports landscape. As a result, the segment offers two main camps of content: (a) sports news without politics governed by ratings, and (b) sites with a "broader editorial mission," which includes espnW, fivethirtyeight, and The Undefeated (ESPN Media Zone, n.d., para. 1). The "broader editorial mission" allows espnW to create and distribute content that is dedicated to, "engaging and inspiring women through sports" (ESPN Media Zone, n.d., para. 1) in a fervent political landscape. Because they operate under the governance of a corporation, however, espnW often appropriates the women's movement through initiatives that involve corporate partners tied to The Walt Disney Company.

ESPN as Sports News Without Politics Because They Are Governed by Ratings

The current U.S. political climate has forced ESPN to straddle the line of how much politics should infiltrate its content. Social movements such as Black Lives Matter and the #metoo movement have become more visible in the last 10 years, and athletes have used their reach to support them. In 2014, LeBron James, Kyrie Irving, and other players wore shirts that said, "I can't breathe" to fight for justice for Eric Garner, a black man who was killed by an officer not indicted for his death (Schoichet, Cummings, & Yan, 2014). The week before, players from the St. Louis Rams protested the shooting of Michael Brown in Ferguson, Missouri, by walking onto the field and putting their hands up in the air. Other silent protests followed, but the election of Donald Trump and San Francisco 49ers Colin Kaepernick sitting on the bench for the national anthem to protest police brutality and the oppression of people of color in 2016 sparked an especially prominent line of player protests (Sandritter, 2017). Players like Seattle Seahawks' Jeremy Lane and

NWSL player Megan Rapinoe followed right away, and many other NFL players joined in, either kneeling, locking hands, or raising a fist in the air in a "nod to Kaepernick." President Trump responded by tweeting that his followers should boycott the NFL. When the NBA champion Golden State Warriors were debating whether or not to go to the White House after their win, President Trump sent out another tweet disinviting them, which has happened with other teams since (Bryan, 2017). If there was any doubt before, politics is officially overlapping with sports.

Some ESPN employees like Jemele Hill joined the conversation about race and sports. In response, in 2017 ESPN issued new political and election guidelines for employees working in news (not in commentary like espnW). The rules allow for political discussion but leadership recommended connecting those discussions to sports (Brady, 2017a). In September 2017, then ESPN President John Skipper explained:

> Sports is intertwined with society and culture, so "sticking to sports" is not so simple. When athletes engage on issues or when protests happen in games, we cover, report and comment on that, ESPN is not a political organization. Where sports and politics intersect, no one is told what view they must express. At the same time, ESPN has values. We are committed to inclusion and an environment of tolerance where everyone in a diverse work force has the equal opportunity to succeed. We consider this human, not political. Consequently, we insist that no one be denigrated for who they are including their gender, ethnicity, religious beliefs or sexual identity. (Brady, 2017b, para. 32)

The leadership at ESPN focuses on sports news without politics because they are governed by ratings according to traditional standards of professional sports in a commercialized landscape. Player protests and social movements have made the company have to address this model.

espnW as Commentary Under a Broader Editorial Mission

espnW operates under different editorial standards than sports news reporting at ESPN, which allows them to address contemporary issues in sport, some of which are political. espnW does this by telling stories and addressing issues that are not typically covered on sports websites. Laura Gentile, Senior Vice President of espnW and Women's Initiatives, says the editorial charter of espnW is "to tell stories that often go untold. There's so many female athletes doing incredible things that just don't get the spotlight. And again, that's not always the world-class athlete. All these athletic experiences are valid, and we try to give a place and a home for those things" (Deitsch, 2017). espnW is a more "inclusive and diverse place" for storytelling than its parent company and Gentile sees this as contributing to ESPN as a business (McGloster, 2016, para. 31).

Beyond storytelling, espnW is committed to, "address issues in sports that potentially go unaddressed" (Deitsch, 2017). For example, when the Ray Rice domestic violence scandal came on the scene, articles on the site went beyond surface-level facts and dove into analysis of sexual assault seldom seen in sports reporting. Gentile prompts authors on the site to stir debate using a point-counterpoint model. They do not shy away from controversial topics and, "call it like we see it" (Deitsch, 2017).

Editorial standards allow espnW to focus on content because they operate based on standards not defined solely by ratings. Gentile says "great content" is the overriding decision about whether or not a story is featured on espnW, not whether or not the story will garner ratings (Dietsch, 2017). espnW is a place dedicated to telling stories about female athletes in a sports media climate where as little as 4% of coverage is about women (Tucker Center for Research on Girls and Women in Sport, 2013). espnW is a beacon in a landscape where so many women-centered sports publications have failed.[1]

2015 and the Emergence of "Women's Initiatives"

Gentile has steered the organization to focusing on women's issues, most notably by creating a "Women's Initiatives" segment in 2015. Part of the focus on "Women's Initiatives" is that espnW employs powerful gatekeepers who are concerned about women's issues as they make decisions and write for the site. The "broader editorial mission" and move toward "Women's Initiatives" allows espnW to create and distribute content that is, "engaging and inspiring women through sports" (ESPN Media Zone, n.d., para. 1) in a fervent political landscape. The shift has been successful from a business perspective.

While espnW still highlights sports performances through features like "Top 10" plays of the week, the site has expanded to have more of a focus on "Women's Initiatives." The move started in 2015 with the promotion of Laura Gentile to Senior Vice President, espnW and Women's Initiatives (Nesheim, 2015). The promotion allowed Gentile to have, "a broader role focused on expanding ESPN's presence in the lives of the many women who love sports" (Nesheim, 2015, para. 1).

The move toward "Women's Initiatives" on espnW has been a planned shift from making women a part of the sports conversation to using sport to engage and inspire women. Gentile recalls the beginning of espnW when senior executives told her to change direction with the site even though she did not agree with the outlook:

I also knew it was something we needed to do in the short-term to keep the dream alive … It's not the be-all-end-all and it's not the forever, but it's what we need to do now.' … we will continue to think critically and we will be able to come out on the right side of this. (Tomb, 2015, para. 6)

Gentile concedes it took time for company executives and espnW personnel to be on the same page about the vision, but she always looked at the "long view" of developing espnW: "we didn't over-promise from the beginning that this was going to be an overnight sensation and we were going to reap incredible, lucrative returns. We were very methodical about it. We knew it was going to take time" (Deitsch, 2017).

Although espnW is more exempt from ratings than other ESPN initiatives, focusing on women's issues through a "Women's Initiatives" segment, employing gatekeepers who are concerned about women's issues, and content that supports women through partnerships would not make financial sense if the site was not successful from a business perspective. The staff of the site started out at five and has swelled to over 50 in eight years (Deitsch, 2017). Website traffic shows growth from year to year and numbers are between five and nine million depending on the measure (ComScore vs. Omniture) (Deitsch, 2017). Gentile is not concerned as much about the amount of traffic as she is about the "right kind" of traffic, which for espnW is women (Deitsch, 2017).

Influencers at the Top
The focus on "Women's Initiatives" is upheld by espnW employing executives and writers who are concerned about women's issues (Deitsch, 2017). When women are in decision making roles, they decide what types of stories are told and which perspectives they cover. Kate Fagan, a columnist and feature writer on espnW, says, "I happen to be on television shows and in production meetings. I also happen to pitch women's sport stories more and fight for them more. So maybe we see them on air more when I am involved" (Walker & Melton, 2015, p. 86). This is especially important because espnW, "provides an engaging environment that offers total access to female athletes and the sports they play, takes fans inside the biggest events, and shares a unique point of view on the sports stories that matter most to women" (ESPN Customer Marketing and Sales, n.d., p. 2). It is one of the only mainstream media organizations that does.

Including women in decision-making ranks is unique in the world of sports. The Institute for Diversity and Ethics in Sport 2014 Associated Press Sports Editors Gender Report card shows an F for gender hiring practices (Lapchick, 2015). Percentages show that 90.9% of sports editors, 86.6% of assistant sports editors, 83.9% of columnists, 86.3% of reporters, and 86.0% of copy editors/designers are men. While research on the impact of female staff members in the newsroom for impacting coverage of women's sports is mixed (Ottaway, 2016), sports editors' values and beliefs have shifted to see the benefit of hiring more women (Laucella, Hardin, Bien-Aimé, & Antunovic, 2017). Including powerful women like Julie Foudy, "the brand's leading voice on pay equity, leadership development, and other issues involving women and sports" (Nwulu, 2017, para. 2) as part of the sports conversation on the site primes espnW to be a "breeding ground for social change in women's sports" (Walker & Melton, 2015).

Examples of Initiatives That Support Women's Issues
While many espnW initiatives like the "Run Mama Run" series documentary and the 45th anniversary of Title IX reflect great storytelling and important political issues, two multimedia campaigns in 2017 are examples of initiatives that especially reflect this mission: international marketing campaigns and the "When I Play" short film.

International Marketing Campaigns
espnW debuted internationally for the first time in Australia and Brazil in 2016. As part of marketing efforts to introduce the site into these countries, the site ran two advertising campaigns: "Invisible Players" and "Inequality Courts." "Invisible Players" was created by the Africa Sao Paulo Agency and debuted in March 2016. The campaign includes two videos: one where people waiting at a bus stop "tested their knowledge" on digitized, disguised athletes, and one where people were invited into a sports arena to undertake the same exercise. The people in the videos had to guess who the athletes were, and all guessed famous male athletes like Neymar or Messi.[2] The videos actually featured WNBA star Maya Moore, pro soccer player Marta Vieira, and big wave champ Maya Gabeira. The last line of the video says, "If you didn't get the answers right, you need to learn more about women's power." Clearly espnW was staking a claim in the international market, and that claim was that they stand for empowerment of women.

The second campaign, "Inequality Courts" ran in Brazil and debuted in June 2017. Also created by the Africa Sao Paulo Agency, the campaign has two parts: a video that exposed differences between male and female athletes in prizes, investment in leagues, and sports in media during actual sport events; and painting public sporting courts to illustrate these differences. The video starts with segments from the documentary created by the Tucker Center for Research on Girls & Women in Sports and Twin Cities Public Television. Then they show a blank screen with the words, "espnW introduces," "Inequality Courts," and "We decided to expose the differences between male and female athletes." Next, they show the *key* to the visuals: blue squares for prizes and media for male athletes, and pink squares for prizes and media for female athletes. They then show instances of placing these overlays in actual competitions and on the streets of Brazil, citing, "During ESPN's broadcast the courts became infographics against inequality" and, for the second part of the campaign, "we didn't stop there," "The fans also saw on the streets what they watched on TV," "The sports courts became an OOH [out of home] and print campaign," and "To report inequality, we engaged sports fans to change this game." Last, the screen flashed, "Equal pay for equal play" and "Let's change this game." espnW came into the Brazil market focused on equality for women in sport. As a result of the campaign, searching for espnW rose 86%, over 13 million people were impacted, 94% of mentions were positive (Ad Forum, n.d.).

"When I Play"

A second multimedia campaign aimed at empowering women was the "When I Play" video as a celebration of Women's History Month, which espnW coined "Women Making History" month. The video features a narrator powerfully reading a poem written by creative director and executive producer Allison Glock (see Appendix A for full poem) over images of everyday athletes skateboarding, boxing, weightlifting, playing roller derby, swimming, and dancing. The last part of the video splices in moments in history from professional athletes and coaches, highlighting women from Pat Summit to Serena Williams. The final moments of the video flash, "W ... Where; W ... When; W ... Why; W ... We; W ... Women" with acoustic piano beats before a page with the espnW logo that says, "For Us/By Us/With Us."

"When I Play" was a success, leading espnW and ESPN.com for most of the day it debuted. It racked up over 7 million impressions and 1.5 million views on Facebook and just over 14,500 views on YouTube (Gentile, 2017). The U.S. Department of State, WNBA, U.S. Soccer, *Good Morning America*, BuzzFeed, Huffington Post, Refinery 29, and MAKERS also showcased the film, adding to its reach. espnW sponsored this video because it represents who they are as a brand: the conduit for those who see their "movement a movement" (Glock, n.d., para. 18).

Appropriating the Women's Movement With Corporate Partnerships

espnW initiatives use the company's reach to appropriate the women's movement in positive ways. While these initiatives are empowering, many involve corporate partnerships that benefit corporations tied to the Walt Disney Company. First, espnW uses sport to cultivate women entrepreneurs and business leaders. Second, "tentpole annual events" bring together senior executives and influencers to strategize about women's sports. These initiatives should be viewed with the caveat that espnW exists as part of The Walt Disney Company and its ultimate mission is to secure dividends for shareholders.

Cultivating Women Business Leaders

espnW sponsors initiatives designed to cultivate women leaders in business professions. While supporting women's development is admirable, setting women up to succeed in business professions benefits large-scale corporations like The Walt Disney Company. A research partnership with Ernst & Young (EY) and the Global Sports Mentoring Program with the U.S. Department of State are two examples of programs that espnW uses to support women in business.

The EY/espnW partnership is a report titled, "Why female athletes make winning entrepreneurs" that ties skills female athletes develop through sports to entrepreneurial success. Interviews from successful entrepreneurs offer advice that promises to help athletes and non-athletes "build market-leading companies" (EY, 2017, para. 1). espnW Senior Vice President Laura Gentile says the research, "solidifies our long-held belief that sports play an integral role in the success of women in business" (EY, 2017, para. 17). By its nature, EY, global leader in assurance, tax, transaction and advisory services for capital markets and in economies the world over (EY, 2017), favors women working in business professions. espnW supports that mission by its affiliation with the research. While women's success in the workplace is essential, research partnerships like these support a very specific type of workplace – one that benefits a capitalist economy that upholds corporations like The Walt Disney Company.

The Global Sports Mentoring Program is entering its sixth year and pairs 17 "emerging female leaders" from countries around the world with "top American female executives from some of the most influential organizations in sports and business" for a four-week mentorship "developing strategic action plans aimed at creating sports opportunities for underserved women and girls in their home countries" (Chozet, 2017, para. 1). The mentees hail from countries like Brazil, China, Kosovo, Nigeria, South Korea, Uganda, and Venezuela. Over half of the mentors represent companies like Burton Snowboards, Eli Lilly and Company, Google, and Under Armour (the other half represent non-profits like the NCAA, NHL, and PGA of America). Creating programs that serve girls and women is admirable, but most of the mentees could at least partially develop programs using a corporate lens because most of the mentors guiding them work for corporations. Pairing mentees with influencers in the American sports sector likely leads to corporate culture because the American sports landscape is so highly commercialized (Coakley,

2009). Ideally this is mitigated by the U.S. Department of State working with the University of Tennessee's Center for Sport, Peace, and Society as part of the program, but the program's mission to "create[ing] more resilient and stable societies" could be affected by corporate partners (Office of the Spokesperson, 2017, para. 2).

"Tent Pole Annual Events" of Athletes, Industry Leaders, and Executives
espnW's "tent pole annual events" (ESPN Customer Marketing & Sales, n.d.), the Women + Sports Summit, in its ninth year, and the Women + Sports, Chicago conference, in its third year, represent the company's divide between supporting women's sports and supporting business. espnW (n.d.) describes the Women + Sport Summit as a "one-of-a-kind event that connects, motivates and enables attendees to gain valuable insights and data points, and collaborate on creating an actionable vision for the future of women and sports." Panels and workshops cover "a wide range of topics, from global access to sports and opportunities for the advancement of women, to the marketing of female athletes and the business of women's sports" (espnW, n.d., para. 3, para. 2). The Women + Sports Chicago conference is similar but focuses specifically on Chicago-area executives. The purpose of the gatherings to "create[ing] positive change and opportunity for women in sports" is important, but the attendees, "female athletes, leaders in the sports world and industry influencers" address these issues from corporate/commercial standpoints (espnW, n.d., para. 1).

espnW addresses important and relevant cultural issues through many of its initiatives. Part of that reach involves connections between the company and corporate partners, and these connections could cause a conflict of interest for the most impactful ways to affect women in sports. When Laura Gentile was promoted to Senior Vice President, espnW and Women's Initiatives in 2015, John Kosner, Executive Vice President, Digital and Print Media for ESPN said, "With the work of Laura and her team, we believe we can significantly expand the impact ESPN has among female sports fans in all our media and enhance the opportunities we can offer our marketing partners to reach women" (Nesheim, 2015, para. 2). espnW operates in a commercial sports landscape, and its affiliation with ESPN and The Walt Disney Company privileges profit above all else (Wolter, 2014).

Discussion

Political economy analysis focuses on the economic ("how values of all kinds are produced, distributed, exchanged, and consumed"), the political ("how power is produced, distributed and exercised"), and how these two aspects work together to shape audience's views of the world (Graham, 2006, p. 494). espnW's "political" initiatives empower female athletes in a context where women's issues are at the forefront of U.S. culture while fulfilling profit imperatives of ESPN.

espnW is not governed by ratings, so its opportunity to publish "political" content that obviously sways toward empowering women's sports is expected. ESPN uses the site's "broader editorial mission" (ESPN Media Zone, n.d., para. 1) as a way to placate fans who demand more in-depth sports reporting. Relegating "political" content to espnW maintains the idea that sports is apolitical, something that has made sports enterprises trillions of dollars (Zirin, 2013). In reality, sports are very political, where "nationalism, patriotism, and military might that festoon every corner" (Zirin, 2013, p. 9) of the sports world, as ESPN has learned covering player protests. The company should evolve as a media organization and cover sports and "politics" in all its businesses.

espnW has used their broader editorial mission to discuss women's sports in positive ways and to employ women in high-ranking positions within the company. This is ultimately in the interest of serving ESPN and The Walt Disney Company's bottom line. The U.S. financial system is capitalist, and espnW's parent company is very successful in that system ($55 billion in revenue and $9.4 billion in net income in 2017). Capitalism is driven by profit and by smashing competition so firms can amass the most money possible (McChesney, 2015). Initiatives of a corporation, then, are about making money, and ESPN uses espnW and corporate connections with other large companies[3] as means by which they can draw additional audience members to their business. The media and sports landscapes in the U.S. are largely commercial (Coakley, 2009), so ESPN's business model works well to draw in consumers. espnW is backed by professional journalists, huge financial contributions from one of the most powerful media organizations in the world, supported by other hugely successful corporations, and gives people an opportunity to consume women's sports in a way that few other outlets have done before (Walker & Melton, 2015).

ESPN has the power to shape the ways consumers conceptualize women's sports, and they do so on espnW with empowering, inspirational stories about female athletes. This benefits the reputation of their business in a U.S. culture that has a heightened focus on women's issues. 2018 has been called the "year of the woman" by many journalists (e.g., Schnall, 2017; Todd, Murray, & Dann, 2018; Yarvin, 2017) because of three major political uprisings (among others). The first is Women's marches "committed to dismantling systems of oppression through nonviolent resistance and building inclusive structures" (Women's March, n.d., para. 1) that have amassed millions of people in protest marches (Bowman, 2018). The second is the #metoo movement, a social media and protest campaign designed to "give people a sense of 'the magnitude" of sexual harassment and sexual assault that has held powerful men like Harvey Weinstein publically accountable for their actions (Gilbert, 2017, para. 6). The third is how many women are running for office–almost double what it was in the previous election cycle–after being disappointed with the 2016 election and Republican Party legislation attacking women (Bowman, 2018; Dittmar, 2017). The context for focusing on women's issues is strongly in ESPN's favor.

Supporting women's sports would ideally come from organizations whose first interest is women and second interest is profit, but few of these organizations exist in a society governed by capitalism. Those that do are not privy to the reach and audience of one of the most powerful sports brands in the world. Reporting on women's sports is 2–4% of total coverage in most publications (Tucker Center for Research on Girls and Women in Sport, 2013), so espnW's scope is welcomed. The potential problem is if the visibility of women's issues diminishes and promoting women's sports is not worth the branding effort, then ESPN's focus on women's sports in espnW may diminish, too. Its history has proved otherwise as the site enters its second decade. Gentile says, "We're very proud about where espnW is right now, but we still feel like we're just getting started" (McGloster, 2016, para. 33). Now it is time to get the stories covered on espnW more regularly transferred onto other ESPN platforms so the positive energy toward female athletes can help transition traditionally male-dominated sport spaces into places where female athletes are more respected.

Notes

1. *Sports Illustrated for Women, Fitness* magazine, *Conde Nast Sports for Women, Sports Traveler,* and *womenSports* (later changed to *Women's Sports and Fitness*) failed because they focused as much on femininity as they did on sports (Creedon, 1998).
2. The list of athletes that people in the "Invisible players" Brazilian ad campaign guessed were (in order): Neymar, Messi, C. Ronaldo, Pelé, Maradona, Ronaldo, Romario for the first clip; M. Jordan, Oscar, L. James, K. Bryant, S. Curry, J. Harden, and S. O'Neal for the second clip; and Medina, Mineiriho, K. Slater, M. Fanning, F. Toledo, A. Irons, and J. Smith for the third clip. Note that all are male athletes and no one guessed any female athletes.
3. One of these connections is with Toyota, who partners with espnW for the Women + Sports Summits and "Everyday Heroes," where the company sponsors $10,000 grants for sports organizations (Toyota Newsroom, 2017).

Appendix A

Transcript of "When I Play" short film

To Whom It May Concern:

What I am doing here is not for you

Not for your judgment or your appraisal

Not for your assessment or your arousal

No boy I know has ever been told he shouldn't play

Couldn't play

I am no longer interested in shouldn'ts

Or couldn'ts

Or rules not written for me

I am not worried about getting too big or too strong

Or too fast

Or too full of myself

I do not agree that "playing like a man" is a compliment

What I am doing here is not

For

You

Movement

Is a movement

My effort, my ambition, my desire

For me

For every woman, every girl

Who dares to see herself as something more

Than a body to be rated

A score to be kept

When I play, I keep my own score

When I play, I know who I am

When I play, I forget how it feels to be boxed in

To be boxed out

When I play, I feel no shame

When I play, I remember

How it feels

To be free

This court This field

This world

Too small to hold me

When I play I know I won't be undone I won't be unsung

My humility

My humanity

My movement a movement

This is not the end of my dream

This

Is where I

Wake Up

References

Ad Forum (n.d.). *ESPNW: Inequality courts.* Retrieved from https://www.adforum.com/creative-work/ad/player/34548765/inequality-courts/espnw

Bowman, K. (2018, March 2). Women in 2018: A look at the polls. *Forbes.* Retrieved from https://www.forbes.com/sites/bowmanmarsico/2018/03/02/women-in-2018-a-look-at-the-polls/#49278e7747e0

Brady, J. (2017a, April 4). New ESPN guidelines recognize connection between sports, politics. *ESPN.* Retrieved from http://www.espn.com/blog/ombudsman/post/_/id/816/new-espn-guidelines-recognize-connection-between-sports-politics

Brady, J. (2017b, September 16). ESPN awash in rising political tide. *ESPN.* Retrieved from http://www.espn.com/blog/ombudsman/post/_/id/871/espn-awash-in-rising-political-tide-2

Bryan, B. (2017, September 23). Trump attacks Stephen Curry, disinvites the Golden State Warriors from the White House in early morning tweet. *Business Insider.* Retrieved from http://www.businessinsider.com/trump-tweet-on-steph-curry-golden-state-warriors-cancels-white-house-visit-2017-9

Chozet, T. (2017, September 27). espnW and U.S. Department of State launch sixth year of global sports mentoring program. *ESPN.* Retrieved from https://espnmediazone.com/us/press-releases/2017/09/espnw-u-s-department-state-launch-sixth-year-global-sports-mentoring-program/

Coakley, J. (2015). *Sports in society: Issues & controversies* (11th ed.). New York, NY: McGraw-Hill Higher Education.

Creedon, P. J. (1998). Women, sport, and media institutions: Issue in sports journalism and marketing. In L. A. Wenner (Ed.), *MediaSport* (pp. 88–99). New York, NY: Routledge.

Davidson, K. A. (2017, February 15). If you thought sports were ever separate from politics, think again. *espnW.com.* Retrieved from http://www.espn.com/espnw/voices/article/18614895/if-thought-sports-were-ever-separate-politics-think-again

Deitsch, R. (2017, March 21). Sports illustrated media podcast with Richard Deitsch [Audio podcast]. *SI Media Podcast.* Retrieved from https://www.stitcher.com/podcast/cadence13/si-media-podcast-with-richard-deitsch/e/49501870?autoplay=true

Dittmar, K. (2017, November 20). Women candidates in election 2018. *Center for American Women and Politics.* Retrieved from http://cawp.rutgers.edu/sites/default/files/resources/a_closer_look_2018_outlook_final.pdf

Dow, B. J. (2006). Gender and communication in mediated contexts: Introduction. In B. J. Dow & J. T. Wood (Eds.), *The SAGE handbook of gender and communication* (pp. 263–272). Thousand Oaks, CA: Sage Publications.

ESPN Customer Marketing & Sales. (n.d.). espnW digital planning guide. *ESPN CMS.* Retrieved from http://espncms.com/pdf/digital-planning-guide.html

ESPN Media Zone. (n.d.). espnW Media Kit. *ESPN.* Retrieved from http://espnmediazone.com/us/media-kits/espnw/

espnW (n.d.). *espnW women + sports summit*. Retrieved from https://espnwsummit.com/event/

EY (2017, May 3). Female athletes make winning entrepreneurs, according to new EY/espnW report. *Ernst & Young*. Retrieved from http://www.ey.com/gl/en/newsroom/news-releases/news-ey-female-athletes-make-winning-entrepreneurs-ey-espn2-report

Foss, S. K. (2004). *Rhetorical criticism: Exploration & practice* (3rd Ed.). Long Grove, IL: Waveland Press.

Gentile, L. (2017, March 7). espnW and ESPN celebrate "women making history" month. *ESPN*. Retrieved from https://www.espnfrontrow.com/2017/03/espnw-espn-celebrate-women-making-history-month/

Gilbert, S. (2017, October 16). The movement of #metoo. *The Atlantic*. Retrieved from https://www.theatlantic.com/entertainment/archive/2017/10/the-movement-of-metoo/542979/

Glock, A. (n.d.). "When I play." *ESPN*. Retrieved from http://www.espn.com/espn/feature/story/_/page/espnW-womenmakinghistory170301/new-brand-film-play-kicks-women-history-month

Graham, P. (2006). Issues in political economy. In A. Albarran, S. Chan-Olmsted, & M. Wirth (Eds.), *Handbook of media management and economics* (pp. 493–522). Mahwah, NJ: Lawrence Erlbaum Associates.

Jason, D. (2017, May 18). Ignition 2017: Learn how the future of sports media is being turned on its head. *Business Insider*. Retrieved from http://www.businessinsider.com/ignition-2017-learn-how-sports-media-is-changing-2017-5

Lapchick, R. (2015, June 10). *The 2014 Associated Press sports editors racial and gender report card*. Retrieved from http://nebula.wsimg.com/038bb0ccc9436494ebee-1430174c13a0?AccessKeyId=DAC3A56D8FB782449D2A&disposition=0&allow-origin=1

Laucella, P. C., Hardin, M., Bien-Aimé, S., & Antunovic, D. (2017). Diversifying the sports department and covering women's sports: A survey of sports editors. *Journalism & Mass Communication Quarterly*, 94(3), 772–792. doi:10.1177/1077699016654443

McChesney, R. (2013). *Digital disconnect: How capitalism is turning the internet against democracy*. New York: The New Press.

McChesney, R. (2015). *Rich media, poor democracy: Communication politics in dubious times*. New York: The New Press.

McGloster, N. (2016, January 5). I want your job: Laura Gentile, founder of espnW. *Elite Daily*. Retrieved from https://www.elitedaily.com/women/want-job-laura-gentile-founder-espnw/1333962

Mosco, V. (1988). Introduction: Information in the pay-per society. In V. Mosco & J. Wasko (Eds.), *The political economy of information* (pp. 3–26). Madison, WI: The University of Wisconsin Press.

Nesheim, J. J. (2015, November 16). ESPN promotes Laura Gentile to Senior Vice President, espnW and women's initiatives. *ESPN*. Retrieved from http://espnmediazone.com/

us/press-releases/2015/11/espn-promotes-laura-gentile-senior-vice-president-espnw-womens-initiatives/

Nwulu, M. (2017, May 4). ESPN signs Julie Foudy to new multiyear extension as leading voice for espnW. *ESPN*. Retrieved from https://espnmediazone.com/us/press-releases/2017/05/espn-signs-julie-foudy-new-multiyear-extension-leading-voice-espnw/

Office of the Spokesperson. (2017, September 21). U.S. Department of State and espnW join forces for the annual global sports mentoring program. *U.S. Department of State*. Retrieved from https://www.state.gov/r/pa/prs/ps/2017/09/274346.htm

Ottaway, A. (2016, July 20). Why don't people watch women's sports? *The Nation*. Retrieved from https://www.thenation.com/article/why-dont-people-watch-womens-sports/

Pringle, R. (2018). On the development of sport and masculinities research: Feminism as a discourse of inspiration and theoretical legitimation. In L. Mansfield, J. Caudwell, B. Wheaton, & B. Watson (Eds.), *The Palgrave Handbook of feminism and sport, leisure and physical education* (pp. 73–94). London: Palgrave Macmillan.

Ritzer, G., & Stepinsky, J. (2018). *Modern sociological theory (8th Edition)*. Los Angeles, CA: SAGE Publications.

Sandritter, M. (2017, September 25). A timeline of Colin Kaepernick's national anthem protest and the athletes who joined him. *SB Nation*. Retrieved from https://www.sbnation.com/2016/9/11/12869726/colin-kaepernick-national-anthem-protest-seahawks-brandon-marshall-nfl

Schnall, M. (2017, December 15). 2018 will be the year of women. *CNN*. Retrieved from https://www.cnn.com/2017/12/14/opinions/2018-will-be-the-year-of-women-schnall/index.html

Shoichet, C. E., Cummings, J., & Yan, H. (2014, December 8). LeBron James and other NBA players don "I can't breathe" shirts. *CNN*. Retrieved from http://www.cnn.com/2014/12/08/justice/protests-grand-jury-chokehold/index.html

Todd, C., Murray, M., & Dann, C. (2018, January 29). A huge 2018 story: More than 500 women are running for major office. *NBC News*. Retrieved from https://www.nbcnews.com/politics/first-read/huge-2018-story-more-500-women-are-running-major-office-n841916

Tomb, D. (2015, October 12). The founder of espnW explains how to start a business within a big company. *Makers*. Retrieved from https://www.makers.com/blog/founder-espnw-business-within-big-company

Toyota Newsroom. (2017, October 4). *espnW and Toyota recognize 5th class of "Everyday Heroes" at 2017 The espnW: Women + Sports Summit*. Retrieved from http://corporatenews.pressroom.toyota.com/releases/espnw+toyota+recongize+5+class+everyday+heroes+2017+espnw+women+sports+summit.htm

Tucker Center for Girls & Women in Sport. (2013). *Media coverage and female athletes* [Video File]. Retrieved from http://www.mnvideovault.org/index.php?id=25506&select_index=0&popup=yes#0

Walker, N. A., & Melton, E. N. (2015). Creating opportunities for social change in women's sport through academic and industry collaborations: An interview with Kate Fagan. *Journal of Intercollegiate Sport*, *8*, 82–95. doi:10.1123/jis.2015-0019

Wasko, J. (2014). The study of the political economy of the media in the twenty-first century. *International Journal of Media & Cultural Politics*, *10*(3), 259–271. doi:10.1386/macp.10.3.259_1

Wolter, S. (2014). "It just makes good business sense": A media political economy analysis of espnW. *Journal of Sports Media*, *9*(2), 73–96. doi:10.1353/jsm.2014.0011

Wolter, S. (2015a). A quantitative analysis of photographs and articles on espnW: Positive progress for female athletes. *Communication & Sport*, *3*(2), 168–195. doi:10.1177/2167479513509368

Wolter, S. (2015b). A critical discourse analysis of espnW: Divergent dialogues and postfeminist conceptions of female fans and female athletes. *International Journal of Sport Communication*, *8*(3), 345–370. doi:10.1123/ijsc.2015-0040

Women's March. (n.d.). *Our mission*. Retrieved from https://www.womensmarch.com/mission/

Yarvin, J. (2017, August 11). Will 2018 be the next "Year of the woman?" *PBS News Hour*. Retrieved from https://www.pbs.org/newshour/politics/will-2018-next-year-woman

Zirin, D. (2013). *Game over: How politics has turned the sports world upside down*. New York, NY: The New Press.

18. Storytelling at the Worldwide Leader in Sports: An Interview With John Walsh, Executive Vice President of ESPN, Retired

Michael L. Butterworth

John Walsh began his career in sports journalism while studying at Scranton University in the 1960s. Over the next half century, he became one of the most influential figures in U.S. sports media. His career took him to *Newsday*, *Rolling Stone*, the *Washington Post*, *Newsweek*, and *Inside Sports*. But Walsh is best known for his tenure with ESPN, where he helped transform the network into the worldwide force it has become. Initially hired to be a consultant to *SportsCenter*, Walsh eventually became Executive Vice President of ESPN. Over the years, he shaped *SportsCenter*, and played a major role in launching ESPN2, *ESPN The Magazine*, and the ESPY Awards.[1] He also provided leadership for the long-form journalism featured on shows such as *Outside the Lines* and the *30 for 30* documentary series. Walsh retired in 2015 after 27 years with ESPN.

Michael L. Butterworth is a Professor of Communication Studies and Director of the Center for Sports Communication & Media, in the Moody College of Communication at The University of Texas at Austin. As a scholar of rhetoric, he focuses on the relationships between politics and sports, with particular interests in national mythology, militarism, and public memory.

On January 29, 2018, I spoke with John Walsh, former Executive Vice President of ESPN. He and I spoke about his time at ESPN, the evolution of sports media in the United States and around the world, and his thoughts on the future of sports media. Portions of the interview have been edited to improve readability.

Michael Butterworth: You retired from ESPN in 2015 after 27 years. So, how closely do you pay attention to what the network is doing and other products it's producing now?

John Walsh: As time passes, less and less. I stay in touch with some of my compatriots and colleagues with whom I was very close—[former Executive Vice President] Steve Anderson, [former Senior Vice President] Vince Doria, chief among them. [ESPN personalities] Bob Ley, Jeremy Schaap, Suzy Kolber, Holly Rowe, the PTI crew, and Chris Berman, of course. I have an interest in it, because I spent so much time there and I spilled so much blood. I try to keep up with the business aspects. I am interested in the state of transition in all media. So, as much as ESPN is refining and reflecting about what the vision of the future is—relatively to cord-cutting, streaming, digital media, Facebook, Instagram, Twitter, and social media—I'm looking at what steps they're taking. I'm always interested in personnel moves—one of my very close friends over the last ten years is [Executive Vice President] Connor Schell, so, I talk to him, oh, once every two months. It's sporadic, but when stories break, obviously, I watch it. For instance, their coverage of Michigan State and the Nassar scandal and gymnastics, I followed the ongoing story and took the time to read online Paula Lavigne's excellent reporting.[2] I get the magazine, and I'll read the big takeouts in the magazine. The fate of *fivethirtyeight*—I helped to recruit and bring Nate Silver to ESPN, so I'm obviously interested in what's happening there. And, I wasn't there for the fits and starts of The Undefeated, but I'm very much an admirer of what [Editor-in-chief] Kevin Merida is doing there, so I keep track of that. [Senior Vice President] Stephanie Druley and [Senior Vice President] Rob King, among many other people, I go back a long way with.

Butterworth: Speaking of the enterprise sites, The Undefeated and fivethirtyeight—obviously, there was a lot of attention on Grantland and it going away after Bill Simmons' departure, do you see the other sites having a kind of longevity that ultimately Grantland did not have?

Walsh: Those two are deeply entrenched now—as was Grantland. Until you see something kind of sparking with stories that people are really following—and I don't mean gossipy stories, I'm talking about what the *Indianapolis Star* started with the Nassar story.[3] It takes a lot of effort to establish new concepts. It's difficult in this day and age with the large variety and the initiatives of individuals and businesses, and what emphases businesses are putting on websites, and streaming, and the acquisition of and licensing for live events. I don't see anybody breaking through recently. Many people are there because they know they have to be there, and everybody on the Internet is taking it slowly because the revenues don't support many sustainable businesses at this juncture. Everybody knows that they will so, for ESPN, television's still the king. I watch *SportsCenter* five to ten times a week and, if somebody asks a question—"Hey, what did you think of the [former ESPN host] Jemele Hill move," or "What did you think of what we're doing with [*SportsCenter* anchor] Scott Van Pelt," I'm no longer qualified to opine.

Butterworth: Let me follow up with you on that because, not too long ago, Bryan Curtis wrote about the imminent death of the "funny highlight guy,"[4] and he was obviously referencing back to the heyday of *SportsCenter* and the "Big Show" with Dan Patrick and Keith Olbermann, and the many others who sort of followed in those footsteps. You were there for those moments and cultivated much of that talent. So, in this changing landscape, how does ESPN remain relevant when it comes to highlights and shows like *SportsCenter*?

Walsh: His observation has a seed of truth but the rationale for it, or the in-depth look at it, no one has really talked about. What highlights are about are storytelling, and when CNN had *Sports Tonight* at 11:30 with Hick [Fred Hickman] and Nick [Charles], they told stories. And, ESPN—whether it was Chris Berman, John Saunders, Bob Ley, Dan and Keith, of course, Stuart Scott, Craig Kilborn, Rich Eisen, Robin Roberts—if you go back and look at those, there were lead-ins to all of those highlights, and there was great care taken. Highlights are stories. Keith could write—Keith is an unbelievable talent for writing quickly and Dan used to labor over getting his well thought-out and well written lead-ins to the highlights—but there were 30 or 40-second stories that led to the highlights that made the highlights a story. Then the humorous part came with appropriate asides, descriptions of out-of-this-world achievements or goofs, and it was a whole different climate and a whole different feel.

Right now, the emphasis is on the volume of highlights. I go back to focus groups—people don't know how to look at and read focus groups. They look at focus groups to *tell* them something, rather than to spend the time to *interpret* what focus groups mean. So, when the focus group *tells* you, "Oh, video, yeah video, I like the video," or, "No, I don't like the on-camera," that's nonsense. So what's really happened is the loss of storytelling. So, when they go from one highlight to the next highlight. … It's impossible to tell a story when you don't take the time, the care, and the research, and the thinking part of it. And, the thinking part of it is really, really significant. Once you've seen the highlight, once you've compiled the necessary research behind what this game's meaningfulness or lack of meaningfulness is, and zeroing in on a focus, it will help you tell a story better. That's what happened. It's not what Bryan is saying, that it's just disappearing because there aren't funny people. There are.

Butterworth: I want to ask you about the storytelling emphasis, because that is a commitment that journalists take very seriously, and you spent two decades in print journalism before you were with ESPN. A lot of the talent that came over to ESPN had that print journalism background before coming there. How important has that been in shaping what ESPN became—to have that many people who came from the print side first?

Walsh: Peter Gammons, who was our first hire, was an information guy, and Peter rarely did highlights. Peter could give you a yarn about how and why a trade happened, or how a free agent signing took place. Adam [Schefter] and Mort [Chris Mortensen], they're similar, they're information people. They made their information into good stories. The print people have been more about information. There are certain people, like Lesley Visser, who are storytellers. So, when she was on, she would be telling stories on the sidelines or back and forth with anchor. The idea of storytelling pervades everything. I mean, Chris Berman is a history major from Brown. [*Outside the Lines* host] Bob Ley is a quintessential "boots on the ground" storytelling-crazed maniac with how much information he can get, how much he can develop an angle on a history. And those guys were never in print— Keith and Dan, they are great storytellers. There is an aspect of storytelling relative to Tom Rinaldi, Jeremy

Schaap and Paula Lavigne, to Chris Connelly, Holly Rowe, Doris Burke, and Lesley Visser that's a different kind of story. It's more of a magazine approach in 60 seconds, and sometimes a long watch. A long read is 30 minutes, a long watch is three minutes. It is essentially what I've always thought: recognizing what your goal is, and your goal is that you have a boatload of material that you're looking at, and then your goal is to put it into a form. And that form can be a book, it can be a magazine piece, it can be a highlight, it can be a special on TV. You take that material and you figure out which parts of the boatload of material or content that I have am I going to utilize, and in what form am I going to utilize them? What are the elements that I need—do I need still pictures for a magazine, where does the video come in for television, and how do I marry all of these elements into what will eventually be the best storytelling vehicle that we will settle on?

Butterworth: In that respect, things haven't changed all that much. Those are things that are constants, right?

Walsh: Go back to the town crier! The town crier could tell a story. It's the intelligence you bring to it, and the intelligence and industry and curiosity and all of the things that go into what makes a really good story and storyteller.

Butterworth: That makes a lot of sense, but we talk so much now about how things are so much different, not just because of technology but that there is a different climate or tone that we're operating in. Do you think that's fair?

Walsh: Yes, there is, and I'm proud to say that ESPN is a player but not really a mover and a shaker in that tone. The tone is opinion, the tone is high volume, the tone is frequently superficial, grandiose, opinion-making to incite the audience. You can tell, what I'm saying here, is that this President [Donald Trump] has made this tone sharper and worse for the people who really know and want to tell really good stories. It's all opinion. Everybody's got their opinion. The leading newspaper storytellers at *The Washington Post* and *The New York Times* are weaving their way through stories and making opinion a part of the story. They're developing a genre.

Butterworth: So, can I play devil's advocate for a moment? Can a network that made stars out of [pundits] Skip Bayless and Stephen A. Smith, and folks like that, claim that it's not participating in that tone?

Walsh: The best opinions are thoughtful, sometimes laced with anecdotes and stories and surprises. Tony [Kornheiser] and Mike [Wilbon] do it every day. Nobody worked harder than Skip Bayless researching what his opinions were. There was a lot of reporting and research in Skip Bayless's opinion. Stephen A. would feed off of them, very well. And they were a great pair together, but I would say, Skip is an example of somebody that came from print and took the best of print, in terms of research and knowing what you're talking about, developing a focus for TV, and presenting it in this high-volume tone that's there. But if you get to the heart of what he was doing, he was somebody that made a viewer smarter about sports, in his own way, and Stephen did the same and was the perfect foil for him. In television, those are the kinds of things that work. I do want to point out that *The Sports Reporters* reinvented the format of the show out of Chicago with Bill Gleason and Rick Telander—they had raised voices, but when Bob Ryan got excited on *The Sports Reporters* or even [Mike] Lupica got excited, you would hear voices rise. The most successful sports talk show in the history of television is *Pardon the Interruption*. And that's because it's intelligent. It's thoughtful. It's got a sense of humor. There's a sense of camaraderie that's going on, and you can feel it. Each of them has their own independent take on whatever it is, and they know how to challenge one another in a respectful and yet argumentative way. That's really what everybody should be shooting for. Often the topics are introduced with a story. You just don't get Wilbon and Kornheiser twice in a lifetime, they're just that good.

Butterworth: That raises an interesting question. The talent plays a large role in this—

Walsh: Oh, personality is everything, no question.

Butterworth: So, given your history with *SportsCenter* and other signature programming with ESPN, how would you say talent acquisition and retention has changed since the time you began there in 1987?

Walsh: Well, it's fascinating to me—one of the biggest changes is that women now have a seat at the desk. I'm proud to say that ESPN was in the forefront of hiring women. Whether it was Linda Cohn, Robin Roberts, Andrea Kremer—

Butterworth: Gayle Gardner.

Walsh:	She wasn't there when I was there, but Gayle Gardner was fantastic. She was the first one to do it every day. And my friend [*NFL Today* host] Phyllis George, she was before anybody, but she was 16 or 20 weeks a year, once a week. She was a pioneer in that respect. But the people who are in the trenches on a daily basis, 52 weeks a year, there's where women have asserted themselves. Look at what Robin Roberts has achieved! I'm so proud of Robin and all these women who have gone out and made young women in college, looking up to them and saying, "You know what? I'm a big sports fan. I could do that." That's probably the biggest trend at ESPN, the hiring of many women on air.
Butterworth:	To follow up on that, ESPN has been the subject, not just recently but historically, of accusations of a toxic inside culture that isn't friendly to women, especially the people at the production assistant level and those who aren't the major on-screen talent. To what extent is that a reality that ESPN has to contend with?
Walsh:	We worked really hard at getting women at places in management. There have been women who have achieved at ESPN. There are now 8,000 employees there. You try to hire the best people, you get the best managers you can, but if you're going to have thousands of employees, there will be people who will be disappointed. You're going to make mistakes. The idea is to deal with them quickly and responsibly to correct the situation, and I think that's what happens at ESPN. We did have many issues, some repeated, with respect for women in the workplace. We tried really hard to address them, not successfully all of the time. There are always mistakes and the best solution is to learn from them.
Butterworth:	To pull the lens up a little, ESPN has been the subject of criticism for other reasons over the years. Are there any of those critiques that you think are fair?
Walsh:	Yes, absolutely. Do we fail on judgments on stories, occasionally? Yes. Do I regret what happened with the promotion of the concussion series that we did with *Frontline*? Yes.
Butterworth:	What part of that do you regret?
Walsh:	I'm very critical of, internally, some of the talk about what it was—the *content* was never affected. The Fainaru [Steve and Mark] brothers reported—nobody touched any part of the content. It was strictly promotion. It was, "Hey, you promoted the most sensational pieces of

things." Anybody who worked for a team in the NFL would be really upset because, you know, as lax as they were for years they're now trying to be responsible about how they do this. So, taking a soundbite and putting it there to represent the hours of really good television and the wonderful book that they wrote—that's a really good book[5]—that's the good part, but we made the promotion sensational to attract larger audiences. I was among the dissenters with the catch-phrase, "The Worldwide Leader in Sports," because I thought there was a certain amount of arrogance to it. But drawing the line, this is very difficult—that subtle line between pride and arrogance, and the absence of humility, that really bothered me.

Butterworth: Was there ever a legitimate possibility that "The Worldwide Leader in Sports" would no longer be the tagline?

Walsh: Oh, there were dissenters in the company and management. Once the decision was made, "Hey, the decision's made, that's what we're going with, get behind it." And that's what people do. It wasn't terrible, it was just a matter of taste. When anyone's naming a show—*Pardon the Interruption*, where did that come from? But people name things, and I keep telling them, "It doesn't matter what the *name* is, it matters what the *show* is." It matters who the people are around the show. When I got there, they were going to change *SportsCenter*'s name and I said, "What, are you crazy? You have eight years under your belt, and you're going to change it?" So, it stuck!

Butterworth: Is that a product of being in a competitive marketplace—"We've got to re-brand, we've got to stay fresh, relevant"—

Walsh: In those days, there was no such thing as talking about "brands," you know, that's the last 15 years, 20 years. So, it was just a product of, "Hey, is this working well enough for us?" And, the problem wasn't the name, the problem was that it needed a boost. When I started there, one of the elements that I was contending with was that the best people were off *SportsCenter* because they had just acquired college football and then the NFL. So, they had to take some of their best people for programming in football. One of ESPN's biggest contributions to the world of sports is that they took what the *NFL Today* was and made a whole network out of it, a whole network of studio shows. And *SportsCenter* was the mothership. The vision for having studio and making studio important was fantastic from [former President] Steve Bornstein. Insightful and visionary. Then, trying to figure out what it was, how many elements were going to go into it, how important was personality, content, how should people talk back and forth when they're hosting shows all pieces of the studio puzzle. There are old stories—[basketball analyst] Dick Vitale is great at telling them—he was there in the beginning, and they would go to Dick and say, "Dick, we need you out there. We need you on the set." He said, "If I go on the set, I'd be there for an hour."

Butterworth: So, even he knows [that he talks a lot]?

Walsh: Oh, yeah, he knows. It was Dick and former baseball manager, Dick Williams, they were the stalwarts. Because baseball and basketball were the volume sports—there were 82 basketball games and 162 baseball games, so you needed someone to talk about what was going on. And those two, you know, it was, "Dick, get the hell out there! You're on!"

Butterworth: Is that, in part, just sort of the good fortune of timing—a personality like Dick Vitale ends up in the position when ESPN is in its very early days, and it just happened to fall together?

Walsh: It was great. I mean, Dick Vitale and Lee Corso, two ex-coaches who did not have what we would call sterling records as head coaches, found their home at ESPN. They, to this day, in their late-70s, mid-80s, they're still there and they're still signature voices for the sports they're associated with.

Butterworth: Thinking big picture, why do you think it's been so difficult for other networks to mount a substantial challenge to ESPN?

Walsh: This is really the simplest answer, and it's really one sentence. ESPN had a 32-year head start.

Butterworth: So, there's just no way to make up for that?

Walsh: It will take a long time, and it will take a lot of money.

Butterworth: Fair enough.

Walsh: You know, first in—but when ESPN was first there, first in wasn't—it was like, "What a terrible idea! 24 hours of sports, my God! What are they thinking up in Bristol? Thank God they're in *Bristol*." And, the reason that there was no competition is that ESPN took a long time to be successful, and it all crept up on everybody. Disney noticed it—well, no; Cap Cities [Capital Cities] noticed this was a good franchise. Cap Cities knew how to run businesses. They got the business on track, they knew how to invest.

Butterworth: If it's the "first in" as you say, and it would take a lot of time and a lot of money to mount a significant challenge, is it also possible that some kind of internal disruption could be an issue? I use that as a way to get at the external narrative about ESPN in some quarters—"Oh my goodness, they're laying off so many people, we've got all this cord-cutting going on, they're imploding." Respond to that allegation.

Walsh: First of all, ESPN is still the major contributor to Disney's bottom line. So, the idea of using the word "implode"—at some point, that stuff is going to even off. I suppose as the generations change and the Baby Boomers fade into oblivion, the young people are finding their own way with the Internet and streaming. But ESPN is very resourceful, so they have these skinny bundles they're doing to keep things alive. They still have 88 million subscribers who are paying a monthly fee of seven dollars and something—

Butterworth: By far, still the highest carriage fee, right?

Walsh: By far.[6] So the rumors of demise are greatly exaggerated. Are they going to find a different business model? Don't you think they're doing models to go direct to consumer at some point? They're all figuring out what the business should be. The real challenge is if Facebook, and Google, and Amazon, and those types of businesses that are very successful—when are they going to jump in, and at what level are they going to jump in? How are they going to make the economics of covering sports viable? It's not an easy problem to solve. Part of the changes that are being contemplated require different skills than the people who have been there for years had. They require not so many people sometimes. So, the people who are working on ESPN Classic—God bless those who have tried to make Classic into a viable network. But it's just not there, so it's a natural attrition for people to leave. It's very sad, because there are people who have families, are in their mid-to-late fifties, some of their kids are going to college, and it's very hard to make those decisions. It's very sad. Unfortunately, there are hundreds of people who have been let go. But they still have 8,000 employees, and they're still hiring. They're hiring people with different skill sets. The one quality, if you're hiring at ESPN, you

	have to be really knowledgeable about sports. You better know what you're doing.
Butterworth:	This story about layoffs and cord-cutting has gotten a lot of traction in the last year or two. One of the other stories that has gotten some similar traction is the suggestion that ESPN has become too political. I would argue, and my scholarship is rooted in the idea that politics and sports have always been connected in various ways—
Walsh:	Tucker Carlson and Sean Hannity going on Fox [News] and talking about stories that they know nothing about. My memory isn't such that I can quote it, but that Jemele Hill story, well, "I can tell you what happened." Well, you know what? You can't tell me what happened because you don't *know* what happened.[7] ESPN covers sports and politics when they intersect. And 99% of the time it's coverage and thoughtful analysis. When on-air people give their own political viewpoint that's dead wrong. ESPN does 50,000 live hours of sports TV and on an annual basis maybe there's five minutes of politics that doesn't belong.
Butterworth:	Jemele Hill is kind of in mind when I have this question for you, which is, how does the network move forward with guiding ESPN's talent with discussions about politics?
Walsh:	[Former Executive Vice President] Mark Shapiro, when he took over [in 2001], he came to me and he said, "John, I want you to establish and run an editorial board." And we established an editorial board to deal with issues—we put out a 22 or a 25-page standards and practices memo that we had everybody read. We continued up until my last days there, we continued to meet once a month. We tossed around issues—those meetings were usually two hours, and they were painstaking with debates back and forth among the senior personnel who were helping to develop exactly what you're talking about. So, 17 or 18 years later, there's nothing new. The policies have been in place. The policy is in place that, if it deals with sports and politics becomes a part of it, go for it. If Barack Obama or Donald Trump are good golfers, go get a golf game with them, and write about it or do a TV piece about it. That has always been a part of what we do. If the NCAA is not diligent in looking after Michigan State, you have to get involved—that's a story. There's politics that might be involved, might not be involved.

And—we were dealing with social media in 2012, 2013, we were developing policies, and those policies were reviewed sometimes on a six-month basis, sometimes on an annual basis, to accommodate what the activity was on Twitter and what was going on, on Facebook. The policy was, "You're the face—when you go on Twitter, you're still working for ESPN. If you want to, go ahead and do it, but we have a policy and there are going to be consequences." But if [Dallas Cowboys owner] Jerry Jones and players are kneeling, and have fists in the air, and all of that, if it's part of the event and you're doing an event, then cover it. You have to cover it.

Butterworth: Aside from the high-profile folks like Bill Simmons and Jemele Hill, and some of the suspensions that resulted from comments they made on Twitter, has there been a less visible pushback against that policy?

Walsh: No, not at all. Actually, when Jemele wasn't suspended the first time, she told John Skipper, and she put it in print somewhere, "Hey, I should have been suspended. I violated the policy, I'm guilty."[8] Then, when she got suspended when she shouldn't have been suspended—on a different Jerry Jones opinion, which had to do with sports and business—she actually said, "It was a make-up call." But, no, there's not a big pushback. And, the people—the guy who runs *SportsCenter* is a lifetime Republican and Bob Ley is an incredible Republican. But, you know what, it doesn't show up in reporting. It doesn't show up in the way they run *SportsCenter*. There's going to be opinions, that's going to happen. But the guidelines are pretty clear. I feel very comfortable about what we did way back in 2012 and the editorial board back in 2001.

Butterworth: Let's move to thinking about the future a little bit. Esports is a particularly interesting area of development and possible growth. Do you have thoughts about esports?

Walsh: No, I don't follow it. I've read a couple stories in the magazine that Mina Kimes has written.[9] It's fascinating—but, would you pay to watch people play games?

Butterworth: I personally would not, no. But there's a lot of investment in it.

Walsh: Yeah, [Dallas Cowboys owner] Jerry Jones, [New England Patriots owner] Bob Kraft, there are people who think there's something there. It's a question of, where am I going to find the new revenue stream of sports, because we're really reaching some limitations on licensing rights. So, personally, I don't see [esports], but who am I? When we talk about the future, and people ask me questions—and I get asked a lot about the future—I want to say, "Why don't you dial it back? Who thought of Twitter? Who thought of Facebook? Who was thinking of these things that are becoming—you know, Google? How did these things develop and become the bedrock of people's experience?" There are people who are visionaries. I wish I were a visionary. And maybe people will go—I can't imagine paying money to go and sit and watch somebody play a video game!

Butterworth:　You mentioned licensing a moment ago—the contracts just keep getting bigger.

Walsh:　I remember as far back as 1985 or 1986, when I was working as a consultant at CBS, and people were saying, "Oh, my God, these licensing rights, they have to be less next time." They're *never* less! The smarter business people, and the more aggressive business people, they all get into sports because they make a dollar, win or lose. If they win a lot, they make a lot more dollars. They're all good businesses, and part of team sports is the exposure to fandom. I do have strong opinions here. I think that starting the networks, the NBA, MLB and NFL networks, they're so narrow, because they're only about one sport. Trying to get new customers—that's the joy of ESPN, that they have a lot of different sports. The variety is important because that's where you can recruit potential zealots for your individual sports. But the rights, the licensing, it's just going to go up.

Butterworth:　Is there a pathway for something like the NFL Network eventually to secure the rights to NFL broadcasts exclusively?

Walsh:　They don't have to secure them, they could just say, "Hey, we're going to do it." They're the owners! Now, whatever revenue the NFL takes in from the broadcasts, are they going to make that money with their own network? I doubt it. So, that's what they have to look at as a business.

Butterworth:　Something like the NFL is a good example, too, of the effort to further internationalize sports—

Walsh:　That's coming. These games in Mexico and London, I think in the NBA and the NFL, that's something I feel confident that we're going to see these international sports.

Butterworth: What do you think those sports media spaces look like? Where are we headed with that—are there particular sports or markets where you expect to see growth?

Walsh: The games are in London, they're in Mexico City. The NFL is piling up the games in London. The NBA has their preseason games in China. So, there's an international feel. MLB has the World Baseball Classic. Hockey, there's big interest internationally. From there, what can they do? They can start to put advertising logos on uniforms—it's all revenue-driven, because the owners want to make more money. That's what they do. And soccer is going to be much bigger here very soon.

Butterworth: I know you're hesitant to address the "future of sports media" question—

Walsh: Well, I just don't know. I mean, look at what's happened with *Sports Illustrated*. I grew up on *Sports Illustrated*, and now they're bi-weekly and for sale again! I don't think it's too distant from them entirely being on your phone.

Butterworth: Well, let's try a retrospective question, then. Upon retirement, you get to reflect on these things frequently. Over the course of your 27 years at ESPN, what do you think the network's most important contribution to sports media was?

Walsh: I just think its very existence—the *idea* that ESPN proved there is a very lucrative business model in a 24-hour, 7-days a week, 365-days a year sports network. And it works. That's a contribution. From my end of it, the culture of ESPN from my time there was one of the greatest cultures ever. I can tell you that I am very close personal friends with everybody who was my boss at ESPN. The nature of ESPN's collaboration and collegiality among employees who were involved in the creation of content was phenomenal. The idea of making whatever we did, whether it was the broadcast of a game or a studio show, we were aiming for the highest quality. I think some of the quintessential examples of that are the *30 for 30* brand, which just grew out of some phone calls and a couple of meetings, and Bill Simmons getting really tired of badgering [John] Skipper and me about HBO doing documentaries. The way that was created was tremendous. Remember, in the beginning the employees were auditioning for jobs they never imagined would exist. They worked tirelessly to make ESPN a real business, going to work and not knowing if you had a job the next day.

Butterworth: Do you have a favorite *30 for 30*, out of curiosity?

Walsh: I was a glorified consultant on it, and I did have opinions. When we finished the first 30 I did this exercise, which I learned in my media experience, of rating them. I had everybody rate them 1 to 30. It was really a great exercise. I used to do this with *The Magazine* and every six months I would take the last 13 copies, throw them down and say, "Put them in order, from what you would say the best is to the worst." Invariably, the top four or five would tell you what works, what are the right things that we're doing. And the bottom five would tell us what to avoid, what not to do again.

Butterworth: So, what were the top *30 for 30*s?

Walsh: I think to this day *The Two Escobars*, that's pretty much rated number one, and I'm guessing it's a very close race with *OJ: Made in America*. That one's a different type. It was very collaborative—it was [film producer] Connor Schell saying, "Hey, I have this idea of doing this on the anniversary of this thing." He ended up finding a documentary filmmaker who had been at HBO, who was involved with the Magic-Bird documentary, [director] Ezra Edelman.[10] It was that kind of combination that got this thing rolling. I'll tell you, what was a great thing about *30 for 30* as it was emerging in its early years, is that there were [a lot of really high quality—whether it was Marcus Dupree or Vlade Divac—they were all really, really good.[11] I would say, if you took the 30 of them, easily 15 of them were of the highest quality, and then there were 10 of them that were damned good. There were five of them, where you say, "You know what, it just didn't work out." The high quality of that first was exceptional, just exceptional. And how about *Catching Hell*?

Butterworth: I could talk to you about *30 for 30* all day, because they're great. But let me throw one last question to you. As you know, the book for which we're doing this interview is a collection of academic studies written by and for sports media scholars. We struggle as academics, sometimes, with being able to bridge the gap with people who are in sports media industries. The book is trying to bridge that gap in some ways, so this is an invitation for you to help us out. What kinds of things should sports media scholars be paying attention to, what kinds of questions do you think we should be asking?

Walsh: You know, at one time I was an academic. [Jokingly] In my youth, I bribed my way into an assistant professorship at the University of Missouri. To your question, I would say, "Where can you get boots on the ground?" There's so much respect for reporting, and I don't think there's enough analysis of talking to people who are reporters and writers. That's stuff that I really love—how people approach things, where ideas come from, how a vision is constructed. I'm especially interested in the early days of media. I'm interested in how things got to be where they are, and what the roots and the history of them are. That's my initial take on it—and, let's ask, "What are we missing?"

Notes

1. A summary of Walsh's career can be found at Kerschbaumer, K. (2017, November 10). Sports Broadcasting Hall of Fame: John A. Walsh—journalist, storyteller, innovator. *Sports Video Group*. Retrieved from https://www.sportsvideo.org/2017/11/10/sports-broadcasting-hall-of-fame-john-a-walsh-journalist-storyteller-innovator/.

2. See Lavigne, P., & N. Noren (2018, February 1). OTL: Michigan State secrets extend far beyond Larry Nassar case. *ESPN.com*. Retrieved from http://www.espn.com/espn/story/_/id/22214566/pattern-denial-inaction-information-suppression-michigan-state-goes-larry-nassar-case-espn.

3. For information on the Indianapolis Star's coverage, see Ryckaert, V. (2018, January 25). Larry Nassar case: What you need to know about the abuser of more than 150 young athletes and the fallout. *Indianapolis Star*. Retrieved from https://www.indystar.com/story/news/nation-now/2018/01/25/larry-nassar-usa-gymnastics-sex-abuse-what-we-know/1066355001/.

4. See Curtis, B. (2017, December 18). The imminent death—and amazing life—of the funny highlight guy. *The Ringer*. Retrieved from https://www.theringer.com/sports/2017/12/18/16790028/espn-sportscenter-anchor-highlights-catchphrases-dan-patrick-keith-olbermann.

5. See Fainaru-Wada, M., & S. Fainaru (2013). *League of denial: The NFL, concussions, and the battle for truth*. New York: Crown.

6. ESPN's carriage fee is $7.21. See Sherman, E. (2016, August 27). Future of TV sports: Pay up or be blacked out. *Chicago Tribune*. Retrieved from http://www.chicagotribune.com/sports/columnists/ct-sports-tv-future-spt-0828-20160826-column.html.

7. Fox News anchor Sean Hannity hosted a panel discussion in response to ESPN personality Jemele Hill's comments about President Donald Trump. See Perez, M. (2017, September 14). Fox News's Sean Hannity gathers panel of White

people to discuss racism. *Newsweek*. Retrieved from http://www.newsweek.com/fox-news-sean-hannity-white-people-discuss-racism-665210.

8. For details on Hill's comments, see Bonesteel, M. (2017, October 21). ESPN's Jemele Hill: "I deserved that suspension." *Washington Post*. Retrieved from https://www.washingtonpost.com/news/early-lead/wp/2017/10/21/espns-jemele-hill-i-deserved-that-suspension/?utm_term=.3be807b095c4.

9. For example, see Kimes, M. (2017, September 15). Game: interrupted. *ESPN The Magazine*. Retrieved from http://www.espn.com/espn/feature/story/_/id/20692051/how-teenage-gamer-became-reluctant-icon-south-korea-feminist-movement.

10. *Magic & Bird: A courtship of rivals*, was produced by HBO in 2010.

11. These films are *The Best that Never Was* and *Once Brothers*.

19. Modern Pathways of Sports Consumption: An Interview With Paul Melvin, Senior Director of Communications for ESPN

MELVIN LEWIS

In 2016, the Walt Disney Company, which owns an 80% majority share of ESPN, purchased a controlling stake in BAMTech, the company that powers streaming video for organizations like Major League Baseball (MLB), HBO, and the WWE (Popper, 2017). The acquisition was to support the launch of a new ESPN-branded streaming service (a technology used to deliver content to computers and mobile devices over the Internet) and a Disney-branded streaming service that launched in 2019 and go head-to-head with Netflix, Amazon, and Hulu. The ESPN+ package included a redesigned app that gives users the ability to stream channels and thousands more live events for a fee (Spain, 2017). This chapter will discuss the challenges ESPN faces in the sports marketplace and the company's vision for the future from the interviewee, Mr. Paul Melvin, facilitated by the interviewer, Dr. Melvin Lewis.

The interviewer, Dr. Melvin Lewis, is an Assistant Professor of Sports Business Management and Fellow of the Alabama Program in Sports Communication at The University of Alabama. Dr. Lewis's current research focuses on sports media, sport-consumer behavior and technology in sports.

Mr. Melvin is the Senior Director of Communications for ESPN's Digital Media, Technology, International and X Games groups. Mr. Melvin oversees day-to-day communications and PR for ESPN's Digital Media, Technology, X Games and International (Europe, Asia, and Pacific Rim) businesses. He is responsible for developing communication and PR strategies and leading a team in U.S. (CT/NY, LA), London and Sydney. Mr. Melvin manages reactive communication and reputation issues, media relations, agencies in multiple regions globally, collaborates with business leaders and other company divisions on cross-functional projects to support various ESPN business priorities. He has spent 16 years with ESPN in New York, London and Connecticut.

A merged transcript of the interview is rendered below.

Melvin Lewis: Paul Melvin:	In general, why are sports fans adopting streaming live content? Sports fans are adopting streaming for the same reason everybody is—it's convenient, available across all the devices that people use today, increasingly offers next generation user interfaces (UI) compliments the look and feel, the presentation and interactivity of a product and has become a mainstream activity. A recent Deloitte study found that—on average—a U.S. consumer spends 38 hours watching video content per week, and 15 of those hours are streaming (Westcott, Loucks, Downs, & Watson, 2018). That is 39%. Importantly, streaming is growing across all demographics, it's not just younger people. In fact, it is especially among Gen X (born 1966–1976). That same Deloitte study showed "In particular, the mobile consumption behaviors of Generation X now closely mirror those of Generation Z (born 1995–2012) and millennials (born 1977–1994)" (Westcott et al., 2018). The fact that content has continued to become more and more available via streaming (some of it exclusively, such as thousands of events that we have offered via ESPN3 for years) is also a major driver. Valuable, highly desired content has always helped drive consumption—across mediums. And sports is the most valuable content in the media ecosystem today—in large part because of the passions involved and the live nature of the content. People are highly emotionally connected to sports, and much of it they want to watch as it happens—making the digital device incredibly important (as it gives them anytime/anywhere access). Streaming is the video technology of the digital device. It is the ultimate real-time drama. Films, characters, drama and comedy also are highly desired—and you have seen them drive other streaming platforms. But sports are truly unique.
Lewis:	Much is being made about how cord-cutters (a person that no longer subscribes to a cable subscription) and cord-nevers (an individual that has never signed up for a cable subscription) would change the fundamentals of viewing sports and interest is heating up. What benefits does streaming provide to the sports fans?
Melvin:	A key factor here is convenience and portability. Streaming is the core delivery technology for digital devices. So video that

you used to only be able to get, first in your living room, then in your living room or on your home computer ... that video can be with you anywhere. Streaming is what allows that to be the case. And those devices—phones in particular —have become so central to our daily lives and so important to how we form our habits.

Something else that cannot be overlooked is user interface. The way the consumer actually interacts with the medium is a really key thing. A great experience in discovering, navigating and engaging with content is powerful. That is an area where streaming has allowed for innovation. New digital pay TV entrants like Sling TV, DirecTV Now and YouTube TV (which people sometimes forget, are also delivered via streaming technology, even though they are packaged in a way that is not fundamentally different than more traditional offerings) have been able to offer new user interface innovations. They make that interaction more of a magical experience. That has been one factor in growing adoption. At ESPN, we've made it a critical point to also be available through these services, most often right from launch. Other "living room" device platforms, like Apple TV, Roku, Fire TV and others, have also been innovating in the area of UI, UX (process of enhancing customer satisfaction and loyalty by improving the usability, ease of use, and pleasure provided in the interaction between the customer and the product) and content navigation and presentation. And I would be terribly remiss not to stress that ESPN has been innovating with user interface on streaming platforms since the launch of ESPN360 (in 2005/2006) and has been developing next-gen experiences for our content on all of the above platforms and even on traditional set top boxes, where we have created bespoke apps (a piece of software which is written specifically for businesses to perform a particular function or set of functions) for the platforms of our traditional TV distributors' boxes, allowing for a more app-like experience with our content.

Lewis: What is the significance of ESPN to millennials, cord-cutters or cord-nevers? Give us a snapshot of the typical ESPN streaming customer. Specifically, who is using your current platforms? Can you provide a breakdown of the user percentages by age and income?

Melvin: ESPN's streaming audience does skew younger than its traditional TV audience. While we do not share or break out users' information, we can share that—overall - ESPN streamers are about twice as likely to be 18–34 year olds than the traditional TV audience, and about half as likely to be 55+. Almost all streaming of ESPN and ESPN2's linear content (programming to start and end at a pre-scheduled time) is now being credited to their Nielsen TV ratings. Adults 18–34 have seen the greatest gains from having that streaming included in the TV rating. ESPN's streaming lift is almost twice as high for 18–34 as it is for total viewers.

Lewis: How is streaming live sports content from ESPN used to impact fan consumption, brand affinity and the overall user experience?

Melvin: For ESPN, this is actually quite simple. We are driven by a very clear mission statement. In fact, it is written in lights on the side of our largest and most technically sophisticated facility at our headquarters (and also in numerous other places around our many offices globally): serve sports fans anytime, anywhere. We take that very much to heart. We also know that sport fans have always been adopters and drivers of new technology. We have seen that first hand for more than 38 years. Every major technology leap has had sports fans at the forefront. So, in order to fulfill our mission, and because we know fans, it has always been imperative that we embrace new technologies constantly. It is often forgotten, but cable television was a brand new and profoundly different technology when we were among the very first to launch on it. We launched ESPN.com in 1994, in the earliest years of the consumer Internet. We were focused on mobile by 2002 and developing purpose-built apps for phones by 2005 (more than a year before the first iPhone). We were one of the main drivers of the adoption of HD (High Definition) television. Many years ago, we began investing in world-class Internet Protocol based infrastructure and private fiber networking (a fiber optic path that connects points within a building, around a campus, throughout a town, or all through a County or State that does not rely on the path offered by the Telephone or Cable companies) that allows us to create, edit, share and move content at the speed of light. These are all things that we have done because they advance our mission and understand fans—and that is ultimately good for our business. Streaming is the same. We began streaming content as early as 2001, with a product called "ESPN Broadband." Our first live-streamed event was in 2003. We launched ESPN360 in 2005, and it became ESPN3 in 2009.

ESPN has been a key leader and driver of streaming. In 2017, ESPN streamed thousands of events and logged more than 430 million hours of viewing, which established a new record for us. At ESPN, we've always had a core belief in the powerful connection that sports make with the remarkable array of fans. We've never underestimated fans' passions and believe it is our job to serve them more thoroughly than anyone else. Today, you cannot do that unless you are leading in streaming.

Lewis: What demographics have the potential to be affected most from the use of ESPN streaming platforms?

Melvin: For ESPN, streaming is currently having the greatest impact on younger adults. However, we know that streaming is now a mainstream activity. It is no longer limited to just younger people. Streaming is now mainstream, and we expect it to be an important behavior for all fans—in some form or fashion—going forward.

Lewis: What is the fan feedback from the Snapchat *SportsCenter* new launch?

Melvin: The reaction has been very positive, and it has really been a success. *SportsCenter* on Snapchat has already grown to 16.5 million unique viewers, with more than two million per day. It has a very young and very loyal audience as well, with over 50% of ESPN's daily audience watched 3x a week, and 75% of the viewers being under age 25.

Lewis: We talked about fans adopting streaming live content earlier, what are the streaming adoption challenges versus fans staying with cable?

Melvin: One of the attributes where cable still wins out compared to streaming is reliability. Qualitatively, buffering/lagging is a known hurdle when it comes to streaming, and the question is what are viewers' tolerance levels when it comes to this for sports. We have generally found that it is far more unacceptable for sports vs. merely annoying for other programming. That is also why we have invested so much in technology and development and work constantly on improving speed and reliability in our streaming products. But it also relies upon the platforms themselves. In fact, the Walt Disney Company recently took a controlling stake in a leading streaming technology company called BAMTech. ESPN is working hand in hand with BAM-Tech as we prepare to launch a brand new and re-imagined version of the ESPN App, as well as our first multi-sport direct-to-consumer streaming service (ESPN+). A big part of the reason why Disney made the investment in BAM Tech was to further build the entire company's technical infrastructure and capabilities in order to deliver world class streaming experiences as they continue to grow to greater and greater scale.

It is also true that, for some consumers in the U.S. and for many in other parts of the world, streaming is a mobile- driven activity and that creates concerns about using up your data package on mobile.

Lewis: Who are the major competitors in your space?

Melvin: We have many competitors—other sports companies, other media corporations, technology companies, telecommunications companies. But this is also not new. We have always had an enormous amount of competition. And, in fact, we have also always been in a rather unique position that many of our competitors are also often big partners. So we both compete and collaborate. That's always been part of the challenge. However, rather than getting overly focused on who are our competitors, we generally tend to think of it in a simpler way; it's simply competition for people's time. If you are staying up late to watch a basketball game that is being played on the west coast, instead of going to bed, then in a way, we even are competing with sleep (at the edges). That's half joking, but only half. In a more real sense, anything that competes for a chunk of a consumer's media consumption behavior is in some form a competitor. However, you cannot allow yourself to spend too much time focused on that, or it takes you away from being mission-focused and audience focused. In our case, Fan focused.

Lewis: Explain how ESPN differentiates from the other streaming companies in sports.

Melvin: The first and main thing is what I mentioned before—sports are unique. A lot of it is live and it is driven by great personal, emotional attachment and investment from consumers. Within that context—understanding that—we have made it a point to invest in the broadest, deepest array of sports rights. We have the rights to bring more sports events live to people than anybody else, and that is an incredible position.

On top of that, we—again—make a clear point to be everywhere fans are, on every platform and medium. ESPN has an incredible, industry-leading position in: traditional pay television; digital pay television (Sling TV, DirecTV Now, PlayStation Vue, YouTube TV, etc.); "authenticated" or TV Everywhere streaming (giving cross-device portability to a pay television subscription); mobile and online news, information, scores, etc.; radio and podcasting; social media; and we are building that leadership position in direct-to-consumer sports streaming now as well. None of that is by accident. We believe that you must be where fans are. Sometimes that even means being there before the specific business model is clear. If you reach fans, engage them and connect with them ... the business will take shape.

Lewis:	What does the future look like three-five years from now for ESPN to stay successful and relevant if streaming content continues to motivate fans as a preferred medium?
Melvin:	Not to be too cute about it, but really, truly—the mission is at the heart of it. Serve sports fans anytime, anywhere—wherever fans are, that's where we'll be—TV, streaming, digital, social, mobile, augmented reality (adds digital elements to a live view often by using the camera on a smartphone), virtual reality (implies a complete immersion experience that shuts out the physical world) ... you name it. When fans decide that they are going to gather on a medium ... we will be there.

Paul Melvin disclosed that streaming is growing across all demographics and sports are the most valuable content in the media ecosystem that drives consumption. Multiple platforms and mediums to absorb live streaming content that exist for sports fans, which provide unique fan experiences, are shifting the way individuals view content. ESPN has made a critical point to be available on digital pay TV services and device platforms from the launch for the user innovative experience.

ESPN believes streaming will have the greatest impact on younger adult fans and that streaming is a mainstream activity. The *SportsCenter* on Snapchat launch has been described as a success with 75% of the viewers being under the age of 25. Melvin added that cable continues to rein champion over streaming due to the reliability of not buffering/lagging and consumers being cognizant of using large amounts of data on mobile devices. Hence, ESPN has invested in technology to improve the speed and reliability in their streaming products. ESPN believes they must be where fans are and their new direct-to-consumer sports streaming efforts show the commitment to differentiation to serve the sports fans. Therefore, the sports enthusiast will have the opportunity to experience the premiere digital streaming platform with ESPN+ for exclusive content and the ESPN television channel. Melvin summed it up best regarding the future of ESPN, "when fans decide that they are going to gather on a medium ... we will be there." Hence, ESPN will remain relevant as they lead the industry to be the preferred sports fan selection for streaming live content well into the future.

References

Popper, B. (2017, August 9). Disney bought baseball's tech team to take on Netflix. Retrieved from https://www.theverge.com/2017/8/9/16118694/disney-bamtech-espn-streaming-netflix

Spain, K. (2017, November 9). ESPN will launch streaming service, ESPN Plus, next spring. *USA Today*. Retrieved from https://www.usatoday.com/story/sports/2017/11/09/espn-launch-streaming-service-espn-plus-spring-2018/850597001

Westcott, K., Loucks, J., Downs, K., & Watson, J. (2018). Digital media trends survey: A new world of choice for digital consumers. *Deloitte Insight*. Retrieved from https://www2.deloitte.com/insights/us/en/industry/technology/digital-media-trends-consumption-habits-survey.html

20. Sports Media in 2020: Patterns, Trends, and Crystal-Ball Gazing

Andreas Hebbel-Seeger and Thomas Horky

The future of sports media is unpredictable, with no clear patterns or trends in sight. By dint of digitalization, many-to-many communication in sports reporting, with multiple layers and meanings, has developed out of the traditional one-to-many mode: the rapidity, the broadcast technology, the players and the object of reporting sports are changing. Declarations about sports media in 2020s can, therefore, only indicate patterns or trends. Nevertheless, this chapter presents several lines of development in an attempt to clarify the perspective on the future.

To begin with, we must not forget, despite sinking ratings for several countries and several sporting codes (Evens, 2017), traditional broadcasting of live sports events on television will certainly remain the most relevant sort of sports media for some time. Mega-events like the World Cup, Olympics, and the Super Bowl continue to achieve widespread coverage in all media (IOC, 2016; IOC, 2018; Kantar Media, 2015) and remain the nation's campfire or society's glue, reliably providing topics for social media. Even though the spread in broadcasting has become more multifarious through various digital platforms, live streams and a range of providers as well as forms of presentation (e.g., OTT)—sports will remain, in the near future too, an item for television sets.

Trends and Developments in Sports Media

An analysis of the current trends in the digitalization of sports media does point to various lines of development which are being formed in different ways. The following compilation is by no means exhaustive, subject to constant change, and can thus be understood only as a general survey.

What is decisively influencing the future of sports media is the changing broadcast technology via digitalization. A few years ago, after a fundamental development of broadcast technology (cable, satellite, Internet), cameras, growing ever smaller and more flexible, mounted on cranes, hung on wires, goal posts or sports equipment, like Formula One cars or skiers' helmets, dominated. In the future, there will be new possibilities for creating images from differing forms.

Video Drones

Looking down from on high, video drones are starting to open a new perspective, in the truest sense of the word. In this, sports are functioning as an incubator for further technological developments and as a catalyst for opening up a mass market (Schierl, 2002). In leisure sports, the increasing trivialization of technology serves a need for self-depiction and self-display, where, through action cams, what always was your sports activity becomes the subject from viewpoints not previously sampled. In professional sports, using video drones allows for documenting sporting action outside of normal sports locations (e.g., inaccessible landscapes) and accompanying activities on the move and characterized by open channels (e.g., sailing), as well as tactical configurations from above.

Independent of the particular context or purpose, deploying drones can, through crashing or loss of control, result in physical dangers for those involved and for spectators. In addition, video drones influencing sporting competitions if guiding (e.g., looking for "wind fields" in sailing) or pace-making (e.g., running or cycling) cannot be ruled out. Moreover, video drones increase the risk of external interference in the form of agitation, or ambush-marketing (Hebbel-Seeger, 2016). At times of heightened security threats, drones present a potential danger from deliberate misuse by criminals and terrorists.

In the context of the professional depiction and communication of sporting events, exploring, locating, and describing video drone use is also driven by the trivialization of drone technology and the concomitant distribution of it on the mass market. We do not intend to go into the ethical and legal implications of using drone technology here but the differentiation pending will soon be performed solely through the quality of the image composition and alignment within the mix of communication, no longer via the nature of content. That is because the effectiveness of unmanned flight systems is increasing in ever shorter cycles, in line with rampant technological development.

If the initial stages saw suitably specialized production firms employing video drones for sports media, then not only has the number of suppliers in this area increased, but so has usage in the semi-professional area, where football trainers are monitoring the team's training with their flying devices. Furthermore, athletes get support to visualize the way they want to perform (Higuchi, Shimada, & Rekimoto, 2011), rowing trainers can study technique from above, or sports promoters offer fans images from on high. With video drones, athletes and teams have a new perspective for documentation and training.

In the case of state agencies, Holten, Lawson, and Love (2014) argue that "despite the actual and potential benefits of UAVs (unmanned aerial vehicles), their future as tools for journalism—and indeed their future as instruments of benefit across many professions—is being challenged by unclear, shifting rules and regulations" (p. 644). The same goes for organized sports, which have been caught largely unprepared by these developments.

The use of video drones in sports media has been a neglected topic in research up to now. We mostly find only general references to their use in journalism, and sports as a topic of reporting has been lacking (Tremayne & Clark, 2014). Yet, no one disputes the importance of video drones for journalistic storytelling, a point made by Gynnild (2014); "The innovation of drones for journalistic purposes will most likely replace, or, more precisely, supplement visual news coverage on the ground with new kinds of aerial views as well as options for aerial close-ups that were formerly unseen" (p. 341).

What characterizes the use of drones for major sporting events is the spatial effect of the images they generate. Goldberg, Corcoran, and Picard (2013) stress the advantages video drones offer general journalism, "if the scale of events is too large to perceive from their ground locations" (p. 21). With a view to sports media, they conclude:

> In addition to breaking news and investigative uses, RPAS can be used in sports coverage of bicycle races, marathons, and football matches where they can provide different visual perspectives than the cable- and track-based robotic cameras. (p. 21)

In the same vein, a Reuters News report refers to possible reciprocal effects of video drone use: "Because application of drones in journalism is just emerging, it is unknown how the public will react to their use" (Goldberg et al., 2013, p. 24).

The area of application for video drones in journalism has primarily been in reporting on crises and wars. In 2016, CNN set up a team tasked with capturing images from areas difficult to access and employed drones for aerial and traffic surveillance. What we have described of drone-operating demonstrates their great advantage for journalism: video drones are cheaper, easier to fly than helicopters, and thus make it easier to report using aerial imagery.

However, it is precisely in sports media where we envision further possible uses, with testing underway. What follows is an incomplete inventory capable of expansion, although we can discern an aestheticization of the space of communication. Using drones in sports media changes spatial perspectives. As far as movement in sports goes, drones enable a new aesthetic, which generates an altered effect on reception. This was tried by Swiss TV, with a bird's-eye view from on the Lauberhorn downhill course in skiing, and it has become a standard at many sports events (Wälti, 2012). In 2013, unmanned flight systems equipped with video cameras were used to display the America's Cup finals off San Francisco, as well as to document the Kiel Regatta. Employing video drones bring about an expansion of media possibilities (Hebbel-Seeger, Horky, & Theobalt, 2017). The variety of camera perspectives were noticeably increased with little effort.

In 2014, video drones were used to broadcast the slope-style contest at the Sochi Winter Olympics. The new perspectives are extending sports media, with regards to a shift in time-perspective (dynamic vs. deceleration), but also with regards to oversight overall (management of training). It is mainly with sports that we can note an alteration of media broadcasts. Using video drones in sports allows new camera perspectives possible through changing positions, which were not available up to now (e.g., water sports), but usage can be restrictive (indoor sports). The alteration of the organization of media elucidates an interesting advantage for using video drones in the area of sports neglected by the media.

Video drones offer a chance for niche sports to generate professional images at their events without elaborate organizational resources. For example, a drone makes current reporting on such codes possible from an effective camera position on high without the elaborate and expensive construction of stands or camera platforms. Using video drones provides an opportunity for gathering unique camera angels (Ciobanu, 2016; Horky & Pelka, 2016). On one hand, compared to crane systems, spidercams or traditional helicopters, video drones represent a cheaper solution for producing videos from an aerial viewpoint. On the other, they open up use scenarios specific to their domain, where they can be used close-in to sporting activities, even with sailing, as "downwash" (i.e., windblast from propellers) is actually negligible, so drones are capable of furnishing a particular closeness to the athletes in action (see Figure 20.1). Beyond that, the modest external dimensions of drones, and their resultant agility, allow an interaction with surrounding objects by flying under bridges or between rows of houses.

Figure 20.1: A drone up close to the action in a yacht race.
Source: Thomas Horky.

360-Degree Video

Depicting a sporting event in the form of a comprehensive take on a particular space, as if from a preset camera position does present just as much a fascination as it does a challenge to storytelling. Here, it is the aspect of presence (Witmer & Singer, 1998) and immersion (Slater & Wilbur, 1997) that play a central role: the more intensively the technology supports viewers' diving into a virtual environment and the nearer they imagine they are to the visualized events, the more intensive the resulting experience becomes.

The basis for this is an experience of presence. It allows people to dive into the situation with the sense of time and space dissolving in the experience of flow (Csikszentmihalyi, 2010).

> Presence is defined as the subjective experience of being in one place or environment, even when one is physically situated in another. As described by teleoperators, presence is the sensation of being at the remote worksite rather than at the operator's control station. (Witmer & Singer, 1998, p. 225)

A highly immersive technology, appealing to as many of the senses as possible, and largely blocking out the outside world while transporting high-quality content as far as technical quality goes, fosters such an experience (Slater & Wilbur, 1997). However, depending on the particular means of production and the production device being used, 360-degree video takes on an increased immersive potential, which in turn, makes the experience of presence fundamentally more plausible. The immersive potential is determined via the way an image segment is manipulated (via drag and drop with a mouse, swiping over the screen, or by steering movement) through the nature of blocking out the outside world (situative context of screen use or VR headset), as well as through the projection quality (screen and video resolution, as well as distance of the eyes from the projection surface) (see Figure 20.2).

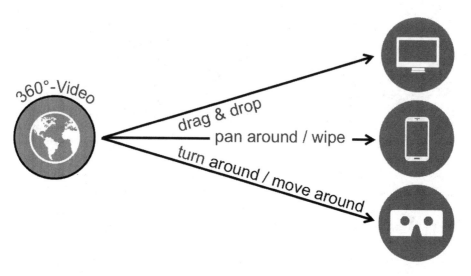

Figure 20.2: 360° video projection equipment and interface.
Source: Hebbel-Seeger (2017).

In comparison to a typical video projection, the experience via user manipulation is potentially more immersive and gains in intensity where the use of head-mounted displays (VR glasses) block out the outside world. Alongside proprietary all-round solutions with integrated monitors, accessed via external computer systems (e.g., Oculus Rift© or HTC Vive©) the comparatively cheap mountings for smartphones, led by Google's paper-based "Cardboard©" glasses, have ensured rapid distribution. With them, the smartphone screen is used as a projection surface, which has to be split when using VR glasses.

On one side, excluding external (visual) stimuli and combining with a narrative choice of image segment via head movement furthers an immersive experience. On the other, you have to accept the limitations in image quality that results from the comparatively closeness of your eyes to the screen and from a smartphone's maximum possible image resolution. When using smartphone VR glasses, the necessary division of the screen for projecting separately to each eye means the image resolution available allows for use of only around half for visualizing the image segment in question. That is why the image quality of 360-degree videos in VR glasses seems mostly inferior when compared to full screen projection (see Figure 20.3).

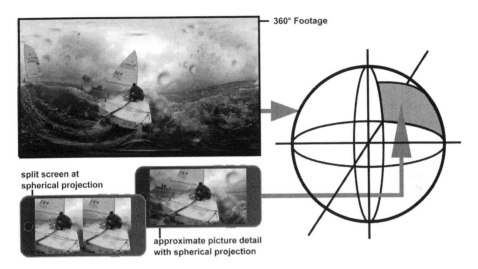

Figure 20.3: A 360° image projection and segment.
Source: Thomas Horky.

Specific camera systems with two or more lenses are needed to produce 360-degree videos. An alternative is to use camera mounts enabling the combination of traditional compact cameras (e.g., GoPro) into a recording unit composed of six and more devices. To display shots as 360-degree video, the video images captured by various lenses synchronically and compatibly must be mounted and combined in a stream or respective data file. Depending on the camera system used, *stitching* in the device happens in real time or is deferred via external software, which offers at least a supporting function.

As noted above in relation to video drones, technological development is progressing rapidly and, to an equal extent, affects the possible quality (image resolution and stability), the processing (stitching), the nature of the construction (dimensions, robustness, water-resistance) usability, as well as price development (accessing the mass market). At the same time, the available bandwidths for online communication are equally expanding as the platforms like Facebook and YouTube succeed in optimizing the algorithms for the data compression of 360-degree contents.

In this situation, it is precisely with sports that the latest developments in 360-cameras become particularly important, as they can generate stereoscopic images in 360-degree space via a suitable number and arrangement of lenses. On one side, 3D projection makes the reception of contents easier, where distances and multi-dimensional positions in space are of central importance (e.g., player and ball in matches) and on the other, visualization 3D enhances the experience of presence. In this way, we can demonstrate marked differences between 2D and 3D projection via VR glasses in the context of an exploratory comparative study on the example of basketball (Hebbel-Seeger, 2018).

A fixed camera position for 360-degree shots scarcely permits attaining any proximity to the respective sporting activity. But, by contrast, the *nearness* to spectator sports is gained. In the context of a sports event, positioning the camera in the spectator area as close as possible to the playing area enables a high degree of immersion, in spite of the mediation. The situative character of (nearly) live experience as spectator replaces the presentation of a sports match. For example, away from the viewpoint of the classical moving imagery with its changing perspectives to differing image segments and a commentary attuned to them. Where previously it was the elements sketched out above that carried the staging of sports events, the 360-degree depiction derives its attractivity from the immediacy of the "dialogue" between the sporting event(s), the spectator reaction(s), and activities (rituals, fan anthems etc.). On the other hand:

> Concert recordings with viewers imagining themselves next to the musicians on the stage, or sports broadcasts from a seat directly on the sidelines, would be interesting. Those are areas which might be the first to become "normal"—a further development of classical television. The camera shooting from the perspective of the Formula One driver is long-established—imagine how you could look around yourself, freely and at will, from this perspective. (Matzat, 2016, para. 6; own translation)

Even if attempts at communicating sporting events in 360-degree live streams have been realized, and the first firms specializing in this form of sports communication are crowding onto the U.S. market (e.g., nextvr.com or vokevr.com), the data transfer rates necessary for 360-degree live stream present as much of a hurdle as the above-mentioned limitations of the end devices required. That is because the principle of in the midst of it instead of just being there (the immersive participation in an event), presupposes the use of head mounted displays, VR glasses, which are experiencing a rapid spread with the use of mobile end devices as projection surfaces. However, in terms of the picture quality, they still have considerable potential for development and will have to apply it to lucratively deliver sports.

A solution focused on the sporting activity, in contrast to the spectator's existence, is a montage carried out on a sports device or on sportspersons themselves. Extending the basic idea of the so-called action camera, users can not just look "through the eyes" of the particular sportsperson, but insinuate themselves into that sportsperson by influencing the visualized activity and being able to look around inside the event(s), like in real life. This allows an extremely immersive experience that would not be available to users in any other way. For example, driving a Formula One car, racing on a snowboard, or sailing aboard a racing catamaran.

In all this, communicating a new perspective on sports does not just aim at changing perspectives, where the users take on the role of actors, but explicitly includes the surrounding space. Sports storytelling has to be largely independent of the relations between environment and the activity of movement in space. Equally independent of the nature of a projection as a 360-degree video or a "typical" projection on a monitor, and has to align itself to the logic of a sequence of movement and a competition's internal dramatic structure. To enable the context of 360-degree video, there are equivalent presentation possibilities available. It follows that not all spaces or every activity involving movement are equally suitable to a 360-degree video. Any selection has to justify why, given a defined aim at communicating, a spatially extensive panorama should be possible so that you can, if necessary, tackle the challenge of providing a structuring arrangement in a complex 360-degree setting where there is a free and fundamentally uncontrollable choice of image segment by recipients. On one hand, you can produce this arrangement by organizing objects in space and, on the other, by keeping to "learned" patterns of communication, where the recipients follow.

The extreme potential of 360-degree video for immersion, in combination with a head-mounted display (VR glasses), makes this technology highly suitable for transporting "experiences" across space and time. Accordingly, the first providers of 360-degree sports content, like the above-mentioned NextVR or LiveLikeVR, are focusing on this visualization technology.

Internal composition as a spatial setting for sports acquires a central role in developing this potential, alongside technical aspects attached to the formal qualities of media production and projection. On one side, the space involved has to offer sufficient possibilities for exploration, and thus have an internal justification for the choice of media, while on the other, users should not lose themselves in exploring that space. The challenge consists in guiding users. Precisely because the technological development in this area is evolving rapidly and 360-degree content is becoming easier, with the end devices for projecting it waxing ever more efficient. Any differentiation via the medium itself alone is growing ever more difficult while the demands on it are increasing. This, however, presupposes submitting the experiments in producing and using 360-degree video on differing end devices and in various use-scenarios to critical analysis, to derive the factors needed for future success.

Mixed Reality

Augmented Reality (AR) stands for an enrichment of our view of the world through additional artificial information; "Augmented reality is a direct, interactive, real time expansion of the perception of the real surroundings" (Broll, 2013, p. 246; own translation). In this sense, 360-degree videos can be supplemented with AR content, when texts, terrestrial information, or biomechanical indices are activated. In the actual sense of the term, AR stands for an expansion of our view of the world in real time, frequently overlaying the real view of the environment with artifacts. In sports contexts, this can be projecting the speed of movement or the distance of a jump onto the inside of ski goggles (Oakley Wave©) or projecting an optimal direction for a swing and the optimal track for the ball onto AR glasses in golf (www.puttview.com). Pokémon Go represents a popular example in the context of digital game playing. Here the user views their environment on their smartphone which shows the device's particular camera viewpoint at that time. This view is overlaid with geo-data relevant to the game and with artificial objects like figures in the game that are integrated into the "genuine" surroundings. The possibility of using VR glasses in AR contexts is being implemented by providing gaps in their mountings for smartphone cameras.

AR is a characteristic of "Mixed Reality (MR), where real and virtual information are mixed without a precise definition of which space (virtual or real) is augmented and which space is augmenting" (Grasset, Mulloni, Billinghurst, & Schmalstieg, 2011, p. 380). MR stands for a mixture of a real (physical) environment with a virtual space. This mixing can basically be envisioned for the entire extent of a "reality-virtuality continuum" (Milgram, Takemura, Utsumi, & Kishino, 1994, p. 283; own translation) from the real world to the virtual, and from a reality augmented by artificial information. Examples include superimposition of data, or objects via surroundings where real spatial features integrate with virtual objects and structures where the surface of a real-world object is endowed with a virtual texture. This extends to virtual worlds "populated" in the sense of an "augmented virtuality" (Milgram et al., 1994, p. 283) by static and dynamic objects as well as subjects from the real world such as three-dimensional whole-body scans in real time are projected into a virtual space.

While the reality-virtuality continuum is defined as one-dimensional through the degree of virtualization, current technological developments demand an expansion in the dimensions of space and time. For example, the real world is combined extensively by real objects from a distant real world being transferred into the immediate real environment (see "Holoportation" with Microsoft HoloLens) that virtualizes the "real world." The component of time becomes significant when it is a question of establishing a boundary to 360-degree video because it can be expanded with artificial contents. However, it does make a difference whether the "mixed reality" is generated in real time and potentially allows interaction with its contents. With MR in the form of 360-degree video, it is a matter of preserved "reality" that only permits optical navigation within a rigid structure of content and time.

> When current practices are investigated; it is seen that the augmented reality applications in the field of sports concentrate on development of expert systems which will substitute or facilitate the training of sports people and help the trainers or on managing competitions in a fair way and presenting the competitions to audiences in a more entertaining and attracting way. (Bozyer, 2015, p. 318)

In sports media MR applications have long been used in various contexts and for various purposes. For example:

- To incentivize ticketing, when tickets are being interpreted as markers by smartphones or computer cameras and trigger superimposing (e.g., game holograms or event locations such as the AR-app of the Phi) (Laird, 2012).
- To activate spectators in the context of a live event, when viewing objects inside an event location with a smartphone initiates casual gameplaying applications, ranging from simple to collaborative use. In addition, channel feeding back into the real context of the event such as the AR-App of the Cavaliers NBA Team (Tepper, 2017).
- For enriching live communication through the distribution of contents like scoreboards, live game data (speed of the ball, number of mistakes) or location-based services (catering, side events). IBM tested the "Seer" project during the 2011 Wimbledon Tournament and Major League Baseball uses the "At Bat" app.

However, it is only subsequent to more recent "VR-hype," driven by the technological development in the smartphone sector, that augmented reality has picked up speed in sports. This has tempted Medal (2017) to declare "augmented reality is the next big move for the sports industry" (para. 1).

In combination with 360-degree video, VR environments have applied a sense of AR to free users from their social isolation when consuming 360-degree contents through VR glasses. Providers like LiveLikeVR are offering 360-degree videos of sports events integrated into a virtual world, which multiple users, with their avatars, can visit communally, making reception into a social experience. Microsoft is pursuing a comparable concept in sports with a cooperative project with the NFL where "Microsoft and the NFL look into the future of football" ("Microsoft HoloLens," 2016). In this, the reception of 360-degree contents proceeds through some glasses (Hololens) by which the real world, and the peers you find in it, remain accessible through AR while video contents are visible simultaneously.

Social Media: The Possibilities for Interaction and Participation

The possibilities for interaction and participation in digital sports media are diverse. Users can at once like/favor, share/forward, or comment on other people's content as well as begin, participate in, or moderate discussions. Thus, placing their opinions at the disposal of a larger community with few limitations, even for a world audience. With mobile end devices, users can network with other users at any time from any place and approach each other via various forms of interaction (Clavio & Walsh, 2014; Frederick, Lim, Clavio, & Walsh, 2012).

For sports journalism, this interactive form remains a curse and blessing. Communicators like athletes, clubs, associations, and leagues have the possibility of sending information directly to internal or external group over social media (Clavio & Frederick, 2014; Whiteside, 2014). On one side, sports journalists gain further research options and frequently find quotable declarations among the profiles of athletes and clubs; while, on the other side, lose autonomy and exclusivity as statements mentioned are already available to the public through social media (Grimmer, 2014).

Web 2.0 has caused the boundaries between producers and consumers to fade visibly. Thus, direct exchange has become possible, without being dependent on traditional mass media as gatekeepers and agents. User-participation in the object/content/topic of communication benefits a mutual connection between fans and their clubs. What is intended and sought in this development is the active participation of users in the production of so-called user-generated content (Williams & Chinn, 2010; Yoshida, Gordon, Nakazawa, & Biscaia, 2014).

Sports are particularly well suited to the fleeting communication in social media. The hurdle seems to be rather low if you want to say anything about a rather entertaining issue like sports. And, beyond that, social media is also an ideal channel for sports communication as their live character suits the principle of sports (Nölleke, 2018).

Up to now, dealing with traditional sports media through social media was mainly limited to superimposing tweets, which are then commented on by moderators and guests. In all the new technology forms, combined with networks like Facebook, Twitter, Instagram, or Snapchat, and YouTube, are offering ever-greater possibilities for interaction between sportspersons and sports reporters. The audience, and every individual user, can be integrated into digital sports media and can participate directly in events.

Media as Sport: Sporting Settings and Virtualization

Ongoing technologization is creating forms of sporting contests, which are influencing sports media ever more intensively. Instead of *sport and media*, we will have to talk much more in the future in many areas about *sport as media* (Hutchins, 2008). What is meant by this is a seamless transition among sports, communication technology, and media content. Examples of esports or drone racing where the contests are comparable with the forms of traditional sporting contests in their structure and sequences (see Hebbel-Seeger, 2012). On one hand, the technical realization is itself becoming an object of sports, and on the other, distribution is not happening often via the traditional channels of sports communication. Digital sports communication is thus becoming an object, where new contests, or, in part, existing sporting matches are being displayed.

In this, the nature of the display is diverse and moves between digital adaptation and simulation of traditional sports like basketball, football or online strategy games, like *League of Legends* or *Egoshooter Counterstrike*. Comparing real football with its electronic variant FIFA18 is not cogent, as it is a matter of respectively independent forms of display. Nevertheless, more intensive approaches are happening on both sides. The large European football clubs are establishing esports departments (see Hebbel-Seeger & Siemers, 2018), while in the U.S., an electronic basketball league and the Madden NFL championship series is gathering speed (Mitchell, 2018). At the same time, esport is adapting traditional sports' league structures, training concepts and development of new talent. What has been an envisaged, and partially accomplished acceptance of esports into the programs of large sporting events like the Asian Games or even the Olympics would then be a sort of merging of both areas.

This has real consequences for media communication. The success of streaming platforms like Twitch is not just due to the live transmissions they offer. Much more, it is a question of the homepage being simultaneously a social network, where spectators can interact with players. The communication between the broadcasters and the spectators is not just limited to a sort of commentary, as we are familiar with from classic sports broadcasts. Broadcasters comment on their own performance and allow themselves to be criticized or praised. For example, via a chat superimposed alongside the actual transmission of a match's events (Breuer & Görlich, 2018). Yet, in conjunction with that, they allow their spectators to vote on the next level or try new things together with their followers. The entire medium and design of the product comes from two directions. Successful broadcasters can belong to one of two categories: those who are informative and those who entertain. In this case, this does not only apply to professionals but also to players from the semi-professional area. In principle, every user can set up an individual channel via Twitch and publish their own gameplay.

These new forms of sports presentation are also driving participation further along in this direction as they enable intensive interchanges between players and spectators. Players communicate their assessment of their performance and open up the virtual doors to their games for the spectators. Social media makes it easier for the professional players to communicate with their fans, to interact and thus, in the final analysis, to build up their own brand (Breuer & Görlich, 2018).

Drivers of Digital Sports Communications

Sports were always a trailblazer in the different areas of journalism. Developments observable on the sports desk mostly turn up just a short time later in other areas of journalism too. Yet, the players in digital sports media do not seem to be the drivers any more.

Sports Clubs, Franchises, and Sporting Associations

There has been increasingly intensive talk about a change in the big players in digital sports media. It was initially the television companies, the big broadcasters and media houses, who had the greatest influence by acquiring licensing rights. Yet the media seems to be increasingly losing importance as drivers in the media-sports complex.

At present, it seems the big associations, like the IOC, FIFA, NFL, and NBA or the big clubs and franchises, like Real Madrid, Manchester United, Paris St. Germain, or the Dallas Cowboys and the New York Yankees are in the driver's seat when determining the way sports media will go. Even an individual athlete, like Portuguese football star Cristiano Ronaldo of Real Madrid, evinces a bigger reach through social media than he does through most of the other media outlets. This is a growing problem for sports journalism, with increasing complaints about competition and reduced access to the subjects of its reporting. One example for the tendency of sports clubs and sports associations to develop themselves into independent media brands is the 2018 decoupling of a media firm also as a provider for the biggest German football club, Bayern München (Nyari, 2018).

How big will the influence of digital Internet organizations like Google, Amazon, or Facebook and Twitter be in future? People have been expecting these firms, not initially interested in sports, to enter the market for licensing rights. Despite a few small attempts, first in cricket and football, later also with the NFL and MLB, there is no comprehensive concept in sight. This could, however, change soon. The first noticeable indication of a changing development is the growing influence of streaming providers, like that financed by U.S. millionaire Leonard Blavatnik, (Perform Group), DAZN in Europe, and the move by Eurosport-CEO Paul Hutton, to Facebook (Sweney, 2018).

Large Sporting Events

Big sporting events like the Olympics, FIFA's Football World Cup, and the European Cup were always milestones in the development of media technology and sports reporting (Wenner & Billings, 2017). Initially, according to global ratings and the 2014 finals in Brazil counts as one of the greatest media events in the world (Haynes & Boyle, 2017; Kantar Media, 2015).

More recently the 2016 Olympics in Rio represented a turning point in the use of innovative media technologies. The Olympic Broadcasting Services (OBS) presented the games in Brazil with over 1,000 cameras (7,200 staff). There were 85 hours of applications in the area of VR in play at the opening and closing ceremonies, as well as in gymnastics. Furthermore, in Germany, parts of the Olympic games could be seen via public broadcasters, ARD and ZDF, as 360-degree live streams. For the 2018 Winter Games in Pyeongchang, the International Olympic Committee (IOC) signed a contract with Intel for using drones, VR technology, 360-degree replay, and artificial intelligence applications. For example, figure skating and ski jumping were presented using a complement of 38 cameras and 5-K technology (Burns, 2017; Price, 2016).

In the U.S., the development is more advanced. Viewers of Super Bowl LI in February 2017 could shift themselves into game sequences in the context of 15- to 30-second video clips presented with up to 38 cameras in 360-degree replay technology. The San Francisco 49ers have tested the use of 360-degree video, to increase spectator participation by incorporating the reactions of viewers while they watched. Before the Tokyo 2020 Olympics and the 2022 Winter Games in Beijing, we can scarcely assess what influence the new large players on the Asian market, like Tencent or Alibaba, will have; as well as on the Arab market, with an eye to the coming 2022 Football World Cup in Qatar.

Prospects

Our deliberations have provided an overview of developments in digitalization and of its influence on sports broadcasting, while looking towards a possible future. After this look forward, prospects can only resemble crystal-ball gazing, yet some long-term perspectives for digital sports media are showing up.

Producers' and consumers' independence with regards to time and space in sports media is growing. Sporting events can be broadcast from all over the world and be received simultaneously or with a delay. On one hand, the form of reception is shifting to individual consumption (e.g. solely over a smartphone). On the other, sports broadcasts are increasingly followed as public viewing by social groups in front of big video screens. This communal use will, in the future, further influence the way sports broadcasts are produced (Horky, 2013).

The narrative technique, or storytelling of digital sports media, is changing. Sports journalists have to acquire distinct skills and additional knowledge in terms of technological applications. Meanwhile, these technical innovations subsequently allow communication with representative possibilities to be markedly enhanced with new experiences for reception. This development is in its beginning stages. We can only discern a few applications with scarcely any structural planning. Even in the highly commercial Bundesliga football league in Germany, innovative media technologies have rarely played any role in presentation or production.

It remains abidingly exciting to anticipate what sort of significance the 2026 Football World Cup in the U.S., as a joint event with Canada and Mexico, as well as the 2028 Olympics in Los Angeles, will have for the development of digital sports media. Innovative media technologies have an exciting future.

References

Bozyer, Z. (2015). Augmented reality in sports: Today and tomorrow. *International Journal of Sport Culture and Science, 3*(4), 314–325. doi: 10.14486/IJSCS392

Breuer, M., & Görlich, D. (2018). Gaming und e-sport—Markt und Inszenierung des digitalen Sports. In T. Horky, H.-J. Stiehler, & T. Schierl (Eds.), *Die Digitalisierung des Sports in den Medien*. (pp. 275–293), Köln: Halem.

Broll, W. (2013). Augmentierte Realität. In R. Dörner, W. Broll, P. Grimm, & B. Jung (Eds.), *Virtual und augmented reality (VR/AR)*. (pp. 241–294), Berlin/Heidelberg: Springer Vieweg.

Burns, M. J. (2017, June 22). Intel bringing drones, VR, AI, replay technology to winter Olympics. *SportTechie*. Retrieved from https://www.sporttechie.com/ intel-bringing-drones-vr-ai-replay-technology-to-winter-olympics/

Ciobanu, M. (2016, May 3). Are drones a new avenue for data journalism? News organisations can use drones to generate data for stories, not just for aerial visuals. *Journalism.co.uk*. Retrieved from https://www.journalism.co.uk/news/are-drones-a-new-avenue-for-data-journalism-/s2/a634331/

Clavio, G., & Frederick, E. (2014). Sharing is caring: An exploration of motivations for social sharing and locational social media usage among sport fans. *Journal of Applied Sport Management, 6*(2), 70–85.

Clavio, G., & Walsh, P. (2014). Dimensions of social media utilization among college sport fans. *Communication & Sport, 2*(3), 261–281. doi:10.1177/2167479513480355

Csikszentmihalyi, M. (2010). *Das flow-Erlebnis. Jenseits von Angst und Langeweile: im Tun aufgehen*. (10. Auflage). Stuttgart: Klett-Cotta.

Evens, T. (2017). Sports viewership goes down: What's up for television sports rights? *International Journal of Digital Television, 8*(2), 283–287. doi:10.1386/jdtv.8.2.283_5

Frederick, E. L., Lim, C. H., Clavio, G., & Walsh, P. (2012). Why we follow: An examination of parasocial interaction and fan motivations for following athlete archetypes on Twitter. *International Journal of Sport Communication, 5*(4), 481–502. doi:10/1123/ijsc5.4.481

Goldberg, D., Corcoran, M., & Picard, R. G. (2013). Remotely piloted aircraft systems & journalism: Opportunities and challenges of drones in news gathering. *Reuters Institute for the Study of Journalism*, Oxford: Oxford University. Retrieved from https://reutersinstitute.politics.ox.ac.uk/sites/default/files/2017-11/Remotely%20Piloted%20Aircraft%20Systems%20and%20Journalism%20100613%20v.2.pdf

Grasset, R., Mulloni, A., Billinghurst, M., & Schmalstieg, D. (2011). Navigation techniques in augmented and mixed reality: Crossing the virtuality continuum. In B. Furht (Ed.), *Handbook of Augmented Reality*. (pp. 379–407) New York: Springer.

Grimmer, C. G. (2014). *Kooperation oder Kontrolle? Eine empirische Untersuchung zum Spannungsverhältnis von Pressesprechern in der Fußball-Bundesliga und Journalisten*. Köln: Halem.

Gynnild, A. (2014). The robot eye witness: Extending visual journalism through drone surveillance. *Digital Journalism, 2*(3), 334–343. doi:10.1080/21670811.2014.883184

Haynes, R., & Boyle, R. (2017). The FIFA World Cup: Media, football and the evolution of a global event. In L. A. Wenner, & A. C. Billings (Eds.), *Sport, Media, and Mega-Events*. (pp. 85–99) London: Routledge.

Hebbel-Seeger, A. (2012). The relationship between real sports and digital adaptation in e-sport gaming. *International Journal of Sports Marketing & Sponsorship 13*(2), 43–54. doi:10.1108/IJSMS-13-02-2012-B005

Hebbel-Seeger, A. (2016). Videodrohnen in der eventkommunikation. In A. Hebbel-Seeger, T. Horky, & H.-J. Schulke (Eds.), *Sport als Bühne: Mediatisierung von Sport und Sportgroßveranstaltungen.* (pp. 326–345) Aachen: Meyer & Meyer.

Hebbel-Seeger, A. (2017). 360 degrees-video and VR for training and marketing within sports. *Athens Journal of Sports, 4*(4), 243–261.

Hebbel-Seeger, A. (2018, April 29). From Seeing to Being?! The experience of presence in360°-video in sports communication. Presentation at the International Association for Communication and Sport. Retrieved from https://www.slideshare.net/ahsHH/from-seeing-to-beeing

Hebbel-Seeger, A., Horky, T. & Theobalt, C. (2017). Usage of drones in sports communication—new aesthetics and enlargement of space. *Athens Journal of Sports 4*(2), 89–105. Retrieved from https://www.athensjournals.gr/sports/2017-4-2-1-Hebbel-Seeger.pdf

Hebbel-Seeger, A. & Siemers, L. (2018), eSport im Profi-Fußball der DFL—Zu Erwartungen, Zielen und Markeneinfluss. *Sciamus, 3,* 42-58.

Higuchi, K., Shimada, T., & Rekimoto, J. (2011). Flying sports assistant: External visual imagery representations for sports training. *Proceedings of the 2nd Augmented Human International Conference (is AH '11).* ACM, New York, NY, USA, (Article 7).

Holten, A. E., Lawson, S., & Love, C. (2014). Unmanned aerial vehicles. Opportunities, barriers, and the future of "drone journalism". *Journalism Practice, 9*(5), 634–650. doi:10.1080/17512786.2014.980596

Horky, T. (2013). Uses of sport communication in groups: Meaning and effects in public viewing. In P. M. Pedersen (Ed.), *Routledge Handbook of Sport Communication.* (pp. 378–387). London: Routledge.

Horky, T., & Pelka, P. (2016). Data visualisation in sports journalism: Opportunities and challenges of data-driven journalism in German Football. *Digital Journalism, 5*(5), 587–606. doi:10.1080/21670811.2016.1254053

Hutchins, B. (2008). Signs of meta-change in second modernity: The growth of e-sport and the World Cyber Games. *New Media & Society, 10*(6), 851–869. doi:10.1177/1461444808096248

IOC. (2016). *Global Broadcast and Audience Report: Olympic Games Rio 2016.* Retrieved from https://stillmed.olympic.org/media/Document%20Library/OlympicOrg/Games/Summer-Games/Games-Rio-2016-Olympic-Games/Media-Guide-for-Rio-2016/Global-Broadcast-and-Audience-Report-Rio-2016.pdf#_ga=2.198005030.825343616.1526661538-697621688.1525555063

IOC. (2018). *Olympic Marketing Fact File: 2019 Edition.* Retrieved from https://stillmed.olympic.org/media/Document%20Library/OlympicOrg/Documents/IOC-Marketing-and-Broadcasting-General-Files/Olympic-Marketing-Fact-File-2018.pdf#_ga=2.26082612.825343616.1526661538-697621688.1525555063

Kantar Media (2015). *2014 FIFA World Cup Brazil. Television Audience Report.* Retrieved from http://resources.fifa.com/mm/document/affederation/tv/02/74/55/57/2014fwcbraziltvaudiencereport(draft5) (issuedate14.12.15) neutral.pdf

Laird, S. (2012, July 21). NFL team enhances season tickets with augmented reality. *Mashable India*. Retrieved from https://mashable.com/2012/07/21/nfl-tickets-augmented-reality/?europe=true#CDc54hDUeuqu

Matzat, L. (2016, March 24). Das endgültige Medium? Über das Potenzial von Virtual Reality für den Journalismus. *Fachjournalist*. Retrieved from http://www.fachjournalist.de/das-endgueltige-medium-ueber-das-potenzial-von-virtual-reality-fuer-den-journalismus/

Medal, A. (2017, October 13). Why augmented reality is the next big move for the sports industry. *Inc*. Retrieved from https://www.inc.com/andrew-medal/why-augmented-reality-is-next-big-move-for-sports-industry.html

Microsoft HoloLens and the NFL look into the future of football. (2016, February 2). *Windows Central*. Retrieved from https://youtu.be/HvYj3_VmW6I

Milgram, P., Takemura, H., Utsumi, A., & Kishino, F. (1994). Augmented reality: A class of displays on the reality-virtuality continuum. *SPIE, Telemanipulator and Telepresence Technologies*, (2351), 282–292.

Mitchell, F. (2018, January 27). Madden NFL 18 Championship Series to Broadcast Exclusively on ESPN/Disney Channels. *The Esports Observer*. Retrieved from https://esportsobserver.com/madden-nfl-18-championship-series-to-broadcast-exclusively-on-espndisney-channels/

Nölleke, D. (2018). Der einfluss von social media auf sportjournalisten. In T. Horky, H.-J. Stiehler, & T. Schierl (Eds.), *Die Digitalisierung des Sports in den Medien*. (pp. 181–207) Köln: Halem.

Nyari, C. (2018, May 16). FC Bayern founds the FCB Digital & Media Lab. Retrieved from https://fcbayern.com/us/news/2018/05/fc-bayern-founds-the-fcb-digital--media-lab

Price, S. (2016). Behind the lens. *Olympic Review*, 101, 32–39. Retrieved from http://touchline.digipage.net/olympicreview/issue101/32-1

Schierl, T. (2002). *Die Visualisierung des Sports in den Medien*. Köln: Halem.

Slater, M., & Wilbur, S. (1997). A framework for immersive virtual environments (FIVE): Speculations on the role of presence in virtual environments. *Presence: Teleoperators and Virtual Environments*, 6(6), 603–616. doi:10.1162/pres.1997.6.6.603

Sweney, M. (2018, January 19). Facebook hires Eurosport chief for multibillion live push. *The Guardian*. Retrieved from https://www.theguardian.com/technology/2018/jan/19/facebook-hires-eurosport-chief-for-multibillion-live-sport-push

Tepper, F. (2017, April 19). An NBA team is turning their scoreboard into an AR basketball game. *TechCrunch*. Retrieved from https://techcrunch.com/2017/04/19/an-nba-team-is-turning-their-scoreboard-into-an-ar-basketball-game/?guccounter=1

Tremayne, M., & Clark, A. (2014). New perspectives from the sky: Unmanned aerial vehicles and journalism. *Digital Journalism*, 2(2), 232–246. doi:10.1080/2167081 1.2013.805039

Wälti, T. (2012, January 13). Mit der Drohne über den Hundschopf. *Tages Anzeiger*. Retrieved from https://www.tagesanzeiger.ch/sport/wintersport/Mit-der-Drohne-ueber-den-Hundschopf/story/10896343

Wenner, L. A., & Billings, A. C. (2017). *Sport, Media, and Mega-Events*. London: Routledge.

Whiteside, E. A. (2014). New media and the changing role of sports information. In A. C. Billings, & M. Hardin (Eds.), *Routledge Handbook of Sport and New Media*. (pp. 143–152). New York: Taylor & Francis.

Williams, J., & Chinn, S. J. (2010). Meeting relationship-marketing goals through social media: A conceptual model for sport marketers. *International Journal of Sport Communication, 3*(4), 422–437. doi:10.1123/ijsc.3.4.422

Witmer, B. G., & Singer, M. J. (1998). Measuring presence in virtual environments: A presence questionnaire. *Presence: Teleoperators and Virtual Environments, 7*(3), 225–240. doi:10.1162/105474698565686

Yoshida, M., Gordon, B., Nakazawa, M., & Biscaia, R. (2014). Conceptualization and measurement of fan engagement: Empirical evidence from a professional sport context. *Journal of Sport Management, 28*(4), 399–417. doi:10.1123/jsm.2013-0199

21. *Visualizing 2020: The Future of Sports Media Panel Discussion*

A Panel Presented at the International Association of Communication
and Sport (IACS) 11th Summit on Communication and Sport

On April 28, 2018 the attendees of the International Association of Communication and Sport (IACS) 11th Summit on Communication and Sport held at Indiana University Bloomington heard from a distinguished panel regarding what might be ahead for sports media in the 2020s. The IACS began in 2002 with the gathering of eight communication and sport scholars at Arizona State University's west campus for the first Sport Summit. Meeting every two years, the Sport Summit attracted more interest from communication and sport scholars and the IACS was founded in 2012. For more information about IACS please visit www.communicationandsport.com.

The editors, with the help of Galen Clavio (Indiana University Bloomington), invited four participants to prognosticate about the future of sports media. After the panel was transcribed, one participant decided to withdraw their participation. The following transcript reports the discussion between the remaining three panelists:

- Bryan Curtis, editor-at-large of The Ringer website where he writes and produces podcasts about sports media.
- Kevin Blackistone, a Visiting Professor at the University of Maryland and writer for *The Washington Post*. Blackistone also appears on ESPN programming such as *Around the Horn*.
- Galen Clavio, Head of the Sports Media Program at Indiana University and the Director of the National Sports Journalism Center in Indianapolis.

Adam Earnheardt, Professor and Department Chair at Youngstown State University and a co-editor of this volume, served as panel moderator. Portions of this panel, specifically some of the audience question-and-answer portion, have been edited due to length and to improve readability.

Adam Earnheardt: What will constitute sport or sports in the 2020s?

Galen Clavio: There's always going to be segments of the sport-watch-
                     ing population that's going to say, "That's not sport and
                     this is," and I think that, to some degree, it's a blurring
                     of the lines between sports and entertainment. Really,
                     it's almost competition-based, I think necessarily, versus
                     being form-based. Esports has obviously become very
                     big. We're watching drone racing get televised on ESPN
                     and ABC. We've seen things that, 10 years ago, would've
                     not only been seen as futuristic but probably wouldn't
                     have been seen as sitting alongside NBA coverage, or
                     things along those lines, popping into the mainstream.
                     Part of it, I think, is due to the audience fragmenting a
                     lot. We're seeing that with sports television, and we're
                     seeing that with social media. I think if you can find an
                     audience that's interested in something and there's a com-
                     petitive aspect, there's going to be some level of sport
                     within that. I don't think we really know, but I think that
                     the paths are there for a lot of different things to fall into
                     that.

Kevin Blackistone: Ted Leonsis, who has now put together Monumental
                     Sports in Washington D.C., which encapsulates sports
                     teams … just launched an esports division. I don't know
                     how he's going to pull it off, but it's more content for
                     Monumental Sports, just as it is for the Big Ten Network.
                     Now I think the idea of sport is always evolving, whether or
                     not it's competition between teams or between individuals
                     or against a time. With all of the different means of broad-
                     casting sports now, NBC, you can watch every Olympic
                     sport if you want to almost all year long on their separate
                     channels. I've got a kid in my neighborhood who is about
                     to enter high school who is already a very accomplished
                     rock climber and potentially going to earn a college schol-
                     arship for rock climbing. Sports seem to be popping up
                     everywhere. I think there's one thing maybe we've been
                     reminded of, this gets back to talking about The Unde-
                     feated, recently about sport is also what it can mean for
                     community building, community bonding around so
                     many issues. What we saw at the University of Missouri and
                     the football team, what we've seen in Sacramento at Kings'
                     games, what we've seen from NFL players and the little bit
                     of leverage that they've been able to apply against owners
                     to get funding for causes that are near-and-dear to their
                     communities. So, I think we've expanded our idea, maybe,

about the impact that sports can have on our communities as a whole.

Bryan Curtis:
I'd just say from the television programming standpoint when we talk about esports, it reminds me also of, if we go back to the 1960s, Roone Arledge running then-third place ABC, right? And what does he do? He goes out and gets the rights to cliff diving and Evel Knievel and speedboat racing, all of which we would not consider to be traditional sports, and he packaged them as *Wide World of Sport*. And, it's driven by what? Competition with the other networks because ABC is in third place and, already, rights fees are already going through the roof way back in the 1960s. He's trying to get cheap programming that he can put on. That strikes me, as we're talking about esports, as really something similar that has been going on in sports television for a long time, which is trying to keep your costs down and try to get a foothold with the competition. I think when we talk about what sports will look like in the 2020s, I think probably pretty similar to today, would be my guess. You'll have your football and your baseball and your big sports staying and also, it'll just be surrounded by a larger constellation of other sports that, thanks to streaming services, thanks to television, thanks to YouTube, just have a bigger foothold in the world.

Earnheardt:
Let's assume for a second that the next superstar athlete is sitting on a couch somewhere eating uncooked ramen noodles. We've heard these stories, right? Where these guys sit for 12 hours at a time playing Madden or whatever. We've heard stories also of the superstar athletes, again the gamers in Korea, who are basically as big as Lebron James here in the United States. There are two parts to this:

1. How do you produce or get ready to produce that kind of content? And, how do you frame stories around that?
2. Are the interviews any different than they would be for a professional athlete?

Curtis:
I think early on we've seen Deadspin and other places do stories about these guys and gals. It's pretty similar, right? The postgame interview does not change appreciably from the usual of, "How big was that performance out there today?" I think the interesting question is also where is this produced because these people we're

talking about who are eating ramen on their couch, do they have cable? Probably not, right? Do they have a streaming service? Maybe. But where are they watching all of this stuff? And are we going to be seeing this in traditional forms? Or are we going to go completely outside the box? We're seeing this on YouTube. We're seeing this on streaming services, that kind of thing.

Blackistone: Certainly, streaming services because they can be so fragmented. I think it was just a week and a half ago ESPN unveiled its brand-new streaming service, to which its invested tens of millions of dollars and built out new studios in the most highly valued property you can find in New York. That's certainly one place it's going to go. I agree with Bryan. I don't know that the way we cover it is going to change because I think that we have a pretty rigid box in which you think about how we cover games and the outcome of games. But the framing may change because the "athletes" in esports are not like the athletes we are accustomed to covering, and I think that at some point, we are going to have to have another conversation about the class of people who are avail to esports and are able to play esports. It might be different than what we have about athletes today.

Clavio: One thing I think that is worth keeping in mind, we've talked a lot about esports here, we're not going to talk exclusively about esports, but something that I think is really interesting is because of the format of esports and the fact that its League of Legends and is available worldwide to people and several other games in that category, from a sports media perspective, you have the possibility of having almost borderless sports competition now. If you're familiar with the Overwatch League, this is something that Blizzard launches this game and they launch a worldwide league where they've got franchises nominally placed in cities in Europe, the United States, Australia, and Asia, and it's televised as such. You have audiences from all of these different countries and much of the competition is going to be on Twitch, which again, isn't tied to any traditional media contract. It's interesting when we think about soccer as the world game, and certainly it is, but FIFA negotiates individual television rights with every country on the map or television entity in every country. We're not seeing that with esports. We're seeing everybody go to these centralized locations for streaming and watching the games there. To me, I think that's a really fascinating aspect to this because it's a complete upturning of how we've thought about media rights within sports, whether that lasts or whether people decide, "Hey, we need to make more money on this or we're going to change the way we do it." That's yet to be determined. Right now, there's a lot of untapped and kind of unknown potential to it.

Earnheardt: That's a nice way to move away from esports, in a way, and get in Kevin's point, too, about what ESPN launched [in April 2018]. How do you see the sports audience watching, and we're talking about the screens question here, how would the sports audience be watching sports in the 2020s? And maybe it won't happen in two years, but toward the late 2020s?

Clavio: Well, to borrow something Bryan said, it'll probably look fairly similar to what it is now, but maybe a little more on stream. I think we're going to see more communal viewing of major sporting events. In 2014 in the United States, really for the first time ever, we had major outdoor watch parties for World Cup games. Who attended one of those in here? Yes, several people did. You think about Germany or Canada, I'm wondering if Canadians ever go inside because every time I see them, they're always outside watching sporting events. It's great. The Toronto Raptors, they won the series last night, and there were what looked like tens of thousands of people outside watching that game. We're seeing hockey. We saw this with the Women's World Cup, certainly. So, I think you're going to see more of that. That kind of communal trend of observing sports games, and rather than it being in a sports bar, it's going to be in larger communal spaces. But, I also think that hand-held streaming devices, they're not going away, and as networks get better, as screen quality gets better and as the streaming services themselves get better, I can still remember back in, I guess it was 2003, CBS, their big thing was they were going to stream the March Madness live, so you were going to be able to watch it on your computer. You'd turn it on and five minutes after the play happens, you see it for five seconds and then it buffers again. It's so much better now, and I think that that's going to continue, as well. The big question is that I don't ever see television networks giving up the contractual relationship that they have now, the leagues might but for the television networks, it's still where you're going to get your biggest single audience at one time, and you can't package it on a Netflix or a Hulu because of the live nature of things.

Blackistone:

Everybody has been following ESPN, obviously. There have been a number of critics out there, Clay Travis, who said the network is dying. I used to cover economics before I got into sports, and if you pay attention to what ESPN is really doing, that's really not necessarily the case. They're transitioning from being, I think, a television sports entertainment company into a screen sports entertainment company. So, they are developing. They purchased a chunk of Hulu, I think it was [ESPN owns 30% of Hulu. This was an all-stock transaction included in the 21st Century Fox purchase]. As I mentioned, they just announced their streaming thing. I know when I walk around Knight Hall at the University of Maryland where the journalism college is based, there are some offices where people have television screens in their office. I always thought, "Why now would you have a television screen?" This building was opened like five years ago … I don't have one but when I want to watch television, I just turn my computer screen into a television screen or of course if I want to see something specific and I'm walking around the hall, I whip out my phone and I find it there. So, it's all about putting it on mobile screens or screens where people can see them everywhere. You talk about communal, that's almost a throwback because I can remember in the 70s and 80s closed-circuit boxing matches at theaters, which were communal. The only difference was you paid a price to get in to whoever was promoting the fight. So, now you put on these communal events, but no one is necessarily making an extra dollar, but it's a cool thing unless you were like us at the, I can't remember which Lakers' game it was where they won the title one year, and we couldn't leave the Staples Center because the party had erupted into a riot. Overturned cars, it was just a mess. So, it's just about delivering things to screens where you can tap into them and see them anywhere. I still have cable at my house for a lot of reasons, but I use Xfinity, and I can plug into Xfinity anywhere and watch whatever I want to watch, so that's kinda cool.

Curtis: I had a mentor who was told 25 years ago that newspapers were dying, same way. His response was, "Well, if they're dying, it's going to be an extremely slow and extremely profitable death." Which is essentially what happened over the next couple of decades. I would sort of say the same thing about sports television. I wouldn't use the word dying, but if I did, I would say it's extremely profitable and I would say an extremely long-time horizon that we're talking about. I think, to follow up on a point Galen made that was really interesting, is right now you have this strange world where the big events that everybody wants to watch are still controlled by the networks and by ESPN. ESPN has *Monday Night Football*, which has a weekly audience of 11 million or something like that. ESPN+ has Ivy League sports, which has a weekly audience of 11. So, essentially, we're still in the network model and whatever screen we're watching this on, we're still on the network model. *Thursday Night Football* is going to stream on Amazon Prime, but they're just picking up the network feed and streaming it, right? It's funny because back in the 80s there was this moment where television networks were run by cost-cutters like Larry Tisch and they were like, "We can't let the NFL go to cable. As soon as that happens, a Rubicon has been crossed and our power and our stature in American life is over." Well, we kind of crossed the Rubicon. Sunday night, at that point, football went to ESPN and went to Turner, but guess what? The networks still are all in the NFL business. I think what's happened is we've kind of repeated that step where we kind of let things go into the streaming world, but we really haven't, right? Because the biggest sports are still on network, and I think that's a huge part of this going forward.

Earnheardt: So, where is all of this leading as we go into the 2020s with the next round of rights are negotiated for professional leagues, for college conferences and so on, how do you see all of this fragmentation, moving to different screens, introducing new sports, how do you see this impacting the rights?

Curtis: I keep hearing, usually with ESPN, "Oh, ESPN is going to get out of business with *Monday Night Football*. It's a money loser. It's so much money. They're cutting costs." I'll believe any network gets out of business with the NFL when I see it. I'll believe that when I see it. For all the problems football has, the audience erosion you saw the last couple seasons. I'll just believe people are going to get out of business with football when it happens. Let me know when that happens. It's funny because I feel for my entire life, networks have been complaining about how much sports cost, and yet, and yet, they continue to pay the bill. Somebody is always around to pay the bills. *Thursday Night Football*, oh we all hated it last year, right? The players hated it. The fans hated it. It was devaluing football. There was football on too many nights, and what happens? FOX comes along and says, "Here's $1 billion. We'd like to put this on, and we'd like to win every single Thursday night in the Nielsen ratings," Because it's still such a powerful thing. Again, to go back to what we've been talking about earlier, I think the networks will continue to control the major rights. I think we'll certainly see an Amazon Prime, a YouTube, somebody getting in on the margins. But, again, I really want to see when that Rubicon is crossed, when there is some real, big, valuable television property that leaves the network world, leaves the ESPN world and goes to there that's not just a niche kind of sport.

Blackistone: I totally agree. Although, I will point to Ted Leonsis again because he has this idea as a sports team owner and the owner of his own distribution platform that he keeps raising the question of, "Well, why should I have someone else charge me for my team?" Right? I mean that's kind of what he has said. He has Monumental Sports. He has really pulled this together, and that's where he's trying to funnel his team through. He's just one guy, owner of three teams … He's trying to figure out a way to break this model. As you said, I don't think that'll happen. Networks continue to pay huge amounts to show these sports because they generate huge audience and they still generate huge advertising revenue. The advertising revenue continues to go up. I don't really see that changing. In fact, I kind of look at it another way now because the networks have now, particularly ESPN, have figured out a way to make, and NFL has helped them, has figured out a way to make the NFL a 12-month-a-year sport. Now people sit around, and they watch the draft and not only the first day of draft but the second day of the draft. Is the draft going on today? Today on television again. You even see basketball has also expanded its part of the calendar. The Big 3 leagues have found people who are willing to pay millions of dollars to put on old guys playing three-on-three basketball, which I just don't get. So, I just think it's going to continue, just get bigger and bigger.

Clavio:

This is the story I've always heard of how the Big Ten Network got started: ESPN goes into a round of negotiations with the conference, and they say, "Hey, this is going to be great. We're going to launch this new network called ESPNU, and the centerpiece of the programming for ESPNU is going to be our Big Ten games," and the Big Ten folks said, "Well, wait a minute. You're going to basically make all of your money off of our content. So, why wouldn't we just do that ourselves." So, that's where the partnership with FOX comes in, and the Big Ten Network gets launched in 2007. It's easy to forget about it 11 years later, but not a lot of people thought this model was going to succeed, the Big Ten Network. The idea that you were going to be able to get any sort of regular large-scale revenue stream the way that ESPN or FOX would be able to provide you. Certainly, if you watch Big Ten Network in the early days, your primary sponsors were like Ro-Tel and companies that maybe you don't think of as topline commercial entities for sports. Now you've got Mercedes-Benz and all of these really topline advertisers because the market was there and has just expanded more and more because of the desire that people have to watch their teams and do so on-demand in a way most of us, as sports consumers, wouldn't have thought of in 2000. What I think is interesting, the reason I started with that story, what I'm really curious about is the standoff that has developed between the teams and the leagues who basically own their own content, which is the product that goes out on the field or on the court. The networks and then the cable companies, who have become kind of the transitive element of the viewing experience. So, now, I mean certainly there are some urban areas where people are buying antennas and cord-cutting and just watching there, but for the most part people are either subscribing to satellite or they're subscribing to cable and that's how they're watching things. And yet, as Kevin points out, he can take his Xfinity subscription anywhere, so who blinks first? Do the leagues and the teams say, "Well, this is our content, and we can make money off it because we've seen the Big Ten Network do it." Does Xfinity or Cablevision or whoever, do they say, "Well, why would we work with the networks when we could basically just take this signal and do something with it ourselves," and then the networks, do they get out of the model of, "We're focusing everything on our television picture," and instead move to a model where we're working on a completely online space or primarily an online space? I feel like everybody is waiting on somebody else to make a move, and nobody has made a move yet. I feel like that's a very fascinating thing for the next five years.

Earnheardt: OK, questions …

Audience member: … I watch much of my sports at home through Reddit, so basically free streams and I feel like a cheapskate saying it, pirated streams. I feel very cheap confessing that here but a few of my close friends do the same thing … I'm wondering about implications of that, surely, its spread in the last few years, the implications for broadcasters or leagues. I'm thinking on one hand I'm not paying directly into the system, yet my eyes are still seeing the advertisements, I'm still more likely to go to the actual games sometimes. It's a bit of a complex situation, but what do you think, going into the 2020s, that poses for leagues and broadcasters?

Clavio: I'll start. It's interesting because it's almost like the reason that many people watch the Reddit streams is because the content is being kept from you. There's a gate. This happens here. I'm a big IndyCar fan, and we don't get the Indy 500 in the Indianapolis marketplace. So, if you're not going to go to the race, you need to go to Reddit because somebody will be streaming the ABC station in St. Petersburg, Florida, and you'll be able to watch it on that. I don't feel morally wrong in doing that, maybe I should. I feel like we're on a 12-step program here or something, like, "Yes, I pirate streams. I apologize." But, there's an interesting conundrum here because so much of the system for media rights is set up around the idea that, I paid for exclusivity, and that exclusivity gets defined market by market. Yet, everybody is using mobile devices. What's the market? What's the gate that you put around the Internet? You can do it but then that kind of defeats the purpose of the Internet. It becomes a much more closed system. I don't know what the answer is necessarily, but I do think that if you're a league or if you're a network you have to be thinking about, "Well, do I want to keep these people who want to watch this from watching it simply because it doesn't fit within this predefined box that we set up 50 or 75 years ago?"

Curtis: I'll just say that I watched a Showtime boxing match on Twitter the other day with somebody filming their television … When I talk to television executives they are maybe weirdly not that worried about this. Of all their lists of problems, that is … probably past No. 10. Cord-cutting is up here and rights fees and all kinds of things. It's way down. It's either to the point where it's not affecting them that much or maybe to the point where you don't think that it's affecting them that much. It's not really on their radar, interestingly. I'm sure it will only become a bigger issue.

Audience member: I just had a question about the digital disruptors out there, Barstool, Bleacher Report, The Ringer, where do you see them going in the future and then traditionally how might they impact more traditional mediums like an ESPN?

Curtis: I did not realize I was a disruptor. I will put that on my next round of business cards. I don't know that it's actually taking a bite out of ESPN at this point. Barstool is almost its own category in this. Somebody asked and said, "What do you want for sports journalism?" and I said two things: more diversity and more good-paying jobs. Those to me would be, especially the writing part of it. Those are my one and two goals. Number-three is way, way down the list because I don't think there's really anything important. So, at the moment, I'm so much more interested in the fact that these places are offering jobs to people in a rapidly disruptive job market. I think Barstool is interesting because I think the biggest effect these have all had, I was talking to someone about this yesterday, is Bleacher and Barstool have really hurt newspapers and mainstream media sources because they're free, because there's a generation of people who have grown up reading them and didn't grow up reading a newspaper and don't understand and could not possibly understand the value the newspaper-style reporting of events is. They just don't know, and they just don't care. When I meet people younger than me they're just like, "Oh, I just read Barstool. Why would I bother with anything else?" I think that The Ringer is probably closer to the old model than a lot of those places. They put out a free product, sometimes it's good, sometimes it's not good, but it's been an alternative. I think when we talk about what's happening to newspapers now, what's happening to other mainstream media outlets, they're really feeling that pressure because it's like, "How are we competing with free?" "If we do a slightly better version of free that costs money, is anybody going to pick us? Especially anybody under the age of 20 or 30?" I think that's a fascinating, maybe unknowable question moving forward.

Blackistone: I think the interesting thing with Barstool, and I'm not a Barstool fan at any level at all, but the interesting thing is how it's been able to go out and get funding and get people to pay them to distribute on their network, which is really interesting. As far as Bleacher, SB Nation, I mean I got out of newspapers in 2006 and shortly thereafter went to AOL when they started up FanHouse and a lot of the people who started up AOL FanHouse went along to start up SB Nation, which is now going through yet another transformative period. I don't see them as disruptors. I really think they prove the growth in sports media. So, while newspapers are shaking out, not necessarily to the fault of newspapers but in a lot of instances as you see in Denver right now just because of predatory investors with bad intentions. These other places have found out how to grow and how to find audience …

Clavio: I'll add this, I think the disruptor is the medium, as opposed to being the outlets. I think Twitter and Twitch and Facebook because of the dynamically different ways that people will consume content and the different things that they'll choose. I mentioned *SportsCenter*'s Snapchat at the beginning. Like that's, "Are you sheering off audience from elsewhere?" or are they just not going to be at that place we thought they were going to be in the first place? So, you have to go somewhere else. I'm actually surprised there haven't been more disruptors, I guess as you would put it, in those spaces. When we see the ESPNs and the FOXs get into it, it's a very traditional approach in most cases to social media and nontraditional methods of reaching sports audiences. I think there's a wide-open avenue for companies and individuals who want to make a name for themselves in the space right now to do it. Primarily, by figuring out, "How do I best utilize Snapchat?" "How do I best utilize Twitter as opposed to the way its developed over time?"

Audience member: Not too long ago, Facebook announced they basically poached the Eurosport guy for TV rights. We know Amazon and Twitter also want to get in on the sports rights deals. I want to know what you all think about this and where you see this going.

Curtis: I'm interested in when that breakthrough is going to happen to get to big stuff from marginal, secondary. It's almost like we had Netflix, but it was only direct video stuff you could watch on Netflix, right? It's a different model. You can't just create your own, you could create your own sport I guess, but the biggest sports are going to be out of reach. Again, I'm sort of waiting for that Rubicon to be crossed where a league like maybe the next NFL contract, maybe everybody will be so pinched in terms of money that they just have to carve out a piece of this. We've also seen with the NFL that they love to be in business with everybody at once …, and they say, "We're just going to carve out a little piece of this for streaming and some for Amazon for whoever wants to give us money." So maybe that's the move.

Clavio: An interesting point about Amazon is that their whole business model is different than these media companies. They're trying to get subscribers, but not subscribers in that we want you to subscribe to Prime just to be there but we want you changing over a lot of your commercial purchasing habits and it's a long game for them as opposed to being a short game. Media contracts end up being relatively short game … So I look at Amazon and I think, "Well, they're going to dabble in it somewhat," but unless it's something that's a core entertainment option for a large group of people, I don't know necessarily that they're going to feel like, "We need to jump in and grab that so that NBC doesn't have it or so that ABC doesn't have it." As far as some of the other big companies that could move into that space that aren't there now, it really comes down to how much of the wheel do you really want to reinvent? If you're an Apple for instance, you certainly have money and you certainly have the infrastructure, but do you want to create sports broadcasting from scratch? If you think about NBC and the way that they have adapted to bringing the Premier League in, they had models to go off of, so it wasn't a huge leap. Trying to jump into something that you've never done before for a lot of companies, it's like, "Why bother when we could have somebody else do that and farm it in?" It's a very interesting spot and it's kind of the fourth wall of the standoff model I was talking about earlier. We've yet to really see anybody, I mean Amazon dipped their toe in it, and Twitter is trying to do stuff, but I don't know if Twitter is even financially important enough to matter in the conversation at this point.

Audience member: I'm going to ask another esport question; I apologize. This one is more about coverage. As networks or professional analysts with esports because of different skill sets that are rewarded, how would networks and professional analysts deal with the possibility that your major competitors that is your champions might be 14 or 12 or 10 without being condescending to them but also being cognizant to the fact that they are children?

Kevin Blackistone: To me the interesting thing about that is that it's really tracking where we're going, we didn't talk about this earlier, where we're going with sports coverage, which is younger and younger. When I was growing up in Washington D.C., if you were a kid playing sports, there was a chance that you would get on TV once and that was in the Turkey Bowl at Thanksgiving on WTTG on channel five if your team just happened to be the team that was picked for that game. Now we're seeing the end of Lebron James' career coming at some point, maybe not soon enough for Pacers' fans. We first saw him on television as a junior in high school. So now you look at ESPN's programming and you can watch high school sports, same with FOX, pretty regularly. To me the interesting thing is, so who's going to be the financial beneficiary in esports? Are those kids going to be able to, and their families, cash in when kids playing high school sports cannot? To me, that's an issue, but my main point is that that track is where we're going now, you can just see more youth sports become a core part in ESPN's programming. They went out and purchased that company, I think it's Rise, which covers high school/youth sports. That's the direction we're headed.

Audience member: This is an esport impacted question, but it's more an Asian question. I was watching the World of Warcraft world championship in Beijing happening last year, I think 80,000 spectators inside the stadium in Beijing. The next big major events are all in Asia. The best soccer player in Germany, Mesut Ozil, his most followers are based in Asia, and Bayern Munich, our biggest club, is doing 24/7 programming in the Chinese language because all of these followers are based in Asia. So, can you talk a little bit on what does Asian people and Asian audience have an impact on the future of sports when you cover esports by streaming and every Asian can see this?

Galen Clavio: You can also look at the way the NBA has marketed itself specifically toward the Asian audience, particularly China. This goes back to something I mentioned a little earlier one, I think, which is this idea of the financial interests in sport will come down to the advertising motivated conceptualization of audience and this idea of, "How do we get the largest audience for the products that our advertisers are trying to market?" Esports provides kind of a blank slate for a lot of advertisers because, again, you're not handcuffed to the same sort of media gating that you would find in traditional televised sports. When you look at something like soccer, football, and because that's so individually player driven in many cases, or it's very brand driven depending on teams, I think that there's a model that can be utilized to try to market into those cultures and into those spaces. With esports, I think where there is an advantage on the esports front is some many of the best esports players in the world are Asian. That is a huge advantage, I think we see it in most sports, you can make that sort of direct cultural connection with the participant. You're going to feel a higher level of affinity that's probably going to be able to translate into more commercial motivation to do whatever the advertising and the programming is telling you.

Earnheardt: Just to kind of wrap up, we like to ask media people who do the things that you do that we study all the time, sometimes we miss something. Is there something we should be looking at going into the 2020s that we should be preparing to study, esports, whatever it is, maybe something that we don't know about that you maybe know more about?

Blackistone: I think you folks do a great job at your research. Going forward, you know one of the things I think about, and we've really been talking about it up here, is the whole symbiotic relationship between sports and sports media, which to me seems to be tighter now and have more of an impact than ever before. Because in order for some sport to go forward, it's got to have the vessel of television or a digital platform in order to survive. And what that means for how information about that sports participants are disseminated to the public, particularly when it comes to journalism. One of the reasons that ESPN is almost always in a quandary is because of their financial relationship with all of the sports that we love to watch. I just think that that's going to become more and more complicated as we go forward.

Curtis: I feel sort of odd answering this question since I write about the sports media and I'm essentially doing what lots of people in this room are doing except with only a bachelor's degree and without footnotes. It's been amazing to sit at panels for the last two days to see the way you guys process stories that I in fact covered very quickly when they were happening. I wrote about the big profile on Jemele Hill last summer, right before Jemele became a political cause celebrated across the United States. To see three different panels involve Jemele at this conference … It's been fascinating to see, going back and putting those events in context that were very, very strange and upsetting when they were happening. I think two really interesting areas of study, at least for me that I would love to see the academic version of, one is just a little bit of what we've talked about today, the erosion and eventual fall of the old forms of journalism. We talked about newspapers and television stations being challenged by and eventually giving way to new forms, right? And how does that affect the way sports media works. That's fascinating to me. The second is something Kevin alluded to, which is politics in the sports media. The newspaper was very, very good at keeping most political rhetoric out of the sports page. Television still does quite a good job of trying keep that over here, but as we've seen with Twitter and everything from Barstool to whatever new media arm you want to name, that's not the way it works anymore. Now these two, political writing and sports writing, have essentially combined, and we're seeing lots and lots of crossover and sports writers being allowed to try to make sense of these things and not just the one or two columnists at the newspaper but everyone in real time at this fascinating moment, whether it's players or Donald Trump or what have you. I just think that that's a fascinating topic, and I can't wait to read more about it.

Editors' Closing Comments on the Changing Sports Media Landscape

As members of this IACS panel discussed, the future of sports media remains bright—but where the industry is headed may be another story entirely. As a college sports network executive told IACS it will likely come down to not only how people want to be entertained, but how people will want to consume their entertainment. The oscillation of sport popularity is a reflection of the symbiotic relationship between sports and sports media. As noted throughout this book, some sports gained in popularity in the 2010s while other sports declined. Cord-cutters also impacted sports content distributors, including ESPN. Sport popularity will always be driven, in part, by its availability, either on a digital platform or through the mainstream media.

The popularity and growth of esports illustrates this symbiotic relationship. The overall demand for esports in terms of viewership is very impressive. The 2017 League of Legends world championship, held in Beijing, drew over 106 million viewers, about 12 million less viewers than the 2018 Super Bowl (Ingraham, 2018, para. 7). The worldwide demand for all forms of sports entertainment (sports news content and live events) remains great. Regardless of how the content is delivered, fan convenience will drive fan consumption.

As the 2020s unfold, the rights for nearly every professional sports league in the U.S. will be up for grabs in a new round of negotiations with prospective media partners. These negotiations, because of the many factors we have noted in this book (e.g., new technologies) will be unlike any others before it. For example, what will existing NFL partners (CBS, NBC, FOX, and ESPN) do if the league demands another gargantuan rights fee increase? Will there be new bidders (e.g., Facebook, Twitter, Hulu, Netflix, YouTube) looking to take more NFL content online (Amazon owned digital rights for NFL *Thursday Night Football* in 2018 and 2019)? Or will the NFL decide to keep more of its games for its own cable and online businesses? Seismic shifts in collegiate sports could also occur in the 2020s with individual conferences like the Big Ten and Pac-12 ready to negotiate new deals in coming years. Can the Big-12 survive without its own conference television network? Will there again be significant conference realignment in the 2020s because of future media deals? These are just some of the questions to be answered in the next decade. When these negotiations are combined with rapidly evolving technologies and changing audience tastes for how and what sports are consumed, it becomes a witch's brew certain to change the sports media landscape for years, if not decades to come.

As always, the future of sports media will come down to one factor: the audience. The dedicated sports fan (whether it be for baseball games or cornhole matches) will always want access to those events and the advertisers will follow where the sports audience goes. Where the audience goes 5 or 10 years from now, or even what device audiences use to consume sports and entertainment, remains the multi-billion dollar question.

Reference

Ingraham, C. (2018, August 27). The massive popularity of esports, in charts. *The Washington Post*. Retrieved from https://www.washingtonpost.com/business/2018/08/27/massive-popularity-esports-charts/?noredirect=on&utm_term=.702cdc97baee

Editor Biographies

Greg G. Armfield (PhD, University of Missouri-Columbia) is an Associate Professor and basic course director in the Department of Communication Studies at New Mexico State University. His research explores the role of cultural identity in sports and organizations. He has authored or co-authored over a dozen refereed journal articles and book chapters, which can be found in the *Journal of Communication*, the *Journal of Media and Religion*, *Speaker and Gavel*, and the *Journal of Communication and Religion*. Dr. Armfield co-edited the first academic book dedicated to the self-proclaimed "world-wide leader in sports," *The ESPN Effect: Exploring the Worldwide Leader in Sports* (Peter Lang). He has also co-edited five volumes of *Human Communication in Action* (Kendall Hunt) with Eric Morgan.

John McGuire (PhD, University of Missouri-Columbia) is a Professor in the School of Media and Strategic Communications at Oklahoma State University. Dr. McGuire's research interests focus on the sports media business, sports announcing, and political reporting. His work has been published in the *Journal of Sports Media, Communication and Sport, International Journal of Sport Communication, Newspaper Research Journal*, and the *Journal of Radio and Audio Media*. Dr. McGuire was co-editor of *The ESPN Effect: Exploring the Worldwide Leader in Sports*, a co-author of *Campaign 2000: A Functional Analysis of Presidential Campaign Discourse*, and has co-authored chapters in three other edited volumes. In addition to his publishing work, Dr. McGuire has won nearly two dozen awards during his career as a radio play-by-play announcer and news and sports reporter. McGuire's broadcast experience has ranged from calling Missouri 8-man football to NCAA national championship games.

Adam C. Earnheardt (PhD, Kent State University) is Chair and Professor of Communication Studies in the Department of Communication at

Youngstown State University, and weekly columnist for *The Vindicator* newspaper, where he has writes about social media, relationships, technology and society. He has authored or co-authored more than a dozen peer-reviewed journal articles, encyclopedia entries, and book chapters. Earnheardt published several books with other communication scholars including his most recent book *Public Speaking in the Age of Technology* (2016). He has served as an expert source on communication, social media, parenting, sports and fandom on various television and radio programs, and in several publications including *Parade Magazine, Psychology Today, Playboy,* and several newspapers and magazines including the *Baltimore Sun Times, Pittsburgh Post-Gazette* and others.

Contributor Biographies

Dunja Antunovic (PhD, Pennsylvania State University) is an Assistant Professor at the Charley Steiner School of Sports Communication and a member of the Women's and Gender Studies Committee at Bradley University. Her research focuses on the intersection of gender, media, and sport in three primary areas: Women in sports journalism, coverage of sportswomen, and new media fandom. Her work has been published in communication and sport sociology journals, including *Communication & Sport* and the *International Review for the Sociology of Sport*, and in edited collections on feminist theory and methods. Dr. Antunovic teaches courses in sports communication, global media, and cultural diversity.

Braden Bagley is a doctoral candidate in the School of Communication at The University of Southern Mississippi with research in the areas of health communication, risk and crisis communication, and sports communication. Specific topics include the opioid crisis, NBA media voting, and community response to disaster. He also earned his MA in Professional Communication from Southern Utah University.

Andrew C. Billings (PhD, Indiana University, 1999) is the Ronald Reagan Chair of Broadcasting and Executive Director of the Alabama Program in Sports Communication at the University of Alabama. His research typically focuses on sport, media, and societal consumption trends.

David Bockino is an assistant professor in the School of Communications at Elon University with an MBA in Sport Management and a PhD in Mass Communications. He teaches classes in both the Communications and Sport Management departments. Prior to joining Elon, he worked at ESPN for eight years (2005–2012) in both the Research and Analytics and International Ad Sales departments, collaborating closely with ESPN offices in Mexico, South America, Europe, Australia, Asia, and the UK.

Ryan Broussard is an Assistant Professor in the Mass Communication Department at Sam Houston State University. He received both his BA and MS from the University of Louisiana before working as a journalist for four years. His primary research interests are the intersection of sports and politics and the sociology of media production.

Michael L. Butterworth is a Professor in the Department of Communication Studies and Director of the Center for Sports Communication & Media in the Moody College of Communication at The University of Texas at Austin. His research explores the connections between rhetoric, democracy, and sport, with particular interests in national identity, militarism, and public memory. He is the author of *Baseball and Rhetorics of Purity: The National Pastime and American Identity During the War on Terror*, coauthor of *Communication and Sport: Surveying the Field*, and editor of *Sport and Militarism: Contemporary Global Perspectives*.

David Cassilo is an Assistant Professor at Kennesaw State University. After earning his BA at Villanova University (2010), David completed a Master's degree in journalism at Northwestern University (2011) and his PhD in journalism and mass communication from Kent State University (2019). He has also worked as a digital media and magazine reporter during this time. His research interests focus on media portrayals of concussion in sport, specifically examining the dialogue about concussions created through digital and social media. His work has been published in several academic journals and has been presented at academic conferences.

Stephen W. Dittmore is the Assistant Dean For Outreach and Innovation in the College of Education and Health Professions at the University of Arkansas. He holds a faculty appointment in recreation and sport management where his research interests have focused on content management in the digital age, including the intersections of sport media rights, government regulation, copyright, and content restrictions. He previously worked in sport media relations in the Olympic movement before entering academia.

Sean Fourney received his doctorate in communication studies from the University of Southern Mississippi in 2019. His research interests include risk, sports, and autoethnography. In 2018, he served as the Public Engagement Intern for New Orleans Homeland Security and Emergency Preparedness which focused on designing, managing, and delivering messages that spread awareness of the "NOLA Ready" Campaign of evacuation procedures during hurricane season. He also has run several NSF Broad Impact Workshops on Communicating Science to Diverse Audiences and worked as a Peer Consultant at USM's Speaking Center. Dr. Fourney began his career in communication as a radio broadcaster. He served as Education Director for the award-winning WESS 90.3FM at East Stroudsburg University where he was also the school's inaugural commencement speaker. He went on to produce for ESPN Radio of the Lehigh Valley before hosting his own talk show on WCHE 1520AM in West Chester, Pennsylvania.

Jonathan Graffeo is a PhD student in the College of Communication and Information Sciences at the University of Alabama. He holds a Master's of Business Administration from Duke University and bachelor's degree in Political Science from Auburn University. Jonathan has served in various legislative and communication roles as a staffer in the United States Senate since 2004. As a doctoral student, his primary research focus is corporate and political crisis communication.

Andreas Hebbel-Seeger (PhD, University of Hamburg) is a Professor at the Hamburg campus of the Macromedia University of Applied Sciences in Germany, specializing in the study of sports and event management. Dr. Hebbel-Seeger has been honored for his innovative teaching methods and creating and implementing multimedia teaching and learning applications.

Thomas Horky is a Professor at the Hamburg campus of the Macromedia University of Applied Sciences in Germany. Dr. Horky is chair of the Journalism and Sports Journalism programs and has worked as a freelance journalist in his home country for multiple media outlets.

Kevin Hull (PhD, University of Florida) is an Assistant Professor in the School of Journalism and Mass Communications at the University of South Carolina. His research focuses on communication in the world of sports—specifically how teams, fans, media, and players interact with each other using both traditional media formats and social media. His articles have appeared in a variety of journals relating to both sports and journalism.

Zach Humphries (PhD Candidate, Kent State University) teaches in the Communication Studies program at Kent State University. His research interests include political communication, sport communication, and media use and effects.

Jared Johnson is an Assistant Professor of Sports Media at Oklahoma State University. He teaches broadcast sports and news reporting and producing classes as well as classes on international media and communication. He holds a PhD in public communication from Georgia State University, an MA in international affairs from Ohio University and a BA in broadcast journalism and political science from Weber State University. He has worked as a news and sports reporter, producer, host and play-by-play commentator. He was a sports editor of the *Athens* (Ohio) *Messenger*, where he also was a beat writer for the Mid-American Conference. He has also reported for and produced TV and radio sports shows in Ohio, Georgia, and Utah.

Jake Kucek is a doctoral student at Kent State University. His research focus is on corporate social responsibility in sports organizations, sports identification and fandom, and social media effects.

William M. Kunz is a Professor in the School of Interdisciplinary Arts & Sciences at the University of Washington Tacoma. He received his PhD in Communication and Society from the University of Oregon. He is the author of *Culture Conglomerates: Consolidation in the Motion Picture and Television Industries* as well as numerous articles and chapters focused on media ownership and regulation. He has worked in sports television at the network level for over 30 years.

Katherine L. Lavelle is an Associate Professor of Communication Studies at the University of Wisconsin-La Crosse, where she is the Director of the Public Speaking Center and teaches courses in Public Communication, Advocacy, and Communication and Sport. Her previous research has explored representations of race, nationality, sex/gender, and other identity issues in sport. She has published work in a variety of communication and sport anthologies, and journals including *Communication & Sport*, and *Journal of Sports Media*. She currently serves on the Board of Directors for the International Association for Communication and Sport.

Melvin Lewis (PhD, The University of Alabama, 2003) is an Assistant Professor in the Sports Business Management Graduate Program and Fellow of the Alabama Program in Sports Communication at the University of Alabama. His current research focuses on sport-consumer behavior and technology in sports.

Anji L. Phillips (PhD, University of Missouri) is an Assistant Professor of Television Arts, and advises radio, television, and film projects in the Department of Communication at Bradley University. Dr. Phillips conducts media research at the intersection of mass/niche and political communication with an emphasis in media effects of both new and traditional media. Telling a good story well is at the heart of her media projects, and how she advises her students to create content. Dr. Phillips is the executive producer of *Stories Beyond the Scores*, which is a sports audio production created for public radio and podcasts.

Xavier Ramon is a lecturer in the Department of Communication of Pompeu Fabra University (UPF). He holds a PhD in Communication from the UPF. He is also affiliated to the Olympic Studies Centre at the Autonomous University of Barcelona (CEO-UAB). His research focuses on media ethics and accountability and sports journalism. He has been a visiting researcher at the University of Stirling, the University of Glasgow, the University of Alabama and the IOC Olympic Studies Centre in Lausanne, Switzerland.

José Luis Rojas Torrijos is a lecturer in journalism at the University of Seville and EUSA Business University. He also participates in the MA programmes in innovation in journalism of Miguel Hernández University and in journalism and sports communication of the Pontifical University of Salamanca, Pompeu Fabra University, European University in Madrid, San Antonio Catholic University in Murcia and Marca-CEU University. He holds a PhD in Journalism (2010) and a BA in Information Sciences (1994) from the University of Seville. His research focuses on sports journalism, ethics and stylebooks.

Miles Romney is an Assistant Professor at Brigham Young University. His research interests focus primarily on national sports networks; specifically, how they frame news and information for audiences on traditional media as well as on social and digital platforms. Miles received his doctoral degree from the Walter Cronkite School of Journalism and at Arizona State University (2016).

Brody J. Ruihley (PhD, University of Tennessee) is an Assistant Professor of Sport Management in Sport Leadership and Management program (SLAM) at Miami University (Oxford). Ruihley's primary research interests lie in the areas of fantasy sport business and consumption, as well as public relations in sport. Ruihley is the coauthor of *The Fantasy Sport Industry: Games within Games* (Routledge, 2014).

J. Scott Smith is an Assistant Professor of Communication Studies at Christopher Newport University. After completing his PhD in Communication Studies from the University of Missouri in 2013, Dr. Smith has focused his research on political rhetoric and crisis communication.

Paul Smith is a Senior Lecturer in Media and Communication at the Leicester Media School, De Montfort University, Leicester, United Kingdom. He has published widely on sports rights and media policy, including articles in the *European Journal of Communication* and *Media, Culture and Society*, as well as a (jointly authored with Petros Iosifidis and Tom Evens) book: *The Political Economy of Television Sports Rights* (Palgrave, 2013).

David Staton is an assistant professor at the University of Northern Colorado. His research interests include new media, sports journalism, ethics and visual communication.

Sarah Wolter analyzes mediated representations of female athletes from a critical feminist perspective. She earned her Master's degree from Minnesota State University, Mankato, and her PhD from the University of Minnesota, Twin Cities. Her research has been published in places like *Communication & Sport, The International Journal of Sport Communication,* and *Journal of*

Sports Media. Wolter is a Visiting Assistant Professor at Gustavus Adolphus College in St. Peter, MN.

Steve Young is a doctoral candidate in the School of Communication at The University of Southern Mississippi. He earned his MA in Interpersonal Communication from SUNY Albany. Specializing in popular culture and social influence, his research interests involve video game studies, sports communication, and digital media with a particular focus on culture.

Index

Lawrence A. Wenner, Andrew C. Billings, and Marie C. Hardin
General Editors

Books in the Communication, Sport, and Society series explore evolving themes and emerging issues in the study of communication, media, and sport, broadly defined. The series provides a venue for key concepts and theories across communication and media studies to be explored in relation to sport. The series features works building on burgeoning media studies engagement with sport, as well as works focusing on interpersonal, group, organizational, rhetorical, and other dynamics in the communication of sport. The series welcomes diverse theoretical standpoints and methodological tactics seen across the social sciences and humanities. While some works may examine the dynamics of institutions and producers, representations and content, reception and fandom, or entertain questions such as those about identities and/or commodification in the contexts of mediated sport, works that consider how communication about sport functions in diverse rhetorical and interpersonal settings, how groups, families, and teams use, adapt, and are affected by the communication of sport, and how the style, nature, and power relations in communication are wielded in sport and media organizations are particularly encouraged. Works examining the communication of sport in international and/or comparative contexts or new, digital, and/or social forms of sport communication are also welcome.

For additional information about this series or for the submission of manuscripts, please contact the series editors or Acquisitions Editor Erika Hendrix:

Lawrence A. Wenner | Andrew C. Billings | Marie C. Hardin | Erika Hendrix
lwenner@lmu.edu | acbillings@ua.edu | mch208@psu.edu | erika.hendrix@plang.com

To order other books in this series, please contact our Customer Service Department:

(800) 770-LANG (within the U.S.)
(212) 647-7706 (outside the U.S.)
(212) 647-7707 FAX

Or browse online by series:
www.peterlang.com